Napoleon and the British

Napoleon and the British

STUART SEMMEL

Yale University Press
New Haven and London

For information about this and other Yale University Press publications, please contact:
U.S. Office: sales.press@yale.edu   yalebooks.com
Europe Office: sales@yaleup.co.uk   www.yalebooks.co.uk

Set in Sabon by SNP Best-set Typesetter Ltd, Hong Kong
Printed in Great Britain by St Edmundsbury Press Ltd

Library of Congress Cataloging-in-Publication Data

Semmel, Stuart.
    Napoleon and the British/Stuart Semmel.
        p.   cm.
    Includes bibliographical references and index.
    ISBN 0-300-09001-3 (cl.: alk. paper)
    1. Napoleon I, Emperor of the French, 1769–1821—Relations with British.
2. Napoleon I, Emperor of the French, 1769–1821—Influence.   3. Napoleonic Wars, 1800–1815—Foreign public opionion, British.   4. Public opinion—Great Britain—History—19th century.   5. Great Britain—Foreign relations—France—1789–1820.   6. France—Foreign relations—Great Britain—1789–1815.
7. National characteristics, British.   I. Title.
    DC202.7.S45 2004   944.05′092—dc22   2004007557

A catalogue record for this book is available from the British Library

Published with assistance from the Annie Burr Lewis Fund.

To my parents

What a change would Buonaparte make in such a scene of liberty and peace—could he but once set his withering foot on this dear island. The state of the rest of the World came into my mind as I stood abstracted, and every other country that my fancy pictured, I thought I saw a dingy lowering cloud hang over it—a beam of light burst through the cloud that enveloped Spain, but it appeared dripping with blood—England alone laid open her peaceful meadows, lit up by gaiety & innocence.

Benjamin Robert Haydon in his diary, 9 September 1810.

Every body knows that it is only necessary to raise a bugbear before the English imagination in order to govern it at will.

William Hazlitt, *The Life of Napoleon Buonaparte*, 1828–30.

Contents

List of Illustrations

Acknowledgments

I have accumulated many debts since I began this project more than a decade ago. Most of my research took place at the British Library and the Harvard College Library. I am very grateful to librarians at both institutions. I thank Harvard's Houghton Library for permission to quote from the Benjamin Robert Haydon papers. My thanks also to the New York Public Library, Butler Library and the Rare Book and Manuscript Library at Columbia University, Van Pelt Library and the Rare Book and Manuscript Library at the University of Pennsylvania, the Library of Congress, the Firestone Library at Princeton University, the Morris Library and Special Collections at the University of Delaware, the Boston Public Library, the Bodleian Library, the Huntington Library, the John Soane Museum, and the Bethlem Royal Hospital Archives and Museum.

A Krupp Foundation fellowship from Harvard's Minda de Gunzberg Center for European Studies generously funded my research in Britain. I also received support from Harvard's Committee on Degrees in History and Literature. A Mellon Fellowship from the Penn Humanities Forum, which allowed me to undertake an unrelated research project, delayed revisions on this manuscript but sustained body and soul. A General University Research grant from the University of Delaware helped me during the final stages of revision, and a university and departmental subvention has underwritten the costs associated with the book's illustrations.

I wrote most of this book while living in two vibrant residential communities that nurtured scholarship and extra-scholarly life: Mather House at Harvard University, and Harnwell College House at the University of Pennsylvania. I am tremendously grateful to Sandra Naddaff and Leigh Hafrey and to David and Ann Brownlee, the faculty masters of Mather and Harnwell respectively. I also thank members of other intellectual communities, albeit ones in which I did not actually reside: the History and Literature program, the Center for European Studies, and the History Department at Harvard University; the Penn Humanities Forum and the History Department at the University of Pennsylvania; and the History Department at American University. I particularly thank my colleagues in History at the University of Delaware for their support.

I have aired some of this book's material at the Delaware Valley British Studies Seminar, two faculty seminars at Penn, the British Studies Group at Harvard's Center for European Studies, a London conference sponsored by the journal *National Identities*, and several meetings of the North American Conference on British Studies. I thank my listeners for many valuable suggestions. Chapter 6 was previously published, in a somewhat different form, as "British Radicals and 'Legitimacy': Napoleon in the Mirror of History," in *Past and Present* 167 (May 2000), 140–75; it appears here with kind permission of the Past and Present Society. A few paragraphs in chapter 8 draw on my "Reading the Tangible Past: British Tourism, Collecting, and Memory after Waterloo," in *Representations* 69 (Winter 2000), 9–37; my thanks to the University of California Press for permission to use this material.

This book began as a dissertation in Harvard's History department. Donald Fleming offered sage guidance and support, even as the project rapidly abandoned high intellectual history for the shores of cultural history. Susan Pedersen asked incisive questions and helped me visualize the project's possibilities. Patrice Higonnet gave encouragement and useful advice. A number of other readers have read and commented on my manuscript. I am deeply indebted to Peter Mandler, whose wide-ranging criticisms of the dissertation helped guide revision of the manuscript. Timothy Alborn and Philip Harling supplied valuable suggestions. Three anonymous readers for Yale University Press proposed a great many improvements. I was fortunate enough to exchange manuscripts with Sudhir Hazareesingh and I benefited both from reading his superb study of the Napoleonic legend in France and from his extensive comments on my own book. Individual chapters have been commented on most helpfully by James Epstein, Lynn Hunt, Margaret Jacob, Maya Jasanoff, Seth Koven, Lynn Lees, Caroline Levine, and Ronald Schechter. I can only hope that I have successfully addressed a few of the problems to which my generous readers have drawn my attention. I should also express my gratitude to my editor, Robert Baldock, for patiently putting up with my endless questions (and to Ann Geneva, for having introduced me to Robert when this project was quite young). Thanks also to Ewan Thompson and Kevin Brown at Yale University Press in London, and to the manuscript's copy-editor Beth Humphries, for their expert editorial and design work.

In listing those who have commented on conference papers, asked or answered questions, and offered advice, I am sure to leave out a great many. (I console myself with the thought that some I do name have likely forgotten the help they provided.) I thank Carrie Alyea, Mark Baer, Daniel Baugh, John Bernstein, James Brophy, Thomas Cogswell, Deborah Cohen, Keith Crudgington, Felix Driver, Donald Ginter, Anne Goldgar, Daniel Gordon, Eliga Gould, Peter Hansen, Mark Kishlansky, Fred Leventhal, Brian Lewis, Patricia Lin, Patricia Lynch, Ann Moyer, Steven Maughan, Andrea McKenzie, Jeffrey Moran, Steven Pincus, John Plotz, Alice Prochaska, Frank Prochaska, Evan Radcliffe, Martin Roberts, Nicholas Rogers, Sophie Rosenfeld, David Ruderman, Benjamin Schmidt, Matthew Sommer, Rebecca Spang, Jonathan Steinberg, the late Jan Thaddeus, Frank Trentmann, Chris Waters, and Owen White. I am grateful to Mark Philp and Alexandra Franklin for introducing me to "Prints from the Curzon Collection: Images of Napoleon 1789–1815," an online Oxford Digital Library collection that they have assembled of some eight hundred digitized engravings; I only wish this amazing resource had been available during my research, rather than after my book had already been copy-edited. I would also like to thank professors from my undergraduate years whose influence on me is, I hope, occasionally visible in these pages: John Brewer, Simon Schama, and the late John Clive.

Rather than list friends beyond the bounds of European history and British studies, I will thank them collectively (and emphatically). But I should give a special tip of the hat to Holly Christensen and Snezana Kordovan, without whom something would have had to give.

This book is dedicated with love and appreciation to my parents. More than most authors, I can truly say that without them this book would never have been written. Many childhood summers spent in London, as well as the inspiring example of my father's books, helped guide me into the study of British history. As a historian, I have profited enormously from conversations with my father, and from the comments of both my parents on my writing. As a son, I feel luckier still.

When Tina Lu started living with this book it was a single conference paper and a disk full of notes. She has coddled, nudged, counseled, consoled, supported, encouraged, corrected, cautioned, cushioned, and clarified. Her sense of balance and proportion has kept life going when the book threatened to overwhelm it, and vice versa. Tina has also made possible two great blessings, both of whom slowed considerably the final stages of this book's production. Tovah Lu and Natalie Semmel helped me not at all in the writing of this book. I am incalculably grateful to them.

A Note on Spelling and Punctuation

Unless otherwise indicated, italics in quotations are original to the sources. Spelling mistakes and typographical errors in quotations have generally been preserved and indicated. Certain spellings that depart from twenty-first century British practice, and which might appear to be the work of an American transcriber—for example, "honor" and "center"—were in fact the spellings employed by late Hanoverians, before a desire to Frenchify British spelling exerted itself later in the nineteenth century. In this sense (and others, including the use of double rather than single inverted commas for quotations, and the placement of commas and periods within rather than outside quotation marks), modern American usage remains closer than modern British usage to "the king's English"—if the king in question is George III.

Introduction

Napoleon to an Englishman is a tempting subject.

Benjamin Robert Haydon, 1831[1]

It is almost needless to state, that everything connected with the late Emperor Napoleon belongs to British history.

Exhibition catalogue for Napoleon's carriage,
Madame Tussaud and Sons, 1843[2]

A book on British conceptions of Napoleon Bonaparte might easily resemble the following outburst of epithets, assembled in 1815:

> the *Corsican!* the *low-minded Corsican!* the *wily* Corsican! the *vile* Corsican! the *once-insolent* Corsican! the *beaten, disgraced, and perjured* Corsican! the *faithless, perjured, craft-loving* Corsican! a *Fugitive!*—an *Adventurer!*—a *blustering Charlatan!*—such a *Fellow!*—a *Scoundrel*, with a degraded character!—an *Impostor!* a *despicable* Impostor! a *notorious* Impostor! an *hypocritical* Impostor!—a *Wretch!* a *desperate* Wretch! *such* a Wretch!—a *Robber!*—a mere *Brigand!* an *atrocious* Brigand!—a savage *Adversary!*—a *Remorseless Ruffian!*—a *Criminal! such* a Criminal! so *infamous* a Criminal!—that *Traitor!* that *Corsican* Traitor! that *audacious* Traitor! that *cowardly and perfidious* Traitor! that *perjured* Traitor! that *Arch* Traitor!—a *Rebel!* an *audacious* Rebel! a *vile Corsican* Rebel! an *usurping* Rebel! a *proscribed* Rebel! an *infamous* Rebel! the *Arch* Rebel! the Rebel *who defies* All Europe!—the *Usurper!* the *Corsican* Usurper!

And so on, and on ("the *degraded* Tyrant!—the *consummate Despot;*—*l'Empereur de la Canaille*"). This is in fact a rather brief extract of a

compilation of phrases used by the journalist Robert Stoddart, editor of
The Times of London.

A great many Britons did despise Napoleon. And the insults Stoddart
used were familiar and well-worn by the time they were collected in the
broadside here quoted, the 1815 *Buonapartephobia*.[3] But Napoleon
occupied a much more complicated and ambiguous place in British
political culture than this string of slurs might suggest. Late Georgian
publications overflowed with such barbs, but it does not follow that
antipathy to Bonaparte was a matter of simple knee-jerk opposition.
Nor, as this compendium of insults—as opposed to the insults themselves—testifies, was Buonapartephobia the only British response to
Napoleon. It was a radical, the publisher William Hone, who gathered
together these instances of Stoddart's heated rhetoric, in order to ridicule
the journalist. Hone was only one of many who responded to the perceived excesses of "loyalism"—the heart-on-sleeve popular conservative
ideology that proclaimed (sometimes in bombastic tones) love for king
and country—with what might be termed anti-anti-Napoleonism. This
latter position sometimes resembled, and it could sometimes become,
flat-out pro-Napoleonic feeling.

This book explores the ways in which Napoleon Bonaparte mattered
for Britain, whose shores were never trespassed by the French revolution's or Napoleon's troops. British forces fought the French from
February 1793 until June 1815, with only a short interlude of peace
from March 1802 to May 1803. Even before his *coup d'état* of November 1799, Napoleon attracted British attention as the young commander
of France's "Army of Italy" from 1796 and as the leader of an Egyptian campaign in 1798. As general, consul, and emperor—and then as an
exile—Napoleon was an object of fascination for British writers and
artists, and for the British people generally. Though many Britons demo-
nized Napoleon, their hatred was often tinged with anxiety and doubt
about their own nation's condition. A vein of sympathy for Napoleon,
moreover, ran through late Georgian political culture. Napoleon's place
in the British imagination was a complex one, for he could be put to
many uses. For a great many observers, both friend and foe, Napoleon
served as a lens through which to scrutinize Britain's own identity, government, and history.

British writers saw their country as the peculiar target of Napoleon's
enmity, and took this fact to be, as one pamphleteer wrote in 1803, "a
glorious and enviable distinction," "the highest compliment, which it is

1. James Gillray, "The King of Brobdingnag and Gulliver," 1803 (Houghton Library, Harvard University).

within his competence to bestow, to our energy and resources."[4] They saw Great Britain—as the Earl of Selkirk declared in 1807—as "the only bar that stands between Napoleon and the empire of the world," and therefore as a nation whose "annihilation" Bonaparte sought with particular zeal.[5] And they took his final surrender to a British ship in 1815 as "perhaps one of the best and one of the most welcome compliments that could be paid" to England's "native independence."[6] One observer after another portrayed Britain's national singularity as if it were inextricably bound up with its relationship to Napoleon.

Geopolitical sense lurked behind these declarations, certainly. Biographers of Napoleon have confirmed his fixation with Britain, a fixation that mingled distaste with admiration. Military historians well know how critical the British armed effort was to Bonaparte's ultimate defeat.[7] But stressing the peculiar relationship between Napoleon and Britain also made a very pleasant story for the British to tell themselves about themselves, as the logician Richard Whately pointed out in 1819. "It *may* all be very true," Whately allowed; "but I would only ask, if a story had been fabricated for the express purpose of amusing the English nation, could it have been contrived more ingeniously?"[8]

There was great narrative satisfaction to be found in reading the Napoleonic wars as a story of single combat between Napoleon and Britain—a satisfaction apparent in Wordsworth's virtual sigh of relief when Napoleon defeated Prussia in 1806 at Jena. Britain now stood "alone," the poet wrote:

> The last that dare to struggle with the Foe.
> 'Tis well! from this day forward we shall know
> That in ourselves our safety must be sought.[9]

Britain's solitary stand against Napoleon demonstrated, for Wordsworth as for others, a certain moral superiority over other European nations. This single combat was a test: a trial of British character, a confirmation of British greatness, an interrogation of British weaknesses. As Britain's special enemy—Wordsworth would suggest a few years later—Napoleon played a critical (if unintended) role in regulating Britain's national character. To maintain its moral compass, Britain needed an enemy like France to contend with: "If the time should ever come when this Island shall have no more formidable enemies by land than it has at this moment by sea" (Britain's naval predominance having been established at Trafalgar in 1805), "the extinction of all that it previously contained of good and great would soon follow." Domestic virtue depended on having an enemy "capable of resisting us, and keeping us at arm's length," Wordsworth continued. "If a nation have nothing to oppose or to fear without, it cannot escape decay and concussion within."[10]

To understand the significance of Britain's war against Napoleon, one must first recognize France's long-standing role in the British imagination as an oppositional figure against which Britons could define their own nation.[11] Enmity between English and French rulers had been a theme since the Hundred Years War—or indeed since the coming of William the Conqueror, as British publications during the Napoleonic wars frequently reminded their readers. More recently, the absolutism of Louis XIV had been associated in British minds with the executive overreach of the Stuart monarchs. Before the revolution of 1789, flaws in the French polity were thought to be linked to defects in the French personality. That pre-revolutionary Frenchmen were purportedly effeminate and frivolous explained their slavish readiness to truckle before authority. Political writers contrasted the French concern with surface appearance with British "sincerity" (an ideal of artless frank honesty not so far removed from French revolutionary notions of transparency).[12] Caricatures contrasted French effeteness with a stolid British manliness. They set France's Catholic (and thus "Antichristian") intolerance against Britain's Protestant liberties, and the overbearing French monarchy against a British executive that in principle represented (even when in practice some thought it threatened) the liberties and balance established by Magna Carta and the Glorious Revolution of 1688. In short, pre-revolutionary France represented the antithesis of Britain. Even the onions and *soup maigre* its unfortunate subjects were purported to subsist on could not compare with the glorious beef and ale that John Bull enjoyed.

While the French revolution dramatically altered British perceptions of the French character, it would not make the cross-Channel contrast seem any less important. The British stereotype of the French had to be modified radically in its details, but the general opprobrium remained. *Ancien régime* frivolity turned into revolutionary savagery, and servility to power became the anarchic repudiation of hierarchy and tradition. A new form of gender indeterminacy took the place of the old one (thanks to overstated reports of French sexual egalitarianism). Students of eschatology, upon reflection, stated that Antichrist must represent atheism rather than popery—which left France's identification as the Beast of Revelations comfortably unchanged. So while the perceived nature of France mutated dramatically, the habitual opposition between things British and things French did not. Britain's neighbor continued to function as an antitype, an "other" signifying Un-Britain. Even for many who sympathized with some aspects of the French revolution—even for those who wished to transplant its spirit to Britain—national difference continued to loom over universal rights, a huge obstacle overshadowing the easy application of French lessons.

The rise of Napoleon Bonaparte, as this book will show, ushered in a new, more equivocal phase in British thinking about France. Napoleon's identity seemed decidedly mixed, his personality protean, his characteristics disputable. His political, his religious, even his ethnic identity did not seem clearly defined; in him, elements of the old and new orders coalesced, merging also with even more exotic ingredients. The very disputability of Napoleon's character—the perceived contradictions in his personality, the way he seemed to straddle categories of analysis—made him a rich subject for interpretation. And his position as leader of Britain's traditional antagonist gave a particular urgency to the puzzle he posed, for the questions raised by his case were inevitably felt to reflect on the British condition. Under Napoleon, France continued to provide the British with a yardstick against which to measure their own national character and destiny. But the lines of measurement now seemed flickering and ill-defined. British national consciousness could not remain fixed in an age where so much attention was given to the shifting nature of Britain's traditional antagonist. Napoleon unsettled Britons' certitudes about their enemy and themselves.

Britons of all political temperaments read in Napoleon's complicated, ambiguous person lessons about their own government and nation. His seizure of power raised questions about the nature of political rule, questions that might readily be reapplied to Britain's governors. The apparent shift in French character as the nation's government was once again transformed—into what many termed a military dictatorship— raised questions about the stability of national identity. These questions of nationality, like those about political legitimacy, resonated for Britons concerned with their own nation's integrity and destiny. Finally, as a figure acknowledged to be of momentous historical significance, Napoleon was a potent catalyst for British discussions of history—of Britain's own past and of the historical process in general. Napoleon, then, figured prominently in British analyses of government, nationhood, and history, in an age that served as a crucible for modern-day conceptions of these subjects.

When Richard Whately drew his readers' attention to how convenient a fiction Napoleon offered to the British nation, he did not really intend them to question the historical existence of Napoleon. Quite the contrary; Whately's underlying argument (he would later become Anglican archbishop of Dublin) was a religious one, that faith in biblical narrative, scoffed at by Humean skeptics, did not differ in quality from the faith that made British readers trust the newspapers' nigh-incredible tales of a man they did not otherwise know. To make his point, he deliberately chose the most inescapable political character of the day, in order to show how indirect was Britons' knowledge of him, how mediated this knowledge was by print culture (itself, Whately noted, an interested party in the question, since tales of Napoleon sold news-papers). Even those wounded or killed in battle by troops purportedly led by Bonaparte—even those thousands who rushed to Plymouth in the summer of 1815 to catch sight of a distant ship bearing a man said to be Bonaparte—had to rely on the self-supporting, if mutually contra-dictory, network of narratives poured forth by the British presses.[13] This book explores those narratives.

Napoleon was inescapable in British culture precisely because he was so variously useful. Using the tool of Napoleon, the British dissected their own identity, constitution, and history. But this self-reflection was seldom complacent. Instead of inspiring easy oppositions between Britain and a French "other," Napoleon raised questions about the condition of Britain. He spurred even the staunchest loyalists to express anxiety about the sturdiness of Britain's national character and the certainty of Britain's national destiny. He inspired cosmic doubts on the part of millenarian interpreters of biblical prophecy, who feared he was a scourge sent to punish the sinful British nation. And he provided British radicals and reformers with a potent instrument with which to investigate the condition of British liberty, a counter-king whose example allowed them to pick apart loyalist conceptions of monarchy and legitimacy.

The intertwined questions of Britishness and Englishness are live wires in historical writing today, as in British society.[14] My title's reference to the British therefore requires some explanation. Readers will note that the great majority of my sources are English, rather than Scottish, Welsh, or Irish. Metropolitan London publications, moreover, overshadow provincial ones in these pages (as they did, of course, in the general printed corpus). Though one key theme of this book is national identity, I do not propose to tease out national or regional variations in concep-tions of Napoleon. I am struck by the similarities and continuities, not the differences, between productions of different geographical origins. Scottish publications, and other writings by Scottish authors, treated France's ruler in much the same way that English ones did. (The sepa-rate question of Ireland lies beyond the boundaries of this study.)[15]

Much recent historical debate has centered on the question of primacy—whether English national identity or British national identity was the more potent or dominant historical force. The problem is posed starkly in the contrast between two highly influential works, both of which present Hanoverian Britain's conflict with France as a critical force shaping Britain's (or England's) thinking about itself. Gerald Newman's study of the growth of *English* nationalism barely mentions the distinction between Britain and England (and thus does not acknowledge the problem).[16] Linda Colley, by contrast, has emphasized the way in which a British national identity was "superimposed, if only for a while, onto much older alignments and loyalties"—loyalties, that is to say, to England, Scotland, and Wales as well as to regions and localities.[17] In response, Newman has criticized Colley for not describing the growth of British nationalism as predicated on, and secondary to, that of English nationalism, a "far more manifold and emotional" ideology.[18]

Insisting on the continued importance of England as a pole of allegiance and identification is more than reasonable. But this need not be done at the expense of Britain. One recent participant in the debate, Adrian Hastings, has flatly contradicted Colley's claim that in times of danger Britain was used as a rallying-cry. He insists that Colley has things backwards, and that *England* asserted itself as a rhetorical touchstone in wartime; as evidence, he offers brief quotations from Nelson and Pitt.[19] Hastings is right to insist on the continued relevance of English identity in the nineteenth century—but wrong to push the more inclusive, multi-ethnic entity to one side. Invocations of England were never in danger of disappearing. But the period that saw Nelson succinctly signal just what it was that England expected every man to do also saw innumerable appeals to Britain and Britons—in, for example, the popular broadsides of 1803, discussed in chapter 2 of this study. Hastings stumbles in seeking to substitute one national primacy for another.

Identity (local, ethnic, regional, and national identity—indeed, imperial identity as well) is not a zero-sum game.[20] English and British (and "Ukanian") national identities developed alongside one another (and also alongside Scottish, Welsh, and Irish identities, though these others did not share England's problem of getting confused with Britain).[21] The threads of national development intertwine in a fashion that ultimately defies extrication.[22] This does not give the historian *carte blanche* to substitute "British" for "English," or to alternate at will. But one must acknowledge that it is not always possible to choose the right adjective—that there is not always a right adjective to choose.[23] No definitive answer to the question of national primacy can be reached.

Indeed, as this book will show, late Georgian observers themselves saw national character as a fragile and unstable thing, prone to intervention and reinvention.[24] During the revolutionary and Napoleonic wars, the salient national contrast drawn by a host of writers was between France and Britain—a Britain whose internal divisions were generally ignored or denied outright. *Pace* Newman (who maintains that by 1789, "the making of English nationalism was over"), contemporaries viewed the French revolution and Napoleon's regime as offering distinctly new challenges to the integrity of English national character.[25] Rather than presenting national identity as solid and fixed, British commentators viewed it as a hostage to circumstance. Napoleon and his regime were presented as external threats to British national character. In addition, British observers were consumed with the fear of degeneracy, the fear that an all too malleable national character had already seen its best days. Contemporaries, in short, saw national identity as plastic, susceptible to imprinting and reshaping by history and indeed by the acts of individuals.

How much of the late Georgian British imagination can we retrieve? In this book, I use a wide variety of sources in an effort to understand the roles that Napoleon played in British thought and culture, both popular and elite. The writings of well-known British literary figures, and the parliamentary speeches of prominent politicians, are here read alongside hundreds of other sources: pamphlets, loyalist and opposition newspapers, caricatures, broadsides, almanacs, poems, paintings, plays, letters, and diaries. Each chapter draws connections between diverse realms of expression and argument.

To better grasp popular conceptions of Napoleon, I look at accounts of popular behavior: the riotous street celebrations of 1801, marking the peace with Bonaparte's France; the bacchanalian Soho coronation of a mock emperor in 1803; the ceremonial destruction of Napoleonic effigies in 1814; the respectful and curious crowds that assembled to view the captive Napoleon in Plymouth harbor in 1815. Another window onto the popular imagination is opened by studying printed genres that demanded no great measure of literacy, if any: broadsides read aloud in public squares and taverns, patriotic songs bellowed in the streets, and caricatures displayed in printshop windows (or "projected" in massive form at moments of public celebration).[26] Plays about Napoleon (some never published, but preserved for the historian because their manuscripts were vetted by the Lord Chamberlain's Office) entertained socially diverse audiences in the years of his reign and the decades that followed. Popular exhibitions of Napoleonic relics reached audiences numbering in the tens of thousands.

Journalism and political pamphlets form the backbone of this study. I try to indicate the dynamic process by which opinion about Napoleon circulated and shifted in daily and weekly newspapers and in monthly and quarterly reviews (and between these and the pamphleteers they reviewed). I give particular attention to a few journalists who most diligently devoted their energies to the problem of Napoleon: not only much-studied figures like William Cobbett, Leigh Hunt, and T. J. Wooler (all of whom might be described as radical), but also the ultra-loyalists Henry Redhead Yorke and Lewis Goldsmith, the moderate John Scott, and the radical Daniel Lovell.[27]

Part of my story is the ideological transformations of individual writers, and specifically their shifts of opinion regarding Napoleon. Generally, these transformations involved moves from the political left to the right. The best-known exception (and one to which I attend closely) is William Cobbett, the man who, in E. P. Thompson's estimation, "*created* [the] Radical intellectual culture" of the period after Waterloo.[28] Cobbett began the nineteenth century as a sturdy loyalist but by the time of Napoleon's first abdication had become his ardent admirer. Some conversions were the products of genuine self-questioning struggles of the soul. Others may have conformed more to Lewis Goldsmith's indictment of Henry Redhead Yorke, who had abandoned his former Jacobin principles to embrace the loyalist cause. Yorke (the then-republican Goldsmith wrote), having once "preached sedition," found that a stint in prison gave him leisure "to calculate, with mathematical precision, the exact rate of interest of *political conversion*."[29] Goldsmith himself, a few years after branding Yorke's transformation a product of self-interest, underwent an even more dramatic political shift in the same direction, and would collect, as we shall see, some attractive dividends.

If I dwell on Goldsmith's case (as I do, particularly in chapter 4), this is because of his prominence as a critic of Napoleon, the unusual degree of state support he enjoyed, and the significance of the case he made for Bonaparte's assassination. The sheer intensity of Goldsmith's concern

with Napoleon also justifies the attention I give to him, as to others especially interested in (in some cases obsessed with) the problem of
Bonaparte. If the history painter Benjamin Robert Haydon—who spent
many days "Napoleonizing" and recording in his diary the impressions
of his reading and musing—represents an extreme case of Napoleon
interest, it is only because of the depth of his personal identification with
Bonaparte, not the amount of time he spent thinking about him.[30] In the
latter, Haydon differed (if at all) only in degree, not kind, from many
contemporaries.

Many of the pamphlets I discuss were published anonymously or pseu-
donymously; others might as well have been, given how little we can
piece together about the lives of their authors. While the bulk were published in London, others came from the English provinces or Scotland—
and many authors of metropolitan tracts had themselves come from far
afield, following a geographical path of self-improvement. Some political writers were gentlemen of considerable means. Napoleon's early
biographer William Burdon was a wealthy owner of Northumberland
estates and coalmines; Capel Lofft, who inundated the British press
with a barrage of letters in the weeks following Napoleon's defeat at
Waterloo, was a former magistrate living on a family estate in Suffolk;
John Cam Hobhouse, later the literary executor of his friend Lord
Byron, followed his father, a baronet and wealthy merchant, into Parliament. But other writers came from more modest backgrounds. The
journalist and poet Leigh Hunt was the son of a debt-laden clergyman.
The careers of Cobbett and of Richard Carlile—who began, respectively,
as farmhand and tinsmith—testify to a political journalist's ability to
support himself through his writing: by newspaper sales, paid advertisements, patronage, government subsidies, or some combination of
these.[31] Lewis Goldsmith's unlikely trajectory reveals that one could be
subsidized first by Napoleon's regime and later by British ministries.

These men, and occasionally women, belonged to a discursive community that may sometimes seem isolated and autarkic, consumed
mostly in conversations about and among its own members. The price
of most pamphlets, and their small print runs, prohibited most people
from purchasing them.[32] But political writers addressed a broader and
more socially various audience, and not only when they were creating
cheap propaganda intended specifically for the masses.[33] The politically
informed class—those men and women who read pamphlets, newspapers, and monthly or quarterly journals—was not a narrow, privileged

elite. A growing segment of the population had regular access to printed political works. By the mid to late 1810s, the liberal *Edinburgh* and conservative *Quarterly* reviews each had a circulation of more than 12,000 copies;[34] each journal thus reached a segment of the population equivalent to that reached today by an American publication selling 280,000 copies, or a British one selling 57,000.[35] A circulation of this order, then as today—but perhaps especially in a day before mass politics and mass media—could make a journal a significant political force.

Newspaper sales were restricted by heavy taxes (of sixpence a copy as the nineteenth century opened, rising to sevenpence after 1815); even most middle-class families could not afford to purchase a daily paper of their own.[36] But coffeehouses and alehouses took in periodicals, including the radical newspapers that play an important role in this book. "Nothing is more common," one loyalist pamphleteer complained in 1812, "than to see pasted upon the windows of the lowest pot-houses, eating-houses, and gin-shops, this inviting bill of political fare: 'The Statesman, Cobbett, and the Examiner, taken in here.'"[37] Subscription reading-rooms spread rapidly; newspapers were hired out by the hour (and then sent to the provinces to make similar rounds); families clubbed together to share subscriptions.[38] Even the illiterate were within reach of papers read aloud at the local tavern, as was the habit with populist radical publications like *Cobbett's Weekly Political Register* and the *Black Dwarf*.[39]

It was not unusual, in short, for an individual newspaper to pass through the hands of a dozen or more readers—to the point even of becoming "illegibly black."[40] William Cobbett, in 1803, estimated that ten people read each copy of his *Political Register*, thus making an effective readership of 40,000.[41] Applying this multiplier (a rather conservative one when compared with those offered by press historians) to the 12,000 weekly copies of the *Black Dwarf* reportedly sold suggests that 10 percent of the British population may have encountered its radical arguments at first hand.[42] Even if we hold such speculative estimates in check, we must acknowledge the social breadth of the newspaper audience and its voracious appetite for news—an appetite especially strong in the war years, when foreign events took on a heightened significance.[43]

The impact of the French revolution on British politics and society has received considerable attention from historians, and while most studies confine themselves to the decade preceding Napoleon's accession to

power in 1799, some also cover the years of Napoleon's empire.[44] Clive
Emsley's valuable study of the effects of the French wars on British
society treats the period from war's outbreak in 1793 through
Waterloo, as does J. E. Cookson's excellent account of liberal anti-war
sentiment.[45] But in general the period of Napoleon's rule has been overshadowed by the years at either end of his career. This is notably the
case for histories of British radicalism, since the 1790s and late 1810s
were crucial moments for radical thought and activity. Though a few
historians have worked to establish the continuity of radical politics over
the period, the years of Napoleonic rule—the years between Pitt's suppression of radical societies and the radical resurgence after Waterloo—
have received little attention.[46] Napoleon's place in the radical
imagination, even after Waterloo, has prompted little comment; one aim
of this book is to show how important, and surprisingly positive, this
role could be.

Historians treating Britain during the French wars have tended to
pitch their tents in either one of two loosely organized camps. By emphasizing the vitality of radicalism, some have portrayed British political
culture as rife with discontent, even primed for revolution.[47] But the last
generation has seen renewed attention given to the wartime loyalty of
many Britons. Revolution, this latter camp has suggested, was averted
not through state repression but thanks to a widely shared satisfaction
with the British constitution and monarchy. According to Colley, the
triumph of British arms over Napoleon—requiring an unprecedented
marshaling of manpower and, as Colley stresses, womanpower—would
be inexplicable in the absence of a sincerely held and *popular* loyalist
ideology that celebrated king and country.[48]

The renewed historiographical emphasis on loyalism provides a salutary corrective to studies too ready to offer radical experience as the
popular experience more generally. Simply because radicals claimed to
speak for the people does not make it so, and the historians of loyalism
are right to identify a broad swath of the British people as in some sense
loyalist. But just as radical history tended to drown out loyalist voices,
so focusing on popular conservative patriotism can marginalize radicalism.[49] Moreover, as Cookson has recently stressed, we must distinguish between full-fledged loyalism and a "national defence patriotism"
that motivated a great many Britons during the years of war (particularly when imminent invasion was feared, as in the spring and summer
of 1803). Many common people, Cookson suggests, were royalist

without being loyalist; moved by a patriotic love of country and king, they were not committed to the blustery anti-reformism of loyalist journals and pamphlets.[50]

This book, by treating radical alongside loyalist discourse and noting their interplay, hopes to neglect neither phenomenon. While not, I hope, allowing radical visions of Napoleon to predominate unduly over the loyalist views that may very well have been more widespread, I do hope to show that radical sympathy for Bonaparte—lurking and half-hearted sympathy, as well as outright endorsement—was an important element of British political culture during and after Napoleon's empire. Though Napoleon's popularity among British radicals rose dramatically after his first exile, he never lacked a radical following. This book also hopes to cast loyalism as a somewhat less self-assured outlook, characterized by doubts and anxieties about the British nation and destiny.

Political terminology poses a challenge for the historian of late Georgian Britain. Many basic terms—notably "liberal" and "radical"— were only just being coined, and were not yet in general use. The strict constructionist response is to prohibit all use of any such words (J. C. D. Clark's blanket condemnation of anachronistic language extends so far as to forbid the word "anachronism" itself).[51] James Sack, by contrast, has deliberately avoided contemporary terms like "loyalist" in favor of the latter-day portmanteau term "right-wing."[52] I have chosen a middle road.[53] Rather than accept Clark's implicit claim that the chicken (the word "radicalism") must have preceded the egg (a phenomenon that the historian can safely term radicalism), I am ready to use the term somewhat before it became common currency.[54] For want of more precise contemporary phrases, I occasionally employ the words "moderate" or "liberal" to describe middling positions.[55] But I have mostly avoided "conservative," as the superior contemporary term "loyalist" more precisely describes the popular ideology of many late Georgians.

This is the first book to undertake a thorough reconstruction of Napoleon's place in the broad political culture of late Hanoverian Britain.[56] While Napoleon's handling by writers prominent in the canon of British letters has received some systematic attention from literary critics,[57] the general tendency of historians has been to take positive or negative opinion about Napoleon as a given, rather than to explore the nuances of an individual's position (let alone to situate this position within the wider intellectual environment).[58] There has been little suggestion of the extent to which Napoleon was perceived by many British contemporaries as a problem with no easy solution. The story of British reactions to Napoleon includes many tales of equivocation and ambivalence, as well as many dramatic about-faces in attitude. Throughout his career, Napoleon had British admirers, but the pool of his support was a shifting one in which ardent advocates could suddenly become harsh critics—and one-time enemies, champions.

While this book's general trajectory is chronological, chapters are for the most part thematically organized and do not hew too closely to the course of either Napoleon's life or his wars.[59] Indeed, many key moments of Bonaparte's career go unmentioned, including some that inspired British interest. I do not wish this book to become a mere catalogue of British reactions to individual battles and conquests, alleged atrocities, and supposed reforms. Some important accomplishments of Napoleon, moreover, inspired surprisingly little contemporary British comment (for example, few British observers seem to have had all that much to say about Napoleon's Civil Code).[60] Bonaparte's military achievements inspired a great deal of comment—but they receive little attention here.

The following chapters focus on several themes that dominated British discussion of Napoleon during his life and in the generation after his death in 1821 (a generation for whose political debate Napoleon continued to be a compelling focus). The most prominent were national identity and the constitution. To these, a third, history, might be added, for the discourses of national identity and constitutional development were both fundamentally historical, posing as they did the question of whether national character and political liberty were stable or in decline.[61] One of the epithets most frequently hurled at Napoleon, "Corsican usurper," drew its force from the double-edged charge it made. Napoleon was branded an interloper because of his birth outside of France and outside of the Bourbon line of kings; he unsettled relations that were thought to be historically constant and ordered. But Napoleon's perceived foreignness and illegitimacy were not simple matters, once they began to be considered closely by British observers.

From the perspective of government or nation—as from the standpoint of religion, nation's close ally—Napoleon proved a slippery figure for analysis. British observers of his rise to power were perplexed by his hybridity in political, national, and religious character. Was France's new leader Jacobin or king; Corsican or French; Catholic, atheist, or something else? Which historical figure might one best compare him with?

By complicating the traditional dichotomies drawn between Britain and France, Napoleon blurred British conceptions of national identity. By muddying the waters of religious logic by which British observers were accustomed to draw a sharp division between their Protestant kingdom and France, Napoleon raised disturbing questions, especially for observers of a millenarian bent, about Britain's destiny. And by grafting the trappings of dynasty onto a political character rooted in French revolutionary republicanism, Napoleon opened a veritable Pandora's box of arguments about political legitimacy, one that would be impossible for conservatives to lock again.

The two themes of nation and constitution were hopelessly interwoven: the debate over constitutional reform was ultimately an argument about national character. Conservative observers feared reform would unsettle the hierarchical fabric of British society, and undermine national tradition. When they denounced "French ideas," it was not only the reforms themselves that horrified them, but also their un-Englishness (whether they characterized this as Gallic or, more broadly, as cosmopolitan, nation-less). French liberty, as defined by the French revolutionaries, seemed a threat to English liberty. Reformers, for their part—at least those working in what James Epstein has called the "constitutional idiom"—maintained that English tradition had already been assaulted, that the once-glorious constitution had been undermined by boroughmongers, pensioners, and sinecurists, and that radical reform was the only way to restore truly English government.[62]

Another set of radicals, as chapter 6 will suggest, rejected the constitutionalist idiom, and embraced French reforms because the English constitution was, in their eyes, either non-existent or hopelessly contaminated. For them, perhaps, the issue of national character could be separated from that of constitutional reform—but only in the sense that they wished to substitute the rational for the national, an actively un- or anti-national set of reforms for the English governmental traditions they saw as poisoned at the source. Spurning the argument from history—the misty-eyed veneration of English tradition (either the historically defined hereditary "legitimacy" of loyalists or the ancient constitution that some radicals wished to rescue)—the anti-constitutional radicals, proclaiming the rights of man in the abstract, also rejected claims of specifically English (or British) liberties.

National character and constitutional rights were integrally connected in the eyes of late Hanoverian observers. The "free-born Englishman" would not have been English without his hard-won liberties (nor would the Scot or Welshman, tacit companions in this category for most contemporary writers). "Take away the theoretical abstract liberty of the subject," wrote the historical painter Benjamin Robert Haydon in late 1819—a few months after the Peterloo massacre, when even a political moderate like Haydon could fear that Britain's governors were contemplating such a theft—"& you take the boast of Englishmen from childhood to manhood, you destroy that conscious distinction between a Frenchman & himself, you weaken the enthusiasm, attachment, to the Country that bred him, & in a few years the spirit of England will be broken down." The fabric of British identity and spirit, typically defined here in contrast to France, could hardly be independent of the political regime that presided over it. National character could be reshaped from above, many feared. Honest, frank John Bull might be made a new man—a far less spirited and independent one—if his governors so chose.

Characteristically (for Haydon tended to view the world through the case of Napoleon, when not viewing it through that of his own troubled professional career), the painter introduced Bonaparte into this analysis of Britain's ills. The now-fallen leader had paved the way for Britain's rulers, Haydon warned: he had "done an irreparable injury to liberty by shewing the feasibility of complete & systematic despotism," and had thus "given the clue" to others in power.[63] This claim, quite a common one, that Napoleon had altered the character of the French, bears some emphasis. One thing the Napoleonic case demonstrated to British contemporaries was the susceptibility and malleability of national identity. If the culture and identity of the ancient Gallic antagonist had been so remarkably remade, first by revolution and then by its sequel, might not Britain itself be altered? For some, the fear was that Napoleon's troops might, by invading Britain, subject and transform it. But many worried that a home-grown decay of national character—instigated not only by continental cultural infection but also by ministerial and monarchical abuse of the constitution—might already be doing Napoleon's work for him.

The peculiar sequel to this wartime anguishing (loyalist and radical) over British liberties was, as this book's final chapters will show, a sort of rehabilitation of Napoleon. The defeated and deposed ruler would gradually lose much of his power as a divisive figure in British political culture. He would become assimilated into British national mythology, his character treated sympathetically in popular song and theater, his case used to demonstrate the contingent and relative qualities of political legitimacy in an age of revolutions. Formerly reviled, Bonaparte would be treated warmly. Indeed, he would be handled with the "fair play" that many had hailed as a central component of English national character. In that sense, at least, John Bull revealed himself to be a sturdy and resilient figure, resistant to the domestic or foreign tampering feared by so many Britons during the wars against Napoleon.

CHAPTER 1

Classifying Napoleon

Each foreign land he dances through,
  In some new garb behold the hero;
Pagan and Christian, Turk, and Jew,
  CROMWELL, CALIGULA, and NERO.

"Harlequin's Invasion," 1803[1]

During the first few years of Napoleon's reign, the relationship between Britain and France veered from war to peace to war again. Individual opinions of Napoleon shifted quickly and frequently. Politicians and political writers debated whether peace was truly possible with this military hero, about whose motives they knew so little. These early years saw, in particular, many radical devotees of Napoleon abandon their admiration—and often their radicalism as well.

Public debate over Napoleon, and individual uncertainty about him, owed much to his perceived enigmatic nature. Attempting to understand and classify him, British observers continually found that he resisted being pinned down (as, indeed, he does to this day). He did not readily fit into pre-existing political or national categories. As a result, the enterprise of analyzing Napoleon opened new avenues of political discussion. The difficulty of classifying him would lead a good number of observers to turn their scrutiny to the very categories that he seemed to elude.

Had things worked out differently, the British might have first come to know Napoleon Bonaparte as the leader of an expedition to conquer England. Returning in triumph from his 1796–97 campaign through Italy—having brilliantly defeated Austrian and papal armies and established a set of republics on the French model—the young general was placed in charge of the "Army of England," whose ships were massing in France's Channel ports. Finding the proposed campaign strategically questionable, Napoleon proposed hitting at Britain by a different path: invading Egypt, as a stepping stone to India.

Napoleon's exact destination, as he departed France, was a matter of much speculation in Britain.[2] Hester Lynch Piozzi (to whom Dr Johnson had unsuccessfully proposed when she was the widow Thrale) hoped his "mysterious expedition" was aimed at "revolutionising the Greek Islands" and "waking the Turks from their long sleep." While fearing the threat Napoleon posed to Britain's Indian possessions, Piozzi still regarded him hopefully as a force of liberation.[3] With Bonaparte's arrival in Egypt came reports of his conversion to Islam. Apparently prompted by a combination of cynical calculation and Enlightenment naïveté, Napoleon had announced to the people of Egypt that the French, too, were Muslims. While he did not persuade the Egyptians, this act convinced many Britons of Napoleon's true foreignness (this French general of Corsican birth was apparently even more exotic than he seemed) and of his shiftiness. Reports of his death in Egypt were quickly corrected; but those of his conversion, and of atrocities committed at his command, would color his reputation in Britain for years to come.[4]

A few later abuses of power would regularly be trotted out as evidence of Napoleon's inhumanity: most importantly, the 1804 kidnapping and execution of a Bourbon prince, the duc d'Enghien, but also the execution of a Bavarian bookseller named Palm and the mysterious deaths in captivity of two alleged English agents, a Captain Wright and the French revolutionary general Charles Pichegru.[5] Still, most litanies of Napoleon's crimes would be dominated by reports of his actions before attaining political power. The charges centered on two events at Jaffa. The French had massacred several thousand Turkish prisoners because Napoleon believed they would again take up arms if released. And Napoleon had reportedly (though many then and since have denied the tale) poisoned his own plague-ridden troops, whom he was leaving behind, for fear that they would fall into less merciful Turkish hands.

So Napoleon's place in the British imagination was already complicated, even before he had achieved supreme political power in his *coup d'état* of November 1799. He acquired a name for himself as more than simply a military figure. His first Italian campaign of 1796–97 marked him as an opponent of the papacy. His wresting of artworks from the rulers whose principalities he besieged there, while encouraging some to view him as a plunderer, made others regard him as a patron of the arts. Some suggested that with the coming of peace, British artists would benefit from the proximity of such a treasure-house of art.[6] Napoleon's reputation as a friend of knowledge was reinforced by his enlisting a troop of scholars in his Egyptian expedition.[7] No wonder, then, that an emblematic portrait published in 1799 paid tribute not only to his military prowess and his "Destruction of the Papal Tyranny and Superstition" but to "his love of Literature and the Arts."[8]

Napoleon's personality had already begun to fascinate. The liberal *Monthly Magazine*, which offered some of the most favorable early accounts of Napoleon, praised this "extraordinary" man not only for his military "intrepidity" and his humbling of Catholic "superstition," but also for his remarkable self-control. "Above all things," the journal suggested in May 1797, Napoleon had "attempted, and in a great measure obtained, the mastery over his passions. He is abstemious at his meals, and was never seen, in the slightest degree, intoxicated."[9] Such accolades help explain the concern of the *British Critic*, expressed in December 1798, that Napoleon had become the "acknowledged idol" of too many Britons.[10]

The coup of 18–19 Brumaire, year VIII (9–10 November 1799) ousted France's Directory from power, and prepared the way for a new constitution designed by the Abbé Sieyès. A decade before, Sieyès had helped usher in the revolution; he thought he would now dominate the new first consul Bonaparte (the other two consuls having been defined from the outset as mere advisors to the first). From the beginning, however, the new regime was identified with the recently returned general. The first task facing British observers was determining the nature of the new regime and classifying the first consul. Where was Napoleon Bonaparte's place in the French political spectrum, defined at one end by Jacobin terror and at the other by Bourbon monarchy? Did he simply represent another form of Jacobinism? Would he oversee a more orderly version of Jacobin democracy (or a more effective Jacobin terror)? Or was he an incipient monarch, bent on founding his own dynasty?

Much parliamentary debate, in the months following Bonaparte's coup, centered on the applicability of the term "Jacobin" to France's new government. Those skeptical of Napoleon's peace overtures tended to maintain, with Lord Grenville, that France "was Jacobin, she is still so."[11] The Pittite George Canning saw Napoleon as the natural product of "Jacobin principles." One should not be misled by any apparent constitutional change, Canning warned: "Though a military despot, [Napoleon] was a Jacobin in his heart."[12]

Determining the nature of the new French government had profound domestic implications. Canning made his remarks as part of a debate over renewing the suspension of habeas corpus: the continued vitality of Jacobinism in France was taken, by friends of the Pitt ministry, to justify repressive measures at home. Hence the sturdy resistance that opposition members offered to the government's labeling Napoleon a Jacobin. In the debate over habeas corpus, the reformer Benjamin Hobhouse (a Unitarian merchant, and father of the radical John Cam Hobhouse) insisted that Bonaparte's power "rose upon the destruction of the Jacobin ascendancy," and depended upon keeping Jacobins "in the lowest state of subjection."[13] Opponents of continued warfare disputed the identification of Napoleon as a Jacobin. The radical brewing magnate Samuel Whitbread asked why war with France continued after Napoleon had achieved "the destruction of Jacobinism" ("by taking all the executive authority into his own hands, destroying clubs, and repressing the licentiousness of the press").[14] Had not demolishing Jacobinism been the goal of the war? The Whig playwright Richard Brinsley Sheridan agreed that Jacobin principles had "stung themselves to death, and died by their own poison."[15] Thus, opposition Members of Parliament—including some who had formerly defended France's Jacobin governments—justified their readiness to deal with Napoleon precisely by the claim that he opposed Jacobinism.

William Pitt had at first been ready to depict Napoleon as an apostate to the Jacobin creed, apparently in the hope that attacking the first consul from the left might win opposition members' support for his war policy. Thus he had announced, in early February 1800, that Napoleon represented not only "every thing that a sincere and faithful royalist must feel as an insult," but also "every thing that a pure republican must detest; every thing that an enraged Jacobin has abjured."[16] In Pitt's initial reading, Napoleon was equally offensive to republican and monarchist. Pitt must have soon realized that this strategy would not succeed; the obvious retort was that offered by Whitbread, that Napoleon's anti-Jacobinical nature negated the rationale for Britain's war policy. Within a few weeks, Pitt was, like Grenville, presenting the new regime as Jacobinical. Jacobinism survived, and was now "centered in one man who was reared and nursed in its bosom." Napoleon was, Pitt declared—in a phrase that would reverberate through British discussion of Napoleon for years to come—"*the child and champion*" of the Jacobin atrocities. Once a Jacobin, Napoleon would always be marked by this "distemper," for "a mind once tainted with that infection, never recovers its healthful state."[17] (Coleridge's response, in 1802, would be that Bonaparte was at best a "parricidal child and champion of Jacobinism.")[18]

The debate depended partly on the inexactness of the contested term. Critics of the ministry commonly complained that Jacobinism was, in the words of Lord King, "a term of abuse indiscriminately thrown on every person who differed in sentiment from ministers."[19] The Whig leader Charles James Fox saw the "indiscriminate cry of Jacobin! Jacobin!" as having "worn . . . out" the phrase.[20] In response to such opposition criticism, the war secretary William Windham was ready to acknowledge some "difficulty in defining" Jacobinism. Insisting, however, that the term did not depend on the principle of universal representation but rather on "the ruin of every thing permanent and dear to man," Windham applied it to Napoleon's regime.[21] Opposition members, recognizing the best defense to be a good offense, deployed the term almost as frequently as ministers, but against the ministry (the government's repressive Irish policy had been "perfectly Jacobinical," Sheridan announced in February 1800).[22] The epithet was indeed being exhausted.

But what did those Britons who still regarded themselves as Jacobins, or republicans, think of Napoleon? That Napoleon was not, from some perspectives, Jacobin enough was made clear by Robert Southey in a letter to Samuel Taylor Coleridge a few weeks after the coup. Rather than denounce Bonaparte for concentrating power in his hands, Southey faulted the new constitution of Sieyès for distributing power too diffusely. The poet mourned the passing of the unicameral Jacobin system, damning the "cursed complex governments," more similar to Britain's own, that had replaced it. The power that might, if still organized as under Robespierre, have "levelled the property of France" and "revolutionised by example" the world, had been dissipated. France had wanted "a Lycurgus after Robespierre, a man loved for his virtue, and bold, and inflexible"; instead, it had Bonaparte, who Southey wished "had staid in Egypt."[23] Napoleon ("the Corsican") and Sieyès had "trod upon my Jacobine corns," Southey wrote a few weeks later, "and I am a thorough English republican."[24]

Southey, who is remembered for his apostasy from radicalism—like his fellow Lake poets Coleridge and Wordsworth, he journeyed from left to right in these early years of the century—would seem to have lost his taste for Bonaparte before abandoning his Jacobin sensibility. Napoleon's coup encouraged Southey to give up on the French, whom he now (echoing Coleridge) considered mere "children." Rather than rest his hopes abroad, he looked to home. "Buonaparte has made me Anti-Gallican," he wrote in the first weeks of 1800; "I remember Alfred, and the two Bacons, and Hartley, and Milton, and Shakespeare, with more patriotic pride than ever."[25] And yet Southey still had not entirely shaken off his admiration for Napoleon. The poet paid a final tribute in a letter to his brother in February. Citing Bonaparte's military career, "the views he entertains as a philosopher—the feelings which made him in the career of victory, the advocate of peace," Southey declared Napoleon "the greatest man that events have called into action since Alexander of Macedon." And even if he had been "the worst of all rascals," Southey added, the British had no right to force a new ruler upon the French.[26]

Southey may have been ready to give up on France, but other republicans had high hopes for the first consul. William Burdon proclaimed his enthusiasm in a series of letters to the radical *Cambridge Intelligencer* in the spring of 1800.[27] Burdon had established himself as a republican during his years at Cambridge, when he was the only Fellow of his college to vote against the university's incumbent MP, William Pitt.[28] Burdon became an inveterate correspondent of radical and reformist publications, and the author of several books, including one of the earliest British biographies of Napoleon. Where Southey had seen Napoleon as a betrayer of the revolution, Burdon would—briefly— regard him as its savior.

In his letters to the *Intelligencer*, Burdon hailed the returned conqueror as a moderator who sought "to reconcile all parties, to conciliate all his enemies, and to dissolve all opposition."[29] Bonaparte had "regenerated France," "redeemed a whole people from moral and political degradation, and improved the condition of his species."[30] Burdon distanced Napoleon from the more "hideous" characteristics of his revolutionary predecessors, and hailed the fact that not "a single instance of cruelty, injustice, or tyranny" could be laid at the new regime's door. Burdon sought, moreover, to link the consul to the revolution.[31] Napoleon's loyalty to revolutionary ideals contrasted sharply with the treachery of the Directory he had supplanted. Burdon redirected the charge of usurpation, commonly aimed at Napoleon, at the very regime displaced by his coup. Not Napoleon, but the men he had overthrown, were "tyrants and usurpers": usurpers, Burdon explained, in having "annulled all popular elections contrary to their own interest."[32] Napoleon, in Burdon's early estimation, had saved the revolution from itself.

Another British radical who would eventually, and most dramatically, cast aside his initial admiration of Napoleon was Lewis Goldsmith, who in January 1801 published *The Crimes of Cabinets*.[33] The crimes in question were the measures that Goldsmith claimed continental governments, in cahoots with the British ministry, had taken to crush French liberties. Goldsmith cited numerous ways in which Britain's cabinet was "resolved to violate the laws of nations," including counterfeiting French *assignats*. Goldsmith had spent a large part of the 1790s on the continent (leading a later critic, one of several who saw Goldsmith's ancestry as a mark of his un-Englishness, to brand him "an arrant wandering Jew").[34] Besides a spell in Germany and Holland, he apparently traveled, if we take him at his word, in the circle of the would-be Polish liberator Tadeusz Kosciusko. Britain's readiness to stand by while Polish freedom was crushed had demonstrated the nation's decline, according to Goldsmith: the Poles, in appealing for British aid, had "erroneously judged by what our forefathers were," not by the present-day species. Goldsmith saw decline also in Britain's having enlisted among the enemies of the French revolution. He invoked the spirits of 1688 to join him in outrage: "Ye revered Champions of that glorious Revolution, whose fragility your present descendants have cause to lament, could ye have believed, that ere the close of the eighteenth century, Britain should join a liberticide conjuration?"[35]

So far, so Jacobinical. But Goldsmith's republican world-view had room, as Southey's did not, for France's first consul. Goldsmith praised the "humanity" of Bonaparte, this "great man" of "boundless talents" whose "moderation and generosity in victory" stood "unparalleled in the page of history." He had come to power by "the unanimous voice of the nation." His government's conduct may not have been flawless, but it was "incalculably more so" than that of "those regular, religious governments that by every crime, art, and every falsehood, have laboured to destroy them."[36] With such panegyrics in his portfolio, it is no surprise that Goldsmith, journeying to France in 1802 after the arrival of peace, would soon find himself employed by the man he had applauded so vigorously.

In early October 1801, the Treaty of London—stating the preliminaries of a peace with France—was announced. The Bury St. Edmunds tanner Thomas Robinson, writing his brother Henry Crabb Robinson (later a barrister and *Times* foreign correspondent), reported a public "tumult of joy" in Bury approaching "madness." The secrecy with which negotiations had been conducted made the announcement all the more surprising. Not too many days before, Robinson noted, the funds had been falling for fear of an imminent invasion. Now, government newspapers had suddenly modulated their language to turn "the atheistical usurper" into "'the august hero,' 'the restorer of public order,' &c. &c.; in fact, everything that is great and good." The shift was so sudden as to remind Robinson of "the transformation in a pantomime, where a devil is suddenly converted into an angel."[37]

Though some described the peace as one of necessity, in which Britain had given up more than France, and others feared it would be unstable and short, few greeted the development tentatively. The *Oracle* newspaper described the peace as epoch-making. "This Peace will undoubtedly form a memoræble æra in the history of the Nineteenth Century," the paper declared, "as it commences a new order of things, which has no resemblance to whatever existed before. Religion, morality, policy, commerce, and industry, must all take a different course from that which they did under the antient order."[38] When jubilant Londoners massed in the streets to celebrate the peace, the *Oracle* could only approve. Could there be a "bosom so callous that would not participate [in] the festival of humanity?"[39]

One such bosom belonged to William Cobbett. The journalist had been shocked by the declaration of peace and by the popular jubilation. He had initially taken comfort from the fact that the issue of his *Porcupine* newspaper denouncing the terms of peace had sold out and had to be reprinted. Cobbett had found, moreover, that the "thinking people" with whom he spoke—"merchants, planters, and gentlemen"— "universally condemned" the terms of peace.[40] But within a few days, his remaining hopes had evaporated. An exuberant crowd had unhooked the horses from the carriage of General Lauriston, one of Napoleon's delegates for the peace negotiations, and pulled him in triumph through the streets of Westminster. Cobbett was particularly shocked by the crowd's having dragged the carriage "through the *Mall*, a place appropriated, exclusively, as a carriage-road, to the use of the ROYAL FAMILY!!!"[41] In a letter to his friend and patron William Windham (who had stepped down from office, with Pitt, a few months earlier, thus clearing the way for the peace-making Addington ministry), Cobbett reported that the behavior of the crowd made him now expect "a revolution with a great certainty as I do to Christmas or New Years' Day [*sic*]." Never before had "an English mob" become "the cattle of a *Frenchman*"; they did so now because they saw Lauriston as a regicide and an enemy of rank and property. Cobbett pessimistically noted that such welcomings of French emissaries on the continent had typically ended in revolt. "God preserve us from the like," he wrote, "but I am afraid our abominations are to be punished in this way."[42]

Cobbett was only made more unhappy by the government's preparing "a great illumination" for public buildings—2,000 lamps, he had heard, at the War Offices and Horse Guards alone—a practice that generally served as a signal for the population at large to light up their houses.[43] On the night of the illuminations, Cobbett refused to light his windows. A crowd attacked his house, breaking his windows while shouting, he claimed, " 'France for ever!'—'Huzza for BUONAPARTÉ!'—'Huzza for the Republic!' "[44] Cobbett blamed the ministry. Illuminations were appropriate for moments like the king's birthday or a great victory, but not for a "measure of *the Cabinet*." Illuminating government buildings meant forcing private individuals to follow suit or be exposed "to the insults and violences of the mob."[45]

But while some Londoners had "hoisted by compulsion" the candles they placed in windows, Cobbett recognized that many others celebrated out of free will. Of those who projected transparencies (large painted caricatures) lauding the peace, "nine-tenths were *republicans*," Cobbett insisted; "*nineteen transparencies out of every twenty, were expressive of attachment to* BUONAPARTÉ'S *person, or to the cause of France!*"[46] Contemporary newspaper accounts do not give much support to Cobbett's claim: though the tradesman whose transparency of Bonaparte bore the motto "Saviour of the Universe" was probably not alone in hailing the French regime, most transparencies seem to have celebrated Peace and Britannia rather than Bonaparte or France.[47] Cobbett claimed that a crowd in front of a printshop had hailed a man who, after making stabbing motions towards a depiction of Pitt, had doffed his hat to a print of Bonaparte and given it three cheers.[48]

Feeling so at odds with the cause of the crowd, Cobbett wrote in terms hardly in keeping with his reputation today as a populist. He decried the "mob" as a "fountain of discord" and "anarchy"—even, in a deliberately chosen Burkean phrase he used both publicly and privately, as a "swinish multitude."[49] In employing the phrase, he took care to note that he did not mean to damn the "sober, modest, frugal, quiet, and cleanly poor," who should "be treated not only with compassion but with a certain degree of respect." Rather, he was describing those who were "headstrong, noisy, growling, slothful, filthy in their carcasses, nasty and excessive in their diet and their drink," and should therefore "be treated with abhorrence."[50]

This effort to distinguish between a good common people and a bad pops up surprisingly frequently in Cobbett's writing. In the *Porcupine*, Cobbett declared his purpose to be "to defend the *people* of Britain against the *populace*."[51] But how to define this people? After the preliminaries of peace had initially been ratified, Cobbett described the news as having been received at Lloyd's Coffee-house, that nexus of the City merchant class, "with a *dumb hollow*," which he attributed to the fact "that nine tenths of the thinking people condemn the peace."[52] And yet just a few days before this he had stated as a certainty that "nine-tenths" (apparently a fraction with which he felt a natural affinity) "of the lower orders of the people" had seen in Lauriston "not merely a BUONAPARTÉ, nor a Frenchman, but a republican, a leveller, one of that nation who have murdered a King, a Queen, a Prince, and a Princess. . . . The people" (Cobbett continued, now dropping the fraction altogether) "here look upon the present French as *a nation of poor men*, who, after a long and arduous struggle, have recovered the possession of that property, and of all those other good things, which the great and the rich had, for centuries, unjustly with-held from them."[53] That Cobbett saw so little overlap between the people and the thinking people must have reinforced his alarm regarding the state of the nation.

The Treaty of London was followed, in six months, by the signing of the Peace of Amiens. One year and two months after this, in May 1803, Britain would again declare war on France. The peace acts as a peculiar punctuation mark in the history of British conceptions of Napoleon. For a brief moment in Napoleon's career, positive accounts of Bonaparte were plentiful—even, as in the case of the government newspapers mentioned by Thomas Robinson and Cobbett, encouraged. The twenty months of peace saw a steady flow of British tourists to France. British artists had a special incentive to visit: in Paris, they could study the extraordinary art collection that Napoleon had accumulated through his

European conquests. Benjamin West, the American-born historical painter and president of the Royal Academy, visited the Louvre, as did J. M. W. Turner. So, too, did a young portrait painter who would make his name by pen rather than brush, William Hazlitt.[54]

A host of journalists and writers, of various political persuasions, made their way to Paris: the poets Walter Savage Landor and William Wordsworth; the barrister John Carr, who for reasons of health had transformed himself into a professional travel-writer; Henry Redhead Yorke, the former Jacobin who, imprisoned for conspiracy from 1795 to 1798, had undergone a political conversion while in captivity (now editor of the government newspaper the *True Briton*). Wordsworth, no friend to Napoleon, scoffed at the

> Lords, lawyers, statesmen, squires of low degree,
> Men known, and men unknown, sick, lame, and blind,

who hastened, "like creatures of one kind," to pay tribute and "bend the knee" to Bonaparte.[55] The "men of prostrate mind," "to slavery prone," that Wordsworth had particularly in mind were no doubt those in the reforming circle of Charles James Fox, who himself, accompanied by Lord and Lady Holland, was fêted by Bonaparte.

It was to Lord Holland that the republican scientist James Smithson— illegitimate son of the Duke of Northumberland and founder by legacy of America's Smithsonian Institution—wrote in December 1801 about his high hopes for the peace. Commenting on the "astonishing" number of French people now docking at Dover, Smithson joked that the two countries seemed likely "completely to exchange their inhabitants." This was no mere quip. Smithson truly believed the peace to demonstrate that "National antipathies are vanished"; he claimed that a new "liberality of sentiment" had "pervaded every order of society, tending to the union of all men into one nation." Smithson scarcely met an individual, he claimed, "who is not in fact become a citizen of the world, who does not already consider the Globe as his country, and express a determination to take-up his residence in that part of it where he can live most secure, most free, most happy, whatever may be the meridian in which this may be."[56] For Smithson, peace promised a world where national boundaries would no longer matter.

In Smithson's dream, however, lay Cobbett's nightmare. Those who did not trust Bonaparte worried about the ever-expanding range of his imperium. The continental borders of France had proved porous to his power; what if the national division marked by the Channel faded away in the same fashion? By August 1802, Cobbett felt that Napoleon had effectively muzzled "the *liberty of the press*, as far as relates to Buonaparté or to his government." What little criticism of Napoleon remained in the British press was veiled in "puns and fables," to the point that soon "not one person in ten thousand will be able to discover who or what is the object of their satire."[57] Within a week, Cobbett's fears proved to be all too justified. Jean Peltier, an émigré journalist, had recently started publishing a royalist newspaper, *L'Ambigu*, in London. Recent pieces in that paper had passionately condemned Napoleon and, somewhat elliptically, appeared to call for his assassination. Now, at Napoleon's behest, the British government brought Peltier to trial for five counts of libel against the consul. Cobbett saw the trial as a confirmation of Britain's status as a "degenerate nation." Britons were now revealed to be "a *beaten* and a *conquered* people," he wrote.[58]

It was generally believed at the Stock Exchange, according to Peltier, "that my acquittal would be considered in France as tantamount to a declaration of war against the First Consul." The presiding judge, Lord Ellenborough, made quite clear in his remarks to the jury his own belief that the publication was a libel.[59] Not surprisingly, the jury, after a seven-hour trial, needed only one minute to pronounce Peltier guilty as charged. Luckily for the royalist exile, Britain and France returned to war before there was a chance to sentence him. Soon Peltier would have plenty of accomplices in libeling Bonaparte.

Attempting to classify Napoleon's political system in 1803, the travel writer John Carr settled on an apparent contradiction. Looking at Napoleon's state, he wrote, one saw the former "antipodes" of "the ancient french and the modern french," the monarchical and revolutionary regimes, "converging." Seeming opposites paradoxically combined in the new regime. In the new state's military features—its creation of "a refined system of knight's service"—Carr saw feudalism. "Seven centuries are rolled back," Carr declared, "and from the gloom of time behold the crested spirit of the norman hero advance."[60] In Napoleon, that is to say, Carr recognized a new William of Normandy.

The significance of the historical analogy Carr employed was at once charged and fluid. As Benedict Anderson has noted, William the Conqueror plays an unusual role in the national mythology of Britain. He is presented to children as "a great Founding Father"—but they are never, Anderson continues, "told 'Conqueror of what?'" because "the only intelligible modern answer would have to be 'Conqueror of the English,' which would turn the old Norman predator into a more successful precursor of Napoléon and Hitler."[61] It was radicals in particular (some idealizing Anglo-Saxon government, some not) who dwelled on the crippling nature of the "Norman yoke."[62] William's role in anti-Napoleonic broadsides was appropriately ambiguous. "The Little Island"—a 1797 popular song whose lyrics were often reprinted during the invasion scare, and whose tune was frequently appropriated for other patriotic ditties—celebrated Britain as "a right little, tight little Island," the favorite of Neptune, of Freedom, and of "BILLY the NORMAN." But the verse following that in which William declared his preference for Britain over Normandy described Harold "bravely defending the Island, / Poor HAROLD, the King of the Island, / Like a Briton, he died for his Island."[63]

The broadsides that overflowed from British presses on war's return in 1803 (scrutinized more closely in the next chapter) presented William more as invader than as founding patriarch, as in an advertised "SKETCH of all the INVASIONS or DESCENTS on the BRITISH ISLANDS, from the Landing of WILLIAM THE CONQUEROR, to the PRESENT TIME."[64] Harold, for his part, stood as a cautionary example of inadequate preparation. One song celebrating "The Men of Kent" recalled that "When HAROLD was invaded, / No discipline he knew, / WILLIAM, the NORMAN, waded / Through blood, and HAROLD slew." The bravery of Kent's men had been revealed in their showing "no submission" to the Norman invader.[65] And so the readers of broadsides were asked to identify with the failed "Briton" Harold rather than the successful "Norman" William, even though the latter was the ancestor of the present king. It was no coincidence that one broadside, imagining an epitaph for Napoleon on British soil, placed it near Hastings, the site of William's victory.[66] Bonaparte threatened conquest as William had; Britons must learn from Harold's error of complacency, so that history would not repeat itself.

William was not the only historical predecessor whom British writers invoked in their efforts to classify Napoleon. From the earliest notices of his military achievements, Napoleon had been linked to historical conquerors like Alexander and Caesar.[67] His arrival at the summit of the French state increased the perceived importance of classifying him with reference to history. Analogies were offered in profusion. He was said

to be a "Sylla" (Sulla), a "modern MAHOMET," "a second Attila," a
Catiline.[68] Cobbett, a few weeks after the Brumaire coup, spoke of
Napoleon's "Prototype, *Cromwell*" (a common comparison).[69] General
George Monck, who had helped to effect the restoration of the Stuarts
after Cromwell's death, was invoked in the early days of Napoleon's
reign, when it was still thought he might want to pave the way for the
return of the Bourbons.[70] Admirers hoped Napoleon would prove "a
second Washington,"[71] or worried that he would fail to take the cue of
the modern Cincinnatus and retire.[72] Comparisons with Maximilien
Robespierre dogged Napoleon: Was Bonaparte a "fac simile of Robespierre"? Or was he a "hypocrite" when he professed his love of France,
where Robespierre had at least been "no *dissembler*"?[73]

Historical analogy meant drawing distinctions as well as links. An
observer might raise a historical precedent in order to qualify an apparent similarity, presenting Napoleon as a flawed or inferior version of
a historical type. The ultra-loyalist Henry Redhead Yorke, though
hardly fond of Cromwell, still wanted to make it clear that France's
consul lacked even the questionable virtues of the Lord Protector. Where
Cromwell had possessed a "saturnine genius" that prevented him from
entering into any project he could not complete, Napoleon concocted
grand schemes he was not able to consummate. This "wretched thing
from Corsica," Yorke proclaimed, was but a "Cromwell in miniature (if
it be not a degradation of the talents of that illustrious hypocrite to associate his name with that of a despicable imp of fraud and malice)."[74] In
similar fashion, an 1803 pamphlet declared that compared with the
"great bad men" Alexander and Caesar, "even in their faults, the Consul
of France is as a pigmy to a giant."[75] The author of an 1809 pamphlet
saw Napoleon and Caesar "*each* trampling on the ruins of a republick,
and lording it over a subjugated people"—but still took pains to point
out that Caesar had displayed "valour" and "modesty," and had been,
"if a modern term may be applied to an ancient character, . . . a gentleman in manners, conversation, conduct, and mind," while Napoleon
was a vain self-flatterer.[76] Napoleon, in short, may have consciously
taken historical figures as models (reportedly carrying Plutarch's *Lives*
in his pocket in an effort "to copy the manners, and emulate the actions,
of antiquity").[77] But few thought his efforts at emulation successful.[78]

The ultimate tendency of such qualification was to admit that
Napoleon was unprecedented, a type unto himself, *sui generis*. There
was, in the words of the minister Gerrard Andrewes, "none like him in

the annals of universal history."[79] The changes he had effected in France
had "no parallel in the records of mankind, and therefore they must be
deciphered and judged by other rules than the mere analogies of
history."[80] Napoleon had broken free from historical models; he defied
classification.

The difficulty of slotting Bonaparte into any one category made the
trope of *hybridity* inescapable in early discussions of Napoleon. When
British writers referred to him as a "monster"[81] or a "mongrel,"[82] the
terms signified more than simply being cruel or low-born. Both terms
had connotations of indeterminacy; they signaled a mingling of characteristics, a straddling of boundaries. From an early point, Napoleon
was seen as "an unclassifiable being," a slippery, enigmatic figure who
did not fit.[83] "In his character there are the greatest contradictions," one
1809 pamphlet would later declare; "at one moment he appears a dwarf,
at another a giant."[84] Napoleon's example muddied the waters of the
traditional opposition between Britain and France. His hybridity complicated the business of national comparison. The mixed signals he sent
made it more difficult to treat France as a simple antithesis of Britain.

First, as we have seen, there was Napoleon's elusive political nature.
By combining "the two extremes of despotism and of democracy: an
Emperor in name, but in act a Jacobin," Napoleon became as "shadowy,
undefinable, and terrific" as Milton's Satan.[85] By mingling the democratic
and, increasingly, the dynastic, Napoleon resisted definition. As a later
chapter will describe, Napoleon's gradual march towards a more conventional semblance of kingship posed an intellectual challenge to
monarchists and republicans alike, as it became increasingly difficult to
distinguish him from other European dynasts.[86]

Second, there was the question of Napoleon's nationality—for many
felt that the key to understanding his regime lay in the interaction
between his Italian birth and the French national character. And third,
as explored below in chapter 3, there was his divided religious identity,
especially significant for pious observers but important to political
commentators more generally. In British eyes, Napoleon was a man who
had "served all gods, and all religions"; "at once an Atheist, a Deist, a
Mahometan, a Christian, a Catholic, and a Protestant."[87]

Napoleon's multivalence was treated as evidence of a deliberate shape-
shifting expertise in the use of disguise. The 1803 verse pointing out
the "new garb" Napoleon wore in each new land suggested that even
his resemblance to historical figures—"CROMWELL, CALIGULA, and

NERO"—was the result of a conscious adoption of costume.[88] Many observers remarked on the divided or shifting nature of Napoleon's identity, decrying him as a "Proteus, who has assumed every shape."[89] He was a Harlequin wearing "the motley coat of a CHARLATAN," according to Coleridge; a "political Janus," in the words of another disillusioned former admirer, William Burdon.[90] There was, wrote Charles Maclean—a medical doctor who had been detained by Bonaparte on the return of warfare in 1803—"not a shape, form, figure, or colour, which this Proteus-like consul is not ready to assume, in order to preserve and to increase his power." Napoleon's religious flexibility, and his readiness to appoint Jacobins and royalists alike, showed him to be "completely destitute of principle," "probably the most complete master of dissimulation that has ever appeared on the great theatre of the world."[91]

Sartorial imagery abounded. Napoleon's sway was portrayed as depending on his mastery of superficial allure—hence the frequent conceit of stripping away Napoleon's surface appeal (his mask or clothes) to reveal his true character. "The greater part of mankind seldom look beyond the surface," one 1803 pamphlet declared, "and see nothing in the victorious General but the laurel of his triumph: it is our present intent to remove this laurel, and, by thus displaying the man in his naked front, enable our readers to estimate him according to his real worth."[92] He was said to operate "under the mask of freedom," and to employ "fustian dignity and trumpery parade."[93] With the language of clothing came that of the theater, equally redolent of dissimulation and trickery. Commentators attributed the French nation's continued servitude to its weakness for "mummery," which Napoleon provided in the form of Catholic ceremonies and state "pageantry."[94] The barrister and former MP William Hunter portrayed Napoleon as "strutt[ing] on the stage, with a sweeping train, in the character of a mock Emperor," "amusing his gaping and frivolous slaves with pantomimical extravagances and dumb show."[95] And an 1809 pamphlet described the members of Napoleon's rubber-stamp tribunate and senate as "mere *automata*" who had carefully rehearsed their "*parts*" for the "*state drama*," a "tyrannical exhibition" whose "performance" was carefully overseen by the army. Again, the point was that Napoleon's theatrical trickery was especially likely to work in France, a nation "naturally prone to vain fancy" and entirely ready to serve as "the echo of this egotism, even to the extreme bombast of extravagant representation!"[96]

As the inescapability of the epithet "Corsican" suggests, few British critics of Napoleon failed to point out that he was a "foreigner" to France, born in Corsica mere months after the Mediterranean island had fallen into French hands.[97] At times, in the British mind, he would take on a more than Italian exotic tinge. Broadside readers were told he was "of a swarthy black complexion," "half-African, half-European, a Mediterranean mulatto," a "CORSICAN MULATTO."[98] The French émigré William Barré compared the "exotic Buonaparte" with an "oriental despot"; an 1803 broadside spoke of "the *Aga of Sultan* BONAPARTE's janisaries."[99] That Napoleon was "an alien to the soil which he has subjugated"—"not a native"—was a refrain throughout his career.[100] William Pitt declared a few months after the Brumaire coup that Napoleon was "a stranger, a foreigner," unconnected "with the soil, or with the habits, the affections, or the prejudices of the country."[101] Hester Lynch Piozzi noted in her diary that Bonaparte was "ruling a Nation not *his own* between whom & himself there is *no Tye*."[102]

Within the world-view offered by the discourse of national character, Napoleon's Corsican birth held great significance. It indicated that his relationship to the French people was not one between equals, and helped explain the nature of his political power over them. Cobbett, writing shortly after the coup, thought it significant that "the being to whom Frenchmen pay constant homage" was not himself French. If, as some claimed, he was Genoese, this would account for his "cruelty and oppression"; if Corsican, he was "a well chosen scourge in the hands of *unerring Wisdom* to chastise that nation which first effectually invaded the freedom, and annihilated the felicity of his native land." Napoleon's behavior (for example, his "criminal indifference" to French prisoners of war trapped in Britain) showed him to bear active antagonism towards France. But Bonaparte had long left simple "retaliation" behind, Cobbett wrote: "the revenge is disproportionate, he heaps cen-tuple slavery on a whole people for the crimes of a few, and visits the sins of the ancestors, without discrimination, on their wretched posterity."[103]

If Cobbett's account of the clash between Italian and French tem-peraments stressed Napoleon's desire for revenge, other observers emphasized the weak aspects of French character, of which Bonaparte was so clearly taking advantage. According to William Hunter, the "stranger" Napoleon saw the French—"light, and volatile, and cring-ing, and submissive"—as simply a "ladder" for himself. He had changed the very nature of their character, according to Hunter, "reduced them

to a state of as abject vassalage as ever degraded the nature of man."[104]
An anonymous pamphlet of 1806 similarly distinguished between
Napoleon's character (he possessed "the characteristic vices of a
Corsican") and "the character of the nation which he governs." It was
through intimate acquaintance with the "levity," "vanity," and "osten-
tation" of the French that Napoleon managed to govern them so effectively; he had these traits in mind when he crafted his imperial title.[105]

The effort to distinguish Napoleon's national temperament from that
of France could even lead to a softening of anti-Gallican language.
William Burdon, Napoleon's lapsed admirer, attributed the consul's
atrocities and "dark ferocity" to the fact that his character "partakes
more of Italian treachery, than of French openness and vivacity." One
ceased to be amazed that a man "bred in a civilized country could be
so coolly cruel" once one recalled "that Bonaparte is of Italian extrac-
tion."[106] Similarly, one 1803 pamphlet explained that the would-be
invaders (though *"rascally"*) were "poor fellows," much "to be pitied,
for the fault is not their's, for all the world knows that they wished for
peace as much as we cou'd do, till that *bloody-minded little Corsican*
forced them headlong into the war." It was simply Napoleon's promise
of plunder and rapine that was compelling the French into an invasion
(and even on this point, the author seemed to suggest grounds for sym-
pathizing with the French, seeing as in reality "the sly cunning rascal
intends to keep all to himself, notwithstanding his promises to his soldiers").[107] But the distinction between French and Corsican did not generally reflect favorably upon the French.[108] As an Edinburgh pamphlet
of 1803 put it, the "base and detestable" French were simply being led
"by a man more atrocious, if possible, than the worst of them":
Napoleon united "the low cunning and revengeful spirit of an Italian,
to the perfidy and unfeeling cruelty of a Frenchman."[109] Napoleon's
nationality, in this reading, exhibited his customary hybridity—and was
all the worse for that. In defying the lines of national classification, he
grafted together the least appealing characteristics of two nations.

If anything, the Italian character was portrayed in even lower terms
than the French. This explains the unceasing loyalist insistence on the
fact that Bonaparte had changed the spelling of his name, from
"Napoleone Buonaparte" to "Napoléon Bonaparte," in order to efface
its Italian origins (a fact that admirers of Napoleon did not dispute—
though they did have a greater tendency to employ the French rather
than the original spelling). One 1809 pamphlet, *The Exposé; or,*

Napoleone Buonaparte Unmasked, self-importantly proclaimed that it would prevent Napoleon's original names "from sinking wholly into oblivion"—that Napoleon could not, "despotic as he may be, force every person to write them after the same way."[110] Napoleon's Italian surname indicated his foreignness. His lack of connection to France lessened his claim to legitimacy—at least so long as one assumed that a nation's king should be of the same nation as his people. Under a Hanoverian monarch, however, the grandson of a German émigré, this was no easy assumption.[111]

CHAPTER 2

National Character and National Anxiety

As to me, I think, the Invasion must be a Blessing. For if
we do not repel it, & cut them to pieces, we are a vile
sunken race & it is good, that our Betters should *crack* us—
And if we do act as Men, Christians, Englishmen—down
goes the Corsican Miscreant, & Europe may have peace.
At all events, dulce & decorum est pro patriâ mori—& I
trust, I shall be found rather seeking than shunning it, if
the French army should maintain it's [*sic*] footing, even for
a fortnight.

Samuel Taylor Coleridge, 3 October 1803[1]

Mary and I sometimes talk of emigration—but where to go
is the question. France is the only country which to my
mind presents any temptation. The language, however, is
an insuperable objection. Buonaparte seems as if he would
make the assumed title of *great nation* a valid claim, and I
fear it is as clear that the sun of England's glory is set.
Indeed I am become quite an alarmist, which I believe is
equally the case with the democrat and the aristocrat.

Henry Crabb Robinson, diary, 27 January 1801[2]

The opening of the nineteenth century saw definitions of British identity
in flux. The Union between Great Britain and Ireland took effect on the
first day of 1801, a product of Britain's war with France. French support
of Irish rebels in 1798 had convinced William Pitt of the necessity of
incorporating Ireland more tightly into the kingdom. Ireland's parlia-

ment, after voting for its own extinction, was dissolved, and one hundred Irish MPs were seated in the House of Commons at Westminster. New official representations of the nation were instantly produced. A new standard, joining the crosses of the English, Scottish, and Irish patron saints, was hoisted aboard navy ships this New Year's Day.[3] The state seal was defaced and a new one delivered to the lord chancellor.[4] A new title for the king was decided upon: among other changes, George III's claim to be king of France (a claim of the English monarchy since the Hundred Years War) was discarded, apparently prompted by a French demand.[5]

The prime minister, William Pitt, shrugged off this pruning of the monarch's ostensible sway as the loss of "a harmless feather."[6] William Cobbett disagreed. Writing in 1804, he would describe the loss of this title as "a sure and certain mark of the debasement of the national mind." The title had kept alive "the memory of the conquest of France" through a narrative chain linking one generation to another: "every son asked of his father an explanation of the meaning of the title of King of France; that generally led to a relation, more or less correct, of the valorous deeds of Englishmen in former times; and the impression thus received was communicated to the next generation." The surest sign of "national decline" was that Parliament and the press had not objected to the loss of the title (though it was still treasured, Cobbett suggested, by the common people, who recognized "that the king is the repository of all that is necessary to the preservation of the national character"). Alas, according to Cobbett, this loss of a national symbol was joined by all too many other marks of national decline, ranging from the suppression of popular rural practices like boxing and bull-baiting to the spread of an "Italian-like effeminacy" among even the countryfolk.[7]

The creation of a new kingdom offered the opportunity to assess Britain's condition in the dawning century. The *Courier* newspaper, in a piece published on the day the Union took effect, welcomed the nineteenth century with trepidation. The nation faced dangerous pitfalls, not least in the continuing war with France. And though the passing century had seen Britain's commerce grow, the *Courier* feared that Britain had, "in proportion" with this success, "departed from the old principles of liberty; a general apathy has seized all ranks; we no longer speak in the firm and manly tone of our ancestors." Hope conjoined with fear at the prospect of a new era: "a friend to freedom," the *Courier* declared, "cannot be without feelings of anxiety."[8]

Many joined in expressing misgivings about the state of the nation, and in employing a rhetoric of decline. The fear that the national spirit of today's Britons might no longer measure up to that of their ancestors would haunt writers in the summer of 1803, when invasion by Napoleon's armies seemed imminent. Even as British writers poured forth a flood of loyalist tracts celebrating domestic liberties and denouncing the nation's enemy, they revealed their worries about stresses and strains internal to Britain.

Recent historical scholarship—reacting against radical histories that emphasized popular dissent and discontent—has sought to demonstrate the strength of popular loyalism during the revolutionary and Napoleonic wars. Such work provides the useful reminder that many Britons adored their king, and despised revolutionary and Napoleonic France.[9] But we should not leap from this finding to the conclusion that wartime Britain was a nation of self-assured optimists. This chapter suggests that the loyalist sense of national identity did not amount to a complacent trumpeting of the unassailable virtues of British character, or a sanguine assertion of the inevitable triumph of British arms. Loyalist pamphlets and broadsides were suffused with doubt and anxiety. Though loyalist writers sought to present the conflict between Britain and France in Manichean terms, they were far from confident about the integrity of the British national character. They celebrated British character as an ideal, and as a historical reality, perhaps—but they were consumed with worries about its present status. William Wordsworth, in October 1803, would write a hopeful sonnet imagining a joyous British victory over French invasion. But not too many months before, he had bemoaned England as a land of "selfish men," "a fen / of stagnant waters."[10]

The loyalist sense of nation was ambivalent, problematic, and troubled. In the British political literature of the late Georgian period—in pamphlets, sermons, and newspapers, and in the scores of broadsides churned out during the invasion scare of 1803—national character did not appear solid and unchanging. Rather, it was presented as a thing that could bend and shift under the influence of a dominant personality, an invading army, or even a merely cultural infection. Loyalist writers told the British people to beware Napoleon and his troops. But they feared equally an internal degeneracy, a decay of the British character that belied any claim to eternal national qualities.

When war returned in 1803, Napoleon ordered the arrest of all British subjects in France, some 10,000 in number. The novelist Frances Burney, visiting France with her French émigré husband, would be detained for ten years. Fears mounted of a French invasion of England. Rushing to piece together an adequate defense, the Addington government called out the militia and created a new Army of Reserve. To complement these organizations, appeals were made for Volunteers to step forward to defend their localities. Hundreds of thousands did so (though many of the recruits appeared to one Norwich gentleman not staunch loyalists but "rank revolutionists").[11] In the face of invasion, many finally abandoned whatever hopes they still had for Napoleon. Within two weeks of the end of peace, his recent admirer William Burdon wrote a pamphlet recommending "unanimity" against the French threat, and denouncing Bonaparte's character.[12]

One of the engines driving the mass mobilization was a propaganda effort perhaps unprecedented in its scope. A profusion of pamphlets and caricatures attacking Bonaparte and warning of French invasion were published in the spring and summer of 1803. In addition, a deluge of handbills—more than a hundred broadside titles—were produced for general circulation.[13] This dense cluster of sources, together with similar works published in the years that followed, provides the cultural historian with an invaluable window onto popular conceptions of Napoleon, and, more generally, onto late Georgian loyalist ideology. While this chapter draws mostly on broadsides, it also looks at anti-Napoleonic caricatures, which spoke in a similar language to the handbills. Though undoubtedly published in much smaller print runs, and enjoying a narrower circulation, engravings likely enjoyed their greatest influence at this moment: during the invasion scare, significantly more titles were published, many overlapping in their messages and imagery.[14]

Broadsides were produced by a host of anonymous writers, whom we now know to have included William Cobbett (still a dogged loyalist) and Hester Lynch Piozzi.[15] The propaganda campaign was coordinated by a relatively few actors, most importantly the bookseller-publishers James Asperne, John Hatchard, and John Ginger. That this bounty of print was overseen by a few zealous entrepreneurs meant that the broadside genre, despite its manifold titles and various forms, was characterized by remarkable uniformity of message and image. The orchestrated nature of broadside production made possible the frequent rearticulation of phrase and argument; working in concert, reinforcing each other's message, the broadsides could establish a codified, canonical reading of the Napoleonic threat. This was especially necessary after the conflicting signals the British public had encountered in Napoleon's first years of power—when the British government had worked to placate Bonaparte, and when many reformers still hoped that he would remain true to the revolutionary ideals that had nurtured him. Though the anti-Napoleonic broadsides had but a brief period of publication, they had, because of their unified message and mass distribution, a long season of influence.

As Cobbett pointed out, the "placarding system" could reach an audience beyond the scope of everyday journalism. Newspapers bore a stamp tax and "could not be pasted on the walls," Cobbett noted; "something more cheap, not so voluminous, and exhibited with greater facility, was wanted to complete, what the daily and weekly prints had so patriotically begun."[16] Though several broadsides claimed to address all Britons, others explicitly targeted the laboring orders. One longer pamphlet, though its title spoke "to all ranks," described itself elsewhere as a "cheap compilation, . . . solely compiled for the instruction of the lower classes."[17] As the *European Magazine* (itself published by the zealous broadside-producer James Asperne) reported, the various handbills were "all calculated to raise in the lower classes of the people a just detestation of the character and base designs of the enemy."[18] As far as the patriot-publishers were concerned, popular prejudice against Napoleon and the French could not be taken for granted.

No doubt direct government subsidy underlay the writing and publication of some works. One contemporary claimed that Cobbett's brief anonymous pamphlet *Important Considerations for the People of this Kingdom* had been "circulated by government at a vast expence"—in such great quantities, indeed, "that the country was overwhelmed with them."[19] Copies of Cobbett's pamphlet, bearing the royal seal, were sent to ministers in every parish in England and Wales, with instructions to deposit some in the pews and some in the aisles ("amongst the poor"), and with broadside versions to be placed on the church door and in other public spots.[20] The ubiquitous and official nature of the pamphlet may well, of course, as this observer opined, have worked against the purpose of the mass circulation, "the people being always suspicious of things thus forced upon their perusal."[21]

We gain some insight into the techniques by which broadsides were circulated from the frank instructions printed at the bottom of many. The general hope and advice was "that those who can afford it, will distribute these Papers among them who cannot."[22] One publisher was reported as having issued "gratuitously" 30,000 copies of an anti-Napoleonic tract (printed "in a very popular form").[23] But this was unusual: publishers did not generally give away their productions but entreated well-off individuals to purchase and circulate them. Bulk discounts encouraged the affluent to purchase broadsides (and some pamphlets) and distribute them widely. A dozen penny handbills might be had for ninepence; a hundred for six shillings.[24] Individual broadsides were gathered into miscellanies that were themselves offered at a bulk discount and "recommended for liberal distribution in every city, town, village, camp, and cottage of the United Kingdom."[25] The social distinction between those whom the broadsides addressed and those who would actually purchase them was frequently mentioned. The publisher of one broadside biography of Napoleon recommended that "Gentlemen" get additional copies printed in their localities "and have them well circulated, particularly on market days."[26] A good number of broadsides urged "Noblemen, Magistrates, and Gentlemen" to purchase, distribute, and post a few dozen bills in order to instruct their neighbors in the "*Cruelty* of the *Corsican Usurper.*"[27] One broadside (not, as it happened, one of the many whose main text addressed itself to women) hoped that "*Ladies*, and Women of all ranks," would assist in the effort of dissemination.[28]

One did not, however, need to purchase or even be given a broadside to encounter its message. Broadsides—when used as directed—would have been spotted on the walls of many public establishments, where they might spur discussions of the French threat. Hence the paradox that the individual handbill with the largest audience is the one least likely to survive and meet the historian's eye. We can only examine broadsides that were unsold, unused, or purchased by collectors—those pasted up for all to see left behind nothing but scrapings. The assumed ephemerality of the documents motivated the collecting of posting-sheets into anthologies so as to "preserve . . . for futurity" what might otherwise be lost.[29]

One publisher "strongly recommended" posting his illustrations of Napoleon's life "in Public Houses, and all Places of Resort."[30] Another suggested hanging his pictures of Napoleon's atrocities in public places—

taprooms, taverns, kitchens, "and all Situations in which common Prints have usually been hung." One might thus reach even the unlettered, he suggested: "Pictures speak to every Eye."[31] Clearly, many individual broadside copies had a considerable audience. And since "hundreds of thousands" of broadsides were circulated (as the *European Magazine* reported in August 1803, at the zenith of broadside production), they provide, as a group, perhaps the single most important evidence of what the British people were being told about Napoleon and France—and of what loyalists feared the British people might be thinking.[32]

Broadsides provided the British with a shared repository of imagery and argument, a pool of common knowledge about Napoleon that was available to nearly all, to embrace, revise, or refute as they saw fit. The actual descriptions that broadsides provided of Napoleon's character and intentions betrayed little subtlety, and may be summarized with some dispatch. But the broadsides deserve further attention because in treating Napoleon they revealed much about the nature of loyalist pessimism. They interwove their discussion of the external threat to Britain with concerns about the domestic state of the nation. Their very *raison d'être* (besides the profit that must, despite the occasional disclaimer, have been involved) was the worry that all too many Britons might find Napoleon a sympathetic rather than frightening figure. In delineating the threat Napoleon posed, they limned (partly by evasion, denial, and elision) Britain's vulnerability to Napoleonic France, the internal weaknesses and divisions that might open up the nation to defeat.

The loyalist broadsides of 1803 took a variety of forms. Among them were songs and odes, both playful and stirring (including one whose instructions suggested it be sung to the tune of the Marseillaise).[33] Several handbills imagined dialogues between Napoleon and John Bull, or between Napoleon and Talleyrand.[34] Mock-theatrical advertisements announced the imminent performance of Napoleon's invasion and defeat in the "Theatre Royal of the United Kingdoms."[35] Some broadsides reprinted loyalist sermons and speeches.[36] Others presented sensationalist accounts of Napoleon's atrocities in Europe and the East.[37] Still others purported to reprint the contents of Napoleonic handbills, in which he had supposedly promised his soldiers free rein—pillage and rapine— once they had landed in Britain.[38]

In finding political fault with Napoleon, the broadsides, significantly, tarred Napoleon as a "despot"[39] rather than a leveler: he was a "tyrant,"[40] broadsides informed their readers, "the most despotic, incestuous, bloody-minded Tyrant that ever disgraced Human Nature."[41] Absent, for the most part, was the epithet "Jacobin," so commonly flung about in the earliest days of Napoleon's reign. When one broadside did warn John Bull about Jacobins, it had English rather than French ones in mind: "a set of unprincipled rascals; who expect to be raised to a precarious, momentary power by French Invasion, and therefore endeavour to persuade their countrymen that France will diminish their taxes, and improve their liberties."[42] Indeed, Cobbett would grumble in November 1803 that journalists (but his criticism applied equally well to handbill-writers) railed against Napoleon "as a despot, not as a demagogue . . . ; as a tyrant, not as a usurper; as a traitor to his people, not to his Sovereign." Cobbett found the prevailing critique of Napoleon too democratic. "Instead of endeavouring to convince the people, that the tyranny, in France, had arisen out of the levelling principle, the London news-writers were, and yet are, continually, crying out against Buonaparté for having destroyed that principle."[43]

That Cobbett overstated the placards' radicalism is evident from the frequency with which broadsides, like newspapers and pamphlets, branded Bonaparte an "upstart" or "usurper."[44] Still, he had a point. One twopenny pamphlet invoked, if only half sympathetically, "the ghosts of the wretched Marseillois and all the Sansculottes" as witnesses of the "luxury and grandeur" of Napoleon's court. Who, after seeing the pomp of the consulate, could "pretend to talk of the extravagance of kings?" the pamphlet asked—a rather backhanded way of defending monarchy.[45] Broadsides tended to appeal not to Burkean hierarchy but to commonality—not to the forces that raised a ruler above his subjects but to those that tied together all members of a nation. While one handbill did note that George III, unlike Napoleon, "was born to fill the Situation he holds among us," it placed just as much emphasis on the fact that the "good old King . . . looks like an honest Englishman."[46] At this high point in what Linda Colley has termed the apotheosis of George III—the renovation of the monarch's and monarchy's popular reputation—the broadsides put little emphasis on the personal qualities of the British king.[47] One song cited his "Christian" and "merciful" nature; a few handbills included grateful references to "our good Old King (God bless him!)" or to "our King (*than whom a better never existed*)."[48] But the very mildness and informality of these tributes suggest that the broadside-writers recognized they were best off employing the figure of Farmer George, the king-as-everyman image introduced in the 1780s.[49]

Even in this guise, George III played only a bit part in the broadside narratives.

Napoleon's perfidy was the central message of the broadsides. His association with the devil was much harped upon.[50] Broadsides branded him as a criminal: an "assassin,"[51] a "ruffian,"[52] "a MURDERER, a ROBBER,"[53] a "Free-Booter,"[54] "the *Leader of a Banditti of Plunderers.*"[55] The broadsides, in addition, painted Napoleon as a creature of "boundless Ambition."[56] His goal, they declared, was "UNIVERSAL EMPIRE."[57] In pursuit of this end, he would stop at nothing.

Napoleon, the broadsides insisted, had committed atrocities wherever fortune took him: in Italy, in Egypt, in Syria, in Hanover.[58] According to some, Hanover had only suffered because it was part of the British king's dominions—a suggestion that augured ill for an invaded Britain.[59] A particularly popular image was that of the ghosts of Jaffa returning to haunt Bonaparte.[60] One "Song of Pity" pictured his bosom as "a hell" because he could not escape "Banquo's ghosts in thousands"; in another song, an invasion of England is averted because "spectres so dire" from Egypt arrive to take Napoleon away.[61] Many broadsides excoriated him for his treatment of Toussaint L'Ouverture, the brave Haitian leader whom Napoleon's troops had "Torn like a felon from Domingo's plain" and shipped to Europe to die in confinement.[62] Even Napoleon's military prowess could be explained away by his cruelty: his 1796 victory at the bridge of Lodi showed simply "that, to obtain his object, he cared not how many lives might perish." One student of his battles declared that any "enterprising general, of ordinary capacity" would have had equal success in Italy—and emphasized Napoleon's cowardice, displayed when he abandoned his army in Egypt.[63]

One critical component of Napoleon's character, alluded to in many broadsides and pamphlets, was his particular antipathy to Great Britain. Whatever horrors Napoleon might have imposed upon other countries, England would *"assuredly be more oppressed in proportion as she is more dreaded, envied, and hated."*[64] Britain ("the Guardian Angel of Europe") was the *"only* country in Europe that has defied his power."[65] The nation's riches made Napoleon covetous, and its constitution stood as reproof "to his own usurped and tyrannical government."[66] Hence his "rooted enmity" towards Britain.[67]

British commentators vacillated on the question of whether Napoleon and the people he ruled shared a common character. But many agreed that something in the French made them peculiarly vulnerable to

Bonaparte. The French were, one broadside declared in 1803, "a nation fitted only to be Slaves."[68] They were "A race accurst," one poet opined, "prone to extremes of ill; / Blood-drinking tyrants, or dust-licking-slaves!"[69] Napoleon's accession to power allowed the pre-revolutionary image of a naturally subservient French population to resurface: Bonaparte managed to rule the French so absolutely because they were "like true spaniels, who ever fawn and lick where they are worst treated."[70]

Other elements of the *ancien régime* reputation also came to the fore in this post-Jacobin age. French frivolity had long been associated with a love of novelty—the desire for change for its own sake. The French were famously volatile, "this hour feeling indignation at a base action, and the next forgetting every impression in new sensations."[71] The flighty inconstancy of the French people—their lack of "moderation and steadiness"—could be cited, as it was by the former revolutionary sympathizer William Playfair, as evidence that they were a people "unfit for freedom."[72]

The characteristic French changeability explained the radical shifts in France's politics. Henry Redhead Yorke, himself something of a political chameleon, had seen the French "assume a variety of dissimilar shapes; at one time frivolous, abject, and superstitious; at another time, starting like Lazarus from a dead repose, and roused to arms and the vindication of national liberty; afterwards the base tools of sanguinary demagogues, furious, vindictive, and cowardly."[73] The fickle French defied classification as Napoleon did; the only consistent aspect of their identity was volatility. Napoleon managed to stay on top, one British visitor to France wrote during the peace of Amiens, by "directing" the natural "levity and the inconstancy of the French; their inordinate propensity to change and novelty" away from his "political being, to extraneous objects; to exploits in the field; to commercial treaties; to colonial augmentations."[74]

Still, even as familiar elements of the French personality reappeared, many agreed that, as John Carr wrote in 1803, the events of recent years had "wholly changed the national character."[75] Yorke described the French *ancien régime* as having been characterized by "urbanity of manners, travels, a natural moderation of sentiment, the decorum of monarchical forms, civilized ideas, and enlightened reason." Whereas these factors had once tempered the "national rivalship" of France with Britain, the new regime allowed "atrabilious envy" to rise to the surface in a "phrensy against England."[76] As proof of France's "degeneracy," Yorke cited "the degraded condition of the fair sex" in this Napoleonic "nation of soldiers."[77] The pamphleteer William Hunter agreed that those French qualities that had once "claimed our respect"—"learning, arts, religion, or morals; the splendour of rank, the politeness of manners, and the refinement of taste"—had now "disappeared; and we now behold a people plunged into every vice, and glorying in every crime."[78]

A *Monthly Magazine* contributor, purportedly "an Anglo-American resident" in Paris, reported in 1808 that the French had changed tremendously in the twenty-two years since his last visit. Parisians had formerly been "gay, frivolous, and foppish." Since then, they had "metamorphosed into a serious, plain-dressing people, whose manners are, comparatively, repulsive, and sometimes verging upon brutality"; their deportment had "roughened" and their hearts had lost their "gentler qualities." The revolution—which many described as a failed attempt to achieve the qualities of Britain's constitution and government—had achieved only a superficial transformation in the French character: "in their endeavours to imitate John Bull, they have assumed his bluntness, without the accordant sincerity of his nature." Not only in dress, but in all respects, Parisians had become "externally *anglicised*."[79]

The mutability of national character, both French and British, was dramatically captured in a March 1803 print by Isaac Cruikshank.[80] A bearded conjuror—Napoleon—has summoned up two figures from the past, and reveals them to their descendants. The obese English apparition of an earlier generation is shocked to see the skeletal thinness of his grandson, who in turn is startled by the powerful figure that his ancestor cut. The gaunt Gallic ghost, by contrast, marvels at the stocky stoutness of today's Frenchman: "Ah mon Cousin," he declares, "vat you eat de Beef & Plum Pudding!!" More seems to be involved here than simply a reversal of the two nations' economic fortunes, a trading of prosperity and want. The post-revolutionary Frenchman has adopted not simply the emblematic foods of England but also sober English dress—in contrast to the modern-day Englishman, whose foppishness, like that of yesteryear's Frenchman, starkly contrasts with the bluff heartiness of the earlier age's John Bull. In short, the physical decline in English character seems to be a consequence of *cultural* degeneracy, of the adoption of continental costume and cuisine.

2. Isaac Cruikshank, "The Phantasmagoria—or a Review of Old Times," 1803 (British Museum).

If Cruikshank was suggesting the English transformation to be domestic in origin, was he attributing the French half of the national exchange to Napoleon himself? Had Bonaparte actually conjured up the French metamorphosis, or was he simply unveiling the startling changes? Some observers did credit Bonaparte with a radical alteration in French character. Broadsides equated the new French nature with Napoleon's own (noting that Frenchmen, like their ruler, were "fierce, blood-thirsty, and rapacious Assassins").[81] William Burdon suggested that such changes could be ascribed to Napoleon, who had transformed the French from "the most polished people in Europe" to "a nation of banditti."[82] Their slavishness made the nation malleable. One recent escaped prisoner remarked, in an extraordinary phrase, that France at the moment had "no character *as a nation*." The French were completely under Napoleon's control, "the mere materials of his power, and the instrument of his ambition"; Napoleon had "completely at his nod the force of a people."[83] He had, to all intents and purposes, reworked French national character in his own image.

Contemporary caricatures alternately portrayed Napoleon as a scorn-worthy mite (he was a "*Liliput* monster," a "mere *insect,* a *pigmy,*" a "Little insignificant Man, not more than fifty inches high")[84] or a quake-inducing "Colossus."[85] In similar fashion, broadsides oscillated between belittling and exaggerating Napoleon's qualities. They thus wavered between optimistic and pessimistic readings of Britain's chances against a Napoleonic invasion. Napoleon (broadsides reported) was talentless from a military perspective—but he was ruthless. His troops were as rapacious as he—and yet any Englishman could take on ten of them.[86]

Many broadsides brimmed with bluster and assurance. Some looked forward to Napoleon's landing in England so that he might there "by British hands . . . die!"[87] He would "turn tail" at "the very sight of our village boys."[88] William Cobbett—who in the season of the broadside would describe a conquered England in frightening detail—had earlier been ready to damn as subversive the very idea that a Napoleonic inva-sion might conceivably succeed: this was "an insult to our countrymen, which none but a jacobin scribbler . . . would presume to commit."[89] In the same spirit, an Edinburgh pamphlet of 1803 now took to task the very outburst of invasion-scare publications for spreading "alarm," "apprehension," and "despondency": invasion was but a "bug-bear" that could not succeed.[90]

A similar warning came from the caricaturist James Gillray, who blasted the broadside campaign as detrimental to the nation. In Sep-tember 1803, Gillray depicted John Bull next to a wall covered with handbills (which bear such titles as "Corsican Cruelties" and "Invasion of Great Britain"). The man responsible for the bill-posting, the instru-ment of his pasting trade in hand, stands next to Bull. The print's title identifies the bill-poster as an "alarmist" (a term of fairly recent vintage, coined as a positive term by Edmund Burke but quickly transformed into a slur).[91] "The Corsican Thief has slip'd from his Quarters," the alarmist tells John Bull. "And coming to Ravish your Wives & your Daughters." To which stolid John responds, undisturbed, "Let him come and be D—n'd!" The alarmist is recognizably Richard Brinsley Sheridan, the Foxite Whig. His true (according to Gillray) Jacobin character is betrayed by the *bonnet rouge* sticking out of his pocket. And thus the foreign, Gallic nature of both the parliamentary opposition and the broadside campaign are at once revealed. By spreading alarm about the threat to Britain, the handbills might, in Gillray's jaundiced view, have the effect of undermining British self-confidence. Thankfully, stolid John seems immune to the handbills' negative message.[92]

Some loyalist publications made it appear as if only the proper will and spirit were necessary for victory over Bonaparte: "As long as we remain united and true to ourselves, we never need to fear the threats or the attacks of France."[93] According to this line of reasoning, national character—being true to one's nature—would by itself prove sufficient antidote to the military threat. Even such rosy portraits of impregnability, however, could come hedged in by caveat and concern. "All we want is to be unanimous," Jacob Bonsanquet declared to a meeting of City merchants in July 1803 (in a speech reprinted in broadside form), "and then we may safely bid defiance, not only to the attempts of France, but to the hostile efforts of the world united." Alongside Bonsanquet's confident assertions, however, appeared his description of two earlier imperial metropolises, sacked because their populations had lolled in "apathy and ease." Rome and Constantinople might have escaped their fate had their nobles, merchants, financiers, "and all the inhabitants" not been so self-absorbed, to the point of hiring mercenaries to protect the state.[94]

A number of writers feared, like Bonsanquet, that over-confidence was even more dangerous than fatalistic gloom. In this cautionary spirit, the pseudonymous Publicola, whose name was attached to several broadsides, criticized some boastful handbills, "the tendency of which was to throw the Country off its guard, by creating an over confidence in its own state of preparation to meet the dangers by which it is threatened."[95] An 1803 broadside letter to Volunteers criticized those "noisy, impotent boasters" who exclaimed, "in the height of bravado, 'Why, let 'em come.'" Such people called anyone who sought to temper their conviction "a friend to Buonaparté, a traitor, a coward, and, in fact, every thing that is bad." They were wrong: the French had demonstrated considerable military talents, "talents we must emulate." In an earlier day, Harold had shown "haughty confidence" in the face of a French threat—and had lost his throne to William of Normandy. The lesson was simple: "He who despises his enemy ensures his own defeat."[96]

The engravers of caricatures faced the same fundamental problem as the broadside-writers: in how menacing a light should the Napoleonic threat be portrayed? The medium lent itself to blunt comparisons between Napoleon and whichever character was chosen to stand in for the British nation. One figure's size or behavior, relative to another's,

3. James Gillray, "Buonaparté, 48 Hours after Landing," 1803 (John Hay Library, Brown University).

could instantly convey to even a casual or unlettered observer the degree of dominance or subservience assumed to exist between the two. Caricatures sometimes portrayed Napoleon as a Lilliputian joke: a small child being spanked by Britannia, or a candle about to be snuffed out by the British constitution (wielded by Britain's king).[97] In two engravings, Gillray portrayed George III as Swift's king of Brobdingnag, scrutinizing with calm amusement a tiny Bonaparte.[98] But Bonaparte could also appear as a menacing giant (though usually, in such cases, he was accompanied by a similarly sized counterpart like Jack Tar, the archetype of the British sailor).[99] At times, Napoleon was opposed to a British statesman—William Pitt, for example, in the well-known engraving "The Plumb-Pudding in Danger," which showed a steaming globe being sliced up by the angular prime minister and the pint-sized consul. Gillray sent a characteristically complex message with this print, which suggested, if nothing else, a certain equality of imperial appetite between Britain and France. Indeed, Pitt is helping himself to a notably larger global portion than is his diminutive counterpart.[100]

When Napoleon was opposed to the emblematic Englishman John Bull, it did not always seem a match of equals. The business of summarizing the English character in the frame of a single individual (or summing up the British character, notably in the female form of Britannia) was tricky. Often enough John Bull's characteristics—his coarse features, his blubbery figure, his plain and sometimes rustic speech—necessitated reading him as but one part of the nation, and not one of high status at that. Dorothy George has claimed John's resemblance to George III in Gillray's "John Bull and the Alarmist"—a claim supported less by John's features (though this Bull does seem a prosperous burgher rather than the usual country yokel) than by the fact that his armchair bears the royal crest. If intended, this was a rare artistic decision: John was usually portrayed as a victim of the political establishment, not its personification.

Just how resilient and resourceful a figure Bull would be in the face of invasion was a trait that varied from print to print. He was sometimes shown treating Napoleon with unrequited politesse, at other times with brusque rage. In some engravings, Bull calmly declared that there was nothing to fear.[101] In others, the two figures wrestled furiously.[102] Caricatures could recklessly downplay the Napoleonic threat: in Gillray's "Buonaparté, 48 Hours after Landing," a joyful Bull hoists Napoleon's "silly Head" on a bloody pitchfork. (The print's upper caption explained "that Policies are now open'd at Lloyd's—where the depositor of one Guinea is entitled [to] a Hundred if the Corsican Cut-throat is Alive 48 Hours after Landing on the British Coast.")[103] But some prints seem likely to have undermined the very confidence they sought to inspire. In one Isaac Cruikshank caricature, John stands with chains restraining his limbs, and a noose (held by a French soldier) around his neck. Bonaparte himself points a gun at John, and brandishes a sword for added effect. John tells Napoleon that if French troops should land, "men, women, & children will all join to tear them to pieces." Stirring stuff—but there was still the small matter of the national representative's seemingly helpless position in the face of French weapons and captivity.[104] If Cruikshank was seeking to avoid both the Scylla of complacency and the Charybdis of panic, he arguably missed his mark.

A more successful balancing of threat and reassurance came in an 1805 Gillray engraving that depicted one national icon coming to the rescue of another. His stallion rearing, George III—as St. George—raises his sword to slay a fire-breathing dragon with the head of Napoleon. The dragon's legs are splayed atop a prone and terrified Britannia, whose shield, bearing the Union Jack, has been knocked to the ground. The postures of maiden and dragon give the assault an almost sexual force. (As we shall see, broadsides commonly warned that a Napoleonic invasion would mean sexual violation for British women).[105] Though St. George was technically the English and not the British patron saint, there seems no reason to read the print's message as one of England saving Britain. Nor must we assume the engraving's point to have been the necessity of monarchy to the nation's survival. What the decision to employ complementary domestic icons managed to do, more fundamentally, was to urge upon the observer the danger posed by Napoleon—but without imbuing the viewer's heart with defeatist fears. The triad of figures allowed Gillray to cast his nation as both victim and eventual victor. Britain could come to its own rescue.

The broadsides were mass productions addressed to the people, not created by the people; we cannot easily assess how they were read. But we can gain some inkling of the target audience's sentiments through the distorting mirror of what authors *feared* their audiences might believe. These apparent documents of loyalist confidence and zeal should in fact be viewed as windows onto the deep unease of the loyalist mind. The fundamental fear of the broadside producers was that there were "some labouring people so deluded, as to think they have nothing to lose if the French should conquer this Island."[106]

The force and frequency with which broadsides sought to reject the claim that an invasion would benefit the poor suggest that this was not so marginal a belief. "No Change for the Worse, a Mistaken Notion" was the title of one broadside addressed to "My poorer Fellow Countrymen": the epigrammatic simplicity of the title's first five words suggests that the author assumed that readers would be familiar with such

4. James Gillray, "St. George and the Dragon," 1805 (Lewis Walpole Library, Yale University).

a line of reasoning.[107] Either such complacency was indeed rampant amongst the lower orders, or their social betters feared it was—or both. To combat the complacent line of reasoning, authors needed to raise it and engage with it. In one broadside dialogue, a "stranger" (whether British or foreign is unclear) asks John Bull: "How can that be your country, in which you do not possess a foot of ground, and in which you are obliged to toil from day to day for a subsistence? It is the country of the rich and great, who possess it; and who, if I might advise, should be left to fight for it at their pleasure."[108] Naturally, John resists the entreaty and asserts his love of country. Still, the author's readiness to voice the stranger's question suggests he did not fear that he was introducing a new, subversive argument to his readers' minds.

One of the most frequently encountered and insistent refrains of broadside literature was that a French invasion would hurt the poor as much as or more than it hurt the rich—that were an invasion to succeed, "the richest and the poorest from that instant are entirely ruined."[109] A laborer, one broadside suggested, "values his liberty," "relishes his pot of porter," and "loves his wife and children fully as well" as any rich man. The French, moreover, recognizing "that the industrious poor are the vital parts of a community," would principally target them—so "the COMMON PEOPLE," the "least able to bear the hardships of Plunder and Desolation," should most fear an invasion.[110]

Some reminded the poor of the benefits with which their nation provided them, and which a conquering France would take away. Should the invasion succeed, one sermon-turned-broadside suggested, the "*lowest individual*" would suffer most: "Not a hospital, not an infirmary, not a charity-school would remain."[111] Broadsides celebrated the hospitals at Chelsea and Greenwich, where military and naval veterans were maintained (in pointed contrast, they added, to France, whose soldiers Napoleon had happily poisoned at Jaffa).[112] One address "to the People of England"—after stressing that the author was "*one of yourselves*," "neither a person of rank nor fortune"—insisted that British economic inequality paled in comparison with that of France. The condition of the British poor, "however deplorable it may seem," was offset by the Poor Laws and by the possibility of social mobility for the industrious.[113] The Poor Laws—"*that noble Monument of national Charity*"—would surely be abolished after a successful French invasion, another broadside predicted.[114]

Broadsides reminded their readers that passivity ("neutrality") in the face of invasion was a crime against all classes, not simply against the rich.[115] An impulse to welcome French armies might well up from a contemptible economic resentment, from "jealousy or *baseborn* envy of superior distinctions."[116] Therefore it was important to note that "mechanics, manufacturers, and labourers" would be worse off under Bonaparte, if only because of the cost of quartering French soldiers.[117] The rich might be the first to suffer, but their misfortunes would mean the evaporation of trade and a consequent plummet in the common man's wages.[118] Invasion would disrupt the grain trade, and the French would "destroy out of wantonness and mischief" what they did not need.[119]

One more optimistic broadside reassured its readers that the French would not gain much from appropriating Britain's physical resources, as "our wealth lies not in gold, or silver, but in the skill, the talents, and industry, in the enterprise and honor, in the heads and the hearts of the people."[120] But this reassurance raised a new worry: that the French would focus their attention on Britain's *human* capital—that able-bodied Englishmen would be enslaved, "turned out in gangs, like galley slaves, and a French guard pricking them forward with bayonets at their A——."[121] Napoleon had "sworn by Mahomet and the Pope," another pamphleteer wrote, that he would turn those Englishmen he did not kill into "*slaves*" in his factories and mines.[122] He would "transport or massacre one half of the people of England for the purpose of tyrannizing the more easily over the rest."[123] English youths—unequaled in their bravery and valor—would be impressed into his armies and "led forth to complete the Conquest of the World."[124] The patriotic song had famously declared that Britons never would be slaves. Broadsides asserted that this most fundamental aspect of the national character would be dissolved by a successful invasion.

The overall aim of the broadsides was to assert unity in the face of potential division. Social tension was denied by claiming that the poor and the rich would suffer equally from an invasion. Domestic political differences, broadsides claimed, were meaningless in the face of Napoleonic invasion. In Hanover, a German Jacobin had "claimed his Protection, as an admirer of the French Revolution! but he found no more favour in the Sight of the *Aga of Sultan* BONAPARTE'S janisaries, than the most loyal *Noblemen in Hanover*."[125] Nor would national divisions within the newly United Kingdom help Napoleon succeed in his conquest: "John Bull, Sandy of Scotland, Taffy of Wales, and Patrick of Ireland" would ignore their differences in the face of the external enemy.[126] One handbill had John Bull, addressing his Irish "brother" Patrick, dismiss French hopes of Irish assistance by claiming himself "quite at ease on that score. In defence of his native land, an Englishman, a Scotchman, a Welshman, and an Irishman, are one and the same people."[127] In John Bull's profession of ease, needless to say—as in the tale of atrocities in Hanover—we should recognize profound unease, the concern that the politically disaffected, whether Jacobin or Irish, would see Napoleon's armies as liberators. It was especially important that the Irish prove their loyalty now, and rehabilitate "the name of IRISHMAN," given the fact that some of their countrymen had in 1798 "been deceived by *French Perfidy.*"[128]

We find further unease at domestic division in the broadsides' treatment of sexual difference—a subject connected to the problem of national identity, given the established genderings of English and French character. Napoleon, the broadsides announced, had promised his followers not only the free pillage of British property but also the sexual violation of British women. All the women of Britain, the handbills warned, were potential victims of "insult and barbarity," of "open ravishment."[129] Napoleon himself did not generally figure as a sexual predator ("that is not in my way," he enigmatically noted in one imagined account)—but broadsides reported that he had promised his soldiers that *they* might "gratify their lustful Passions with the Violation of the Chastity of our Wives and Daughters."[130] Just as British prosperity made the islanders special targets of French avarice, so too did the "unrivalled beauty" of British women increase their vulnerability.[131]

The threat of rape was presented as a blow to men as much as to women. The worst aspect of the "brutal violence" to which the French subjected women was that the gratification of "their furious passions" was not even "their chief object in these atrocities." The French soldiers' true target was male, their "principal delight" being "to shock the feelings of fathers and brothers, and husbands!"[132] Broadsides often defined and addressed women in relationship to men, treating them as intermediaries and catalysts. It was as *"Wives and Daughters of our People"* that women would be violated.[133]

Sexual violence was presented as a great social leveler and unifier, in two senses. First, the high might be made low (in Hanover, it was reported, "WOMEN OF THE HIGHEST RANK" had been "VIOLATED BY THE LOWEST OF THAT BRUTAL SOLDIERY"). But the prospect of rape also argued against the claim that commoners would have nothing to lose from a French invasion: "the poorest honest Labourer, who has a Mother or a Sister, a Wife or a Daughter, has, in truth, as much reason as the highest Duke in the Land" to fear invasion.[134] Rape leveled the investment in British loyalty. Neither poverty nor riches would protect a woman from sexual violation, any more than the right politics would save a republican from death at the hands of the French armies. Broadsides that told rich women they were not safe from an invasion army fulfilled the secondary purpose, perhaps their true chief aim, of telling poorer women that better-off women were in the same boat—and that they knew it. The audience ostensibly addressed, in other words, was not necessarily the audience actually targeted. By the same token, the woman-directed broadsides undoubtedly envisioned male readers as well—men who might be shamed or coaxed into loyalty through imagining women reading these pieces.

As men were told to see themselves as the victims of sexual violence against women, so women were informed that they might be the linchpin in the defense of the nation against the French. Handbills ordered women to shrug off their accustomed passivity, even blamed them for this passivity. But in summoning women to an active defense of their land, broadside authors could not hide their unease at the prospect of an energized female population. Wartime mandated a shift in gender boundaries—but the broadsides feared this change at the same time as they urged it.[135]

Women were assigned powerful but ambiguous positions in the project of patriotism. *Buonaparte in Britain!*, a "cheap compilation" whose compiler encouraged the country's "wealthy proprietors" to circulate it among the poor, forthrightly declared that it was "peculiarly" woman's duty "to reprobate the doctrines of the French." As mothers, women instilled patriotism and religion in the minds of children. Now the very "constitution . . . depend[ed]" on women persuading their fathers, brothers, lovers, and husbands not to place their faith in France. This was, on the face of it, high praise for the role women played in the fabric of the polity. But the pamphleteer believed women would recognize the dangers of French republicanism not because of cerebral astuteness but because of their instinct for corporeal self-preservation. Women would recognize that the "diabolical principles" of republican France clashed with the "sacred inviolability" of their bodies. The very nature of French government now amounted to a system of "obscenity" and "prostitution": France (once the haven of chivalry) was now "one immense brothel," where the women had gained a sort of equality by becoming "as ferocious and abandoned as the men." Republican France, the author told his female audience, regarded "the violation of your persons" as one of the "rights of man!"[136] The French were "as much the enemies of the Virtue and Chastity, as of the Religion and Liberty of Europe."[137]

A woman's concern for her body would provide a necessary counterweight to the revolutionary sympathy she might find in her men. The pamphlet's suggestion that a woman could persuade her father "not to countenance a plan of government which would prostitute his dear girls" implied that without a daughter he might well have considered welcoming the French. Republicanism was also to be expected from many a young man—unless his sweetheart pointed out to him that under the French she would suffer "a common intercourse with the most brutal of mankind." Female bodily integrity depended on the British status quo, for the "happy frame" of British government, permitting neither seraglio nor convent, recognized "the rights of women" as no other did. Thus women would save Britain through personal self-interest. On their physical well-being rested "the morals, the freedom, and even the happiness of the empire at large."[138]

Broadsides sought to convince women that the nation's future depended on them—but hedged any declarations of women's importance, restraining generous offers as soon as they were made. A number of invasion broadsides adopted a female voice, such as "Old England" speaking "to her Daughters," "An English Woman," or "Britannia"— or as an imaginary "Female Association for Preserving Liberty and Property" ("comprising the Ladies of the United Kingdom," and boasting Britannia as "Presidentess"), whose name intimated new possibilities for female civic action. This association's creator, however, could not resist describing the group's plan as "drawn up, and settled in the most material parts, by one of the most eminent Statesmen and elegant writers of his age."[139] If women were to play a critical role in the new war, this role was to be articulated by men.

Even as the formal organization of women was suggested, women were warned against too public a role. A pamphlet ascribed "national preservation" to the "courage, fidelity, and patriotism" of women found "in every page of our history."[140] But broadsides that scolded women for being passive and frivolous creatures also told them they could not possess "rights of a political hue."[141] While with one arm summoning British women to battle—invoking "Queen Boadicea, and a thousand other heroines"—broadsides sought with the other to hold back the raised spirits.[142] The women to whom broadsides gave voice disavowed interest in being "a *British Joan of Arc*" or in becoming "Amazons" (they would not "so much as let their *nails* grow for the defense of their country").[143] Women's military role would be expressed solely through the weaponry of their sexual allure. One pamphlet, after calling on "the spirit which animated . . . the heroic Elizabeth," quickly explained that actual military tasks could be left to men: women had been "furnished ... with other arms"—their beauty and charms. Jealousy would be the mainspring of British female loyalty: British women had, according to the broadside, been outraged by Napoleon's having sent over "*troops of Female Freebooters*" during the peace—French women "with characters as *light* as their *arms* and *accoutrements*." To resist these forces, members of the Female Association would defend king and country by employing "our *tongues* and hearts, our eyes, eye-lashes, lips, dimples, and every other feature." They would "avow the *Loyalty* of our princi-ples, in every word we shall utter, and every *change of dress* which, under the magic influence of fashion, we shall assume" (notably by wearing only British manufactures). British women would deploy their weapons like (Bowdlerized) Lysistratas: they would "not ... have intercourse with any man, nor accept his hand in a dance, nor lean upon his arm for support, who is not ready to use them in the defense of his *King and Country*."[144]

Suggesting that sexuality could serve as a weapon, though, raised fears as well as hopes. One broadside anonymously penned by Hester Lynch Piozzi told women they had been "gay and airy long enough" and must now "cease to be frivolous": frivolity, in the form of fraternization with the French troops, might lead to treason. Piozzi blamed Cortés' conquest of the Aztecs, and Napoleon's recent Italian triumphs, on the native female populations. Napoleon's armies would assuredly be defeated within three weeks of invading Britain if only they were "shew[n] no Favour" by women (who should "never betra[y] by a Look or Gesture where any Treasure is concealed, but suffe[r] Death rather than divulge a National Secret").[145] If women could save the nation, then they might damn it just as easily.

Much physical devastation was prophesied in the broadsides of 1803: rape, slaughter, pillage, economic meltdown. But perhaps the most sig-nificant devastation augured by the broadsides was cultural. Handbills warned that an English (and it was generally English rather than British) way of life was at stake, that the greatest danger the French posed was to the English culture and even language. These warnings cannot be entirely disentangled from predictions of the dismantling of freedom of the press and the subversion of the Magna Carta.[146] National culture and political fortune were seen as linked; there was an unbreakable con-nection between a people's mores and its constitutional circumstances.

Some of the changes foreseen from a French conquest would be culinary. "English Porter, and English Bread and cheese, would be out of Fashion," and no exertions would be sufficient to procure "a Slice of English Roast Beef, if Bonaparte should be allowed to prescribe what is good for us."[147] These threatened gastronomic alterations would debilitate the physical body, indeed shape it into a new national form: French foods, "instead of heartening and strengthening you, would reduce you presently to the Thinness and Skinniness of Frenchmen."[148]

Food had symbolic importance beyond the nutritional. Diet had been a principal imaginary dividing line between British and French cultures in the eighteenth century. The "roast beef of old England"—hailed in Fielding's song (still familiar enough to serve as the tune for an anti-Napoleonic ditty) and in Hogarth's engraving—stood as evidence of the links between national prosperity, diet, and political freedom.[149] Roast beef was, as Roy Porter has written, "the Englishman's sacramental meal"—a mainstay of popular political celebrations, a touchstone of prosperity, an emblem for the national character.[150] Significantly, the broadside that predicted roast beef's disappearance was addressed to the writer's "poorer Fellow countrymen."[151] That even a common laborer might find beef occasionally affordable, and could turn his nose up at the thought of dark bread, was a culinary fact invested with huge political significance. As Cobbett would later note, "the people of England believed firmly, that the French people were most wretched creatures, and that their general diet was broth made of cabbage-leaves, and such stuff, together with frogs roasted, and now and then a bit of *sallad* [*sic*]."[152] After an invasion, one pamphlet reported, the English would be forced to "live on black bread, and work for sixpence a day."[153] The word-play may not have been deliberate, but it might as well have been, in one broadside's query: "Would *Soup-maigre*, think you, suit an English Constitution?" As the body was worn away by the enemy's "sour rat-gut Liquor," so too would the body politic deteriorate.[154]

The fabric of quotidian life would be rent by a French invasion, broadsides repeatedly suggested; Napoleon would rearrange not only cabinets but daily life. The French would not "be fit for any of our manly Games," one broadside claimed: rather than engage a group of Frenchmen "in a Match at Cricket," Englishmen "might as well attempt to play with so many Monkies." The men in Napoleon's army came from "a giddy, thoughtless, volatile, frivolous, Race, completely the Reverse of ourselves in Sentiments, Manners, and Amusements."[155] All native children between four and twelve would be sent abroad to learn French, their parents forced to pay for their maintenance and their older siblings *"fined or flogged"* for speaking English. England would "become a province of the Republic, in which the French language alone shall be spoken, and French laws obeyed."[156] Few imagined a Napoleonic Britain in more nightmarish dystopian detail than William Cobbett, who foresaw a scheme of classification that would tear apart the English nation. The French would "divide us into separate classes; hem us up in districts, cut off all communication between friends and relations, parents and children" (splitting families up in order to indoctrinate children "in their own blasphemous principles"). French invaders "would affix badges upon us, mark us in the cheek, shave our heads, split our ears, or clothe us in the habits of slaves!"[157]

With invasion, the nation would lose what held it together. The national character would wither with the society's internal ties. Napoleon would convert Britain "into a department of his grinning, miserable, mock Republic."[158] Britain's military heroes and statesmen would be shot in Hyde Park, and London would be renamed *"Bonapart-opolis."*[159] Britain—its distinctive national traits effaced—would become indistinguishable from France. Broadsides diagnosed a French desire to "annihilate our name as a nation," and described Bonaparte as "the determined extirpator of the British name." Britain, they warned, would suffer "utter destruction as a nation," and "the very character of an Englishman would be lost."[160]

The broadsides of 1803 stand as a high-water marker of British invasion fears. After Nelson's victory at Trafalgar in October 1805, France's status as a naval power would be irreparably compromised. The war now seemed to some a stalemate between "the Leviathan of the land and the Leviathan of the waters."[161] There was frustration in this—Leigh Hunt suggested that Britain's naval power could have "as little effect on the military sway of NAPOLEON, as the whale of the Atlantic can have on the lion of the deserts"—but also some security.[162] Fears of French soldiers on English soil subsided.

Still, warnings continued to be sounded in the idiom of the 1803 handbills. In 1807, the evangelical abolitionist James Stephen anonymously published *The Dangers of the Country.* Echoing the broadsides, Stephen argued that an invasion would target not simply the government but everyday British culture. Napoleon would abolish habeas corpus and juries, as well as the Riot Act. The "British multitude" would have to abandon "their hisses, their cat-calls, their Green men"—the very apparatus of carnivalesque political protest—lest they unleash the lethal powers of the Napoleonic state. Respectable extra-parliamentary organizations would come under threat, and the English "might soon find it dangerous to assemble beyond the limits of a family circle." "Every distinguishing feature of our national character, would be offensive, or alarming to our new masters," Stephen wrote. "An entire revolution in our manners, our feelings, and opinions, must be effected, before we could have such rest as the prostration of habitual servitude affords." The new regime would require the English national character to transform itself into its *alter ego*. "The next generation, if not the present, would be all *frenchified*, and debased, even below the vile standard of our oppressors." English "children would become in morals, as well as allegiance, *Frenchmen!*"[163]

While Stephen would emphasize the external threats to English national character, others, we have seen, suggested that national culture and identity could weaken from within. Even without an invasion, the essence of British character might be weakening, the national fabric fraying in a manner that would make military occupation superfluous (if also more likely). If the British needed to fear the French, this was ultimately a result of their own flaws in character, their own fall from a historically defined grace.

In Britain's past lay the resources with which the nation's character could be defended. Halfpenny war songs reminded their listeners of the martial bravery of "lion-hearted RICHARD," Edward III, Henry V, and the Duke of Marlborough.[164] One caricature showed Elizabeth I's ghost gesturing at a painting of the Spanish Armada's defeat, and Bonaparte recoiling in horror.[165] Broadsides invoked the victories at Crécy and Agincourt, where English armies had overcome larger French forces. In their linking of these names to more recent British victories, such as those at Acre and Aboukir,[166] the handbills might seem, at first reading, to be suggesting that certain qualities of English character existed outside of history, and would naturally dictate triumph should the French be foolhardy enough to invade. One historian has seen in the 1803 broadsides an unconcerned boasting about "continuity across time."[167] But the historical name-dropping was not meant to induce complacency. History was invoked not as salve but as goad. Lurking beneath the proud invocation of ancestral triumph was the nagging worry that the national character was less hardy than it once had been.

In the effort to remind present-day Britons of an earlier age's vigor, even ancestors who had resisted overreaching monarchs (the "Shades revered! of those whose blood / Fanatic STUART's arm withstood") could be invoked.[168] Wordsworth's "Lines on the Expected Invasion" appealed both to those who would stand "by the Monarch's side, / And, like Montrose, make Loyalty your pride," and to those

> who, not less zealous, might display
> Banners at enmity with regal sway,
> And, like the Pyms and Miltons of that day,
> Think that a State would live in sounder health
> If Kingship bowed its head to Commonwealth.

Admirers of Civil War royalists and republicans should resolve to "have one Soul" in the face of the French threat.[169] Citing the touchstones of radical patriotism, some loyalists hoped to subsume internal difference and meet the "friends of liberty, those who were stigmatized as Jacobins" on common ground.[170]

History's measuring-rod had been carved not only by Edwards and Henrys but by unspecified "forefathers" who had "detested the *slavery of France*"—unglorified John Bulls against whom present-day Britons might gauge their own achievements.[171] The reader of broadsides encountered not only Elizabeth's rallying speech but also charts of how many weapons and men each London ward had contributed in 1588 to repelling the Armada. Surely a people now "ten Times more numerous" and "Opulent" should "imitate the noble example of such Ancestors."[172] Such calls for emulation were common.[173] Britons were told they had "a splendid part to fill," and should "act up" to their "ancient character."[174]

But imitation was an inherently uncertain and derivative objective. (Were not Napoleon's own purported theatrical character and emulation of historical figures generally taken to indicate moral failing?) The bond between past and present could break. The notion that British qualities were a patrimony, a "*noble* Inheritance" handed down from one generation to another, stirred up doubts, for a patrimony could go astray.[175] Lurking underneath so many loyalist celebrations of past glory was concern about present decay.

This sense of loss motivated loyalists to call for quite literal inspiration, to proclaim their hope that the spirits of yore would possess present-day Britons. The minister David Rivers, whose *Discourse on Patriotism* had gone through four editions by 1804, invoked the "shades of departed heroes," asking them to "hover round us, and inspire us with a portion of that heroism which distinguished you!"[176] Though one broadside imagined British ancestors lying "snug and quiet," not likely to "rise to haunt us, as they say the Egyptian Ghosts do the Murderer of Jaffa," others clearly wished that just such a haunting might take place.[177] "Your fore-fathers call to you from their graves," an "Englishwoman" told her fellow countrymen; "their warning voice tells you, that you would soon find the perfidy of [Napoleon's] heart."[178]

Just as they were linked in time to their ancestors through the narration of courageous resistance, so the present generation was linked to the future through the tales that might some day be told about their own deeds. As one broadside put it: "The babes of posterity shall lisp with pleasure, MY GRANDFATHER BEAT THE FRENCH; MY UNCLE HELPED TO DRIVE THEM AWAY."[179] "Posterity" was invoked frequently: an unspecified future moment from which spectators might look back and view the present historically; proleptically, present-day readers were asked to do the same.[180] The future of Britain depended on letting the "divine spirit" of British ancestors "animate us"; Britons should "figure to ourselves millions and millions to spring from our loins, who may be born freemen or slaves, as Heaven shall approve or reject our efforts."[181]

The necessity of appealing to the ancestral spirit—what might on first glance seem the triumphalist certitude that past victories would become future ones—turns out to have been driven by a deep uncertainty as to whether the nation's once-great character survived. Again and again, broadsides expressed the fear that Britain had passed its zenith, that the national character had weakened or dissipated. The aim was partly to shame today's Britons by having them recall the brave anti-Gallican actions of their forefathers.[182] Cobbett rhetorically asked whether his countrymen would (by yielding to Napoleon the nation for "which our fathers so often dyed the land and the sea with their blood") "thus, at once dishonour their graves, and stamp disgrace and infamy on the brows of our children." In denying that Britons had indeed "so miserably fallen," Cobbett was denying that they had "in so short a space of time . . . become so detestably degenerate."[183]

By raising this spectre of decline ("shew, that in TWO THOUSAND YEARS, you have not degenerated"), broadsides sought to galvanize their

Wonder! look at that and tremble !!!

Defeat of the Spanish Armada

The Ghost of Queen Elizabeth !!

5. William Holland, "The Ghost of Queen Elizabeth," 1803 (Houghton Library, Harvard University).

readers.[184] In one handbill, the ghost of a shopkeeper ennobled by Henry VIII for his archery skills rose from the dead to chide present-day Londoners for letting "the exercise of Arms" atrophy—but still hoped it was not the case "that the Character of *Englishmen* has degenerated since my time."[185] Some feared this fall had already occurred. David Rivers detected only "dissipation," "luxury and licentiousness" in the present day; he saw "a frivolous and effeminate spirit" and "a dereliction of manners" in his fellow Britons. The condition that Rivers diagnosed revealed itself in sexual frankness (with a French inflection): "Our young men become *petit maitres*, and our young women are early habituated to a bold and indelicate conduct, and to a *costume* more analogous to courtezans, than modest females."[186]

Between the lines of even the most rousing patriotic song could lie anxiety about the trajectory of British history:

> Rouse we, BRITONS, let them see
> How unchang'd the British name?

Let the ruffians know that WE
Are IMMUTABLY THE SAME.

Shew them, that age to age bequeathes
The British character complete;
That 'tis the SELF-SAME SPIRIT BREATHES,
And the SELF-SAME HEARTS THAT BEAT.[187]

The song acknowledged—if through sturdy denial—the possibility that
national character could degrade with time. To proclaim, as an Ealing
troop of Volunteers did, the necessity of demonstrating that "Britons
have not lost the Spirit, nor abandoned the principles of their forefathers," was to acknowledge the need to resist a dimming of the national
temper. All too easily, Britons could imagine their own nation following
in the footsteps of other liberal states that had declined—most recently
the republic of Venice, "the eldest Child of Liberty," whose "extinction"
at Napoleon's hands Wordsworth mourned in a sonnet.[188] The worry
expressed by the abolitionist William Wilberforce (to a large audience,
as his words were broadcast in handbill form) quietly haunted many
broadsides: "We bear upon us but too plainly the marks of a declining
empire."[189]

The nature of these marks of decline was described, ardently and
repeatedly, by the journalist Henry Redhead Yorke. The former Jacobin's
writings provide further evidence of the essential pessimism of Franco-
phobic patriotism, evidence of the degree to which hatred of the other
was predicated on anxiety about the self. Yorke's writings—particularly
once he launched his own *Weekly Political Review* in the spring of 1806
(reportedly with ministerial assistance)—teemed with outrageously
violent characterizations of the French.[190] He recommended killing captured French prisoners of war in Spain, declared it "lawful to kill a
Frenchman whenever and wherever he can be caught," and branded the
French an "execrable race" who "should be hunted and slaughtered like
beasts of prey." Those Frenchmen who survived battle "should bleed
under the dagger of assassination, and be hanged upon the first convenient tree," he added.[191]

The danger posed by Napoleonic France arose partly from the fact
that Napoleon's overarching imperial strategy was to efface national
sentiment from the countries he seized. Bonaparte wished "to eradicate
every principle of patriotism from [the] breasts" of his new subjects,
Yorke wrote, "to convert them into *citizens of the world*, that is, to pave

6. C. Williams, "The Consequence of Invasion or the Hero's Reward," 1803 (Houghton Library, Harvard University).

the way for universal monarchy."[192] But Yorke worried that the English seemed to be taking care of this on their own. His bloodthirsty Francophobia was joined by a deep unease regarding "the degeneracy of our national character."[193] Yorke's fear that the English character was being contaminated by French culture was nothing new.[194] But rather than decry, as many others had, the dissipation and effeminacy simply of the Francophile English ruling classes ("*Frenchified* members of the house of commons," for example), Yorke, like Cobbett, diagnosed a "rage for French fashions" extending beyond the social elite to more humble Britons.[195] The people—"the body of the nation"—were "effeminate" and "emasculated by the superficial education and trifling character of the times." Even the sins of Britain's governors could be laid at the door of the people. Yorke employed a telling phrase (he was one of the very earliest English writers to use it) to indicate the nature of the problem: "I have shewn that the people themselves are the real sources of all the evils complained of, and that the ministers only partake of and are actuated by, *the spirit of the age*, which I have proved to be a wicked and perverse spirit." Attributing agency to the *Zeitgeist* meant offering a measure of absolution to the nation's leaders: government ministers were symptoms rather than causes.[196]

Yorke, Cobbett, and others who warned of degeneracy worried that British virtue and *virtu* had grown frail, that British culture—not simply the amusements and fripperies of an elite, but the daily life of the people—was losing its distinctive character. The spectre of French effeminacy may seem a strange one to have evoked in the face of the French army's purported brutishness, but it was difficult to discuss degeneracy without this key marker. France may have become a hypermasculine nation of rapacious soldiers, but the contagion of effeminacy with which the bluff Englishman had been diagnosed was still identified as continental (with Italy occasionally serving in France's stead, as when Yorke censured Madame Catalini, a singer recently arrived on the London stage, for working to convert the "once high-minded" English people "into a nation of Sybarites, to sink in soul and body, into despicable Italian effeminacy").[197] A deep, seemingly inescapable anxiety over the state of the British nation ran rampant through British loyalism in the early years of Napoleon Bonaparte's reign. While striving to set up a sharp distinction between the British and French nations, British commentators found "Britain" and "France" alike to be fragile constructions, susceptible to interference from governors, open to undermining by foreign influence, liable to degeneration, capable of being effaced altogether. The discourse of national character—one of the key languages through which the British sought to explain Napoleon—was premised on the eternal possibility and perhaps inevitability of national change and decay.

Curiously, in the season of the broadside, William Cobbett managed to voice the same concerns as Yorke would, but in a fashion that reflected critically on the very phenomenon of loyalist patriotism. Despite himself participating in the propaganda production of this "age of Placards," the ever-contrary Cobbett detected evidence of historical degeneracy in the vulgarity and violence of the broadsides themselves. He was troubled, first, by the inconsistency of the newspapers that had laid the groundwork for the broadsides: while many of the epithets they ladled upon Napoleon were appropriate, the terms were "scandalous" coming from organs that had so recently "extolled his character." The handbills, following the newspapers, "conveyed some striking and useful truths to the people"—but too many of their authors "seemed to vie with each other, who should invent the most shameful, incredible, and ridiculous falsehoods, conveyed in the lowest, most foul and disgusting language." Handbill writers had sought to "'writ[e] to the level of the meanest capacity'"—but in so doing had "sunk far lower than the meanest, and absolutely carried their sinking propensity so far, that the very rabble cried *shame*."[198]

A scene in which John Bull, Sandy, Taffy, and Patrick described in blood-curdling detail what they would do to Napoleon suggested to Cobbett "a set of cannibals dancing round a roasting prisoner of war." Graphic prints showing Bonaparte's bloody head on a pike (including one engraving that suggested Volunteers might win the attention of "a whole bevy of females" by parading around with "ghastly and bleeding French heads") struck Cobbett as "shocking and disgraceful exhibitions, the tendency, and the sole tendency, of which is, to prepare the people for acts of cowardly barbarity."[199] The broadsides, Cobbett feared, despite the truths they had spread about the Napoleonic threat, had "imprinted on the character of this nation a stain, which will not be easily effaced." The propaganda campaign was itself a sign of national decay.

Much like Coleridge, who saw a French invasion as a trial of whether the English were "a vile sunken race," Cobbett preferred national destruction to national degeneracy. "Neither liberty nor life is worth preserving," the journalist concluded, "if to be preserved only by infamous means; and, as to my country, much rather would I, that England should be utterly destroyed, than that Englishmen should be accounted that cowardly, blood-minded, braggart race, which, from the recent labours of the press, the world would naturally suppose them."[200]

CHAPTER 3

The Pious Proteus and the Nation's Destiny

'Tis not the POPE,
   Nor the Popish priest,
   Nor yet TOM PAINE;
     But BONAPARTE,
     He is the BEAST
     That's to be slain.

"The Beast, a Sure Word of Prophecy," broadside, 1803[1]

Posterity will hardly know how to reconcile the proverbial courage and sense of our countrymen with the expression of such fears as they will find in the predictions and revelations of the preachers and politicians of the present age; who, by helping out the Apocalypse with an anagram, behold in this warrior sometimes the Horned Beast, at others Apollyon himself.

John Cam Hobhouse, 1816[2]

The years of war against revolutionary and Napoleonic France witnessed a great burst of British interest in the more esoteric parts of the Hebrew and Christian Bibles—the prophetic books, in particular Isaiah, Ezekiel, Daniel, and Revelations. The two best-remembered representatives of this eschatological fervor were vilified in their time as mad, and perhaps understandably so. Richard Brothers announced himself to be Prince of the Hebrews—including the "invisible Hebrews," the unwitting British descendants of the ten lost tribes—only to be removed to an asylum in 1795 (partly, no doubt, because he saw God's hand behind the French revolution). Joanna Southcott, after publishing more than sixty prophetic pamphlets, declared herself in 1814 to be pregnant with Shiloh, the son of God. She died shortly after this prophecy failed to be realized—in her mid-sixties.[3]

Millenarian beliefs, however, were not the province solely of these two self-declared prophets and their followers (tens of thousands, in the case of Southcott). Scores of British tracts, by both Anglicans and Dissenters, were published on eschatology during the years of Napoleon's rule. A great many of these claimed that Scripture, properly deciphered, explained contemporary political and military affairs.[4] In a Britain that historians have painted as fairly crawling with itinerant preachers, it may be assumed that the geographical and social reach of apocalyptic beliefs stretched far indeed.[5] While it has been suggested that millenarianism was especially alluring to the poor, to whom it may have offered a vision of radical social change,[6] most of the audience for millennial ideas remains hidden from the historian's sight. By emphasizing printed studies of the prophetic books, this chapter necessarily privileges the writers themselves, and the literate and fairly well-to-do men and women most likely to have encountered religious pamphlets and books. A final section of this chapter will suggest that chiliastic readings of Napoleon circulated more broadly—but even here, our dependence on the printed word means that we are left with many questions about the general population.

Late Georgian writers on prophecy were not detached from mainstream political culture.[7] Some found prominent publishers. Some exegetical works went through several editions in the space of a few years (incorporating revisions reflecting new diplomatic and political developments) and spawned additional American editions and responses. Prominent journals reviewed some of the genre's offerings, and through their summaries offered writers on prophecy a larger audience than they could reach through pamphlets alone. And while some reviewers treated exegetical works with mockery or a polite incredulity, others offered respect and praise.

The core of this chapter examines loyalist and radical millenarian readings of Napoleon—by Anglican and Dissenting writers, some with Oxford degrees and others (to judge from appearances) with little formal education.[8] But it was not only writers in the prophetic idiom who concerned themselves with Napoleon's religious significance. Many "secular" writers on politics regarded Napoleon's religious identity—for example, the extent to which he could be described as Catholic—as a critical component of his political personality. Prophetic writing should be situated within the broader British effort to classify Napoleon in terms of religion. So before examining religious readings of politics, this chapter will consider political readings of religion.

By unsettling the political-religious ideology of British Protestant patriotism, Napoleon's perplexing religious character raised fundamental questions about Britain's place in the world and in the providential scheme.[9] The chapter begins by considering opinions on the matter of Napoleon's religious intent. Had he set out to be the friend of the Catholics, the Protestants, the Jews? Why? Did he aim to restore religion in France, or to crush it? These were questions that concerned writers of all religious persuasions, or none; at issue was Napoleon's own motivation, not God's ultimate scheme. The chapter then considers eschatological opinion: efforts to explain Napoleon's actions in terms of God's overarching plan, and to predict the destinies of Bonaparte and the British nation through the interpretation of Scripture. A final section briefly suggests the extent to which commentators in other, less obviously pious areas of discourse shared the concerns of exegetical writers. The vision, invoked by writers on prophecy, of a providential scheme— the belief that Britain's struggle against Napoleon should be read as a momentous event in God's design—appeared in spheres far removed from the esoteric realm of scriptural analysis.

Religion and power were inextricably intertwined in the political imagination of early nineteenth-century Britain. France's religious status was felt to have deep political implications for Great Britain. The puzzle of Napoleon's religious policy demanded solution because of the light it was assumed to shed on the moral status of the British nation. While some loyalists drew self-affirming lessons from the new French regime, other writers believed that Napoleon's example offered a rebuke to Britain's religious path. Demonstrating Napoleon's presence in Scripture prompted some to celebrate the destiny of the British nation, but others to question it.

Anti-Catholicism was deeply embedded in the collective historical imagination of British Protestants. Catholicism was associated with tyranny at home and abroad.[10] Protestant memory associated the persecutions of Mary Tudor with the Armada that her widower husband, Philip II of Spain, later sent to attack England. Charles I's marriage to a French

Catholic princess seemed of a piece with his attempt to exert arbitrary power at the expense of Parliament. James II's apparent desire to emulate Louis XIV's absolute rule was assumed to have been fueled by his conversion to Catholicism. James's reputed master-plan against English freedom provided the pitch-black backdrop for that blazing triumph of liberty, the Glorious Revolution.

Xenophobia, anti-Catholicism, and fear of domestic tyranny dovetailed in the British world-view, each reinforcing the others. And this ideological edifice was cemented by an esoteric biblical typology that confirmed the Roman Church's perfidy. Protestant writers identified the Roman Catholic Church, and by extension Europe's arbitrary Catholic dynasties, with the apocalyptic forces described in Scripture: Antichrist, the Beast, the Whore of Babylon, and so on. The identification of Catholicism with Antichrist and his minions was a basic and assumed element of the interpretive framework of eighteenth-century Britons. Caricatures cast Antichrist or the Beast alongside, or in the place of, figures representing the pope and continental monarchs.[11] But the coming of the French revolution shook the foundations of this sturdy ideological construction. By negating a basic assumption on which the logic of British Protestant patriotism depended—the Catholic nature of the French "other"—the revolution threatened the coherence of the entire model. The enormous shifts in France's religious policy dictated dramatic adjustments in the British world-view.

A nation that had once seemed the very model of Catholic superstition and intolerance now, briefly, presented itself as a paragon of reason and of ecumenical tolerance—extending, in the period from 1789 to 1791, liberties to Protestant and Jewish minorities in a fashion that put to shame British reformers' failed efforts to obtain "relief" for Jews, Catholics, and Protestant Dissenters. Then, just as suddenly, with the onset of war in 1793, France's religious identity was again transformed. With the coming of war, French anti-clericalism gained strength; ecumenicism was replaced by the persecution of majority and minority religions alike, and deistical tolerance mutated into atheistical intolerance. Britons found themselves at war with France once again, but this time they faced an enemy whom they could no longer plausibly associate with the Catholic Beast.

If one held to the established eschatological classification of Catholicism, then France's liberation from the chains of superstition and papal subservience ought to be welcomed. But many British writers were unwilling, for reasons of both politics and faith, to embrace the new atheist regime, preferring an alliance with France's Catholic foes. To make sense of the new oppositions that were playing themselves out on the stage of Europe, British writers began to consider the possibility that Antichrist should actually be identified not with Rome but with the unbelief of republican France.

This new wave of scriptural analysis had hardly begun when French religious policy, already a moving target, became a murky one. The dechristianizing program of France's Jacobin government had at least been easy to characterize. (Robespierre's deist parry against the atheist thrust—his cult of the Supreme Being—would hardly, to the Protestant mind, seem any less inimical to Christianity than the irreligion he denounced.) Napoleon's rise to power brought a new ambiguity to the religious identity of France. Napoleon refused to conform to any single religious type. He seemed suspended at some intermediate position among the available religious categories.

The young general was at first regarded as an enemy of Catholicism: the liberal *Monthly Magazine* hailed him in 1797 for humbling Catholic "superstition" in Italy; a 1799 iconographic engraving by an English admirer included a "Tiara, Fetters and Monkish Cowl" to indicate Napoleon's "Destruction of the Papal Tyranny and Superstition."[12] With his expedition to Egypt, Napoleon began to be characterized as in some manner allied to Islam—not an entirely unreasonable claim, given his conciliatory attempts to assure Egyptians that the French were good Muslims. His Concordat with the Catholic Church—the qualified embrace effected in 1801—made British observers wonder if the new consul was directing France back toward its traditional Catholicism. His behavior towards the Jews of his empire would even lead some to suggest a special Napoleonic link with Judaism.

Napoleon's hybrid signification complicated the British debate over France's religion. Consensus on the identity of Antichrist (and on the identities of the other apocalyptic figures whom the revolution had so rudely uncoupled from their time-honored referents) was unlikely, if agreement could not even be reached on the more basic question of whether Napoleon was restoring Catholicism or destroying it. Napoleon could be described as an instrument of God, or as the enemy of God's chosen people. His actions could be interpreted as indicating a glorious future for the British nation—or as proving that Britain had lost God's favor. His place in British religious thought was peculiarly destabilizing.

Napoleon's national identity, we have seen, and the nature of his government, were routinely portrayed as combining diverse, even mutually antagonistic, elements. His religious affiliation defied classification just as much. The indeterminate religious identity of this *"Christianiz'd Mussulman-Papist"* provided an easy target for British wits, high and low.[13] On town streets in 1803, one could hear the ballad-sellers sing that Napoleon was a "Disciple avow'd of the Mussulman school; / A Papist at Rome, and at Cairo a Turk, / Now this thing, now that thing, as best helps his work."[14] At the theater, one might hear him described as "A *mongrel* Mussulman, of *Papal* growth, / *Mufti* and *Monk*, now *neither*, or now *both*."[15] An English Jew, responding to Napoleon's 1806 convocation of the Sanhedrin, suggested that if "the *Temple* of *Solomon*" was still standing, "the High Priest of Jerusalem would be as much an object of the French Emperor's *hypocritical homage* as the reigning successor of St. Peter."[16]

Napoleon's religious oscillations were a stock ingredient in British descriptions of his career. Many felt that his religious indeterminacy indicated a self-serving, purely instrumental relationship to religion.[17] But for some liberal writers, the very fact that France's leader had not convincingly aligned himself with a particular dogma showed him to be "superior to vulgar and narrow prejudices."[18] He tolerated religious dissent, wrote the *Annual Review*, in contrast to "other sovereigns" who "have belonged to some fragment of their nation" and have "abridg[ed] the liberties . . . of unestablished worshippers." Unlike Britain's own king (a contrast this writer clearly intended), Napoleon stood as "a common father of his people; not the subservient apparitor of his archbishop."[19]

Napoleon's British sympathizers could justifiably claim that he had welcomed religion back to France, in a fashion that asserted the rights of religious minorities. Napoleon had, by the Concordat, recognized Catholicism as the religion of the majority of the French, but had refrained from establishing it as the state church. He had seen to it that not only Catholic priests but Protestant ministers as well were made salaried employees of the state. He had, moreover, to the surprise of the papacy, appended to the Concordat a set of "Organic Articles" that imposed restrictions on the Catholic Church in France. Napoleon's ecumenical policies, in short, could readily be interpreted as favoring no one creed.

Nonetheless, and most surprisingly, many British observers concluded that the new French policies would naturally favor, of all religions, Protestantism. Many in late Georgian Britain felt that Protestantism, the most "rational" religion, would naturally emerge the victor from a fair contest of faiths—that religious tolerance would ultimately produce not religious diversity, but the triumph of a single creed.[20] Such logic suggested to many that Napoleon's ecumenicism would foster, through benign neglect, the ascendancy of reformed religion.[21] The clergyman Edward Hankin, for example, praised France's leader for having restored religion, and declared "that more pure and rational forms of devotion will gradually prevail" in France.[22] Some writers regarded Napoleon as an active antagonist of Rome.[23] Even after the Concordat, some remained convinced that Napoleon hoped to crush the Catholic Church completely.[24] An 1814 poem hailed Napoleon for having "done a deal in his day, / For Popery's ruin, tho' in a rough way."[25]

Others believed that any favors performed for Protestants were inadvertent. Many felt Napoleon would ultimately ally himself with atheism, or with the Catholic Church. The prolific Lewis Mayer portrayed Napoleon's "clemency to dissenters" and "general tolerance to all sects and parties" as but temporary. The religion that "answers his purpose best, will have the preference, should he obtain universal power," Mayer wrote—and this religion would be "popery," which was "admirably adapted to serve as a tool of state, to quench every spark of civil and religious liberty; to prevent combinations against despotism, and to hold men under an absolute subordination to an usurped power." Mayer yoked France's revolutionary atheism to its traditional Catholicism: the frontispiece to one of his works showed a friar and a sansculotte together approaching Napoleon to present him with his imperial crown, partners in their abject subservience to the upstart ruler. But Mayer made it clear that France's essential Catholic character would prevail.[26] For Mayer, no major realignment of eschatological typology was necessary. Many writers on politics agreed that Napoleon would ultimately find Catholicism most convenient for his despotism. As for his antagonistic stance toward the bishop of Rome, might he not intend to steal the papal tiara for himself?[27]

Napoleon's ambiguous ties to the Catholic Church cast a shadow over British discussion of the rights of domestic Catholics. Anti-Catholics, who had traditionally damned domestic "papists" by linking them to Britain's continental enemies, could treat Napoleon as yet another Catholic monarch. The ultra-loyalist journalist Lewis Goldsmith, writing in 1811, painted Napoleon as "virtually the Pope of Rome." As a consequence, Goldsmith argued, Catholic emancipation could have devastating results for the United Kingdom. Why did British and Irish Catholics press for reform at a moment when their Church was associated with "the inveterate and declared enemy of their government"? Why, Goldsmith pointedly asked, "if those who advocate it are truly loyal, and not under Corsican influence," did men support a measure which they knew would "irritate" the mind of their sovereign, "already too much and too unhappily distracted" by his mental incapacitation?[28] Goldsmith's argument turned all seekers of Catholic emancipation into crypto-Bonapartists, heedless of their monarch's well-being and desperate to genuflect before the imperial puller of papal strings. Now that "BUONAPARTE and the POPE of Rome is one and the same thing," restrictions against Catholics were justified more than ever before.[29]

Parliamentary friends of emancipation, in an 1811 debate, had to acknowledge Napoleon's apparent power over the Church of Rome. But the Irish Protestant reformer Henry Grattan insisted that measures could be taken to ensure that "a French pope" would not control the nomination of bishops in the United Kingdom. Grattan reminded the British that their nation's allies, Napoleon's enemies, were largely Catholic, and that French troops had helped "pull down the antient fabrics of superstition in the countries subjected to their arms."[30] Samuel Whitbread added that although Napoleon "had the pope in his power indeed," removing restrictions on Irish Catholics would actually decrease Napoleon's potential influence in Ireland. The fierce ongoing Iberian resistance to Napoleon, moreover, showed that Catholicism did not imply docility, least of all in the face of foreign tyranny.[31] Even the notorious anti-Catholic Patrick Duigenan, when he rose to denounce Grattan's measure, emphasized the limits of Napoleon's tolerance of Catholics—in order to recommend that the British government emulate the French refusal "to leave those people quite uncontrouled."[32] For Duigenan, the emperor's caution was evidence that a wise (or crafty) leader would limit the power of his Catholic subjects, and set barriers against the papacy's interference in his domain.[33]

British visions of Napoleon's relationship to the Christian churches, it is clear, ranged across the spectrum. He was described as the friend of all sects, and as the enemy of all. He would bring about the triumph of French Protestantism, and its destruction. His religious tolerance was exemplary; so were his religious restrictions. For those who tried to pin down the proteus, Napoleon could be Protestant, Catholic, dechristian-izing atheist, or religious liberal. But other elements besides Christian ones vied with free-thought or atheism in the British classification of Napoleon. His exploits in the East, and his reforms at home, led many observers to inquire into the Corsican's peculiar relationship to the Jewish people. Did he mean to rehabilitate French Jews, or to expel them? Was he setting himself against European Jewry, or trying to enlist it in his cause?

Napoleon's position regarding the Jews was genuinely ambiguous; his-torians today continue to debate the liberality of his position.[34] He eman-cipated Jews in the lands his armies conquered, but his actions within France can be read as a scaling back of the rights that France's Jews had won in the revolution's early years. Napoleon convoked an assembly of Jewish notables in 1806, and then, more famously, the Grand Sanhedrin in 1807 (named after an ancient rabbinic court). In his dealings with these bodies, he revealed himself as ready to restrict Jewish activities, including occupational and marital choice—albeit in order to speed, by force if necessary, the assimilation of Jews into the French national fabric (and into the fabric of the empire: the Sanhedrin included representa-tives from Italy, Spain, Portugal, and Germany). The "consistory" he created, for the self-policing of the Jewish community, was a particu-larist body that had more in common with the corporate structure of *ancien régime* society than with the revolutionary principle of univer-sality. And yet Napoleon's pronounced interest in Jewish welfare led many British observers to hail the Sanhedrin (which many commenta-tors mistakenly called "Sanhedrim") as a demonstration of religious tolerance. One writer claimed that the Jews' "years of tribulation were ended at the time that Sanhedrim arose."[35] The radical William Hamil-ton Reid argued that Napoleon's Jewish policy offered a great improve-ment on that of the previous revolutionary regimes—since under the Jacobins "privileges were not *really enjoyed* by any class of persons, not even the sanguinary Rulers themselves."[36]

Reid's 1810 letter to the *Gentleman's Magazine* prompted an angry response from Robert Atkins, author of a history of the Jews. Atkins maintained that the Sanhedrin marked a worsening of the Jewish con-dition in France, the substitution of "military despotism" for "compar-ative freedom." The assembly's members had "exchanged . . . the purity of their Religious principles for modern Atheistical dogmas." That this apostasy had been forced on them was evidenced by the Sanhedrin declaration which thanked the Christian clergy of preceding ages for their kind treatment of the Jews. The declaration proved that Napoleon had "deprived [Jews] of the power of expressing their real sentiments, and made them appear to the world as the voluntary denunciators of their ancestors, and the pliant tools for promoting his ambitions and blasphemous views." Atkins sensed, moreover, that Napoleon hoped to employ the Jews as "useful instruments . . . to promote his ambitious projects."[37]

Others joined Atkins in asserting that Napoleon intended the Jews to serve as tools of his empire. F. D. Kirwan, who translated the Sanhedrin's *Transactions* in 1807, claimed the Jews had been relatively happy under the Bourbons, and had won new liberties thanks to the revolution. Greed and suspicion had motivated Napoleon's convocation of the Sanhedrin. By making it clear that Jewish rights were revocable, Napoleon hoped to blackmail the Jewish community; the new consistory would turn rabbis into state spies. Moreover, Kirwan saw little sense in Napoleon's exhortation to the Jews to take up unaccustomed occupations— "mechanical trades and husbandry"—unless he wished them to become an autonomous nation, outside of France. So Napoleon planned to re-establish the Jews in Palestine, a scheme that would bring him one step closer to the conquest of Egypt. No "distinct nation in a land of their own" could survive were it "wholly composed of merchants and traders." Napoleon wanted Jews to take up new occupations not to further their assimilation into France, but to prepare them for removal from it.[38]

Kirwan's sympathies lay with France's Jews, not with Napoleon. Still, the Sanhedrin's apparent obedience disturbed the Englishman. The assembly's members, in their effort to placate Bonaparte, seemed blithely ready to neglect "the precepts of their law" and succumb to "the contagious infidelity of France." Kirwan accused French Jews of having "profanely" incorporated the names of Napoleon and Josephine into religious ceremonies. By "acknowledg[ing] France as their country, without any restriction," Kirwan wrote, French Jews were guilty of a "heinous dereliction of the tenets of the Mosaic law." Kirwan was only partly comforted by the hope, not entirely complimentary to the Jews of France, that they had "feigned" their devotion to Napoleon.[39] Kirwan's position—as an English Gentile cautioning French Jews as to the proper degree of assimilation they might undertake—should be read in the context of British Protestant millennialism. The coming of the end of days depended upon the Jews' conversion to Christianity. But many believed that Jews must remain a distinct people until they returned to Palestine, where they would finally be absorbed into Christendom.

While Kirwan did not mention English Jewry, other writers feared that Napoleon's policies, whatever their governing intent, might lead British observers to regard Jews as enemies-within, a community whose true loyalty would now naturally direct itself to the French nation. William Hamilton Reid urged readers to dismiss the thought that English Jews might share the allegiance to Napoleon of their French co-religionists. Jewish loyalty in France did not imply Jewish disloyalty in Britain.[40] An 1808 pamphlet by an "English Israelite" similarly defended the patriotism of English Jews.[41] Napoleon's original scheme, the author claimed, had been to enlist Jews "under his Imperial banners, and thereby dissolv[e] their loyalty and allegiance to the other Sovereigns of the Earth." Napoleon saw the Jews "as a magazine of wealth and of oriental knowledge," who might help him "carry on his plans of conquest and plunder in Asia." By extending religious tolerance, Napoleon believed he might harness the loyalty of Jews everywhere; he felt "that in their having no temporal prince of their own nation, he could the more easily withdraw their allegiance from all the other kings, princes, and potentates of the earth."[42] But Napoleon, the "English Israelite" continued, had wrongly underestimated Jews' allegiance to the lands they inhabited, and especially that of British Jews, whose "mild and merciful Prince" had given them "every immunity, and indulgence, granted to others not of the Established Church."[43] By prostrating themselves to Napoleon, French Jews (the author's "*former* co-religionists") had engaged in an act of "venal apostacy."[44] The unyielding patriotism of non-French Jews "who have refused to adopt France for their Country, or Napoleon for their Prince," would now prompt Napoleon to show his true colors. Napoleon would now reveal his aim to be the "projected subversion, and final extermination, of the religion of Judaism, in France."[45]

Even in these distrustful accounts of Napoleon, writers saw a peculiar affinity between Napoleon and the Jews. Though he planned to rid France of the Jewish people, Napoleon was thought to be scheming to employ them as instruments of his world dominion—trying to fashion himself into the Jews' king. For analysts of Scripture, the ultimate consequence of Napoleon's encounter with the Jewish people was an especially riveting question. On the outcome of Napoleon's Jewish policy, many believed, hinged the fate of the British nation.

In works of early nineteenth-century eschatology, one finds a rich debate over the British nation's destiny. Both supporters and opponents of the war saw it as an event described in prophetic Scripture. Reading the Bible would reveal the nature of Napoleon, and the fate of the British and French peoples. Those who wished to place current events into an eschatological framework needed first to demonstrate that the Bible's descriptions of apocalyptic figures applied to actors on the contemporary world stage. The most notorious method of achieving this was the attempt, as one skeptic put it, "to silence opposition by the letters of Napoleon's name."[46] Writers who wished to identify Napoleon as Antichrist performed arithmetical exercises upon his name or personal history to reveal "the number of the beast," as described in Revelations: 666, a number that British Protestants had long associated with the Roman Catholic Church.[47]

Thus the pamphleteer Lewis Mayer counted the number of Roman emperors and popes; added to this host all those individuals who had (during certain periods) been "the heads or sovereigns of the nations alluded to by the horns of St. John's first Beast, Rev. 13" (the kings of the Roman empire's myriad successor states, from France and Spain to Hungary and Sardinia); noted "many exceptions"; and reached the astonishing conclusion that there were 665 such rulers prior to Bonaparte himself, the 666th.[48] The *British Press* reported that the Latin abbreviations "DUX CL I"—representing Napoleon's roles as military leader, consul, and imperator—added up, as Roman numerals, to the same revelatory figure.[49] Cabbalistic manipulation of the letters in Bonaparte's name could produce similar results. One pamphleteer reached the desired number 666, but only by summing up the letters in "Nicolais Buonaparte" or (closer) "Napolean Buonaparte"[50]—an orthographical technique similar to that which had, a few years earlier, irked a *Monthly* reviewer (who thought "farcical" one author's reasoning on the basis of a Greek-lettered "Bonneparte").[51] While loyalist interpreters of Scripture sought to identify Napoleonic France with the Beast, critics of Britain's war could turn the same weapon to their own devices. The anti-ministerial exegetes James Bicheno and Ebenezer Aldred showed that LUDOVICUS (Louis) added up to 666.[52] The technique was

embraced by friend and foe of governmental policy alike—if in the face
of skeptics like the *Scourge* correspondent who confessed himself unable
"to discover the period of time when letters possessed this numerical
value."[53]

Eschatological writers on Napoleon can be divided into two camps:
the loyalist majority who supported Britain's war policy explicitly or
tacitly, and the opposition minority who denounced it. Associating
Napoleonic France with Antichrist and the Beast (as loyalist writers did)
necessarily meant loosening, in British Protestant minds, the Catholic
Church's traditional monopoly on eschatological bogeymen. It was difficult to promote Napoleon's regime to the first rank of millennial threat
without giving the impression that the Catholic Church was now less
menacing than it had been made out to be—that, in the words of
Thomas Witherby, one of the first to link Napoleon to Antichrist, "the
idolatry of the Roman church" was "not so bad as the idolatry of the
great antichrist to come."[54]

This eschatological demotion amounted to a revolution in typological thinking. The political consequences of the semiotic shift were
described, at the end of the Napoleonic wars, by the young radical John
Cam Hobhouse. Hobhouse chastised his fellow countrymen for "sacrificing our former interpretations to our present interests, our prophecy
to our politics." His disapproval arose not from an investment in these
"former interpretations" but rather from an antipathy to the new
geopolitics that brought Protestant Britain into alliances with illiberal
Catholic dynasts seeking, among other things, the restoration of the
pope's patrimony. The new alliances brushed the wrong way against
long-held assumptions of British Protestant patriotism. The new
loyalist exegesis, as Hobhouse pointed out, smoothed out these ruffled
feathers by demonizing Napoleon and lessening the negative connotations of Rome. By identifying Napoleon as "the Horned Beast,"
loyalist exegesis had freed Britons to ally themselves with the papacy,
the power with whom the devil "had been, in every British heart, so long
allied."[55]

The millenarian Thomas Witherby, in his 1800 pamphlet on the
restoration of the Jews, dropped unambiguous hints about Antichrist's
identity without actually naming Napoleon. Revelations, according to
Witherby, described Antichrist as resembling Caesar: "A GREAT
WARRIOR," "not of a royal house," who "may pretend to be the patron
of peace," but only of "a peace in which all is to be placed under his

7. "An Hieroglyphic, Describing the State of Great Britain and the Continent of Europe, for 1804." Frontispiece to Lewis Mayer, *A Hint to England; or, A Prophetic Mirror; Containing an Explanation of Prophecy that Relates to the French Nation, and the Threatened Invasion*, 1803 (British Museum).

control."[56] Other loyalist millenarians made more explicit charges. The prolific Lewis Mayer maintained that biblical references to Lucifer, the dragon, the false prophet, Gog, "Abaddon and Apollyon, the angel of the bottomless pit, the king of the locusts, the beast with two horns and head of the anti-christian powers," all alluded specifically to Napoleon. Bonaparte's government was the second Beast described in Revelations (successor to the first, France's monarchy). The fact that the second Beast arose "out of the earth" indicated Napoleon's "springing forth from the lower classes of society, and suddenly grasping the supreme authority, through treachery and dissimulation." And the famous passages from Revelations describing the mark of the Beast had two contemporary meanings, "civil and ecclesiastical": the mark referred both to "the seal, ensign and cockade of France," and to France's "embracing the errors of the church of Rome, and joining her communion" (for Mayer continued to identify Napoleonic France with Rome).[57] The claim, in the following verse of Revelations, that "no man might buy or sell, save he that had the mark," was a clear indictment of Napoleon's attempt to exclude British trade from the European continent.[58] Indeed, a careful reading of Scripture would provide British readers with a vision of their struggle's end: Napoleon, the Bible revealed, would be "slain with the sword in the land of Palestine, in the fifth year of his reign" as emperor.[59] No wonder, perhaps, that Mayer stopped publishing after 1809, the fifth year of empire, after which point Napoleon's continued tenure of office might have seemed a mockery of the exegete's claims.

The exegetical writing of George Stanley Faber, by contrast, would not be halted even by Napoleon's death. Faber was the most prominent of the loyalist exegetes to address the problem of Napoleon, and probably the most learned. Faber was by temperament a syncretist, who in some works drew erudite, Casaubon-like links between pagan, Jewish, and Christian beliefs.[60] Few contemporary students of Scripture neglected Faber's analysis of Napoleonic France; no work on prophecy in the years following 1806 was complete without a critical consideration of the claims made in his two-volume *Dissertation on the Prophecies.* The work went through several editions, English and American, and attracted the attention of prominent periodicals. The *British Critic*, after resisting the *Dissertation* for several years, finally gave in when a fourth edition made it "impossible to deny that the work has commanded attention"; the journal now devoted more than ten pages to a close, if critical, consideration of the book's argument.[61] A graduate of University College, Oxford, and a former Fellow and Tutor of Lincoln College, Faber was thirty-two when he put the finishing touches to his *Dissertation* in late December 1805, in the immediate wake of Nelson's victory at Trafalgar.[62] He would live until 1854, long enough to claim that Napoleon III's rise confirmed the interpretation he had formulated nearly half a century earlier.[63]

Faber repeatedly insisted in his works that figures like Antichrist represented not individual human beings, but communities or intellectual tendencies. He did not, therefore, follow the eager lead of Lewis Mayer, promiscuously connecting Napoleon to almost every available millennial type. More cautiously, Faber claimed that Antichrist stood not for Bonaparte but for *"the tremendous infidel power of France."* (Indeed, Faber argued that Antichrist was "a sort of generic name" that could describe atheist opinions "lurking in the Church even in the earliest ages"—although not until the present day did one see Antichristian sentiment "embraced *without disguise* by a whole nation.") Napoleon was significant only in his capacity as head of the infidel power, Faber declared: "if [he] were slain tomorrow, and if one of his generals stepped into his vacant throne, no event would have occurred which were worth prophetic notice."[64]

This broad definition would prove useful on the eve of Napoleon's fall. In May 1815, during the Hundred Days, Faber would point out that his own interpretation—unlike that of his rival interpreter, James Hatley Frere, who "fancies [Napoleon] to be a personal Antichrist"—would not skip a beat if Napoleon should die. Prophecy singled out the revolutionary government, not the individual. But within a few weeks, Faber's interpretation was in more trouble than Frere's: Napoleon still lived, but his regime had clearly ended (more definitively so than in 1814, when Faber had held tight to the fact that the Allies had allowed Napoleon "to hold a sovereignty however small"—as emperor of Elba—and thus "preserved the line of the revolutionary government unbroken"). Hence Faber's eventual thrill at the revival, by Napoleon's nephew, of the "sword-slain French Emperorship": the regime had been restored, just in time for Antichrist to be thoroughly destroyed, as Faber had long predicted, in the apocalyptic 1860s.[65]

ith atheist France, rather than with the
against the grain of British Protestant tra-
Church of Rome would be punished at
the papacy with the biblical "harlot" and
hat Rome did not answer to Antichrist's
olics had never denied God or Christ).[66]
ed though it was, popery would have to
menace to infidel France.

Faber, like so many commentators, characterized Napoleon as a hybrid: "*a motley monster*, . . . inwardly *an atheist*, outwardly *a papist*." Similarly, the French nation's superficial return to Catholicism masked a continued infidel, and thus Antichristian, identity. "It is unreasonable to suppose," Faber maintained, "that all the people of France, even fickle and volatile as they are, should suddenly have turned with sincerity from *Atheism* to *Popery*." Why this dissimulation? Because if atheistical France had destroyed the papacy, as it had been on the verge of doing, prophecy would have been outpaced; the onset of the millennium would have come too soon. "Hence, rather than one jot or one tittle of all God's word should fail, *the infidel king* has become, by the overruling providence of God, a supporter of the very superstition which he had once laboured to destroy." God had intervened so that the divine plan could keep to schedule. Also illusory was Bonaparte's apparent indulgence of

Protestantism: a tyrant like Napoleon would naturally view any religious dissent "as a secret mark of disaffection."[67]

How, then, did Protestant Britain fit into God's millennial design? Faber maintained that the Bible predicted the Jews would be restored to Palestine by "*the prevailing protestant maritime power of the day.*" He advised caution in identifying this power as England (though his exultant reference to Trafalgar as a victory for "the great protestant maritime power" indicated that he felt some confidence in the identity of the Jews' restorer).[68] Others were less circumspect. Faber's fellow Oxonian Henry Kett, "one of His Majesty's preachers at Whitehall," wrote that Britain fit Ezekiel's description of Tarshish, the opponents of Gog and thus servants of the Lord.[69] Lewis Mayer determined that England was "the mountain of the house of the Lord," and predicted the nation would restore the Jews to Palestine.[70] But the conclusion that the Jews' exile would end soon was resisted by writers who feared that this restoration would come prematurely. Thomas Witherby insisted that the Jews could not be repatriated until they acknowledged the "justice" of "their long-continued dispersion."[71] Faber likewise warned against any scheme to bring European Jews to Palestine "in *an unconverted state*" (but felt that Napoleon's self-interested scheme to that end would backfire, prompting "*the maritime power*" to restore to Palestine the Jews it had already converted—which in turn would lead the unconverted Jews of Antichrist's empire to embrace Christianity).[72] Faber's great rival, James Hatley Frere, similarly expected Napoleon to declare himself the Jews' messiah and "lead some of them back to the Holy Land." Frere underscored the cosmic significance of such a scheme by announcing that Napoleon would "plant his tabernacles in the valley of Megiddo"—the town better known as Armageddon.[73]

Many loyalist exegetes believed that God would make the British people "instrumental in bringing home the remnant of the true Israelites."[74] As Ralph Wedgwood proposed in a chaotic 1814 pamphlet, the task of restoring the Jews to Palestine was "perfectly congenial with British principles, and a prevailing disposition of her most enlightened christians." But for a few writers, Wedgwood among them, the role of deliverer was not sufficiently grand for the British nation. According to Wedgwood, Britain's great enemy Napoleon, just sent to Elba, was either Satan himself or the servant of a Satanic pope. Wedgwood noted that the Hebrew for covenant was "Brit," "the original name of our land." This and other circumstances (such as Britain's free press) led Wedgwood to ask that his readers not only view Britain as the Jews' ally but at least "for a moment consider Britain . . . the new Jerusalem descended from above." Prophecy spoke, according to Wedgwood, not of the Jews but of the British: the Scriptures revealed that *the British Empire is the peculiar possession of Messiah, and his promised Naval Dominion.*[75]

Lord Liverpool's correspondent Augustus Markett reached the same portentous conclusion in an 1813 letter. God had bestowed many "temporal and spiritual blessings" upon England, Markett wrote: the Reformation, the Glorious Revolution, an "insular Situation" separating England "from all nations as the Jews by their civil and religious society." These blessings, and England's rivalry with France ("the great Enemy of Christianity") clearly indicated the nation's special role in the providential scheme. "In short the Lion of England, seems for the present to have taken Place of the Lion of the Tribe of Judah."[76] The light the prophecies cast on Britain was not reflective but direct: it was not in the Bible's description of the Jews' deliverer that Britons should recognize themselves, but in its description of the Jews.

No one erased the Jews more effectively from the chiliastic equation than James Hatley Frere, for whom scriptural reference to the Jewish nation was but "a symbol . . . of that *nation* which now stands in the situation formerly filled by the Jewish nation, as the chosen people of God." All biblical references to the fate of Israel were for Frere predictions about "the Israelitish Nation, or Protestant British Nation": Britain now occupied the position that the Jewish nation had formerly held "as the chosen people of God." Frere admitted that Bonaparte had so far appeared to be an instrument of divine punishment of the papacy and Islam. Soon, however, Napoleon would reveal himself as the enemy of true Christianity. Sufficient proof of Bonaparte's true status lay in his hostility to the British nation. It was Napoleon's war against Britain, God's chosen people, rather than any particular act in the religious sphere, that allowed Frere to brand him the "Infidel Power": an enemy of Christianity, a chiliastic partner of popery and Islam.[77]

Frere's conception of Napoleon as an instrument in the hands of God was a well-established component of loyalist exegesis by the time he published his work. Napoleon's ambitious efforts to attain entirely selfish ends would, it was held, bear fruit unrelated to, or even antithetical to, his goals and interests. He would accomplish God's will unawares. Hester Piozzi, citing in 1796 the improved situation of Dutch Jews under French occupation (and expecting the same soon for Roman Jews), believed French troops were acting out the script of prophecy unwit-tingly.[78] Their individual actions, though they did not realize it yet, were part of a greater plan. Others agreed that Napoleon, "without knowing or intending any such matter," was fulfilling prophecy, acting in a fashion "unquestionably divine."[79]

Many were agreed, then, that Napoleon—though very likely himself one of the characters described in Revelations—chastened and destroyed other millennial enemies of the Lord. He punished those that had strayed from the path of true Christianity. The question then arose, in the minds of all but the most sanguine: had the British nation, like the penalized lands of the continent, also strayed?

Even the most fiercely patriotic and anti-Gallican reader of Scripture conceded that God's favor depended on Britons living within his law. Beneath their triumphalist skins, many loyalist exegetes betrayed a seething anxiety on the question of Britain's future. Some pointed out the stumbling blocks that might trip up the nation in its service of God. One anonymous pamphleteer, writing in 1809, feared that Faber might (by misdating the "second woe" of Revelations) have mistaken a past ordeal of the Protestant Church for one that was yet to come. And if such a punishment were due, "where can it fall so effectually as on this Island?"[80] So while Joanna Southcott reassured her followers that "If Buonaparte entered this nation, he should not conquer it; for the Lord would protect this nation from destruction, for the sake of Believers," others were not so complacent.[81] Even the optimistic Lewis Mayer warned Britons, at the 1803 height of invasion fears, that it was only "by humbling themselves before [God] as a nation" that the British would "find shelter amidst the approaching storm."[82] Without ques-tioning the war, or their typological identification of Napoleon, loyalist exegetes could harbor a deep uncertainty about the outcome of the coming chiliastic conflict.

Pro-war exegetes in the age of Napoleon, in short, should be assigned to the most moderate category of "holy nationalism," as defined by Conor Cruise O'Brien. They believed, that is to say, not in a "holy" or "deified nation," but in a "chosen people." They displayed, to quote O'Brien's definition of this mildest category, "not only national pride, but also humility, anguish, fear, and guilt," and felt that God could "use other peoples as instruments of their punishment." Even in the appar-ently self-satisfied assertions of some that God had redirected his attentions from the Jews to the Britons, one detects the recognition, in O'Brien's formulation, that "God, having chosen one people, [could] simply drop it for another." The British might lose God's favor as the Jews had before.[83]

Loyalist interpreters of Scripture, then, did ask worrisome questions about the national fate. But unlike their opposition counterparts, they believed that Britain would retain God's favor. Loyalists first raised the seemingly risky question of whether Britain itself, as a nation once attached to the Church of Rome, might be part of the Beast that Providence would destroy. They then dissociated Britain from the Beast, citing theological difference or the passage of time.[84]

What separated loyalist from opposition exegesis was, by definition, the position taken on Britain's war with Napoleon.[85] The two interpretive camps were further distinguished by their treatment of Britain's eschatological identity and destiny. Where loyalists insisted that Britain ought not to be identified with "mystic Babylon," opposition exegetes feared that the British nation was part, or even the heart, of the Beast that was destined to be destroyed. At the very least, opposition readers of Scripture warned that Britons had misread the signs of the times and risked obstructing the path of Antichrist's true enemy.

Despite the differences between the two camps, one should note the similarities—the symbiosis, even—between loyalist and opposition eschatology. Just as the loyalist vision left room for anxiety about Britain's fate, so did some anti-war analysis allow that Britain could indeed have been God's "chosen people," had the nation's governors only acted properly. James Bicheno, the most prolific figure in the prophetic assault on British policy, felt Britain was a "favoured isle" that had lost its way.[86] Opposition writers should not be excluded a priori from O'Brien's category of believers in a "chosen people." They stressed the negative aspects of "holy nationalism," but worked within the same paradigm. Robust patriotic pride had a soft underbelly of self-doubt, and it was this doubt that the anti-war exegetes labored to express.

In refusing to "transfer from the church of Rome to the democracy of France, the odium attached to antichrist,"[87] anti-war exegetes rejected the typological revolution set in motion by loyalists. They resisted the eschatological demotion of the Catholic Church that logically followed from pinning Antichristian labels on Napoleon and France. Opposition exegetes emphasized (indeed exaggerated) the extent to which loyalists lessened the traditional taint of Rome. In opposition eyes, the loyalist reinterpretation of Scripture was a mere loincloth of justification for Britain's ill-judged foreign policy. If loyalist exegesis delivered the rationale for an alliance outrageous to the Protestant world-view, opposition exegesis, by contrast, held tight to the anti-Catholicism of the traditional schema, and in so doing raised new questions about the national destinies of France and Britain.

Lewis Mayer exaggerated when he claimed that "the enemies of episcopacy"—that is, Dissenters—"hold up Bonaparte as an angel of light, and a supporter of the Protestant faith."[88] Still, it is true that the most prominent opposition exegetes were Dissenters, more distant doctrinally from the Church of Rome than high-church Anglicans. Dissenters not only displayed greater hostility to Rome but detected excessive Roman influence in the established Church. Thus James Bicheno mischievously suggested that the anxious Anglicans who rallied against Napoleon, Catholicism's foe, may "have been seized with the fancy that some near degree of kindred subsists between themselves and the consecrated orders of the Roman hierarchy."[89] Bicheno, a Baptist minister from Berkshire, was joined in his opposition to loyalist exegesis by Ebenezer Aldred, a Unitarian minister from Derbyshire, and by the Londoner William Hamilton Reid, free-floating in his Dissent, but a Unitarian at the time of his exegetical writing.[90] Like the more secular John Cam Hobhouse (raised as a Unitarian), these writers condemned Britain's new alliances and questioned the wisdom of war against Napoleon. They reacted against loyalist arguments, "so flattering to the general prejudice, so congenial with the inveterate hatred cherished against France, and so well calculated to buoy up our hopes of ultimate success."[91] They rejected the hubristic claim ("Gross delusion! and shocking perversion of the sacred Prophecies!") that Britain was *the Israel of God.*[92] In seeking to determine Britain's true millennial identity, as well as that of France, Bicheno and his colleagues reached more unsettling conclusions.

Bicheno's eschatological career began in 1793, with a work entitled *Signs of the Times*. Bicheno would publish at least ten other titles during the years of war with France, and *Signs* would go through many editions (both English and American). Like more secular "friends of liberty," Bicheno blamed French revolutionary excesses on the aggression of Britain and its allies. From the war's earliest years, Bicheno maintained that Britain should remain at peace lest it find itself struggling against God's purpose. He insisted on the "folly" and "sin" of allying with Catholic powers.[93] Bicheno pointed to the glorious tribulations that continental "despots" and the pope now suffered as a result of French actions; whatever the crimes of France's governors, surely such blows against tyranny and superstition indicated the French to be "instruments

to scourge the nations for their sins."[94] "Kingdom after kingdom falls;

[...] is annihilated"—Bicheno wrote in 1799,

[...]d the pope to surrender most of his ter-

[...] any sensation is produced [in Britain],

[...]tion against the instruments whom God

[...]ing to fight against Napoleonic France,

[...] appointed it "the public executioner of

[...]on to our ruin."[95]

Bicheno feared that Britain might itself be one of the nations deserving punishment by the divine scourge. Britain, Bicheno warned in 1803, would be judged not only for the sins of its individuals— swearing, drunkenness, adultery, sabbath-breaking—but also for what he termed *"national* sins," and *"national* crimes": the nation's "public corruption," "passion for commerce," colonialism, and participation in the slave trade. To prevent invasion, "radical reform, both political and moral," was necessary, Bicheno wrote; otherwise "GOD WILL BE AGAINST US; . . . our endeared constitution and liberties will soon be lost, and our country ruined."[96] Like loyalist exegetes, Bicheno sought "to distinguish between the crimes of the instruments and the equity of Providence," and stressed that "the principal actors in the great drama" unfolding on the European stage were "unconscious . . . of the parts which they are acting in the tragic accomplishment of the awful decrees of heaven."[97] In viewing Napoleon's personal goals and scruples as, in a sense, irrelevant, Bicheno drew a picture of Napoleon that was hardly more flattering than that offered by the rival interpretive camp. But when he turned to the subject of Napoleon's Jewish policy, Bicheno suggested that France was performing a providential role more positive than punitive. Making matters worse, this role could have been Britain's, had only Britain's governors been more keenly attuned to the dictates of Scripture.

Given the "piety" and "generosity of Englishmen," Bicheno wrote, one might have expected Britain to help restore the Jews to their ancient homeland. Britain's alliance with Turkey allowed the Baptist minister to hope, in a 1799 pamphlet, that the British government might encourage the Turks to give Palestine to the Jews. But the moment passed: by the second edition of 1807, Constantinople was in the French camp and

Napoleon had convened the Sanhedrin, which seemed to bode well for the "speedy restoration" of the Jews. Isaiah's reference to Tarshish, it seemed increasingly clear, described France, not England. Napoleon would not only be the heaven-sent scourge of European Catholicism, but also the prophesied restorer of God's chosen people; getting in his way would amount to "waging war against the providence of Almighty God." An ill-ruled Britain had allowed its role to be stolen by the French emperor: "I wish," Bicheno concluded gloomily, "our prospects were more promising."[98]

Bicheno's arguments were contested by Faber and by Witherby; his prolific output received attention in the monthly and quarterly journals. Ebenezer Aldred, by contrast, garnered few reviews with his *Little Book* of 1811. The provincial clergyman presented a biting radical critique of British policy similar to Bicheno's; if anything, Aldred left even less room for escape from Napoleonic punishment. Aldred rejected the loyalist Henry Kett's claim that "infidel" France figured in Revelations (nothing in the relevant verses, Aldred insisted, "has the least analogy to infidelity, or the hacknied [*sic*] word, Jacobinism").[99] Aldred mocked the common desire to identify Napoleon, on the basis of a similar name, with Apollyon, "the angel of the bottomless pit" described in Revelations.[100] Instead, he argued that the Antichristian figures in Scripture pointed to Britain.

While noting the "dissipated and dissolute" ways of Britons, and the unprecedented prevalence of "Sodomy," Aldred's emphasis was not on the moral behavior of individual men and women but on the political sins of the nation. He believed Scripture to have singled out Britain for her sins: by the seven heads of the Beast in Revelations, he wrote, "I suppose the Protestant succession is meant"; clearly God would visit his wrath on "a monarchical Island having seven successive kings, rulers, or heads" (of whom the Prince Regent, who had just assumed his father's powers, was the sixth).[101] The forehead-mark of Revelations referred to "a general system of bribery and corruption" (that is, the system of Old Corruption lambasted by British reformers): those with the mark "*were willing to take a subsidy.*"[102]

But the greatest of Britain's national crimes, according to Aldred, expressed itself on the stage of the world. It was Britain's empire that most appalled Aldred: the nation's role in "the massacre of millions" in the Indian subcontinent and "the hellish traffic in human beings" to the West Indies ("there to be used as beasts of burthen to fill the coffers of our over-grown merchants"). Both colonial oppression and the slave trade had been sanctioned by Parliament. They must therefore be considered "national crimes," "very great evils" that "call for the judgments of a God of justice."[103]

When Aldred invoked the Whore of Babylon elsewhere in his pamphlet, it was not to denote Rome. Instead, in an extraordinary twist on Protestant typology, Aldred maintained that the Whore was to be found in Britannia's own representation on the new English halfpenny. This figure was

> an harlot, with wet drapery from the hips upwards, and which causes the parts to be exposed; a loose garment thrown over the thighs and legs, but so as to permit them to be very *conspicuous*; the feet, arms, bosom, neck and head, completely bare, and in the very attitude of invitation. If the engraver had designed an harlot he could not have depicted one more accurately.[104]

Britain herself was the woman of sin decried in Scripture, according to Aldred. All that British Protestant exegesis had traditionally foretold for the Church of Rome was actually in store for the British nation.

A pseudonymous pamphlet of 1807 presented its criticisms of British policy, and its grim prognosis for Britain's national fate, in terms even harsher than those offered by Bicheno and Aldred. Written by a man calling himself "An Advocate for the House of Israel," the pamphlet featured a title whose first words—*Sanhedrin Chadasha*, "new Sanhedrin"—were spelled out in Hebrew letters, and which promised to consider "the question, 'whether there is any thing in the prophetic records that seems to point particularly to England?'" In the millenarian tenor of his argument, and in his readiness to appeal to scriptural prophecy, the "Advocate" would have seemed not too different from the clergymen-authors already encountered. Contemporary readers may have been surprised, then, when the "Advocate," three years after his pamphlet's publication, revealed himself in the *Gentleman's Magazine* to be the radical pamphleteer William Hamilton Reid, a man whose other works offered little discussion of religion and much sharp criticism of the British political establishment.[105]

Reid's secular publications hailed Colonel Gwyllym Lloyd Wardle's revelation of a "torrent of corruption" involving Frederick, Duke of York, the army's commander-in-chief, and denounced the war policy that had allowed "rivers of British blood" to be "uselessly shed in Spain

and Portugal." Reid held that the government could reasonably claim
to have brought prosperity to Britain, but only because its war policy
had killed "the refuse of society, and check[ed] the exuberance of population": the government, he darkly warned, had a vested interest in
encouraging "*eternal war*" so as to evade the nation's real economic
(indeed Malthusian) problems. Reid traced this social predicament to
the new factories being built—at which "poor John Bull has lately been
taught to fly into raptures," despite the threat they actually posed to the
welfare of most tradesmen.[106]

Reid spoke the language of national decay, but (unlike Henry Redhead
Yorke, for example) pinned the moral deterioration of the British people
on the actions of their governors. He emphasized that Britain's "degeneracy" was rather "chargeable to its government and to the great, than
to the people at large," and that the actions of men like Wardle might
bring about a "moral regeneration" and "restore the best constitution
in the world to its pristine vigour." Still, Reid acknowledged that the
acts of Britain's rulers had fundamentally altered the general character
of the people. The taxes imposed by Pitt's government, according to
Reid, had changed everyday behavior: they had "altered the once free
open temper and the blunt manners of John Bull." Pitt had imposed
restrictions (like the window tax) that tended "to the total prohibition
of social intercourse." In this, he resembled an earlier William: "William
the Conqueror changed the English customs; William Pitt succeeded but
too well in changing the English character." Pitt injected alien elements
into England more effectively than foreigners themselves, according to
Reid: while it was "poor French Protestant refugees" who had brought
the habit of eating offal to London, it was not until Pitt's administration that this "humiliating" practice was taken up by Englishmen.[107]

Reid clearly enjoyed playing with the dichotomies of national difference—presenting anti-Gallicans as a more subtly insidious enemy of
British culture than were Britain's Francophiles. In the same spirit, he
worked to turn the loyalists' favorite insults back against their habitual
employers. Entrenched political interests had formerly "intimidated the
honest and well-meaning by the mad infuriated cry of *Jacobins*, Con-
spiracies, No Popery, &c.!" They had headed off reform by impugning
the loyalty of would-be reformers. Now, however—thanks to men
like Wardle, those "truly great men of the age, who have undertaken
the Herculean task of cleansing this Augean stable"—the bombs
of imprecation were exploding in their hurlers' hands. "The spells of

Jacobinism and No Popery will no longer obey their old masters," Reid maintained. The British public now recognized that the greatest threat to proper government came from within government itself: "the increasing good sense of the country is beginning to fix the character of Jacobin upon those whose actions, [now] exposed . . . to public censure, would most infallibly tend to bring the Sovereign and his Government into contempt."[108] The real enemies-within were the men warning Britons against enemies-within.

A sense of paradox, then, or of reversal, characterized Reid's political writing: prosperity built on the back of eternal suffering; the anti-Gallican as agent of foreign influence; the anti-Jacobin as Jacobin. This same sense informed his pseudonymous pamphlet of 1807. The cosmic relationship that the "Advocate" drew between the English, the French, and the Jews resembled in many particulars the relationship described by loyalist exegetes. By dramatically shifting the polarities of the loyalist argument, however, Reid produced startling identifications of the Beast and of the New Jerusalem. *Sanhedrin Chadasha* would be interesting enough if motivated by a satirical desire to assault his political enemies with a bludgeon from their own arsenal. But Reid's pamphlet seems heartfelt, not only in its argument for lessening British legal restrictions against Jews but also in its scriptural reading of contemporary events. Reid would criticize, in his Wardle pamphlet, the suggestion "that 'God in his providence interferes not with the management of human affairs.'"[109] The radical writer—a member, around this time, of the Unitarian Thomas Belsham's famous Hackney congregation—was sincere in his embrace of scriptural exegesis.[110]

Reid read and praised James Bicheno, but he departed dramatically from Bicheno's predictions for the future of the Jews. Where Bicheno warned (as had Kirwan, the translator of the Sanhedrin *Transactions*) that Napoleon might soon restore Europe's Jews to Palestine, Reid maintained, against all established eschatological reasoning, that the prophecies did not in fact predict the Jews' return to their ancestral land. It was wrong to assume that "the Millennium could not commence till the Jews rebuilt" Jerusalem, Reid argued; "the prophetical idea of the New Jerusalem" mentioned in Revelations "is more applicable to a *state* or *condition* than to a place." Scripture described not the Jews' physical return to Jerusalem, but the reinstatement of the political and civil rights they had enjoyed in ancient Palestine. The New Jerusalem, then, would be the "city, kingdom, or empire" that "restor[ed] all men under its dominion to the free exercise of their civil and religious rights, not excepting even the *Jews*."[111]

An overly hasty reading of Reid's pamphlet might allow a reader to mistake the author's meaning, for Reid characterized the New Jerusalem in ways that had often been used by loyalist exegetes to describe Britain as God's favored nation. He noted that the New Jerusalem would be "situate[d] among the ten apostate kingdoms, who had given their power to the Beast, and made themselves tributary to Mystical Babylon," and would "surpass the rest as much in the favour and distinction of the Deity as ancient Jerusalem had done before." Reid's ambiguity served both as playful tease and protective evasion. His further summation of scriptural prophecy made it clear—without naming names—that Reid had Napoleonic France in mind when describing this "New Jerusalem state." The New Jerusalem, he wrote, would be "the principal instrument in pulling down Mystical Babylon, and destroying the antichristian systems of tyranny and religious persecution" (as well as the Holy Roman Empire, that "stubborn confederacy begun by Rome papal"). The military success of the nation in question would itself indicate its millennial status, Reid suggested (though here again he allowed himself an inch of wriggling-room, given the loyalist trope of Britain standing alone against Napoleon): "At this time of day there can be no necessity for naming that Empire, which, notwithstanding an opposition, unprecedented in the history of the world, has successfully contended with all the powers that opposed it."[112]

By drawing attention to the unnamed leader of the apocalyptic polity, Reid cemented the identification of France as the New Jerusalem. An early section of the pamphlet, describing current events, saw "a Hero, a Legislator, whose vast conceptions embraced all the parts of legislation, . . . restoring [the Jews] to society . . . and, in fact, [giving] them a country"—a description that tallied with Reid's later assessment of Napoleon in the *Gentleman's Magazine*. Reid stated that the Prince of the New Jerusalem "should deliver the people of Israel, . . . and take away their reproach among the nations." The full force of Reid's identification hits one on reading his characterization of the Jerusalemic leader, and thus of Napoleon, as a "distinguished human character, or agent of the Messiah."[113] None of the moral ambiguity found in Bicheno's portrayal of Napoleon—no suggestion that Bonaparte, though performing as an instrument of God, had his own self-serving agenda—

is present in Reid's description. Reid identified Napoleon unproblemat-
ically with a messianic program.

Where did this leave the British nation? Not, clearly, where loyalist
exegesis positioned it, as either the Jews' restorer or a new chosen
people: Reid's pamphlet explicitly criticized the British for not advancing the cause of the Jews (instead they displayed an "absurd propensity"
for converting them).[114] Loyalists had celebrated Britain's intrepid defiance of French charms and arms; Reid, by contrast, regarded Britain's
solitary status as incriminating. Noting that "almost every kingdom that
once formed the Great City, or antichristian empire," had seen "destruction poured out upon" it, Reid concluded that the seventh vial spoken
of in Revelations was

> reserved for some one of these kingdoms, which may be called the
> seat of the Beast— . . . the place where Satan or the great adversary
> dwelleth. This kingdom is that which, after seducing many others to
> protract theirs and its own destruction, will, probably, hold out longer
> than all the rest . . . and even contend alone; but yet, after all, being
> an integral part of the Beast, must be given to the burning flame.[115]

And where loyalist writers, trumpeting Britain's navy and commerce,
had dwelled on the radiant example of Tarshish, Reid turned up another,
less optimistic biblical reference to seafaring merchants: the destruction
of the maritime trading city of Babylon.[116] Reid answered the typological shift of loyalist exegesis with one of his own, turning Babylon and
the Beast into spectres of Britain's possible fate.

The national pessimism offered by opposition exegetes articulated a
more extreme version of loyalist fears. Even those who gladly branded
Napoleon a millennial threat found themselves worrying about the providential verdict on the British nation, often in terms quite similar to those
found in opposition pamphlets. The line between the two interpretive
camps could blur. Ralph Wedgwood, for whom Napoleon was Satan,
and England a potential New Jerusalem, still groaned about "the
national debt, which has arisen by national sins," and "the extreme
pressure of our excessive taxation," and noted in his January 1815
postscript that the end of war saw "our Christmas roast-beef and
plumb-pudding [sic] . . . dearer than ever, and likely to be still more
so."[117] Only now would Britons, according to Wedgwood, see whether
their government was "a son of the true church." All depended on the

conduct of the nation's governors: having crushed "the French Devil, Napoleon," the government now needed to ensure "that there is *no want* to her people, by restoring all things to her depressed subjects." If the government failed—if there remained "a poor man in Britain"—"it will be only from such miserable mismanagement of this abundance, as will merit the curse of heaven."[118] Francophobia and anti-Catholicism did not cancel out severe millennial anxiety about the future of Britain, and the nature of the nation's governors. The "dawn of Christian perfection" may have arrived; still, the outcome for Britain remained uncertain.[119]

Works on prophecy were directed to an audience presumed to be well versed in Scripture—or at least patient, literate, and interested enough to follow the intricate arguments offered in the pamphlets' pages. What sort of a role did Napoleon play in the religious imaginations of other Britons, everyday English women and men who, if literate, were unlikely to read religious works with limited print runs? Where, other than in works of scriptural exegesis, might Britons have encountered the notion that Napoleon's actions raised questions about Britain's providential destiny? One can approach this question both by looking for types of print media explicitly devoted to the themes treated in exegetical works, and by considering more broadly the extent to which the metaphors and assumptions of the prophetic idiom circulated in society at large.

Some sermons—of those that were printed and survive to be read today—did speak in the voice of prophecy. Three of Bicheno's pamphlets reprinted the text of sermons (offering analysis similar to that of his other works, but less dauntingly arcane in their citation of chapter and verse).[120] The Anglican minister G. J. Skeeles delivered a sermon, at the coming of peace in 1814, interpreting Napoleon as having been "an instrument in the hand of God to punish the wickedness of France."[121] But when printed sermons addressed the subject of Bonaparte, their rhetorical affinities were often with loyalist broadsheets rather than prophetic explications.

The title of one published sermon, *Obedience to Government, Reverence to the Constitution, and Resistance to Bonaparte* (1803), conveys the tone and message of many such works. While its author, Charles Edward Stewart, chaplain to the Sheriff of Bury St. Edmund's, did mention that Napoleon was "THE PROFESSOR AND DISBELIEVER OF ALL RELIGIONS; APOSTATE FROM HIS SAVIOUR; BLASPHEMER OF HIS GOD," this came only at the end of a string of more secular epithets ("THE

violator of treaties, the plunderer of defenceless and neutral
nations, the oppressor of his allies, the murderer of his prisoners, the poisoner of his sick").[122] None of these marks against
Napoleon's character was taken to indicate apocalyptic significance,
and the sermon's chief emphasis was on the obedience to government
mentioned in the title. Stewart preached politics from his pulpit, but
not an eschatological reading of contemporary events.

Sermons were expected to perform a political function. Prominent
periodical journals, which devoted many pages to reviewing religious
works, praised printed sermons for "breath[ing] a loyal, a patriotic, and
a pious spirit," or for aiming "to impress the minds of the hearers, especially those of the lower class, with a just sense of the present critical
state of the country."[123] A respected minister could play an important
role in alerting his parishioners to the Napoleonic threat. But reading
Napoleon in the light of Scripture did not have to mean claiming that
the Bible described contemporary politics. When a Newcastle minister
delivered a sermon drawing "an analogy between Nebuchadnezzar
and our Consular enemy" in 1803, he was offering a moral lesson, not
claiming that the Scriptures spoke specifically about the present day.[124]

For a genre more immediately concerned with linking Napoleon to
Britain's providential fate, one should look to the astrological almanac.
Other than the Bible itself, almanacs had served as perhaps the single
most important vector of literacy in the early modern period—considered numerically, the most significant source of printed information.[125]
Content varied from title to title; many almanacs presented medical and
agricultural rather than political advice. But the British almanac with,
by Napoleon's time, the greatest circulation—selling 365,000 copies in
1802, more than all competing titles combined—functioned largely as a
forum for the political ruminations of its editor.[126] Henry Andrews' *Vox
Stellarum* (attributed, as today a British almanac continues to be, to the
already long-dead Dr Francis Moore) offered regular analysis of Britain's
military conflict with Napoleonic France.[127] In addition to Andrews'
almanac, British readers could peruse several competing "nativities," or
horoscopes, of Napoleon Bonaparte published between 1805 and 1814,
which speculated on such matters as how long France's leader would
live and whether his death would be a natural one.

William Cobbett suggested that the Company of Stationers, which
published all the major English almanacs, "serve our rabble, in this
respect, in the stead of priests."[128] But how appropriate is it to treat

astrology alongside scriptural exegesis? Besides the fact that both genres presented mundane events as dictated by higher powers, was not the mystical-scientific discourse of astrology at odds with the religious account offered by tracts on biblical prophecy? In a word, no. The pagan language of the stars did not oppose itself to that of Scripture. Henry Andrews gladly cited in support of his predictions not only the opposition of Jupiter and Saturn, but also the books of Revelations and Daniel.[129] Similarly, an 1805 astrological pamphlet on Napoleon's "nativity" employed familiar prophetic language, characterizing France's leader as "a dreadful scourge" for Europe and warning Britons to repent their "national sins" which stood as "awful and alarming *signs of the present times.*"[130] The astrological and scriptural discourses were highly compatible. Both, moreover, could evade simple determinism. The astrologer urged repentance, reform, alteration even in the face of heaven-sent fate: actions could be taken to deter the punitive hand of Providence, the stars' unbending course notwithstanding.

The above plea that Britons repent their "national sins" came in an 1805 nativity in which Thomas Orger called for a re-evaluation of British policy towards France. From Napoleon's chart, Orger predicted that Bonaparte would become more pacific and "complacent," "devising wholesome laws, that shall conduce to the well governing of the people."[131] Within months, John Worsdale published a rival, anti-Napoleonic nativity, which accused Orger of giving an erroneous time of birth for the Corsican. The true figure revealed not the "*good-natured creature, full of honor*" that Orger had described, but "the *image of a murdering* DESPOT!"[132] The stars revealed that Napoleon would become increasingly detested and would die a violent death.[133] Further nativities, published in Leeds and London, likewise served as vessels for the language of the loyalist broadside. One author portrayed Bonaparte as a man who "might have been the general benefactor of the human race" but had instead acted like "a fiend of hell, a demon of darkness, . . . let loose upon mankind to effect its extermination."[134]

In the early years of the French revolution, Henry Andrews' almanac, the *Vox Stellarum*, had treated France with sympathy (suggesting in 1797, for example, that the revolution "may possibly be of God, and designed to issue in Good").[135] Though ambivalent about Napoleonic France, as many revolutionary sympathizers were, Andrews repeatedly insinuated that the heavens themselves frowned on Britain's war.[136] With its enormous circulation, the *Vox Stellarum*—one of the few "political"

texts some readers were likely to read in a given year—may have played
a crucial role in forming British popular opinion of Napoleon.

The keystone of the *Vox Stellarum*'s world-view, like that of much
opposition exegesis, was anti-Catholicism. Andrews' initial presentation
of Napoleon, in the almanac for 1799, was favorable, based on the
young general's having "annihilated" the papal power. Andrews noted
that France would serve as an instrument of "Discipline and Trial" to
Protestant nations.[137] Napoleon's Concordat with Rome did not elimi-
nate Andrews' confidence that the papacy would soon decline; Andrews
now praised the new French regime's tolerance of Protestantism as evidence of Rome's coming fall. As late as 1810, Andrews could celebrate,
on Protestant grounds, Napoleon's military actions: he noted the delight
Britons must feel at the liberation of the Spanish people. Napoleon's
Iberian exploits led the *Vox* to forecast, once again, the imminent demise
of "the *Roman* Antichrist."[138]

Though he made some reassuring noises about the unlikelihood of a
successful Napoleonic invasion of England, much in Andrews' account
reflected poorly on the condition of the British nation.[139] He noted
Britain's continued sins ("Swearing and Lying, and Killing and Stealing,
and committing Adultery").[140] He suggested that similar corruption had
led to the defeat of other nations by French armies, and prayed that
Britain would "not provoke the overwhelming Blow, by outwearing the
Goodness and Mercy of Omnipotence."[141] But Britain's greatest crime,
Andrews suggested, was continuing to fight, even while the heavens
favored ending the war. "Cursed are the unjustified War-makers,"
Andrews declared, adding that while other nations made peace with
France "*Britain*, unhappy *Britain*, kept behind, and continued the wide
wasting War!"[142] Though England had so far escaped "that over-
whelming Blow" felt by other nations, "we are still groaning under the
Pressure of very heavy Taxes, and other Burdens, never before known;
[England's] Manufactures and her Commerce at this Time [are] greatly
crippled, and her Streets are filled with great Complaints, so that every
Mouth is extended to execrate the War, and all its dreadful Miseries,
and suffering thousands sigh for the Return of Peace."[143]

Discontent would be unavoidable as long as the war continued,
Andrews warned.[144] He repeatedly insisted that peace was "the earnest
Desire of Thousands."[145] Who then was to blame for the continued war?
Andrews murmured darkly about a "wilful and obstinate Party, in high
Stations of Life amongst us." During the peace of 1814–15, Andrews

feared that some in Britain might have an interest in a return to war: "Those who for a long time have made a Trade of War . . . may be very reluctant to have their Swords beat into Plough-shares, or their Spears into Pruning-hooks."[146]

Britain's leading almanac writer offered, in short, a radical critique of the British political establishment very similar to that provided in the exegetical works of Aldred or Reid, to an audience numbering in the hundreds of thousands. But references to a providential design, and more specifically to Napoleon's antagonistic role in that design, were scattered even more broadly through the political literature of the period. One might never touch a work of exegesis and still be familiar with the notion of Napoleon (or France) as a divine "scourge," sent to punish sinful Europe—or with the notion that Britain might be an instrument in the hands of Providence.[147] In the face of such examples, William Hamilton Reid's claim, towards the end of his work on the Sanhedrin, that "public writers are, in a manner, compelled to adopt the solemn language of divine inspiration," does not seem so far-fetched.[148] Reid (citing "celebrated" political writers who quoted Revelations and described the French as "symbolical locusts") hoped to suggest that works like his own should not be dismissed as obscure examples of "religious melancholy"; any scoffing readers who might rate higher the worlds of politics and commerce should realize "that persons of their own stamp and character" were using biblical phrases to describe the imminence of danger to Britain. For Reid, the prevalence of such language was itself an indicator of the age's millennial significance.

Some references to Providence may have been rhetorical tics or pious bromides, of little importance to the speaker or writer, but it would be a mistake to dismiss providential language as mere surface gloss. Exegetes and political commentators alike felt the need to argue against providential fatalism. The agricultural writer Arthur Young warned his readers that God's role in the European conflict did "not in the smallest degree lessen the duty of every power resisting, to the uttermost, the attacks that are made upon their liberty and independence."[149] Spencer Perceval, prime minister in 1811, while concurring "in the sentiment that we were in the hands of an over-ruling Providence," insisted that "even though this individual may have been raised for purposes inscrutable to us, . . . it is . . . still our duty to resist him in that career." Napoleon might well have been intended by Providence for some "great end," the evangelical Perceval agreed—but Britons, in turn, "may also be chosen

instruments in the hands of Providence to raise up some great good out
of the evils of his injustice."[150]

Perceval was responding to the radical Samuel Whitbread, who,
in condemning Lewis Goldsmith's proposal to assassinate Napoleon,
had let slip the remark that Bonaparte's life was "in the hands of an
over-ruling Providence, and if for purposes inscrutable to the short-
sightedness of man he had been raised up to his present formidable
eminence, vain would be the efforts of feeble human means to counteract
the dispensations of Providence." After Perceval's response, a chastened
Whitbread remarked that he "trusted that no expression of his would
be construed into the declaration that he was a fatalist, or that he
thought it impossible to resist the power of France."[151] But such
determinist conclusions hovered inescapably about any eschatological
reading of Napoleon. William Cobbett—who steadfastly refused to
"dra[g] Divine Providence into the discussion" of politics—pointed out
the self-defeating implications of loyalist exegesis: if Napoleon had been
an instrument in God's hands, then his oft-reported atrocities were
"attributable to Divine Providence." How "horrible" it was, Cobbett
acidly added, if Napoleon were to be punished by God for doing what
God had "enabled him, and *compelled* him to do."[152]

The novelist and translator John Byerley warned that "by dissemi-
nating the idea that he is an instrument in the hand of Providence,"
British observers were performing a great service for Napoleon. If one
accepted the premise that Bonaparte was "a scourge from heaven
to punish the wickedness of mankind," then one should cease warfare
lest one "fight against God."[153] A series of letters in Lewis Goldsmith's
ultra-loyalist *Antigallican Monitor* similarly criticized Southcottians
and Methodists—and even some Protestants who otherwise enjoyed
"the character of good sense"—who considered Napoleon "as a superhuman genius, and silenced all opposition on the subject by an appeal
to the Scriptures." The "fatalism" inherent in this "widely diffused
conviction," the author cautioned, played into Napoleon's hands.
By "admitting human agents as . . . accelerators" of the millennium,
one lent assistance to those who wished to further "the Utopia of
Revolutionists."[154]

In identifying eschatology as a system of thought that would
naturally—even in the hands of his fiercest enemies—favor Napoleon,
these writers recognized the sense of helplessness, or at least uncertainty,
that lurked within so much loyalist exegesis. Millenarian fears that

Napoleon was a scourge sent by God to punish a sinful nation—a concern even more pronounced in the radical interpretations that accused Britain of "national crimes"—formed a counterpart to the anxious visions of decline presented in broadsides. For radical and loyalist exegetes alike, Napoleon represented something more than the individual man, something integrally connected, if opposed, to the destiny of the British nation. Intimations of Napoleon's cosmic significance would continue to echo in more "secular" writings on history, even when specific scriptural references were forgotten.[155]

CHAPTER 4

The Imperial Sans-culotte

Why not acknowledge the sovereignty of the Corsican dynasty now, as well as afterwards? If the monarchy is not hereditary, it must be, what is worse, elective. Where and when is a boundary line to be drawn between an usurpation that creates a new government, and the possession which legitimates the usurpation? Titles of empire can neither be judged of by common rules, nor subjected to them. As power confers, so power must uphold, them.

Monthly Magazine, Oct. 1802[1]

Learn'd Genealogists, declare who can,
From what imperial stock proceeds this Man?
Time-honour'd CHARLEMAGNE, does thy rich blood
Pour thro' his veins its pure unsullied flood?
Ye BOURBONS, can NAPOLEON's annals trace
Their course illust'rous thro' your royal Race?
Ah no! his Mother was AMBITION dire,
And black HYPOCRISY his Hell-born Sire!

[Matthew Rolleston], *The Anti-Corsican*, 1805[2]

In two caricatures—one published in January 1806, the other in June 1807—James Gillray presented Napoleon as a maker of kings. In the first, Napoleon is a baker, pulling fresh "imperial gingerbread" out of his oven—German electors whom he has transformed into satellite monarchs.[3] In the second, Bonaparte has been planting rows of "Royal Pippins," whose upper branches—human heads wearing crowns—have been grafted onto older trunks. His sabre, emblem of his military might, bears the label "Corsican Grafting Knife."[4]

By the time of the second engraving, Napoleon had begun crowning members of his family and seating them on ancient and new European thrones (a development foreshadowed in the first print's basket full of "True Corsican Kinglets for Home Consumption & Exportation"). But both caricatures extended their gaze beyond these continental developments, to Britain. Waiting on a shelf next to the baker's oven stands a batch of "Little Dough Viceroys, intended for the next new Batch." Among them we recognize members of the British opposition, including Sheridan and Fox, each with a crown and sceptre. Similarly, Napoleon the gardener is preparing to plant the crowned pippin of Lord Moira, the Irish peer and advocate of the Prince of Wales. Still waiting to be grafted are branches with the crowned heads of the radicals Sir Francis Burdett, John Horne Tooke, and William Cobbett.

In both engravings, Gillray was airing the common loyalist plaint (made with varying degrees of seriousness) that British politicians deemed insufficiently tough on Bonaparte hoped to benefit from a future Napoleonic regime in Britain. The caricaturist emphasized the ramifications that a Napoleonic dynasty might have on Britain's monarchy. As Napoleon and Talleyrand prepare to plant the Moira tree, three of the recently departed "talents" who had governed since William Pitt's death in early 1806 hack away with axes at the sturdy royal oak supporting the British crown. For the loyalist Gillray, the health of Britain's monarchy was endangered by the planting of new royal trees on the continent. In making this connection, the artist had much company. Across the political spectrum, British discussions of Napoleon commonly turned into broad-ranging analysis of monarchy and political legitimacy, analysis that insisted on viewing domestic rule in the light of foreign developments.

Loyalists sought to treat Napoleon's claim to power as different in kind from the claims of Europe's established dynasties. But this required raising the more general question of what constituted legal power. This in turn allowed radical critics of British policy towards Bonaparte to pounce on the loyalist definitions and claims. In discussions of legitimacy, as in those of national character, Napoleon proved a slippery subject, one who revealed the porousness of supposedly airtight classifications. Because of his complicated and shifting political identification, he brought to the surface the ambiguities of legitimate rule, not least as

8. James Gillray, "Tiddy-Doll, the Great French-Gingerbread-Baker; Drawing out a New Batch of Kings," 1806 (Houghton Library, Harvard University).

they revealed themselves in the case of the troubled British monarchy. Simplistic loyalist contrasts between Bonaparte and established monarchs were continually foiled by radical respondents, in whose arsenal pro-Napoleonic arguments were an important weapon.

Napoleon's efforts to emulate hereditary monarchs drove away many of his early republican admirers (Wordsworth was not the only writer, nor the first, to liken the French people's renewed embrace of kingship to a dog licking up his vomit).[5] But his actions did not reassure loyalists. The friends of hereditary monarchy believed Napoleon was cheapening the currency of dynasty by mimicking its forms; they were loath to give up identifying him as a Jacobin, and felt that his coronation augured the collapse of Europe's dynastic system. But even as Napoleon's apparent embrace of hereditary dynasty repelled some republicans, it opened up rhetorical pathways along which other radicals could assault loyalist pieties. The very similarity that Napoleon, unlike his revolutionary predecessors, now superficially bore to Europe's monarchs made him an especially potent tool in the radical critique of hereditary government.

Parallels could easily be drawn between his usurpation and the similarly unsavory origins of established dynasties.

"Usurper" was one of the most common terms of abuse hurled by British loyalists at Napoleon Bonaparte. This was true even before Napoleon claimed an imperial crown and began fashioning a hereditary dynasty to supplant the ancient Bourbon monarchy.[6] From the very first British parliamentary debates after his coup, Napoleon was defined in opposition to the Bourbons, even though it was a revolutionary government that his coup had extinguished. "Upstart" was an allied epithet. Either term, especially if accompanied by an adjective denoting his foreignness to France, sufficed to denote him. One did not need to name Napoleon; "the Corsican Usurper" would do. In drawing attention to Napoleon's supposedly humble, and certainly not regal, roots, those who employed such barbs wished to underscore his social distance from hereditary rulers. He was an "upstart Ruffian" from an "upstart family," "an obtrusive upstart, who has jumped into the Throne of France."[7] This "mushroom Emperor"—rooted only, as this popular image suggested, in dung—exhibited a "total want of inborn majesty, / Of calm and unassuming dignity, / By Heav'n vouchsaf'd to rightful kings alone."[8] The "mean subaltern" Napoleon was provided with improbably low ancestry (his mother "a most notorious prostitute" and madam, one of his siblings fathered by a friar) or was simply described as having "sprung from Nobody knows whom."[9] This made him "wholly deficient in all those principles of probity with which men of elevated birth and high hereditary expectations are generally inspired."[10] Coleridge, in 1811, endorsed the British loyalist practice of terming Napoleon by his family name rather than the first name by which he ruled: "Whilst he is called by the name of his reputed father, the Scrivener of Ajaccio, the memory of his pristine meanness continues; with his meanness we associate his crimes; with his crimes we confirm his infamy; with his infamy we perpetuate our resistance."[11]

Charges of low birth and of political illegitimacy often nuzzled up against one another, as when the journalist Lewis Goldsmith, after his conversion to anti-Napoleonism, termed Napoleon an "upstart Usurper."[12] In this regard, the terms "legitimate" and "legitimacy" should be considered. Remarkably, they seem to have acquired a specific political significance in English only around the time of Napoleon's reign. Prior to this, the terms referred first to the state of having been born in wedlock and consequently enjoying recognized filial rights (the only sense in which Dr Johnson defined "legitimate"), and later to being genuine, lawful, or regular. In the former sense, the terms did, of course, feature in many political discussions of hereditary monarchy. Descent and sovereignty comingled. Whether or not a monarch's child was a bastard could have the most profound political significance—as, for example, in the disputed case of James II's son, who some thought had been smuggled into the maternal bed in a warming-pan.[13] But using the words in such a context did not amount to distinguishing hereditary rule from other forms of political sovereignty. Today, "legitimacy" may seem an indispensable keyword for the analysis of constitutional conflicts, and one whose relationship to birth, and thus to hereditary succession, lies in the mists of ancient time. It is salutary, then, to recognize how recently the term entered political discussion, and the controversial manner in which it did so.[14]

The introduction of "legitimacy" into British political discourse seems to have been directly connected to the peculiar case of Napoleon. His superficial similarity to a king, in the wake of France's republican experiment, made it necessary to distinguish him from other monarchs by dwelling on the quality he lacked, that of hereditary descent from a line of kings. Perhaps the earliest appearance of the new usage came in 1801, when the *True Briton* newspaper contrasted the "obtrusive upstart" Napoleon with France's "legitimate Monarchs."[15] The adjective occurred frequently in discussions of Napoleon (an 1803 broadside, for example, called on the French to remove Bonaparte from "his usurped station . . . and hail the return of their legitimate prince").[16] Goldsmith employed the word frequently—as when he bemoaned Napoleon's placing members of "his own bastard family on the thrones of ancient legitimate monarchs."[17] In accusing the entire Bonaparte clan of bastardy, Goldsmith was not claiming that every member had been born out of wedlock, but rather that Napoleon and his siblings had been born outside of dynasty. Even as we chart the emergence of the new usage, however, Goldsmith's language should remind us that the older meaning lurked underneath the surface (as it perhaps still lurks). The double meaning was present in contemporaries' minds, as occasional word-play suggested[18]—not least because it was a common loyalist tactic to question the purity of Napoleon's mother, and thus Napoleon's paternity.[19]

As Bonaparte inched his way towards dynasty—he became "consul for life" in 1802—the charge of usurpation took on new relevance and force. Shortly before empire was declared in May 1804, the kidnapping and execution of the duc d'Enghien, a Bourbon prince residing in Germany, threw into stark relief the opposition between Bourbon and Bonaparte. French soldiers, crossing the Rhine in the dead of night, seized the duke; charged with conspiracy (he reportedly confessed to being in the pay of Britain), he was summarily tried and executed. Enghien's death joined the atrocities at Jaffa as key evidence against Bonaparte's humanity; the name of this "murdered Prince! meek, loyal, pious, brave!"[20] would be invoked even more often than those of Toussaint, Palm (a German bookseller executed for selling an anti-Napoleonic work), or Wright (an English captain who died mysteriously in a French prison).[21] Napoleon, who had had nothing to do with Louis XVI's execution (he was in Corsica at the time), could now be directly tied to the killing of a Bourbon—though defenders would try to pin the blame on Talleyrand. William Burdon, in the biography of Napoleon he published late in the year of Enghien's death, suggested that the killing had been motivated by a desire to prevent further attempts on Napoleon's life. But this was no excuse for "a deed of horror which can hardly be parallelled [*sic*] in the history of the most savage nations."[22] More than simply a blow against an individual or a family, Enghien's execution was seen as an assault on the very system of hereditary monarchy. Napoleon, if unchallenged, would kill other sovereigns, "because, whatever rank Buonaparte assumes, he is unable to change his birth; and, guilty as he is, he will consider every good prince, as much a censuring enemy as a proud superior."[23]

Enghien's execution was a fitting prologue to the proclamation, within a matter of weeks, that France's consul would become an emperor. In the plebiscite held to determine whether Napoleon's position would be hereditary, an overwhelming majority approved (a predictable result, given the equally lopsided votes that had endorsed him as first consul and then consul for life). And so Napoleon joined the ranks of the European dynasts—indeed, in the grandness of his title, leapfrogged ahead of them.

Would Napoleon's elevation tend toward the reinforcing or the weakening of other dynasts' power? In the eyes of a sympathetic *Annual* reviewer, writing around the time empire was declared, Napoleon had, by restoring "monarchy (or the government of one) in his own person," disarmed the "arguments and war-whoops" of the followers of Burke. Bonaparte could no longer be defined in opposition to monarchy. Arguments that had formerly justified waging war against a Jacobin France now served "to stabilize his institutions, to render popular his government, and to facilitate the progress of his authority from a life-long to an hereditary, from an anonymous to a titled sway."[24] A less well disposed *Oracle* admitted that Napoleon's elevation put "an end to all that republican influenza which at one time threatened to overturn all the thrones in Europe." Europe's monarchs might well feel that "if the force of France is to be in the hands of a single person, it is at least as well that he should wear a crown and wield a sceptre, as the red bonnet and poniard of the Jacobin Club."[25]

Other observers, however, were less sure that the impact of Napoleon's coronation on European dynasties would be benign. The *Times* declared the "black and inauspicious day" of the coronation to have "sealed the fate of every established and legitimate monarchy on the continent of Europe." With the single exception of Britain's monarch—whose title was "the charter of liberty to his subjects"—no sovereign could "sleep quietly in his bed" after the French innovation.[26] William Burdon likewise believed Napoleon's "burlesque upon monarchy" would "in the end overturn every throne in Europe," since it would tempt other "artful and ambitious men, to excite the people to revolt."[27]

One such instance of emulation had already taken place in the months between the announcement and the consummation of Napoleon's coronation—but not by a low-born adventurer. When in August 1804 the Holy Roman Emperor Francis II, fearing the imminent demise of his ancient empire, assumed as Francis I the new title of emperor of Austria, British journalists viewed Francis' action as a moral victory for Napoleon and a singular setback to the cause of hereditary monarchy. The immediate effect of Francis' assumption of a new title, British commentators agreed, would be to reinforce Bonaparte's claim to imperial power. The loyalist *Morning Post* maintained that France's ruler would be happy "to see an emperor newer than himself, and whose recognition is, as it were, a creation of sovereignty on his part."[28] The opposition *Morning Chronicle* agreed that Francis had provided Napoleon with a springboard to legitimacy. The *Chronicle* positively reveled in the prospect feared by the *Post*—that others, George III in particular, might follow Napoleon and Francis: "By-and-by we shall have every king of Europe an emperor, and every petty prince a king. Emperors will become as plenty as volunteer colonels, and the title is likely to be worth as much."[29] For the *Chronicle*, Francis' move was a tremendous strategic blunder. Francis had in effect declared that all titles "arise from the caprice of the individual who assumes them." By adopting a new title, he had undercut his own and all ancient titles:

> It is one of the best securities of titles, that their origin is obscure, that the mass have been accustomed to reverence them for their antiquity. But those who respect the sacred rust of antiquity that adorns the title of emperor, cannot help laughing at new emperors and self-created princes. Imagination has no room to play, when the deceit is so gross, and novelty is of itself incompatible with the principle of nobility.

One senses some glee on the part of the *Chronicle* journalist ("sacred rust" is not the language of a writer disturbed by a shiny new dynasty). Francis had revealed hereditary rule to depend upon a willful suspension of disbelief; he had unwittingly unleashed "one of the most decisive strokes of jacobinism which has been struck since the French Revolution." And unwitting was the proper term. Francis' action illustrated the "stupidity" of monarchs; he "exhibited monarchical government naked and deformed, to the scorn and derision of its enemies."[30]

The Bourbon prince's death, the Corsican usurper's coronation, and the Austrian potentate's mimicry all led observers to cast Napoleon as a menace to hereditary dynasty. But Napoleon's emulation of the forms of monarchy simultaneously offered the highest tribute to that institution. In the years following his coronation, Napoleon took steps to place his family members on the thrones of Europe. His brother Joseph became king of Naples in 1806, and then of Spain in 1808—at which point Napoleon turned Naples over to his brother-in-law, General Joachim Murat. Louis Bonaparte became king of Holland in 1806—though Napoleon, irritated at the political and financial costs of Holland's too great autonomy, forced him to abdicate in 1810. Jerome Bonaparte was made king of Westphalia in 1807. In addition, Napoleon began, as one observer noted in 1806, to effect marriages and alliances with "the great continental families of the second order; whom he elevates to the first rank." By "entwin[ing]" these established vines "about his parent stock," the mushroom emperor sought to make "his roots strike deep into the soil, while sovereign princes repose under his branches."[31]

Napoleon, then, while unearthing some ruling families, had a grafter's interest in maintaining certain roots.[32] Creating one dynasty, he needed to preserve others. The consummation of Napoleon's pact with dynasticism came in 1810, when—shortly after ending his childless union with Josephine—he married Maria Louisa, daughter of the Austrian emperor Francis I. (Caricatures mocking Napoleon's sexual inadequacy naturally followed.)[33] The union of the Bonaparte and Habsburg bloodlines was made complete in March 1811, when a son was born to France's imperial couple. The infant Napoleon, made king of Rome, was predictably the object of British ridicule and hostility. Henry Redhead Yorke chillingly declared that the child (a "baboon" born of "the young prostitute whom [Napoleon] calls his wife") "is to be pitied—he *must* perish for the crimes of his parent."[34] Few newborns have inspired such hatred. The young Napoleon represented the perpetuation of the Bonaparte dynasty into future generations. He tied Napoleon to the future; and his Habsburg blood rooted the new dynasty in the distant past.

Napoleon's Habsburg marriage was manna for critics wishing to highlight his inconsistency. "Before this," one unsympathetic pamphleteer wrote, "Bonaparte stood on his own ground as high as an usurper could stand; he now truckles to principles which he has ridiculed."[35] But it was a blow to sympathizers, some of whom would later blame Napoleon's fall on his embrace of the ancient monarchy. In 1813, as it grew ever more conceivable that Napoleon might fall from power, Cobbett would attribute the possibility of collapse to Bonaparte's having married a niece of Marie Antoinette—an "act of treason against the cause of democracy."[36] Napoleon's imperial marriage locked him into a new set of principles, Cobbett wrote; now he must "endeavour to support himself as a mere wearer of a crown."[37]

Napoleon's complicated political status—apparently hybrid, like his national character and religion—invited debate over what made a ruler lawful. His gradual, determined march towards dynasty naturally placed the foundations of his rule at the forefront of political argument: few British commentators could consider Napoleon without raising the question of political legitimacy (if only by hurling the insult "usurper" at him). Discussions of Napoleon's claims to power, furthermore, often led to analysis of the British king's own right to rule.

Questions of British and French legitimacy circled tirelessly around one another in the years of Napoleon's rule. Reformers and radicals regularly took up loyalist criticisms of Napoleon and turned them against the British monarch. The ground had been seeded in the early days of France's revolution. The Dissenting minister Richard Price, in a

November 1789 address best remembered for Edmund Burke's blistering assault on it, had hailed the changes in France. Price drew parallels between current events in France and the revolution that had brought William of Orange and Mary Stuart to the throne in 1688. The glory of Britain's revolution lay in its having defined popular approval as the true base of monarchical power. The forced departure of James II had demonstrated that Britons had a "right to chuse our own governors; to cashier them for misconduct; and to frame a government for ourselves." Britain's monarch held his throne by the pleasure of his subjects. His very legitimacy (the "lawful" nature of his rule, to use the term Price employed) depended upon the fact that he could be removed at any moment. George III, Price declared, was "almost the only lawful King in the world, because the only one who owes his crown to the choice of the people."[38] George's right to rule did not depend upon his ancestry, but upon popular approval. Price proffered his allegiance to the British king with one condition attached: that this loyalty be eternally retractable.

When Napoleon acceded to power, then, British political commentary had already begun to explore precisely the problems his case would raise in a new form. In addition, Napoleon's rule happened to coincide with a period of crisis for the British monarchy. Scandals and indications of instability were persistent: late Georgian Britain offered critical observers an unusually large number of opportunities to interrogate the foundations of their government. And so the spectacle of Napoleon, a walking case study for the student of legitimacy, could not help but trigger associations with domestic politics. Napoleon unsettled the categories by which lawful rule was defined, but domestic politics ensured that these categories did not seem very stable in the first place (and that some political participants had an interest in making them seem even less stable). Hence the tendency of discussions of Napoleon's rule to revert continually to the subject of Britain's own monarchy.

There was a long period of intellectual rehearsal for the crisis of legitimacy that eventuated in the regency of 1811–20. George III's mental illness of 1788–89, prompting steps towards establishing a regency, had subsided quickly enough—but worries about his capacity would continue to haunt political observers, even years before his final illness led to his son being made Prince Regent in 1811. Thus one reader of Cobbett's *Political Register*—in 1804, when the king's condition had again asserted itself—worried that the king's state should not be overseen simply by "a secret committee of ministers and physicians" but by Parliament; another warned of the danger of a "sort of tacit usurpation on the part of ministers," which would in effect "depose the Sovereign, set aside the succession, and place the servant on the throne of his master."[39]

George's family members had difficulties of their own. In 1806, the rumor spread that Caroline, the estranged wife of the Prince of Wales, had had an illegitimate daughter; friends of the prince demanded that his own daughter Charlotte be removed from the mother's custody. And in 1809 there was the dramatic revelation, by the MP Colonel Gwyllym Lloyd Wardle, that the mistress of the Duke of York—the king's second son, who as commander-in-chief of the army controlled many a military plum—had taken bribes to encourage those fruits to fall in the right direction. The scores of public meetings called to support Wardle provided renewed impetus for electoral reform; more immediately, if only temporarily, the public dissection of the duke's behavior led him to resign from his military post.[40]

All these scandals inspired not only gossip but serious philosophical argument. Each development in the royal drama stirred up the cauldron of debate over monarchy. When one MP declared that the Duke of York, if guilty as Wardle had charged, should not simply resign from his post but be removed from the line of succession altogether, Henry Redhead Yorke responded that this amounted to "that fundamental principle of jacobinism which the nation had indignantly rejected," "the hateful and exploded doctrine of the right of cashiering kings and princes." James I himself would have approved of Yorke's unbending rejection of any deviation from the hereditary line of succession. No matter what the duke had done (and Yorke decried his adultery), his place in the succession must be preserved. Anything else, Yorke declared, would amount to "elective monarchy," which was to say "the worst, and weakest, and most anarchical form of government that can be imagined."[41]

When loyalists raised questions about Napoleon's legitimacy, they could not do so in a political vacuum. Discussions of Napoleon triggered domestic associations, if often unintentionally. Napoleon's example touched sensitive nerves in the British body politic, to the frustration of loyalists and the delight of radicals. And so loyalist discussions of Napoleon overflowed their intended channel, and raised issues that radicals could exploit in unexpected fashion.

Special dangers arose when the cruder devices of popular satire were employed against France's ruler. Consider, for example, the 1804 ceremony conferring imperial status upon a humble London muffin-vendor. In the eighteenth century, in the tiny community of Garrat, south of London, the practice had arisen of regularly electing a humble, often crippled, laborer to the imaginary position of mayor of Garrat (or "member for Garrat").[42] John Brewer has closely studied the development of this popular amusement, characterizing its saturnalian proceedings as "a burlesque of authority"—a mockery of state ceremony that verged at times, in patrician perception at any rate, on a subversive critique of the political establishment. In its later years, according to Brewer, the Garrat election lost its force as a radical political device, and became "a reactionary trope" employed by the opponents of popular politics to tar their adversaries as disorderly revelers. The election's meaning passed from the hands of its participants to those of its critics. Brewer traces the Garrat elections up to the 1790s, at which point the trail seems to go cold. The apparent demise of the ritual, he conjectures, was in part a reaction to the French revolution: patrician terror of the populace, together with a new radical emphasis on "respectability," meant that popular and polite culture alike recoiled and withdrew from the "political dialogue" Garrat had provided.[43]

Press accounts from 1804, however, reveal that the Garrat rite still had some life in it as the new century began. The ritual's practitioners retained the ability to reconfigure the meaning of the ceremony—not simply to have signification thrust upon their actions by conservative critics. In the autumn of 1804, Garrat's electors employed their parodic devices against the presumptions of France's ruler. The Garrat ritual was transmogrified, on the face of it, from radical carnival into loyalist bacchanalia. The menace of French political innovation did not dampen but rather served to invigorate the rough satire of London popular politics.

In mid-October 1804 (five months after the proclamation of Napoleon as emperor and two months before his coronation), London newspapers reported a new development in the polity of Garrat. On the afternoon of 15 October, readers learned, "a full meeting of the electors of Garratt took place at the King's Head, in Compton Street, Soho, according to proclamation, for crowning the renowned and august Sir Harry Dimsdale, Mayor of Garratt, *an Emperor*."[44] The coronation, for which the "paraphernalia of royalty" were supplied by the owner of a masquerade shop, took place soon thereafter, in the Soho public house that served as "Imperial palace" for Dimsdale (in daily life a "deformed" muffin-dealer). The *General Evening Post* reported the event:

> Before eight o'clock, the electors that attended exceeded, by several hundreds, the numbers who could gain admittance; every part of the house was crowded to an overflow, till His Imperial Majesty ascended his throne—in the parlour—where he gave audience to his officers of state, commonly called link-boys, and to his legion of honour, as commonly called chimney-sweepers; after which His Imperial Majesty Harry I. of Garratt, went up stairs, where another superb throne was prepared in the club-room. This throne was formed by placing a chair on a sofa, over which were, in large transparent letters, the words, '*Long live the Emperor!*'[45]

One account added that a group of Volunteers had presented themselves as bodyguard to Dimsdale, after the crowd (who, to be fair, *had* given a halfpenny each to witness the entertainment) began to murmur discontentedly at the absence of an actual crown. In the end, a punchbowl was placed upon Dimsdale's head. Order was preserved, and Garrat's mayor beat Napoleon to an imperial throne.[46]

This surreal vision of Garrat's muffin-seller emperor with a court of ragamuffins was a sort of *tableau vivant*, a living, breathing caricature of the planned proceedings across the Channel. Yet like so many satires, its political message was complicated. One is led to ask (as when confronted by an ostensibly loyalist print depicting a fine-featured Napoleon next to a brutish John Bull): who exactly was being lampooned?[47] Authority in general was as much the target as Bonaparte was. When Dimsdale had trouble drawing his sword, he remarked (to "the greatest uproar of laughter and applause") that he was "a peaceable Emperor, and that was more than the subjects of every other Potentate could say." The *Morning Chronicle* saw Harry's patriotic speech as a "caricature of the declarations which are too frequently made in exalted situations with as little sincerity as Sir Harry's."[48]

Dimsdale, in his grateful address to "his loving subjects," had contrasted his own empire of license with the tyranny of Bonaparte. Unlike Napoleon, Dimsdale would not make his subjects slaves, and needed "no *Mamelukes* to protect me from the daggers of the distracted relatives of *those I have murdered.*" This was because "Harry I. is not a *Corsican*, he is an *Englishman*, and *English hearts* engender no such crimes, and need no such protection." To underscore his promise of good behavior, Dimsdale added a second pledge. Should his subjects tire of him, he would be "off in the twinkling of a pig's whisper," Dimsdale promised; "I'll *bundle* directly! *Dare every Emperor say as much?*"[49]

In suggesting how easy it would be to remove him should his subjects have second thoughts, Dimsdale, whether wittingly or no—or perhaps the correspondent who claimed to report his words—was siding with Price against Burke, in support of the right to cashier a king. The emperor Harry offered his subjects precisely Price's vision of conditional rule. His suggestion that he would "*bundle* directly" if asked would have been reason enough for Burkean loyalists to find his coronation, as reported, troubling (the patriotic anti-Gallicanism of the performance notwithstanding). Dimsdale's readiness to be cashiered contradicted not only Napoleonic praxis but British loyalist dogma.

William Cobbett went so far as to ask whether the satire was "*really aimed at Buonaparte*" or at a subject closer to home. Cobbett described the event as having begun as "the brilliant conception of a rich loanmaker" (financiers being far from the most sympathetic of figures in Cobbett's world-view) who, losing his nerve, had allowed the event "to descend to, and be improved on by, the newspapers and the mob."[50] The mock coronation made Cobbett question the people's loyalty:

> How could the anthem of "God save great George our King," sung in burlesque, be meant as a satire on the Emperor of France? I think one may perceive through the whole scene, and the description of it, something that it is by no means wise for magistrates to encourage, and that may, if only a little improved upon, tend to the producing of events far from laughable. In short, we may by such means, degrade ourselves, our country, and our government; but never shall we thereby whiten one hair of Napoleon's head, or blunt the point of one of his half million of bayonets.[51]

The Soho ceremony struck Cobbett not only as evidence (like the previous year's broadsides) of English decline, but as a portent of domestic upheaval. Even if aimed at Bonaparte, the satire posed just as sharp a threat to Britain's king, according to Cobbett. By drawing attention to the foundations of Napoleon's rule, the Soho satirists could not help but raise questions about Britain's own monarchy.

The same years that would see William Cobbett change from friend to critic of British policy on Napoleon saw Lewis Goldsmith transform himself from a Napoleonic operative into a recipient of British state largesse. Goldsmith had repaired to Paris during the peace of Amiens. For his activities there, we rely largely upon his own testimony (a rather uncomfortable reliance). He became editor of *The Argus, or London Review'd in Paris*, an English-language Paris newspaper overseen by Talleyrand. The newspaper, according to one escaped English prisoner, functioned as a machine for the laundering of French state disinformation. In order to make more believable the "ridiculously false statements relative to England which appear in the daily papers in France," such statements were first placed in the *Argus* and then translated back into French and "inserted in the Moniteur (the French Government Gazette), which does not scruple to quote the *Argus* as an authority."[52] The *Argus* was published in English, as another commentator pointed out, "to keep up the idea, that it was smuggled over from England."[53] Jean Peltier, whose libel trial Cobbett had taken as evidence of Britain's decline, maintained that in addition "the French government subscribed for a thousand copies . . . and distributed it with profusion in foreign countries, and particularly among the late rebels of Ireland." This explained the journal's "invitation to English sailors, to desert and repair to France, where they would find better treatment, better food, and higher pay than in the British service."[54]

When he later sought to distance himself from the anti-British content of the *Argus*, Goldsmith would insist that he had "published only 49 numbers" of the newspaper in late 1802 and early 1803, "which, at 3 a week, make the time I was concerned in the publication, not quite four calendar months."[55] And indeed, the content of his issues was less inflammatory than later numbers, after the return of war. In the fall of 1803, after Goldsmith's departure, the *Argus* would describe the English government as a "most atrocious tyranny" which "all mankind ought to rise up [against] and exterminate," and would predict that on arriving in Britain Napoleon would "meet with a numerous and brave, though oppressed peasantry, who with joy and gratitude will hail him as the deliverer of their country!"[56] Goldsmith's *Argus*, by contrast, proclaimed a love of the English constitution and laws ("if administered with a benevolent and patriotic spirit").[57] But it lambasted, for example, Britain's "long, lawless and sanguinary career of pillage, havoc and devastation in the East, where murder has been reduced to rule, and robbery to science!"[58]

Contemporaries who knew of the *Argus* probably did not distinguish between one or another period of its development.[59] Certainly the later numbers help us to understand what Goldsmith's association with the newspaper (a journal notorious enough to figure in more than one Gillray print) would have meant to his fellow countrymen.[60] Even the later, self-exculpating Goldsmith would admit that the newspaper had, during his tenure, printed "articles of an obnoxious nature against the English government, and the whole system of English policy." He prided himself, however, on not having allowed Talleyrand to insert pieces criticizing "*the English monarch, or any branch of the royal family*," and maintained that this refusal had been the grounds for his dismissal.[61]

Goldsmith's initial account of his life in Napoleonic France, presented to British audiences in 1810, implied that he had been an innocent civilian, certainly no imperial operative. When war had returned in 1803, Goldsmith narrated, he found that the French authorities did not wish to detain him. At liberty and unemployed, he had taken a position as "a law agent and a *sworn* translator" (a position he likened to that of a notary public); in this capacity he had "access to the first persons in office." His continued fidelity to the British constitution was demonstrated, in Goldsmith's account, by his having begun to translate Blackstone's *Commentaries* into French.[62] All very innocent, if not yet offering much evidence for his claim that he had "had opportunities of knowing Napoleon Bonaparte better than any man in Europe who is not a Frenchman."[63] Soon, Goldsmith would come to recognize that his value as an ultra-loyalist journalist lay in playing up, not in muting, his radical past. Regularly mining his own personal history for copy, Goldsmith would reveal that he had been a trusted emissary of Napoleon's, who had, among other tasks, been entrusted with the job of approaching Louis XVIII with a proposal to place him "at the head of a considerable nation" if he gave up his claims to the French throne.[64]

Goldsmith returned to England in 1809. Unsurprisingly, he was required to spend some time in custody. His professed intent now was not to write on politics but to resume his career as a notary public and "atone for the indiscretions of my youth!"[65] But the year following his return, Goldsmith published two anti-Napoleonic works.[66] In *The Secret History of the Cabinet of Bonaparte*, he offered his considered opinion on the character of Napoleon, "the greatest murderer and assassin of whom there is any record in history." Goldsmith's former hero and employer had turned out to be bisexual, incestuous, epileptic, and scrofulous; he had killed a pregnant lover and was prone to random acts of violence. Never before had there been "in one human being such a combination of cruelty, tyranny, petulance, lewdness, luxury, and avarice." In defense of his own apparent change of heart since the *Crimes of Cabinets* and the *Argus*, Goldsmith offered the first of many self-justifications. He did not, he wrote, "retract one syllable of the *principles*" that had motivated his 1801 *Crimes of Cabinets*. Not he, but Napoleon's British apologists were "apostates" to the principles of liberty they had once proclaimed.[67]

Whether or not Goldsmith's journeyman effort against Napoleon was subsidized by the British government is unclear. It was tremendously successful: in 1810 and 1811 the *Secret History* went through at least ten British editions (and one in New York). Perhaps this triumph recommended Goldsmith to the government. Certainly his personal story—his conversion following a journey into the beast's belly, his pose as a consistent friend to liberty—would have seemed ideal credentials for the job of anti-Napoleonic propagandist. At any rate, Goldsmith was soon the recipient of one hundred pounds from Spencer Perceval's ministry to print and circulate "Prospectus's, hand Bills, Posting Bills, Advertisements" for a new weekly newspaper he proposed to edit, as well as another hundred "for a Journey to Lancashire, Yorkshire, & Scotland, to establish agents." Within two months of the paper's first issue, published in January 1811, the Treasury had agreed to provide him with an impressive £1,200 per annum—a fantastic sum, given the fact that less than £10,000 was available for subsidizing the entire British press.[68]

So, at any rate, Goldsmith would state in 1814, when it looked as if the already ebbing flow of cash might be cut off by a later administration, that of Lord Liverpool. In truth, Goldsmith was never entirely certain of the steadiness of state subsidy. A September 1812 letter to the Regent's brother the Duke of Cumberland, with whom Goldsmith had earlier met, reported uncertainty as to whether the Treasury intended to offer "permanent support" or not. Goldsmith's letter to Cumberland points us, in addition, towards two characteristic concerns that would mark most issues of the *Antigallican Monitor*: Goldsmith's tendency to self-mythologize and his belief that the British nation's greatest enemies lay within the kingdom. "I can assure your Royal Highness," he told the duke, "that Bonaparte as well as his dupes on the Continent not only wish the Antigallican to be suppressed but myself exterminated, this wish is not confined to persons on the Continent it is equally the ardent desire of persons in this country."[69] That Napoleon had innumerable supporters within the borders of the United Kingdom, and that Napoleon feared Lewis Goldsmith above all his other foes: these would be the *Antigallican*'s continued refrains.

The domestic enemy, according to Goldsmith, had many faces. To begin with, there were Goldsmith's own "calumniators," those who accused him of apostasy. These individuals were "the hired agents of Napoleon,"[70] as were many British reformers who sought "the destruction of the Government of this country in order to seat themselves in the places of their masters."[71] Reformers received from Bonaparte sums "from 20 to £50,000 sterling . . . to disburse as they think fit, and to pay for articles written in the disaffected prints; and whenever such seditious articles appear, to purchase a large number to distribute *gratis*, and otherwise inflame the public mind" and "encourag[e] riots."[72] Luddite frame-breakings in Nottinghamshire—indeed all riots that *appeared* to have their grounding in domestic unhappiness—should be attributed to "the agents of NAPOLEON in this country, the correspondents of the English special *Bureau* at Paris," who paid the Englishmen a weekly stipend.[73] Colonel Despard's plan to assassinate the king had been a scheme of "the Committee of Buonaparte . . . organised in this country."[74] The assassination of Goldsmith's patron Spencer Perceval, if not actually planned by Bonaparte's agents, had at least been inspired by the speeches of Napoleon's radical apologists in Britain, in particular Sir Francis Burdett.[75]

Goldsmith detected pervasive Napoleonic influence over British journalism; he reported that Napoleon "had two London Weekly Papers in his pay."[76] Goldsmith's insinuations about one editor, Daniel Lovell of the radical daily newspaper the *Statesman*, resulted in a libel case in the Court of King's Bench in May 1812, in which Lovell and Goldsmith, through their barristers, traded accusations of treachery. Lord Ellenborough, the Lord Chief Justice, presided; his instructions to the jury left little doubt about his antipathy to the plaintiff Lovell, already in Newgate for an 1811 libel against the government. The jury found for Goldsmith.[77] Though fear of legal action generally made Goldsmith stop short of identifying individuals as Napoleon's pensioners, he was happy to decry them as Napoleon's apologists. He equated William Cobbett's having "gone over" to the Foxite opposition in 1804 with enlistment under "the banners . . . of a base murderer and robber," and questioned Cobbett's choosing "to advocate the cause of Napoleon, immediately after he had murdered the Duke d'Enghien, tortured

Pichegru and Captain Wright, made himself an Emperor, &c. &c."[78] Even many newspapers that did "not go the full length of praising our enemy," according to Goldsmith, still "endeavour[ed] to raise a mutiny in our armies, and attack all our Institutions."[79] Jean Peltier himself was not immune from the charge of seeking "the favour and patronage of Napoleon": Goldsmith insinuated that only financial support from Napoleon could account for Peltier's ability to distribute "libels" of Goldsmith so widely, even having them "thrown down the areas of houses."[80] Goldsmith suspected that even London's newsagents, guilty of "wilful irregularities" in the delivery of the *Antigallican*, were responding to "*Corsican Agency.*"[81]

Goldsmith, we see, felt that Napoleon's forces were targeting him personally. Napoleon wished to "crush" (and perhaps kidnap) Goldsmith because there was "no political writer in Europe who knows so much of Napoleon Buonaparte and his mock court as I do."[82] A selfless bravery was one component of his self-fashioned persona: in the wake of Perceval's 1812 assassination, Goldsmith announced that he would "not be dismayed, were I even to learn that the assassin's dagger was sharpening for me."[83] Goldsmith assigned himself a key role in the dramatic tale he wove.[84] Napoleon must recognize that he had no greater literary enemy: "if the recording of the actions of Buonaparte carries guilt with it," Goldsmith modestly proclaimed, "*I confess myself to be the greatest criminal on earth.*"[85]

From an early moment in its publication, the *Antigallican Monitor* distinguished itself from many other loyalist organs by its fervent advocacy of Bourbon restoration.[86] (Henry Redhead Yorke, by contrast, was arguing in 1811, the year Goldsmith launched his paper, that the Bourbons could "be laid aside, like worn-out broomsticks"—"for, between ourselves, we never cared much about them.")[87] Even a reluctant Lord Liverpool (complaining in 1814 that Goldsmith had "received more money than has been given by Government to all other periodical Publications put together for the last few years") admitted that the journalist "may have rendered some service by his writing up the cause of the Bourbons at a Time when that cause was almost forgotten."[88] Bourbon restoration was not, however, the policy proposal for which Goldsmith would gain his notoriety. That recommendation, whose reverberations would be felt in parliamentary debate, was that the "*Imperial Sans-culotte*" (as Goldsmith frequently termed Napoleon, capturing in a phrase the oxymoronic political nature of France's ruler) be assassinated.[89]

The debate over assassination—or, as its proponents would phrase it, over tyrannicide—was well developed by the time Lewis Goldsmith made his proposal in 1811. Assassination figured prominently in the public imagination of early nineteenth-century Britain.[90] There was the 1802 plot against George III, which led to the execution in February 1803 of Colonel Edward Marcus Despard and six of his fellow conspirators. There were several attempts on Bonaparte's life.[91] A plan to stab Napoleon as he reviewed his troops was foiled in 1803: it was this scheme's discovery that had prompted the duc d'Enghien's arrest. The French government claimed that a number of would-be assassins had British connections, just as Napoleonic influence was suspected by some to lurk in the background of Despard's plot (one of the colonel's associates, after all, had named his son "Bonaparte").[92] The age, we see, had a heightened awareness of assassination, not least as it might figure in Anglo-French relations. As a result, there was a continuing debate over the propriety of the practice.

The debate over assassination shadowed that over legitimacy and usurpation. Claims about king-killing *were* claims about legitimacy. One side held that there was a point at which a ruler had so little right to rule that his death was warranted. This was the position of George Ensor, for example, a writer on Irish and occasionally radical subjects who in 1806 praised the Roman law "by which every citizen was commanded to kill an usurper," and scoffed at the "modern canting by the abettors of usurpation, that assassination is shocking."[93] The opposing perspective ruled assassination out of the question in all cases, even against a despot. The loyalist *Courier*, outraged at the "diabolical" attempt in 1801 to kill Napoleon with an exploding device (the so-called "infernal machine," whose detonation killed a number of bystanders), declared there to be "something so cruel, and at the same time so cowardly in assassination, that no situation and no circumstances can divest it of its atrocity, or palliate its enormity."

The political contours of the debate were not simple. Some loyalists recognized the dangers of endorsing assassination, even of Britain's usurper enemy. For assassination was the most radical and immediate means of cashiering a king. Though a convenient argument in the case of Napoleon, the justification of tyrannicide could all too readily be applied to other figures of authority (as indeed it would be after

Napoleon's fall).[94] Historically, the argument was associated with those critics of divine-right monarchy who proposed a right of resistance to tyranny; James I, by contrast, had insisted that even a tyrant could only be judged and punished by God. It is not surprising, then, that the anti-Napoleonic *radical* Ensor upheld tyrannicide, while many loyalists refused to condone such a proposal.

In the brief peacetime of 1801–03, recommending Napoleon's assassination could even be deemed a crime; Jean Peltier had ample reason to distance himself from such advocacy, of which he stood accused. In his introduction to the printed account of his trial, Peltier noted the irony of his trial's taking place on the very morning of Despard's execution. Would-be regicides were being hanged, drawn, and quartered while a royalist journalist went to trial for libeling a man he held to be a regicide.[95] His antipathy to Napoleon notwithstanding, Peltier made sure to deny that he himself had called for assassination. Indeed, he would "probably have let judgment go by default," he claimed, if he had faced a simple libel charge. "But I was accused of having provoked the French to an act of assassination," a charge "which would have fixed an indelible stain on my character."[96] Though he believed Napoleon to be a usurper, Peltier could not, publicly at any rate, recommend assassination as a means of restoring France's rightful ruler.

The brief peace between Britain and France produced a strange, ironic *pas de deux* on the part of the prosecution (led by the attorney-general, the future prime minister Spencer Perceval) and the defense in the Peltier trial. The peace-making government felt compelled to brush away any suggestion that the means by which Napoleon had arrived at power mattered. Though its ministers would soon, with the return of war, freely apply the epithet "usurper," the government held for now that Napoleon was "to be respected as if his ancestors had enjoyed the same power for a number of generations." Napoleon was "*de facto* the chief Magistrate."[97] The attorney for Peltier's defense could hardly disagree: he was James Mackintosh, whose 1791 *Vindiciæ Gallicæ* had defended France's revolution against Edmund Burke. Whether "a government be of yesterday or a thousand years old," Mackintosh declared, "whether it be a crude and bloody usurpation or the most antient, just, and paternal authority upon earth, we are *here* equally bound by his Majesty's recognition to protect it against libellous attacks." Prosecution and defense alike, then, claimed that usurpation was irrelevant: Mackintosh simply denied that Peltier had actually called for assassination.[98]

Others, however, once war returned, felt no qualms in recommending tyrannicide. In this regard, the most significant development was the revival of a seventeenth-century treatise advocating Oliver Cromwell's assassination. *Killing No Murder*, a 1657 royalist pamphlet, was republished in 1804 as an appendix to *The Revolutionary Plutarch*, a loyalist collection offering biographical vignettes of France's rulers and generals.[99] Having perused the lives of Napoleon's generals, ministers, and relatives, one might then read this essay that, as the *Plutarch*'s compiler explained, "points with equal force at a Protector—or a Consul."[100] The popular historical analogy between Cromwell and Bonaparte was being invoked yet again, this time with a deadly prescription attached.

The *Plutarch*'s message was not lost upon contemporaries. Henry Redhead Yorke quoted from the 1657 pamphlet in an 1804 denunciation of Napoleon (and he would invoke the eponymous phrase "Killing No Murder" again in 1809, as the title of his piece calling for the merciless slaughter of French soldiers in Spain).[101] The *European Magazine* greeted the republication of the seventeenth-century "masterpiece of reasoning" by hailing its tyrannicidal thesis. The work's argument remained topical, the magazine explained: "though actually levelled at Cromwell, the arguments will suit any other usurping Tyrant as well as him."[102] The short-lived liberal *Annual Review*, while recoiling in outrage from the argument for tyrannicide, was no less certain of its relevance to contemporary politics. In a review of *The Revolutionary Plutarch*, the *Review* (edited by the Unitarian chemist Arthur Aikin, member of a prominent Dissenting clan that included the *Monthly Magazine*'s editor, as well as the poet Anna Barbauld) called on the British government to disavow any plan to kill Bonaparte, and on the British public to abhor works "whose direct tendency is to degrade the generous and high-spirited patriot into the lurking assassin."[103]

The notion that Britain might play a role in killing Napoleon was kept alive by Charles James Fox's announcement, soon after becoming foreign secretary in February 1806, that he had been approached by a would-be assassin seeking British help. Fox expelled the man from Britain, and wrote to Talleyrand to warn him; this display of openness begat peace negotiations (though the talks ended unsuccessfully shortly after Fox's death that September). Cobbett, when the story was publicized in an 1808 pamphlet, would suggest that the entire affair had been "a matter of mere contrivance, as completely as any 'incident' of a play-house piece"—Talleyrand had arranged the episode so as to bring Britain to the negotiating table. One of Cobbett's correspondents went further, pointing out aspects of the account which suggested that Fox, hoping for peace, had simply fabricated the tale.[104]

Whatever the case, the story fed the continued discussion of the propriety of assassination. Leigh Hunt's new journal the *Examiner* pronounced in early 1808 its disgust with those politicians who spoke wistfully of Bonaparte's assassination. Such talk was "beneath the dignity of a nation like ours," Hunt declared; assassination was "the weapon of cowards."[105] A loyalist pamphlet of 1809 similarly proclaimed that "the benevolent and humane English" could not possibly have been "engaged in attempting to dip their hands in blood, like Buonaparte."[106] Even Lewis Goldsmith initially refused to countenance assassinating Bonaparte.[107] In 1802, he had declared assassination to be "a crime, from which every liberal mind must recoil with *instinctive horror*."[108] As recently as the 1810 *Secret History*, he claimed that Fox's visitor had been sent by Napoleon, who had wished "to inveigle our ministers into an encouragement of so abominable an act as that of assassination, in order to throw an odium upon them."[109] It was, he suggested, an insult to suggest that the British government might possibly condone such an act. Goldsmith's attitude soon changed.

Goldsmith's brief for assassination was first voiced in a pseudonymous letter proposing to found "a Society"—on the model of radical societies like the Jacobins, the Illuminati, the London Corresponding Society, and the United Irishmen—"to be called the *Anti-Corsican Institution!*"[110] Two weeks later, Goldsmith quoted the jurist Emeric de Vattel: "As to those monsters who, under the title of Sovereigns, render themselves the scourge and horror of the human race, they are savage beasts, whom every brave man may justly exterminate from the face of the earth."[111] Where once Goldsmith had cited the law of nations against Napoleon's enemies, he now employed it against Bonaparte.[112]

The "grand object" of the Society was "the destruction of NAPOLEON BUONAPARTE."[113] And should that object "happily be accomplished, let it be resounded from one end of the world to the other, that Napoleon Buonaparte owed his destruction to Lewis Goldsmith."[114] Goldsmith recognized the objections that might be raised to his proposal: "Assassination, considered abstractedly, is certainly repugnant to the feelings—and British feelings, especially, shrink from it, as an act of the greatest cowardice and baseness." But it was a peculiarly appropriate punishment for Napoleon, "the very means which he has himself so often employed."[115]

Goldsmith's proposal was brought to the attention of the House of Lords by the leading Foxite Whig, and former "Friend of the People," Earl Grey, who was outraged at this "open incitement to Assassination."[116] If this "atrocious" proposal were not "stigmatized and reprobated as it deserved," Britons should worry for their nation's reputation abroad. Grey received from the ministry the answer he desired, though it was not one that would please the editor whose newspaper the ministry secretly funded. Marquess Wellesley, former governor-general of India and now foreign secretary in Perceval's administration, declared he "fully coincided" with Grey's view of the "horrid" doctrine Goldsmith had proposed. Wellesley proclaimed he had never seen the newspaper in question.[117]

Goldsmith quickly rose to his own defense. Reading the Lords debate, he wrote, he had momentarily feared he was in France; the statements he read seemed as if spoken under an "arbitrary and oppressive system of government." Wellesley's declaration he excused, "for no British Nobleman can be the advocate of assassination." The minister had simply been laboring under a misapprehension because Grey had left out a key portion of Goldsmith's argument.[118] As Goldsmith now reminded his readers, he had explicitly denied any intention "to organize a band of *Chevaliers de Poignard.*" He had in fact hoped to form "a band of Writers and Printers, who, in a very short time may accomplish the tyrant's destruction": his society would not act physically against Bonaparte but would simply rouse the people of the Continent to such action.[119] The distinction Goldsmith took pains to draw did little to persuade his critics.

Samuel Taylor Coleridge, in the loyalist *Courier*, agreed that Napoleon's death would "be the greatest blessing, which by any human event could at present befall mankind." Coleridge "would not cross the gutter to save Buonaparte from death by whatever means it was coming upon him."[120] Still, he allowed that assassination was "abhorrent to the nature of an Englishman."[121] Coleridge settled on a position of historical agnosticism. One could not truly tell what the "general consequences" of an act would be, only the immediate ("*real*") ones; one could not tell whether killing a tyrant would have any results beyond the individual.[122] Assassination was not tyrannicide unless the act killed tyranny as well as tyrant—and the national circumstances that had created one tyrant were likely to create another; the hydra's body was likely to grow a new head.[123] Assassination, therefore, like "revolutionary resistance to established authority" (Coleridge mentioned Magna Carta and the revolution of 1688), could only be approved of "*retrospectively.*" Goldsmith's writings, consequently, were "not only indefensible, but absurd."[124]

As the liberal monthly the *Scourge* pointed out, Goldsmith had placed the ministry in an "unpleasant and ridiculous" situation. The *Scourge* had no doubt that Perceval had formerly supported the editor whom Wellesley condemned in the Lords—making it "a pity either that the one should have employed him, or that the other should be unacquainted with the fact."[125] The awkwardness of the government's position was confirmed a few days later in the Commons, when Samuel Whitbread asked Perceval to distance himself from Goldsmith's proposal. The subject was not only one "intimately involving the character of the British government" but also, Whitbread noted darkly, one involving "the welfare and safety of every individual of the royal family." Allowing Goldsmith's proposal to circulate uncondemned would confirm Napoleon's belief that British agency lay behind the earlier attempts on his life. Whitbread cited the loyalist claim that Napoleon was plotting to kill Britain's king: if this were true, then Goldsmith's talk was especially foolhardy, inviting as it did "retaliation." In becoming "the advocates of assassination," the ministry "exposed the persons of their sovereign and his family" to a "vital danger." Presented with an argument like Whitbread's, a minister could do little more than assent: Perceval, in his response, duly acknowledged that Goldsmith's system, if established, would indeed "involve the world in calamities greater than any by which it had yet been afflicted."[126]

The next month's *Scourge*—after Goldsmith had riled the magazine by making noises about libel—joined Whitbread in suggesting that the *Antigallican*'s logic tended ultimately towards the assassination of Britain's own ruler, the ostensible opposite of its goal. The magazine first objected to Goldsmith's "cowardly" technique of insinuation: how dare he threaten libel for being termed a "convicted spy" when he constantly wrote much worse about individuals who, unnamed and thus unable to seek redress, could be clearly recognized from his descriptions? The fact that he stuck to innuendo rather than denouncing his suspects to the ministry (and thus, presumably, preventing them from collecting further stipends) suggested there was no truth in "this story of the *editors in the pay of Bonaparte.*" The *Scourge* professed to be especially shocked by Goldsmith's "infamous" insinuations about opposition aldermen and

commoners in the City of London's governing body, the Court of
Common Council. Goldsmith had expressed his doubts that these men
would pray for Napoleon's destruction, adding the emphatic line, "*We
know for whose destruction they would pray*." How, the *Scourge* asked,
could the ministry support "a renegado scribbler, who has so little sense
of truth and decency, as wantonly to accuse a large body of respectable
men of praying for *the death of the king*"? This seemed the sort of language which, if made by an opposition journalist, would result in "an
ex officio information." If anyone deserved "the thanks of Napoleon,"
it was Goldsmith, "who insinuates into the minds of one half of the
nation, that the other half are rogues and jacobins; and diffuses, by
every infamous and cowardly artifice, the principles of discord and
distrust."[127]

After this contretemps, it is perhaps remarkable that any British
ministry continued to keep Goldsmith in its employ. But Goldsmith did
not give up his scheme, and the state did not give up its subsidy.
Goldsmith continued to recommend "a moral and political assassination," to be achieved by raising the Bourbon standard and distributing
"Papers . . . in the Armies of the tyrant."[128] He offered as precedents for
Louis XVIII's placing a price on Bonaparte's head both a similar reward
the British government had offered for the Stuart pretender to the crown
in 1715, and also Napoleon's own killing of Enghien.[129] Goldsmith also
sought to convince the government to fund his plan. He clearly had his
"band of Writers" in mind when he proposed to the Duke of Cumberland, in the fall of 1812, "a kind of office distinct & separate from any
of the Government offices, the object of which should be for the persons
employed in that establishment to write pamphlets, to reply to articles
written in the disaffected prints, but principally to write pamphlets in
all languages to be distributed on the Continent." This ministry of
propaganda would, Goldsmith continued, "be under the direction of the
Foreign Office, and the Treasury."[130]

Despite repeated denials of being the government's pensioner,[131] Lewis
Goldsmith would receive thousands of pounds from British ministries
between 1810 and 1830. The money ebbed and flowed, and he would
have to reassert his financial claims from time to time, but his correspondence suggests the well only ran dry when the revolution of July
1830 replaced France's Bourbon monarchy with the cadet Orléans
branch. Goldsmith primed the pump of government aid in 1814 by
threatening to leave for France, from whose newly restored king, Louis

XVIII, he claimed to expect "a lucrative situation."[132] In early 1824, he concocted the notion that he might issue passports to British travelers in France and thus collect a stamp tax upon them. To sweeten his proposal, he told the foreign secretary George Canning that if his plan were accepted he would "give up my Paper," now being published as the *British Monitor*, "& have done altogether with writing." He would, moreover, give up his plan to publish his memoirs, "which I am now preparing for the Press & which I intend to bring out in about two months."[133]

This was blackmail: Canning would surely recognize that a memoir by Goldsmith might offer damaging revelations about British ministers. Canning rejected Goldsmith's proposal, but appears to have offered the journalist, as an alternative, a position as what Goldsmith would later term Canning's "confidential agent" in Paris. After some haggling over the pay (Goldsmith first held out for £1,000 a year, noting that Paris was "expensive if you keep good company & pay visits to *great men* which can only be done in *Carriages*") the journalist agreed to give up his paper and report secretly from Paris for two hundred pounds a quarter. There was relief in the Foreign Office: as Canning, or perhaps his assistant Joseph Planta, noted, the government was already paying Goldsmith nearly this much to publish the *Monitor*, "& his Paper is a *Discredit* to us rather than an advantage."[134] Goldsmith moved to Paris, and sent Canning regular bulletins and newspapers. The memoir was never published. Goldsmith seems to have collected an additional four hundred pounds a year from the Treasury—so he would claim, at any rate, in a subsequent, apparently unsuccessful appeal for back pay.[135] We need not feel too much concern for Goldsmith's fortunes in later years. In 1837, his daughter married Lord Lyndhurst, the former and future lord chancellor.

Goldsmith might easily have been cut off from the wellspring of government money at a much earlier moment. His assassination proposal, made only a few months into his journal's career, but repeated incessantly thereafter, did not derail his career, even though it embarrassed his benefactors. Despite the apparent feelings of several government officials that he had overstayed his usefulness, Goldsmith continued to collect regular payments for decades. The case of this career propagandist demonstrates, if nothing else, how readily bad money could chase good in the crepuscular world of government-financed journalism and intelligence.

Lewis Goldsmith was not alone in claiming that Britain swarmed with Napoleonic sympathizers. The "secret plottings of . . . internal enemies" figured frequently in loyalist accounts of the national condition.[136] Napoleon would address his bulletins to the "*internal* adversary more dangerous, because less visible," who would "perfectly understand his meaning, however dark and oracular."[137]

Though conspiracy-minded loyalists discerned widespread pro-Napoleonic sentiment in wartime Britain, recent historians of British radicalism have not. J. E. Cookson, in his important study of "anti-war liberalism" from 1793 to 1815, draws a distinction between radical feeling for Napoleon before the peace of Amiens and after it. Early identifications of Napoleon as the revolution's legatee dissipated with the return of war, according to Cookson; "friends of peace," as they called themselves, now found Bonaparte as much of a despot as the loyalists did. The remaining opposition to Britain's war policy was voiced in pragmatic and strategic terms—not, Cookson states, as political sympathy for Napoleon.[138] J. Ann Hone, in her ground-breaking work on London radicalism in the early nineteenth century, does note that two former leading figures in the London Corresponding Society, the wine merchant Maurice Margarot and the shoemaker Thomas Hardy, continued to extol Napoleon in the later years of his reign. But she makes little of this, and her general conclusion is that sympathy for Napoleon dried up as evidence of his "expansionist mien and imperial ambitions" became too overwhelming to deny.[139]

Cookson and Hone are right about the intellectual trajectory of many British radicals. And if some bade farewell to Bonaparte in order to stay true to their republican faith, others let Napoleon's sad example justify a complete renunciation of radicalism. Napoleon's ambitious grasping for dynasty helped inspire the cynicism and conservatism of the Lake poets Coleridge, Wordsworth, and Southey. Perhaps it helped reinforce or intensify the anti-reformist spirit of Henry Redhead Yorke, after his prison conversion in the late 1790s. William Burdon toned down his reformist language once he soured on Bonaparte (though enough republican feelings lay dormant in Burdon to blossom when Napoleon later professed a return to revolutionary ideals).[140] In short, many who had once embraced France's revolutionary example refused to endorse Napoleon's regime. The more Bonaparte came to resemble a hereditary dynast, the less, some felt, he could be held up as a counter-example.

Still, loyalist claims about Napoleon's British admirers were not mere paranoid fantasy. To a much greater degree than has been recognized, many British radicals continued to have kind words to say about Napoleon, and continued to use him as a cudgel with which to chastise their own rulers. There was a continuous, if at times attenuated, tradition of British radical admiration of Napoleon, stretching from the earliest days of his military career through his consulate and empire and on into the period of his exile. It would be an exaggeration to claim, as one *Antigallican Monitor* correspondent complained, that "every thing Napoleonic" was praised in certain quarters of the opposition press ("Cobbett, the *Edinburgh Reviewers, Statesman, Examiner*, &c. &c.").[141] Turning to these journals, one finds both applause and reprimand for Napoleon. But that applause, indicating fissures in the anti-Napoleonic front, deserves attention. Napoleonic France provided British radicals with a tool to dissect the claims of British ministers and loyalists. Some radicals might best be termed mere anti-anti-Bonapartists, who regarded Napoleon as an evil lesser than the continental dynasts he opposed, or who rejected the excesses of loyalist rhetoric. But others found it difficult to mute their thrill that Napoleon was—in the words of one English admirer, Anne Plumptre—"creating a new æra in the history of mankind."[142]

The young Leigh Hunt, in the weekly *Examiner* newspaper he and his brother John launched in 1808, repeatedly drew attention to the flaws in Napoleon's character. But he offset each criticism of Napoleon with an equally telling reproach of Napoleon's enemies. True, Napoleon was not "*Great*"—he was too much a creature of ambition for that. Still, "it must be confessed that his fortune has thrown him into an age when he is almost literally without competitors." Napoleon's motives were not commendable, to be sure. But the emperor was achieving desirable ends: "a great part of Europe will be much alleviated by the destruction of [the] feudal system."[143] Even when damning Napoleon as "a man who would exterminate liberty from the face of the earth," Hunt noted that Bonaparte's downfall would not by itself liberate Europe—since "the overthrow of one tyrant is not the destruction of all."[144] For each aspect of Napoleon's regime Hunt criticized, it seemed, he could find another one to praise. "An Englishman very properly looks with disgust at the condition to which NAPOLEON has reduced the press in France," Hunt wrote—"but it must be allowed that the revolution . . . has obtained France many benefits, although *political liberty* is not among the number."[145]

Hunt did not exempt Britain from his criticism of established governments. He cautioned his countrymen not to throw the first stone at Bonaparte the usurper and conqueror—for "an abuse of power is the same in Asia as in Europe, and . . . an East Indian would have much greater reason to cry out against the usurpations of England." Any Englishman who supported Britain's "monstrous excesses of ambition" in the subcontinent, Hunt declared, "should not dare to say a single word against the FRENCH EMPEROR."[146] Even Hunt's argument for containing Napoleon's ambition drew attention to the moral defects of Britain's government: "if we suffer him to take civilized kingdoms one after another purely because they do not deserve to be defended, . . . we may at last apply the same exquisite delicacy to ourselves, and leave him to conquer our own country because we may chance to have a corrupted constitution and a contemptible heir-apparent."[147] To fight successfully against Napoleon, one must "imitate what virtues he may possess, and scrupulously . . . avoid his vices." Napoleon's "anger and ambition will do nothing for us," Hunt wrote—but he added (thus implicitly attributing these qualities to Bonaparte) that "promptitude, vigilance, temperance, and the studious encouragement of intellect will do a great deal, and virtuous motive added to all these, will do every thing." In short, Britain should emulate Napoleon's sharpening his sword "*upon*," rather than "blunting it *against*, the temper of the age."[148]

Napoleon, in this presentation, was a distinctive creature of the age, in step with the particular historical moment. He was also, Hunt argued, a product of the nation that had crowned him. It was "natural for the fickle and vain-glorious French" to choose "conquest and slavish glitter"—rather than to choose freedom, as the British had when they had placed the house of Brunswick on the throne. But French vanity did not diminish Napoleon's right to rule, Hunt insisted. "Their vain-glory, instead of making Bonaparte an usurper, has made him a *legitimate* Emperor."[149] Being rooted in the present and in the French national character was itself Napoleon's title to lawful rule.

Napoleon found an even more stalwart defender in Anne Plumptre, a novelist and translator from the German and French, who had lived in France from 1802 to 1805. Like Hunt, Plumptre balanced each of Napoleon's alleged sins with a British equivalent. But reading Plumptre, one feels that she, more than Hunt, actually wished to clear Napoleon of the charges against him. If Hunt seemed genuinely to struggle with the problem of Napoleon, Plumptre came off as a devoted apologist. Her

public defense of Bonaparte, presented in her three-volume *Narrative of a Three Years' Residence in France* published in 1810, was in fact a pale shadow of her private adulation of the man. Henry Crabb Robinson, an inveterate transcriber of his contemporaries' dinner conversations, would in later years recall her remarking that the British nation would "be all the happier if Buonaparte were to effect a landing and overturn the Government. He would destroy the Church and the aristocracy, and his government would be better than the one we have."[150]

In the *Narrative*, Plumptre compared Napoleon's burning of an Italian town with the British immolation of Connecticut towns decades earlier. Like Hunt, Plumptre drew parallels between Napoleon's actions (specifically in Syria) and Britain's in India (specifically the storming of Seringapatam).[151] Plumptre defended the killing of the duc d'Enghien (that central exhibit in the case against Napoleon as usurper), drawing a moral parallel between this act and the price Britain had put on the head of the Old Pretender in 1715. If the British act had been justified, so too must be the French one.[152] Besides defending Napoleon's foreign policy, Plumptre celebrated his domestic achievements. Others saw Napoleon as a despotic crusher of French liberties; Plumptre felt Napoleon was working to transform the French national character into one that could sustain liberty. While the Jacobins had erred by giving the French an "extended system of liberty" too quickly—and thus had effectively introduced a new tyranny—Napoleon had introduced a system of education which would teach future generations to understand freedom's "true nature," and not to chase blindly after "wild and impracticable theories." Though "absolute," Napoleon's government would sow the seeds of "a rational system of freedom." Bonaparte had already increased the French people's liberties by overturning the "fabric of religious thraldom"; even in the turmoil of war, he had nurtured French agriculture, industry, art, and science. Until he was "left in a situation in which it is possible to establish freedom," Plumptre declared, "we are not authorized in calling him a tyrant."[153]

In portraying Napoleon as a figure whose restraints on liberty could be excused because they would ultimately increase the freedom of his subjects, Plumptre was joined by the *Statesman*—the evening paper, founded by John Hunt, whose Newgate-bound editor Daniel Lovell would take Lewis Goldsmith to court. In one 1811 piece, for example, prompted by Napoleon's visit to the Netherlands, the newspaper defended Napoleon by contrasting his government with those he was

overturning. Most continental nations had formerly been "subjected to the worst of tyrannies, under an insolent and fanatical priesthood, who taught the Kings of the earth that they were Gods, and that their subjects were merely playthings destined to amuse them here below." When one compared the former state of these nations with their current condition, one had to conclude that continental dynastic changes were "calculated to promote the happiness of the human race." Like Plumptre, the *Statesman* was ready to mortgage fragile present freedoms for sound future ones, and to justify current restrictions by claiming the peoples of the continent to be unready for true freedom. The government Napoleon brought to Europe's nations was not necessarily "fashioned according to the true principles of freedom," the *Statesman* admitted. But that was only appropriate, for "the great mass of the Continental nations" were "as yet too ignorant of what constitutes political liberty."[154]

Even those who generally defended Napoleon could draw the line somewhere. The Spanish war provides an interesting case. It was French "butcheries" in the Spanish peninsula that finally drove the *Monthly Magazine*, Napoleon's frequent defender, to scathing censure of the emperor. The *Monthly*, in 1811, reviled his Iberian actions as those of a "monster" and "merciless Assassin" driven by "insatiable ambition." The Spaniards' war was one "*of* PURE DEFENCE *against the most unprovoked aggression*," it declared (though it added that applauding Spanish self-defense did not mean approving Britain's forward role in the conflict).[155] Lord and Lady Holland, too, took Bonaparte to task for his Spanish actions, even as they extended him their sympathy in other areas. In Spain, where the Hollands had cultivated friends who they hoped would lead the nation Whiggishly forward, Napoleon seemed the enemy, as elsewhere he seemed the friend, of constitutional liberalism.[156]

Samuel Whitbread, a satellite in the Hollands' social system, similarly supported the Spanish resistance, while still pressing for negotiations with Napoleon.[157] In his Commons assault on Goldsmith's assassination scheme, however, Whitbread drew moral parallels between Napoleon's sins and those of the British government. Before telling "the Spaniard that he had a right to assassinate the emperor of France because he invaded Spain," one should "recollect how recently Great Britain had attacked an unoffending nation, with whom she was not at war," namely Denmark. Like Hunt and Plumptre, Whitbread also played the Indian trump card, reminding his listeners of "the march of British armies over

the guiltless countries of Asia, for the purpose of deposing their unoffending sovereigns." Napoleon's actions in the peninsula were wrong, but British actions elsewhere were equally iniquitous. Loyalists would do well not to talk too much of assassinating Bonaparte, lest they inadvertently justify a Zealander's or Indian's wish to revenge his nation upon Britain's monarchy.[158]

But even in the Spanish case, some reformers rushed to praise Napoleon's actions. Leigh Hunt maintained that Napoleon would, by handing Spanish sovereignty to his brother Joseph, "certainly present them with a better Monarch than their own." A Bonaparte in power would do away with the "execrable" Inquisition, thus turning the Spanish people into "a military instead of a priest-ridden people" ("and perhaps the poets and the painters will once more revive when there are men to praise and actions to paint"). In short, "French innovation, and French manners, and I may add, I am sure, French improvements, will ere long, give a new tone to Spanish society." Though "unlucky for us" that Napoleon brought improvements to the lands he conquered, Hunt concluded, it was "very lucky for the conquered nations: and though he certainly could do us no good by enslavement, since the only good we want is the perfect enjoyment of our constitutional liberty, yet it is a truth which posterity will acknowledge, that the nations he overthrows are usually in want of such a conqueror."[159]

While hailing Napoleon for crushing the Inquisition, opposition writers took Britain to task for hypocritically supporting the Catholic *ancien régime* in Spain while persecuting Catholics at home. Anne Plumptre, writing in 1810, lamented the "great anomaly" of Protestant Britain fighting for the "most pernicious and oppressive" version of Catholicism abroad while subjecting domestic Catholics (who practiced their religion "under an amended form, and curtailed of every thing materially exceptionable") to "grievous and galling restrictions."[160] John Scott Byerley similarly argued that the ministry's readiness "to revive all the horrors of the Inquisition" did not sit well with its craven acquiescence at home to the "senseless cry of 'No Popery'" and its keeping Ireland in "chains."[161] Byerley even managed, paradoxically, to make the Spanish resistance to French occupation reflect well on Napoleon. If the Spanish struggled, it was because the emperor had given them the freedom to do so: "Under the old government, they were mere beasts of burthen; they now breathe, their eyes are opened, and they feel they are men."[162]

In defending Napoleon against his critics, opposition writers worked to undermine the belief that Bonaparte had less of a claim to rule than hereditary dynasts. Even when representing the royalist Jean Peltier, James Mackintosh could not resist noting how "scarcely applicable" the term "usurpation" was to Napoleon's seizure of power, given that the period preceding his was not one of stable rule but of "anarchy."[163] Anne Plumptre pointed out in 1810 that if the reports of Napoleon's low birth were true, that would only make his achievements more impressive, given his "having surmounted in a manner so truly astonishing, the obstacles presented to his advancement by a total want of birth and education." Plumptre hastened to add that the reports of Napoleon's inferior background were false, and that Napoleon was "descended from one of the most ancient and illustrious families of Florence."[164] Democrat or no, Plumptre recognized the value of a gentle birth.

A number of opposition writers worked to defend Napoleon's legitimacy by equating his origins with those of Europe's other rulers. Leigh Hunt, for example, pointed out that many European states were ruled by "various political tyrannies similar in their origins to that now exercised by BONAPARTE." These other states, however, unlike Napoleon's, were "weakened by age and rendered contemptible by sloth and ignorance."[165] Hunt reminded his readers of how recently Britain's own ruling Hanoverian dynasty had come to the throne.[166] Reasons for distrusting or fighting Napoleon there might be, but his usurpation, in Hunt's account, was not among them. Plumptre likewise noted that Napoleon reigned "by the same title that the house of Hanover reigns in England, by the wish of the people." Both leaders owed their power to their subjects' readiness to dispose of rulers not to their taste.[167] Usurpation, in this reading, served as a foundation for the very liberties Hanoverian Britain enjoyed.

The terms thrown at Napoleon could readily be hurled back at loyalist targets. (Henry White's weekly newspaper the *Independent Whig*, in contesting the 1809 elevation to viscount of Arthur Wellesley—whose efforts in the peninsula the newspaper castigated—insisted on referring to the general's "UPSTART FAMILY.")[168] The terms' applicability to Napoleon could also be disputed directly, a tactic employed by William Cobbett at a surprisingly early moment in the journalist's trajectory from loyalist to radical. Just after Napoleon's 1804 coronation, when many British commentators were reacting with horror at the apparent act of self-aggrandizement, Cobbett defended Bonaparte against both the epithets "upstart" and "usurper." An "aversion to upstarts" was perfectly praise-worthy, Cobbett agreed. But true upstarts were those who had risen "by low and base arts," or through patronage. Those, by contrast, "who have risen, however suddenly, by deeds of arms, are not upstarts": neither Napoleon nor Nelson could be described by this term. "Extraordinary talents, exerted in rendering great public services, whether in the cabinet or the field, are a fair foundation for rank and power."[169] Cobbett took issue also with the label of "usurper," which implied that Napoleon lacked the support of the French people. There was much evidence that Napoleon was in fact popular, not least the plebiscites that had approved his advances in rank: "though the collecting of the suffrages of the people might be a mere mockery, yet, the dynasty of Buonaparté has, in appear-ance at least, been established by the choice of the French nation."[170] That put Napoleon ahead of many other rulers.

Cobbett was not yet, in 1804, an advocate for Napoleon. But that he was ready, at this early moment, to offer any defense at all is significant. Napoleon may have been more important to Cobbett's political trans-formation than the journalist's biographers have suspected. Cobbett's swimming against the current of British politics in the second half of this decade—his leftward transit during a period in which so many writers were tugged from republicanism to conservatism—has been a central problem for students of his life. A number of factors propelled Cobbett to the left, and allowed him to turn himself into probably the most prominent voice of British radicalism. These transforming factors included rage at the corrupt system of financial reward for government favorites (a rage stirred up when Cobbett was himself offered a profi-table "slice" of a government loan in 1803), disgust at the flogging of English soldiers (a punishment which, he wrote, Napoleon himself did not inflict upon his troops), and a two years' imprisonment for libel (resulting from his denunciation of flogging).[171] The point is not that a growing admiration for Napoleon necessarily drove Cobbett's radical-ization. It is significant enough that sympathy for Napoleon was one of the several ways in which Cobbett's burgeoning radicalism manifested itself. Cobbett could readily have transformed himself into a radical reformer, even a radical critic of the war, without embracing Napoleon; indeed, the standard narrative of British radicalism would almost demand that he do so. That, instead, Cobbett increasingly turned to Napoleon to make his points (and, incidentally, started using the Gallicized version of the Corsican's surname rather than the loyalist

"Buonaparte") provides further evidence of the important role the French emperor played in British radical thought even after the peace of Amiens.[172]

Cobbett was incensed by the hailstorm of epithets that poured down on Napoleon. "Any fool may call Buonaparté a monster," he wrote. "Nothing is easier; but, let any one shew me what valour or what sense there is in such reviling."[173] And why call him "the Corsican"? Bonaparte's "*Corsicanship*" did not bear on his qualities as a leader.[174] Why a tyrant, "as if he was the only one in the whole world"?[175] And why a military despot, considering the fact that the French people now enjoyed "a criminal code, a civil code, and a commercial code, framed with infinite labour and care, deliberately enacted, and solemnly promulgated"?[176] Cobbett repeatedly reminded his readers of the 1802 libel trial of Jean Peltier (which at the time the journalist had denounced as craven submission to France's leader). After Cobbett's own imprisonment for libel, the tale of Peltier, revolving as it did around freedom of the press, especially rankled. If it had been unlawful during the peace of Amiens to use "*hard names*" towards the man who had during the trial been acknowledged to be sovereign of France, it should still be, Cobbett reasoned.[177] In 1811, Cobbett made much of the fact that the current prime minister, Spencer Perceval—who now gladly branded Bonaparte a tyrant and worse—had prosecuted the Peltier trial.[178] Cobbett asked for consistency, refusing to call Napoleon a tyrant "until such a change is made in the practice of the law, as will authorize me to call him a tyrant in *time of peace* as well as in time of war."[179]

The accusation of tyranny had never really appealed to Cobbett. Back in his loyalist years, the journalist's chief problem had been the democratic aspects of Bonaparte's rule, not the ruler's despotism.[180] As Cobbett himself became more of a republican, he viewed these aspects of Napoleon's regime in a more favorable light. France, he declared in 1812, was "a *republic*, except merely in name." Its nobility and clergy had "*no privileges* distinct from those of the people"; the revolution had "created, *totally created*, a middle class in society; and, though one man has the executive government in his hands, the *society is essentially republican*, and all its manners are, and will be, those of a republic."[181] This was now a good thing. In some sense, it was not Cobbett's view of Napoleon that had changed, but his opinion of the categories with which he judged Napoleon.

Much of what Cobbett wrote during the First Empire might best be termed anti-anti-Napoleonism. In one 1808 piece, he claimed to have no "friendly feeling" towards Napoleon, but maintained that Bonaparte had done no harm to the English constitution—while much had been done by "the corruptors, the corrupted, the peculators and plunderers, in England, Ireland, and Scotland." These men, Cobbett announced, were "the best friends that Buonaparte has in this kingdom."[182] Loyalists branded reformers as traitors, but the "boroughmongers" posed the real threat. The "hirelings of corruption," those who claimed reformers were friends of Bonaparte, would in fact "not hesitate a moment *to let him in rather than see the people of England in possession of the right of choosing freely the members to serve in the parliament.*" They would "gladly make a bargain with Buonaparté and betray the country into his hands" if reform were the alternative.[183] Reformers ("*Jacobins and Levellers,*" in the phrase that Cobbett borrowed from their detractors) were in fact the country's greatest strength and hope. What use would be the "*quiet good sort* of folks" who remained silent (in public) about reform, should Napoleon's troops land in England? "These Quakers in politics will be something worse than Quakers in war.—Common sense says, that in the hour of real danger, the fate of the country must depend upon the disposition of the *active* and *zealous* part of the people, and these are *all* for reform."[184]

In the later years of Napoleon's regime, Cobbett increasingly went beyond mere criticism of the anti-Napoleonists. He began to endorse elements of Napoleon's rule, some of which stood in pointed (if tacit) contrast with Britain's government. The Code Civil knew "nothing at all of *religious distinctions,*" Cobbett wrote—nor, he added in capital letters, of tithes. Napoleon had not reinstated the game laws the Jacobins had abolished.[185] Moreover, as Cobbett pointedly noted, it was Napoleon who had introduced trial by jury to France—no small matter to a journalist who spent many pages denouncing the inroads that British executive power was making into the jury system.[186]

One tactic repeatedly employed by Cobbett was to protest against an anti-liberal measure of Napoleon in order to focus attention on a similar abuse in Britain. Through this device, Cobbett managed, in an article ostensibly decrying a recent French act allowing arbitrary imprisonment, to criticize the House of Common's 1810 imprisonment of the MP Sir Francis Burdett. The "greatest evil of all," Cobbett noted (this at a time when Burdett's uncertain fate was occupying the overwhelming bulk of the *Political Register*'s attention, and inflaming Cobbett with even more than his accustomed vitriol) was "the power, exercised by Napoleon, or by some other part of the government (it is no matter which) of sending men to prison, and keeping them there for an *indefinite term*, without *any trial*." Condemning the French people—but implicitly also the British—for accepting such tyranny, Cobbett seemed to be advocating actual armed resistance in defense of Burdett's rights: "would not the people, if they had common sense and common spirit, ask him [Napoleon] whether it would not be better to be killed, to be hacked to pieces, in an endeavour to recover their liberties, than to drawl out life for a few years longer under such a load of misery and infamy?" That Cobbett's eye was more on Westminster than on Paris was underscored by his description of the Napoleonic decree as "recently passed, or said to have been passed."[187] Even as he ostensibly condemned Bonaparte, he raised doubts about the existence of the French decree he was nominally criticizing.

Like a number of his fellow radicals, Cobbett answered complaints about Napoleon's empire with reminders of Britain's own imperial might and expansion. In sheer numerical terms, Cobbett observed in 1811, the British had, since the beginning of the French revolution, added "a number far surpassing all those whom Napoleon has added to the empire of France." Having just conquered Java from the Dutch (who were now ruled by a Bonaparte), Britain had "at one single dash, conquered more subjects than Napoleon has conquered all together." Cobbett doubted that this conquest would "tend to convince the nations of Europe, that Napoleon alone has the rage of conquest and ambition in his breast."[188] As for the liberty enjoyed by the British king's far-flung subjects, Cobbett responded to criticisms of French press restrictions by pointing out that comparable constraints had been imposed in British India.[189]

Empire did not play much of a role in British debate over Napoleon. How could it, when one side, the loyalists, generally refused to engage with the question at all—refused, that is, to dignify with a response the radical comparison between Britain's colonial efforts and French expansionism? (One notable exception was the vaguely millenarian Scot who recommended placing the Prince Regent's brothers on the thrones of India, Canada, and the Netherlands—an idea, he gladly admitted, "*tout à fait à la Napoleon*, and in fact borrowed from him."[190]) Nor would it be right to exaggerate the relative importance of the imperial comparison within the broader arsenal of radical argument; this was but one arrow in the quiver, and was employed only occasionally. Still, many radicals defending Napoleon did reach for this rhetorical weapon. For

Cobbett—as for Hunt, Plumptre, Whitbread, and the millenarians Aldred and Bicheno—such comparisons served as exculpatory evidence in the case of Napoleon's empire, but at the same time contributed to the indictment of Britain's rulers.

In 1809, Gillray would depict Cobbett hailing "that Idol of all my Adorations, his Royal & Imperial Majesty, NAPOLEONE!" The artist exaggerated Cobbett's Napoleonic sentiments in order to portray him as a traitorous internal enemy (he drank his "favourite Toast of Damnation to the House of Brunswick" with a bottle of "True Napoleone Spirits," according to the caricature).[191] But Gillray was not conjuring Cobbett's Napoleonic sympathy out of thin air (even if it had yet to blossom in its full glory). Around the same time, Cobbett scrutinized a new loyalist device designed to celebrate Britain's monarch—the royal Jubilee of 1809—by comparing it with similar festivities in countries ruled by Napoleon. His effort here, comparable to efforts undertaken by Hunt and Plumptre, was to blur the difference between the foundations of Napoleon's and of George III's power.

The Jubilee sought to honor George III in the fiftieth year of his rule.[192] Cobbett questioned how sincerely a nation engulfed in war and associated economic ills could celebrate its good fortune. Furthermore, he suggested that the very objection that loyalists made when Napoleon's subjects celebrated their ruler could be applied to the British case. Loyalists regarded any sign of popular approval for Napoleon as stage-managed or fear-induced. Why should not these objections be addressed to Britain's Jubilee, this supposed outpouring of spontaneous, authentic, loyal joy?

Over a period of weeks, Cobbett worked to connect Britain's Jubilee to continental celebrations of Bonaparte. He threatened to publish, alongside accounts of the upcoming British festival, "the brilliant accounts of the *loyal* celebrations in honour of the Buonapartés."[193] His point was double-edged: he sought both to recognize the possible sincerity of Napoleon's subjects and to question that of George's. If the people of the continent "drink, gorge, and sing anthems, in honour of a man, whom they wish at the devil," Cobbett wrote, then the British people might well do the same: "there may be a *doubt* of the sincerity of our jubilee."[194] A few days after the celebration, Cobbett went further, suggesting that in fact the British jubilation was the only insincere one. Britons' celebration of their monarch, he suggested, had relied on "giving the ignorant and the hungry victuals and drink, in order to make them shout for joy." On the continent, by contrast, "whole nations, unbought with either bread or beer, are proclaiming their admiration of our enemy."[195] The professed loyalty of Napoleon's subjects, unlike George's, seemed spontaneous and genuine.

Again and again, British discussions of Napoleon's legitimacy circled back to become discussions of domestic power. The coronation of Napoleon led some to speculate that the very fabric of hereditary monarchy would unravel. The Soho coronation, designed as a satire on Napoleon's monarchical emulation, prompted Cobbett to worry whether one could mock Napoleon's authority without implicating George III's. Goldsmith's proposal to assassinate Napoleon inspired Whitbread's warning that British foreign policy might unleash a deadly vengeance upon Britain's royal family. The loyalist language of legitimacy roused Plumptre and Hunt to remind their readers of how very shallow were the roots of the house of Hanover. And the Jubilee spurred Cobbett to argue that George III's relationship to his subjects was at least as troubled as Napoleon's with his. Each loyalist criticism of Napoleon, it seemed, could be picked up by radicals and brought to bear on Britain's government and policy. And, by implication at the very least, on the character and honor of the nation: as Cobbett wrote in 1804, and reiterated in 1810, there was, "amongst the mass of [George III's] subjects, . . . an habitual, an hereditary persuasion, that the King is the repository of all that is necessary to the preservation of the *national character*, in which the heart of every man, however humble his condition, tells him that he has a share."[196]

British radicals were not the paid Napoleonic agents of Goldsmith's imagination. But some prominent radicals did defend Napoleon against loyalist charges, and did celebrate a number of his qualities. They used his example as a rod against which to measure the legitimacy of other monarchs, not least Britain's own. Radical writings on Napoleon form a key thread in the early nineteenth-century British discussion of political legitimacy. The critical stance radicals took towards loyalist opprobrium of Napoleon helped shape their understanding of how political power was constructed. If Napoleon provided some writers with a bridge from radicalism to loyalism, he provided the radical movement with a bridge connecting the revolutionary sympathy of the 1790s with the post-war radicalism of the late 1810s.

CHAPTER 5

From Elba to St. Helena

Were I disposed to moralise, there is before me the finest field that ever opened to the eye of mortal man.—*Nap the Mighty*, who, but a few months ago, made the sovereigns of Europe tremble at his nod; who has trampled on thrones and sceptres, and kings and priests and principalities and powers, and carried ruin and havoc and blood and fire, from Gibralter to Archangel—*Nap the Mighty* is—*gone to pot*!!!—"I will plant my eagles on the towers of Lishbon"; "I will conquer Europe and crush great Britain to the centre of the terraqueous globe"—I will go to Elba—*and be coop'd up* in Limbo!!! "But yesterday; and *Boney* might have stood against the world; now none so poor as do him rev'rence."

Thomas Carlyle to Robert Mitchell, 30 April 1814[1]

Which of ye, ye long-headed ones of the earth ever dreamt that little Nap, tired of fretting out his heart in Elba— would rise Phoenix-like disdaining "the limits of his little reign" and once more front the world—determined to die "with harness on his back"? Your calculations are ruined for NAP is on the field! And now poor d——l! when so many men that wield sceptres, and paving-shovels—when so many people that have diadems, and gridirons are com- bined against thee—why should *I* be thine enemy?—No! fight thine own battle—and come what speed thou mayest for me.

Thomas Carlyle to Robert Mitchell, 25 March 1815[2]

Princes are now but performers, strutting for an hour in the grandeur of royalty, and the next, perhaps, walking as footmen in attendance on those who before waited on them;—the crowns of Empires are changed with the evening.

John Scott, *The Champion*, 26 March 1815[3]

After Napoleon's abdication in early April 1814, effigies of the fallen leader were constructed, and then destroyed, in many provincial towns. In Yarmouth, Norfolk, 8,000 people, seated at a table three-quarters of a mile long, dined on roast beef, plum pudding, and strong beer—potent symbols of Englishness—as a figure of Napoleon, positioned atop "a pyramid of tar barrels," was set ablaze. An inscription told the crowd that it was witnessing the "funeral pile" of the "Buonapartean dynasty."[4]

The sight of English minds in "such a phrenzy" disgusted William Cobbett, who was sure the effigy-destroyers had been spurred on by the loyalist press. The radical journalist took comfort, though, from the sequel to one such mock execution. In the Lancashire manufacturing town of Bolton, Cobbett reported in the summer of 1814, townspeople—believing Napoleon's fall would help open the continental market to their products—had celebrated the abdication by hanging a wooden Bonaparte. Soon, though, as French manufactures flowed into markets where Britain had formerly lacked competition, cotton goods fell to their old price. The people of Bolton, according to Cobbett, came to see the error of their ways. As if in contrition—as if seeking to mollify a deity they had offended—they announced that Napoleon was "most innocent" of the charges they had laid against him. They "raised his effigy from the grave; washed it from all the impurity which it had contracted in the earth; re-crowned it, and placed it in a situation where, as I have been assured, it is looked up to with respect, instead of terror and abhorrence." Napoleon had been forgiven, and crowned again by Cobbett's countrymen. The British, Cobbett concluded (taking the Bolton incident as emblematic of a broader tendency), were "now returning to their senses."[5]

The British political temperament hardly underwent a transformation as sudden or entire as the one Cobbett described in 1814. But the year or so following Napoleon's Bolton exhumation and coronation did see a dramatic alteration in British attitudes toward Bonaparte and France. In 1814, the liberal *Edinburgh Review* had welcomed Napoleon's replacement by a Bourbon king, and had excoriated the fallen emperor as a tyrant and despot; even the radical *Statesman* had sought to put the best face on the Bourbon restoration, portraying it as a triumph of French revolutionary—and English constitutional—principles. The disappointing reality of Bourbon rule, the excitement and hopes raised by Napoleon's Hundred Days of power in the spring of 1815, and the perceived maltreatment he suffered after his defeat at Waterloo all changed the manner with which the British treated Bonaparte. By the time a ship set sail carrying the twice-abdicated Napoleon to St. Helena, members of the British opposition were praising his past accomplishments with a forthrightness seldom seen during his reign.

News of the Allied entry into Paris, and then of Napoleon's abdication, was greeted in Britain by loyalist jubilation.[6] The exiled Louis XVIII— Louis "*le désiré*," his advocates now proclaimed him—rode victoriously down Piccadilly. (Byron refused an offer of seats to see "Louis the Gouty . . . wheeling in triumph, . . . in all the pomp and rabblement of Royalty.")[7] The London printshops displayed grand transparencies: Wellington and the Cossacks putting Napoleon to flight; Napoleon debasing himself before a skeletal Death, while his conquerors raised the Bourbon standard.[8] Cheering crowds greeted the Prussian king and the Russian emperor in June 1814 as they docked at Dover, toured London, and received honors at Oxford.[9] Friedrich Wilhelm and Alexander were made Knights of the Garter at Carlton House, and Doctors of Civil Law at the ancient university (Metternich, Blücher, Count Lieven, and the duke of Wellington shared in the latter honor).[10] Alexander found himself being lauded as a kind of antithesis to Napoleon, a "Christian Conqueror"; even the *Monthly Magazine*, sympathetic to Napoleon during his reign, was charmed by Alexander's earnest attentiveness.[11] Meanwhile, as Louis settled into his throne and into what he controversially declared to be the nineteenth year of his reign, Napoleon accustomed himself to the smaller empire of Elba, over which the Allies, at Alexander's urging, had granted him sovereignty. Elba was an island of a mere 140 square miles—an empire whose new ruler, moreover, was forbidden the company of his own wife and son, who, representing the vitality and future of the dynasty, had been taken to Vienna.

Some thought exile too good for Napoleon. Dorothy Wordsworth felt

NAPOLEON BONAPARTE.

CHEF DE BRIGANDS;

at his Post of Honor.

9. Frontispiece to Lewis Goldsmith, *Buonaparte, an Outlaw!!! An Appeal to the Germans, on the Necessity of Outlawing Buonaparte,* 1813 (Yale University Library)

he should either have been "fought . . . to the Death," or, if he surrendered himself as a prisoner, "tried for the murders of the Duc d'Enghien, of Pichegru, of Captain Wright—of Palm." The income that the Allies had granted him was a particular "folly," for he would "convert it into power."[12] Walter Savage Landor, in a pseudonymous pamphlet, recommended death or life imprisonment for Napoleon. As to whether "this military Marat" should be assassinated by a royalist or executed by a

Jacobin, Landor pronounced himself "indifferent." The killer need not get tied up in legal niceties. By placing himself "beyond the laws," Bonaparte had been "outlawed by his own subscription."[13]

Lewis Goldsmith, familiar with the political risks of advocating assassination, had insisted in early 1814, months before the abdication, that he did not "recommend the private murder of NAPOLEON," but rather hoped Bonaparte would be brought before a "Grand European Tribunal." Goldsmith's proposal, in support of which he cited his favorite jurist Emeric de Vattel, presaged the international courts of a later day. Every state would send two persons "skilled in the law of nations, in history, and diplomacy, to assist as Judges" to the tribunal, which would show Napoleon's principles to be those of "a disturber of the public peace and tranquility of the world." Napoleon's "accomplices" would be sure to testify against him, if they knew their lives depended on it. Goldsmith generously offered himself as a witness as well, reminding his readers of his special knowledge of Napoleon; all he required in exchange for his valuable testimony would be safe conduct during the tribunal. The obvious conclusion of Napoleon's trial would be the Corsican's death: Goldsmith compared him to a "robber and murderer," who would end up "executed on a gibbet." It does not seem to have occurred to Goldsmith that one of his scheme's merits—that it would "establish a precedent for the punishment of wicked Sovereigns"—was likely to dissuade Europe's dynasts from following his advice, not persuade them.[14]

In the spring of 1814, Goldsmith continued to weave back and forth— protesting and finger-pointing all the way—between advocacy of assassination and denial of this advocacy. In late March he recommended giving "the coup de grace to the Usurper." Louis, "the legitimate Sovereign of France," should "set a price upon the Usurper's head."[15] But two weeks later, Goldsmith denied desiring Napoleon's death. Napoleon should instead be brought before a tribunal, where (Goldsmith bitingly added) he might retain as his counsel those prominent Whig advocates, "the Chevaliers ROMILLY and MACKINTOSH, and Mr. BROUGHAM."[16] Reports of Bonaparte's planned sovereignty in Elba brought Goldsmith's anger flaring back to the surface the following week ("why, in the name of Heaven, suffer such a wretch to quit the political stage with such pomp?"). Still, he denied wanting Napoleon to be killed—only "whipped every day and exposed to public view."[17] May found Goldsmith once again denying he had ever wished "to organise a plan of assassination," though he admitted that assassination might have *resulted* from his plan of distributing anti-Napoleonic literature.[18] And by late July, he was again voicing his regret that Bonaparte had not "expiated his crimes on a gibbet."[19]

The spring of 1814 gave birth to the charge (one that would be expressed after Waterloo as well) that Napoleon should not have allowed himself to survive his fall from power, that the only reasonable conclusion to his career as French emperor was death on the battlefield or by his own hand. Goldsmith berated him for "not even hav[ing] the courage to die like NERO." A religious man, Goldsmith allowed, might have reasonably refrained from suicide—but since Bonaparte was "a complete Atheist," his "abject behaviour" could signify nothing other than cowardice.[20] The caricaturist George Cruikshank engraved "Little Boney" declining the offer of a pistol and thus demonstrating he had not "one spark of courage left."[21] The Tory *Quarterly Review* contrasted Napoleon's behavior with that of an English "Usurper," Richard III, who had at least had the good grace to be "found dead in the field of battle, with his sword in his hand, and his crown on his head."[22]

The charge of pusillanimity was most vehemently presented by Byron, whose anger at Napoleon's shrinking from death stood in direct proportion to an earlier admiration.[23] Surely if Bonaparte was to "abdicat[e] the throne of the world," he could at least have done so at "the height of his sway, red with the slaughter of his foes."[24] Bonaparte's "crouching catastrophe" demonstrated "the utter wreck of a mind which I thought superior even to Fortune."[25] Byron vented his spleen in an anonymously published *Ode to Napoleon Buonaparte*, which went through ten editions in a matter of months.[26] Napoleon had chosen to "live a slave" rather than "die a prince," the poem declared. The world had "spilt her blood" for one who now "hoard[ed] his own."[27] In response to Byron's *Ode*, the opposition monthly the *Scourge* offered the objection that Goldsmith had sought to preclude: "in a Christian country," surely the poet should have "reprobated the act of suicide," rather than "taunt[ing] Napoleon with not committing it."[28] But the charge would have remarkable staying power. Serving as emperor of a token island seemed an unlikely and ignoble end to a career like Napoleon's. Many shared Byron's perception that "the man of thousand thrones" now seemed "a nameless thing / So abject—yet alive!"[29]

Perhaps the most remarkable fact about British political opinion in the spring of 1814 was the opposition's readiness to accept a Bourbon restoration. One cannot appreciate the full significance of the left's Napoleonic sympathies a year later, during the Hundred Days and after Waterloo, without recognizing, through comparison with this earlier moment, that the later sentiment was not automatic or preordained. William Cobbett was one of the opposition journalists least willing to embrace the returning Bourbons, but even he maintained that Napoleon's fall from power was "in a great measure" deserved. Cobbett attributed Napoleon's loss of popularity, and consequent defeat, "to the alliance he formed with royalty, to his contemptible vanity, to his hankering after hereditary fame, and to his sacrificing many of the political rights of his people to his cursed ambition, and his inordinate desire to aggrandise his own family."[30] Only by watering down his original democratic principles, and becoming no better than Europe's other hereditary dynasts, had Napoleon lost his power.

Cobbett did celebrate the peace made possible by Napoleon's abdication. Men like Cobbett had thought peace was possible with Napoleon, and "were called Jacobins for that opinion." Peace had now come, if a peace without Bonaparte, and would force those who had let the nation be "blind-folded" for a generation to come clean. No longer could the "scare-crow"—"the political and military Devil" of Napoleon—be used to distract the British people. "The *bugbear* is gone: The *hobgoblin* is destroyed: Reason will now resume her sway."[31] Soon, however, he feared the worst. For Napoleon, Cobbett intimated a swift and suspicious end ("We shall hear, I dare say, that he has *put an end to his existence*; and then there is an end of him and his dynassty [*sic*] for ever"). But peace itself might be served a similar deathblow. Like the almanac-writer Henry Andrews, Cobbett worried that too many Britons had benefited from the war, and would now find their livelihoods in danger. Not only the contractors who had woven the spider's web of Old Corruption, but also the biscuit-makers, the dock workers, the army tailors, the army surgeons—and their relations—might have an economic interest in war's renewal. It was no surprise to Cobbett when *The Times* responded to Bonaparte's defeat with a declaration of "NO PEACE WITH JAMES MADISON." Something like eternal war seemed necessary for a society subsisting on the spoils of battle.[32]

One of Cobbett's correspondents made the best of the abdication itself by claiming it as an act that, demonstrating as it did the emperor's subservience to the "*people's wishes*," should be studied by Europe's other monarchs, and by their subjects. "Russians, Prussians, Austrians, and

Germans of every denomination will ask, have the people then such rights? Have the people such powers?—Reflexion follows." By bringing about "this abdicating lesson," the Allies had, inadvertently, "given the death blow to despotism all over civilized Europe." The writer exempted Britain's own king from this sentence. George "(God bless him) can do no wrong"—which was to say he was a powerless constitutional figure, not to mention a man whose lingering ability to do wrong had now been assigned to his son the Regent. The prescription for Britain was parliamentary reform, which could no longer be held at bay by "the flimsy excuse, *that this is not the time, for we are at war.*" Cobbett echoed his correspondent's diagnosis.[33]

Cobbett's critique from the left did not leave much room for welcoming the returning dynasty. But other opposition journalists, in framing their accounts of Napoleon's fall, suggested that Louis XVIII might indeed make an acceptable and constitutional monarch. The *Edinburgh Review*'s Francis Jeffrey pronounced his delight at the prospect of peace, at the fall of the "Tyrant," and at "the liberation of so many oppressed nations." His 1814 farewell to Bonaparte was ambivalent. "History" would "not class [Napoleon] quite so low as the English newspapers of the present day," Jeffrey suggested. The fall of this admittedly "very hateful individual" served as a warning against conquest, against ambition, and against schemes of universal dominion—but if these lessons were properly learned from Bonaparte's example, then "we should almost be tempted to say that the miseries he has inflicted are atoned for; and that his life, on the whole, will have been useful to mankind." Though expressing satisfaction at the Allies' not having recognized the Bourbons "till they were invited to return by the spontaneous voice of their own nation," the *Edinburgh* characterized the Bourbon restoration as "an act, not merely of wisdom, but of necessity."[34] Things had come full circle: a Bourbon restoration seemed "the natural and only certain *end* of that series of revolutionary movements, and that long and disastrous experiment which has so awfully overshadowed the freedom and happiness of the world. It naturally figures as the final completion of a cycle of convulsions and miseries." But the *Edinburgh* attached a warning to its blessing. The French nation displayed "no great love or spontaneous zeal for the Bourbons." Louis would have to be a limited monarch; the arbitrary rule of his predecessors had led to the family's expulsion.[35] As for Louis' new constitution, Jeffrey expressed only partial optimism. It resembled Bonaparte's constitution—and that had turned out "to be no obstacle at all to the practical exercise and systematic establishment of the most atrocious despotism that Europe has ever witnessed." Even a well-designed constitution could only flourish in the proper circumstances, and circumstances were not favorable in France. The French "character and habits," the people's "vivacity" and "raised imagination," made them impatient, "too ambitious of perfection—too studious of effect, to be satisfied with the attainable excellence or vulgar comforts of an English constitution."[36]

A surprisingly warm welcome was offered the new Bourbon regime by one of Lewis Goldsmith's *bêtes noires*, the radical, anti-war *Statesman* newspaper—a journal Goldsmith had alleged to subsist on the largesse of Napoleon's government. The paper was edited by Daniel Lovell from the confines of Newgate prison, to which he had been consigned for libel in 1811.[37] The *Statesman* has received little attention from historians,[38] but the radical daily was an important voice on the British left in the 1810s. The subscription list for relieving Lovell's debts, after his final release from Newgate in 1815, reads like a roster of prominent British radicals: Samuel Whitbread (who before Lovell's release had described the editor as "perhaps, the most oppressed man in the kingdom"),[39] the duke of Bedford, Sir Francis Burdett, Earl Grey, Major John Cartwright, Lord Holland, and the marquis of Tavistock all contributed to the cause, as did Napoleon's early biographer William Burdon.[40] In addition, the paper had a less elevated set of readers. "Fifty-two Friends to Freedom, at the Green Man, Preston" banded together to give two pounds to Lovell's fund; the denizens of a Nottingham pub raised three pounds, and those of a Dartford establishment raised close to four. The compositors of the *Liverpool Mercury* gave one pound, ten shillings.[41] Lovell's paper, in short, seems to have enjoyed a wide and socially diverse readership. Lovell was a prominent enough figure to be thanked (with Cobbett) in public resolutions at more than one reform meeting in 1818.[42] The *Statesman*'s essays not only tell us about the political theory of the radical leadership, but also open a window onto popular radicalism.

The *Statesman* would, as a later chapter shows, be a key forum of pro-Napoleonic sentiment in the Hundred Days and after. Its initially sympathetic reading of the Bourbon restoration, then, is especially significant. The paper claimed to find in the restoration not a "Counter-revolution" (as some claimed) but instead the victory of revolutionary

principles.[43] The new constitution was "in its fundamental principles
... the same as the first of 1791." It resembled the English constitution,
the newspaper declared; in fact, it was superior, granting salaries to sen-
ators, limiting the life of the legislature to five years (not seven), guaranteeing freedom of worship and preserving the "Code NAPOLEON ...
with only a change of name!!"[44] One correspondent captured the paper's
mood perfectly: liberty had been "secured under this revived Monarchy,
with the one unimportant head, the harmless expletive, the Idol without
homage, the gross expence of which is winked at for the occasion." A
figurehead Bourbon king, and indeed his descendants, could be tolerated
("however little ability" they displayed) because the new regime actually amounted to "the final establishment of republicanism!"[45] Of all
people, according to the *Statesman*, it was the friends of "rational
freedom" who should celebrate the Bourbon triumph.[46] Napoleon had
only his own "obstinacy" to blame for his fall from power; the Allies
had given him an opportunity to negotiate peace.[47] The *Statesman*,
moreover, now realized that Bonaparte had indeed "been a very atrocious tyrant" (a conclusion it declared could not have been reached
earlier, because the "rancour, and prejudice, and servility" of ministerial
journalists had disqualified the anti-Napoleonic press as a source).[48]

The *Statesman*'s readiness to renounce Napoleon and put a good face
on the restoration must have stemmed partly from the simple desire for
peace. Some might cynically add that pronouncing admiration for
Napoleon now, with almost the entire British nation wallowing in
victory, called for a greater degree of courage or foolhardiness than even
Lovell possessed, after years of Newgate incarceration. Yet Lovell was
not alone on the left in his initial optimism regarding the Bourbon
restoration of 1814—or in his rapid subsequent disenchantment. The
Monthly Magazine welcomed the restoration in its May issue: the new
regime would be a liberal one, it trusted, since the Bourbon family,
marked by "mild virtues and passive character," were to rule "as constitutional monarchs." The magazine especially approved of the apparent fact that Napoleon and his followers were not to be "insulted or
proscribed" by the new regime."[49] By the following month, the *Monthly*
was already expressing its concern that "intriguers" surrounding Louis
(and also the "incendiary" writers of "certain unprincipled London
papers") might steer the restored king away from the liberal settlement
he had promised.[50] By July, the *Monthly* felt that France's constitution
had been "injudiciously subverted"; constitutional language now pro-

vided a mere façade, the journal declared, behind which "unlimited and arbitrary power" might scheme.[51] No kind words remained for the Bourbons by the *Monthly*'s August issue, which lambasted Bourbon press censorship. In Napoleon's day, French papers had been rich in discussion of literature and science, according to the magazine; now they were full of little more than "apolog[ies] for shackling the press" and "sneer[s] at civil liberty."[52]

The guarded optimism expressed a few months before had evaporated. The British left's initial goodwill towards the Bourbons had dried up, and nostalgia for Bonaparte had begun seeping in. The stage was set for a new British attitude to Napoleon—should circumstances somehow return him to the world stage.

Napoleon's place in the British political and historical imagination might have been very different had he remained on Elba, occupant of the island's "mimic throne."[53] An emperor still in name, but merely nominal, Napoleon's fate seemed risible rather than noble, his circumstances more cozy than unpleasant. Elban exile was a fate Napoleon had negotiated for himself, not one unilaterally imposed upon him: as Goldsmith acutely noted, it was "a condition far more humiliating than if he had been shut up in a dungeon; as in that case it might be attributed to the superior force of his enemies, whereas now he submits to the degradation of accepting the Sovereignty of this little insignificant island."[54] Napoleon's tiny new empire fitted him like a pair of trousers several sizes too small—a costume more likely to provoke a smile than to command respect or arouse sympathy. One contemporary caricature showed Bonaparte "seated on a lump of rock smaller than himself, in the midst of the sea, apparently in most melancholy mood."[55] The "great disproportion between the size of the place and of its inhabitant"—the way "his arms . . . hang over its narrow boundaries"—led the journalist John Scott, editor of the moderate weekly the *Champion*, to think the print had "a very touching character."[56] Scott's sympathy for the confined isolate presaged reactions to the St. Helena exile. But we can safely assume that many of Scott's contemporaries read the engraving in a less respectful spirit.

This is not to say that Napoleon had no British admirers during the period of his Elban reign. But while his absence from France could be regretted by disappointed observers of the Bourbon restoration, his current state was hardly one to inspire the poet or enrage the

THE SORROWS OF BONEY,
or
Meditations in the Island of ELBA!!!

CONTINENT OF
EUROPE

ELBA

10. "The Sorrows of Boney, or Meditations in the Island of Elba!!!," 1814
(Houghton Library, Harvard University)

humanitarian. The *Edinburgh Review*, as if reviewing a novel, had, in the spring of 1814, remarked on the "unsuitable" nature of Napoleon's "catastrophe." There seemed to be a disparity between the hero's colossal deeds and his pedestrian denouement: the end of his career seemed "incongruous with the part he has hitherto sustained."[57] Few such objections would be aired in the wake of Waterloo: though some loyalists would still seek to portray Napoleon as a coward for refraining from suicide, the immediately mythologized defeat in Flanders appeared an appropriately grand conclusion. The second time around, Napoleon scripted a more acceptable end to his story.

One can imagine a counter-historical scenario in which Napoleon might have become a focus for liberal British sympathies even without a daring escape from Elba, a brave march through France, and a quasi-republican Hundred Days: rather than escaping he might have been *removed* from Elba. Napoleon's tenure on the island was far from secure; it was not clear, in early spring 1815, that he would be suffered to remain there. During and after the Hundred Days, Napoleon's British defenders would frequently cite the rumor that the Allied powers had, at the time of Bonaparte's escape, been on the verge of forcibly transferring him to a more secure exile on St. Helena.[58] This, to the minds of many, absolved Napoleon of his pledge to remain on Elba: he had to break the Treaty of Fontainebleau by a pre-emptive escape lest the Allies break the treaty by a coercive removal. To understand the ways in which British opinion changed after Elba, we may usefully think about a hypothetical world in which Napoleon did not enjoy a second period of power. Had the supposed Allied plot succeeded—or had a British ship caught the emperor before he reached French soil, and whisked him away to more secure custody—there would have been a St. Helena without a Hundred Days, an onerous imprisonment without an electrifying popular embrace or a character-renovating second reign. Bonaparte would very likely have found British sympathizers in his adversity, men and women ready to console the fallen hero and excoriate the Allies' treatment of their prisoner—but without the Hundred Days, fewer Britons would have defended Napoleon as a leader (as opposed to a victim). The apparent rapture with which the French people greeted the returned exile in the spring of 1815, and the manner in which Bonaparte managed to suggest that his new regime would avoid the excesses of its earlier incarnation, prompted many British observers to reconsider his political nature. The Hundred Days encouraged republicans and liberals alike to voice their support for a man from whom they no longer anticipated tyranny. He had, to their satisfaction, largely cleansed himself of the stain of imperial ambition.

No British ship caught Bonaparte as his ship left Elba; Colonel Neil Campbell, the commissioner stationed there to keep an eye on him, was in Italy consulting an oculist. Some wondered why stricter precautions had not been taken to keep the emperor on his island. Well before the escape, the *Quarterly* had expressed concern that Napoleon should reign on an island so centrally located, an island situated "in the focus of all Buonaparte's crimes," surrounded by "the scenes of his usurpations" and offering "a center of unrestricted communication" among them.[59] After Napoleon's landing, a rumor circulated in France that Britain had deliberately released Napoleon, wishing to unleash the dogs of civil war on Albion's eternal enemy.[60] Sir James Mackintosh, in the *Edinburgh Review*, dismissed the "absurd" rumor but understood its prevalence, given "the criminal supineness" of the British ministry (combined, paradoxically, with its "almost frantic security"—its desire to move Napoleon off Elba to a more secure location, word of which was enough to have induced him to leave). Mackintosh complained that if one had set out to find a residence "most dangerous to France, all sagacious searchers must have pointed to Elba."[61] Walter Savage Landor expostulated that Elba had been "a rat-trap open at both ends."[62] Leigh Hunt complained about the island's central location: "Had the Sovereigns been studying Mr. BENTHAM's Panopticon, they could not have contrived their old enemy a more snug and ingenious situation for inspecting all that was going on about him."[63] One anonymous pamphleteer felt the escape smacked of something beyond mere incompetence. Why, he asked, had not Napoleon been guarded in a fashion appropriate to "the first man of the age," rather than as one might watch over "an irregular subaltern"? The writer insinuated that the escape had something to do with the fact that the foreign secretary, Viscount Castlereagh—that "crooked, cunning, compromising politician"—had consorted at the Vienna negotiations with the equally wily Metternich.[64]

The shock of Napoleon's escape was soon overwhelmed by the spectacle of his welcome. Landing in Provence on 1 March, with a retinue scarcely more than a thousand in number, the emperor of Elba marched north. Troops were sent to stop him, but rather than fire on their former general they rallied to his side. The ranks of his army ever swelling, Napoleon proceeded toward the capital at a remarkable pace. No blood was shed. By the time he reached Paris, less than three weeks after touching French soil, it was clear the Bonapartist tide would not be stemmed by internal forces. Louis fled to Ghent, hoping to convince foreign powers that Bonaparte must again be removed.

Both friends and foes of Napoleon used superlatives to describe his "Phoenix-like" rise from political death, and treated his triumphant return as an event unique in history.[65] As Napoleon marched toward Paris, Wordsworth, fearing the worst, wrote that Bonaparte's reinstatement as emperor would be "the most disheartening event, and the most discreditable to human Nature, that History has yet had to record."[66] John Scott, editor of the *Champion* weekly, fumed that Bonaparte's return to power would make the French people "detestable" until "the latest ages of future time."[67] Other observers, if more friendly to

Napoleon, were equally sure about the momentous and unprecedented character of his escape.[68] Thomas Babington Macaulay, fourteen years old, found his moral reservations about Napoleon shattered by the enormous daring of his effort to reclaim power. "All my detestation of his crimes, all my horror at his conduct," he wrote to his mother, "is completely swallowed up in astonishment, awe, and admiration, at the more than human boldness of his present attempt."[69] And Byron announced that he "forg[a]ve the rogue for utterly falsifying every line of mine Ode—which I take to be the last and uttermost stretch of human magnanimity." The poet declared himself "dazzled and overwhelmed," and entirely "reconciled" to the hero whose pusillanimity he had previously denounced.[70] Millenarians assigned even greater significance to the news. Faber saw Napoleon's return as reinforcing his identification of "the revolutionary government" as Antichrist (the earlier exile had seemed to disprove the theory).[71] And "the best informed and leading" Methodists, according to one concerned observer, were "electrified" by Napoleon's reappearance because it "fulfil[led] their predictions."[72] Many, in short, would have understood William Cobbett's declaration, soon after receiving word of Napoleon's arrival in Paris: "feel as we will; say what we will, this is the grandest, the most magnificent spectacle, that ever presented itself for the contemplation of the human mind."[73]

The astonishment of the moment may partly account for the excitement with which formerly muted or unspoken opinions burst into the open, and for the sudden shifts in attitude that occurred at both ends of the political spectrum. On the right, Lewis Goldsmith, who from the "very commencement" of his newspaper had "constantly maintained" the necessity of placing the Bourbon family back on the throne of France, now announced he had no particular brief to argue for the dynasty. It had never been his intention, he now claimed, "to *force* any sovereign upon France."[74] A later generation, familiar with the mechanics of the bicycle, might have recognized the sound of Goldsmith furiously back-pedaling: though he did not acknowledge Napoleon's popularity (attributing his return to power solely to the approval of the military), Goldsmith now gave up his claim that the Bourbons were much loved.[75] Their behavior since Louis' restoration, Goldsmith wrote, had undermined their case. It was "one thing to put down Buonaparte, and another, quite distinct, to set up the Bourbons," Goldsmith declared. British self-defense demanded the former—"but as to the other, that is the affair of France and Frenchmen, not ours."[76]

On the left, William Burdon, in a series of long letters to the *Statesman*, jettisoned his long-standing antipathy to Napoleon and returned to his earlier advocacy: he saluted Bonaparte as potentially "the greatest man the world ever saw."[77] The former magistrate Capel Lofft, a long-time correspondent to the *Monthly Magazine* on astronomy and other non-political matters (so prolific a contributor that by 1807 he had his own entry in the magazine's index), now became, of a sudden, one of the most outspoken and enthusiastic advocates Bonaparte had ever found in Britain.[78] Sixty-three years old when Napoleon escaped from Elba, Lofft had as a younger man written tracts in support of parliamentary reform, prison reform, and religious toleration; he had helped found the Society for Constitutional Information and had been an early critic of Burke's *Reflections on the French Revolution*. His handwriting was practically indecipherable; it seems remarkable that editors ever bothered to read his letters, let alone publish them with such great frequency.[79] Yet the *Statesman* and the *Morning Chronicle* would overflow, in the spring and summer of 1815, with letters from Lofft (more than twenty in the *Statesman* alone). In May's *Monthly*, at the bottom of a letter concerned with gleaning-rights and Hebrew translation, Lofft gave a foretaste of his thoughts. He hailed the "most sublime and bloodless of revolutions" that France had just witnessed. Napoleon had shown he possessed "a calm and a great mind, above all passion and revenge."[80]

The radical press now took up Napoleon's banner more openly—no longer simply opposing war, but actually rallying in support of Napoleon's rule. Radical writers directed some of their effort to arguing the strict legality of Napoleon's actions. Cobbett and others, in response to the loyalist charge that Bonaparte was a "traitor" or "rebel," pointed out that the Treaty of Fontainebleau had given Napoleon full sovereignty over Elba. He was not, therefore, a subject of Louis, but an independent sovereign, and as such entitled to invade France because the Allies had withheld his promised income and the Italian duchies that should have been handed over to his wife and son.[81] But radicals did not limit themselves to arguing on the basis of legal technicality. Many unapologetically described the new regime as democratic and liberal, and Napoleon as a man reborn, a very phoenix indeed.

For many, the ease with which Napoleon advanced through France seemed sufficient proof of his popular support. Cobbett declared that if Napoleon were "not now fairly *chosen* by the people of France, never was man fairly chosen in this world."[82] (That Napoleon had "STAKED HIS LIFE" on the success of this enterprise also served, according to Cobbett, to discredit imputations of his cowardice.)[83] The political theorist William Godwin, like Cobbett, reached for a historical superlative: "Never did a sovereign ascend the throne of any nation under such astonishing evidences of general favour, as Bonaparte has just now ascended the throne of France."[84] For the *Statesman*, the popular welcome of Napoleon in Paris showed him to have been "chosen by the unanimous voice of the Empire he governs."[85] In short, wrote Capel Lofft, Bonaparte's return to power was the "unquestionable act of a whole nation."[86] From which it followed that it was meaningless to distinguish, as some loyalists wished, between a war against Napoleon and a war against France.

Napoleon, crafting the public face of his new regime, sought to present a more liberal, republican front. He announced the abolition of the slave trade. He called in Benjamin Constant, his long-time liberal critic (whom he had removed from the Tribunat over a decade earlier), to produce an *Acte additionel* to the constitution, offering a mild extension of political representation and guaranteeing trial by jury and freedom of expression. The loyalist *Courier* dismissed the new constitution as "a mere manœuvre and trick," not likely to convince the French—but British radicals acclaimed Napoleon's reforms.[87] His abolition of slavery would "consecrate" his regime "to latest posterity, as deserving of the thanks of the human race," the *Statesman* declared.[88] William Burdon, studying the *Acte*, concluded that the overwhelming majority of Britons would, if given an "honest vote," reject a war based on nothing more than the French nation's having chosen "to have a better Constitution" than that of Britain. Constant's *Acte* did have the "radical defect" of not being truly republican, Burdon wrote—but then again, the French were "not fit for a Republic" anyway.[89] Cobbett, who had traced Napoleon's fall to his imperial ambitions, endorsed the new regime, which he termed "essentially Republican." Like Burdon, Cobbett attributed any shortcomings not to the leader but to the nation he ruled over: the new government came "as near to the standard of liberty as the character and genius of the French people, and the state of Society in France will permit."[90]

Many on the British left, then, believed Napoleon had indeed reformed himself, had cast off the sins of imperial ambition and tyranny, and won "a victory over himself."[91] Bonaparte had managed to efface his past actions, the *Statesman* declared, and ought to be judged anew, by his "future conduct" alone.[92] The emperor had "profited by his short period of adversity more than the BOURBONS by their twenty years of exile and calamity," wrote Burdon.[93] Save the French themselves, "no nation has a right to try him for his past misconduct," the born-again Bonapartist continued. "He is now a new man."[94] The original principles of the revolution had come to the fore once again, Burdon claimed. One could discern in Napoleon's new regime "the commencement of a new era, or rather . . . the completion of that which was begun twenty-five years ago; for the French Revolution has now nearly returned to the point from whence it set out."[95]

When the news of Napoleon's landing reached the diplomats assembled at Vienna, they quickly issued a declaration stating that Bonaparte had "placed himself without the pale of civil and social relations." He had forfeited "the protection of the law"—had destroyed "the only legal title on which his existence depended"—and thus had "rendered himself liable to public vengeance." The French would rally round their "legitimate sovereign," the Allies hoped, and "annihilate this last attempt of a criminal and impotent delirium"; if not, the sovereigns of Europe would come to the aid of Louis.[96]

By singling out Napoleon, as opposed to the French people, as the Allies' target, the declaration appeared to call for Napoleon's murder, and thus stirred up again the debate over assassination. One *Statesman* contributor saw the declaration as the fruit of Lewis Goldsmith's earlier proposal.[97] Whitbread decried the declaration's "designat[ing] an individual for assassination."[98] William Godwin, the eminent radical philosopher, was equally outraged. Using the pen-name "Verax," he wrote to the opposition *Morning Chronicle*, hoping to dissuade Parliament from a new war. Commanding the French to reject Napoleon could only be counter-productive, Godwin wrote, rendering the returned leader "infinitely more dear to the people of France, than he ever could be before." It was ludicrous—a thing of "perfidious irony"—to command an entire population to abjure its *de facto* leader and thus commit treason. France being a fiction ("an artificial individual, the creature of the reasoning faculty merely"), the command was actually directed at "thirty millions of souls, scattered over a wide extent of territory, acquainted only in small knots and circles with each other's faces, and still less acquainted with each other's judgments and inmost desires." But even beyond the impracticality of the Allied demands, the sovereigns' peremptory refusal to suffer Bonaparte as leader defied "a first principle in the law of nations, that no state or confederacy of states has a right to interfere in the internal government of another state."[99]

Godwin worried that the new war against Napoleon would be particularly brutal; its conclusion would be nothing like that which had ushered in the Bourbon restoration a year before.[100] The Allies had already given a hint of their bloodthirstiness—a signal that they had "repented of their humanity"—by pronouncing that Napoleon had forfeited "his legal title to existence." But the bloodshed would not stop with Bonaparte. France itself would be "annihilated," Godwin declared; Europe would witness "the entire destruction as a nation, of one of the most eminent nations on the face of the whole earth." By this he did not quite mean the extermination of France's population (though he certainly anticipated suffering on a massive scale); more that France would be weakened so much as to "never hereafter be a member of the commonwealth of Europe," and that the war, unlike any previous one, would be mercilessly continued until the enemy's government "shall cease to exist."[101] Others joined Godwin in forecasting "a war of extermination" (Samuel Whitbread's phrase).[102] The opposition magazine the *Scourge* took *The Times* to task for exhibiting "a singular and disgusting propensity to the slaughter of the human race": the endless epithets that the loyalist newspaper applied to Napoleon ("monster, miscreant, arch-fiend, rebel, traitor, conspirator, scum of the earth, ragamuffin, and robber") would inflame British passions, the journal warned, and help bring about "the extermination of six hundred thousand human beings" in France.[103]

This was a harsh charge, but the words used by pro-war advocates could indeed be brutally final. A year earlier, Goldsmith had repeatedly warned that it would not suffice to remove Napoleon from power; rather, "every germ of the French Revolution" must be "destroyed" or "annihilated."[104] The revolution, according to Goldsmith's chillingly modern metaphor, was an "epidemic disorder": "to perfect a cure it must be entirely rooted out from the political system," lest it "break out afresh."[105] Now, a year later, the inveterate pamphleteer the Reverend Edward Hankin used similarly wide-wasting language to criticize the claim that war would be waged not against France but against Napoleon.[106] While Hankin felt Napoleon should have been killed in 1814 rather than sent to Elba, he knew that deposing Bonaparte now would not remove the root danger France posed to Europe. The military system was too solidly entrenched in French life.[107] The French population had become "a military horde," "a more tremendous monster" than Napoleon himself: were Bonaparte to fall, the military would simply replace him with another general. The situation called for more than the mere removal of a leader. The bulk of the French army would have to "be exterminated," Hankin wrote, "or be removed to distant regions"—possibly Russia, or some uninhabited Pacific isles "where necessity calling forth their industry and talents, and compelling them to abandon their predatory habits, they may, in a course of years, make to society some amends for the atrocities which they have committed." Along with having to submit to this enforced mass exodus (or, if necessary, this "utter extermination of the military horde"), France would be compelled to "submit, for many years, to pay for the support of a foreign army within her own territory"—the only means by which the remaining French population might "assume the habits of social life."[108]

Hankin was one of many who looked back on the years of revolution and empire and concluded that the French national character had been transformed. Writing early in the Hundred Days, an anonymous British pamphleteer had traced the weakness of the restored Bourbons to the fact that the returned emigrants could no longer "speak the language or wishes of the people," a people whose character had "wholly changed."[109] And the minister John Chetwode Eustace, visiting Paris during the first restoration, had claimed that revolution and war had "gradually *dis*civilize[d] the nation": another generation of revolutionary rule would have seen France "inhabited by monsters, and Europe . . . compelled to wage against it a war of extermination."[110]

Hankin was unusual, at this juncture, in calling explicitly for a war against the nation rather than the individual. The ministry tried to emphasize that it only objected to Napoleon, and that any government not Bonapartist would be acceptable. The opposition raised a collective eyebrow at this avowal. George Tierney protested in the Commons that it was "unprecedented in the history of the world, to commence a war for the mere purpose of getting rid of one man."[111] Godwin pointed out the absurdity of claiming to allow the French to choose any leader other than "the man of their choice."[112] Few believed the Allies would actually stomach any regime besides a Bourbon one. The effective choice, it seemed—the ministry's protests notwithstanding—must be between Napoleon and Louis.

Just as revealing as Burdon's or Lofft's sudden bursts of enthusiasm for Napoleon—or as Goldsmith's abrupt backtracking on the subject of the Bourbons—was the hesitation felt by the moderate journalist John Scott. Scott had spent the spring of 1814 dithering over which was less desirable, the continued rule of "the remorseless, restless, and false soldier" Bonaparte, "firmly seated in his despotic authority," or the imposition of the Bourbons against the will of the French people ("the whole moral of the French Revolution effaced").[113] Now, in the Hundred Days, Scott had to face again the troublesome choice between Bourbon and Bonaparte. Which evil was the lesser?

Scott claimed to pride himself on offending both ministerial and radical tendencies.[114] He recognized the failings, and indeed the instability, of the system that opposed itself to Bonaparte ("the system of the Allied Princes"). The peculiarity of his argument lay in his citing precisely these defects as reasons for preferring a Bourbon to a Napoleonic restoration. The system opposed to Napoleon taught the public a useful lesson through its vices: it demonstrated "the connection between profligacy of conduct and imbecility of mind,—which is one of the most salutary exposures that can be made." By "withhold[ing] what is desirable," hereditary monarchy spurred observers to value and seek proper goals. Napoleon's regime, by contrast, devalued useful principles in a fashion that cheapened them. In opposition to those who forgave Napoleon his faults because of his apparent regard for intellect, merit, and talent, Scott condemned the ruler because his association with such virtues corrupted them. "Angels have been by him converted into devils,—that is to say, he has extracted all their excellence and beauty from high pursuits and great achievements, and while he has seemed to promote and encourage them, has been perverting their very natures."[115] In short, Bonaparte coopted intellect, while monarchical government "provoke[d] the opposition of intellect." Consequently, Napoleon's system stifled change, while the Bourbons would inadvertently encourage it. Napoleon's despotic system, in part because of the strength it drained from real virtues, would outlast any traditional despotism, according to Scott. The old chains were less burdensome than the "new and heavy fetters forged by Buonaparte" precisely because "we were day by day disencumbering ourselves" of them. The "abuses" of the old system were unlikely to survive for long, Scott maintained, "but if this new tyranny can establish itself, its effects will be extensive and lasting."[116] It was the very modernity of Napoleon's system, its appropriateness to the times, that made it so dangerous. Bourbon rule was less harmful, precisely because it was anachronistic.

Scott scoffed at Napoleon's claim to have freed the press (predicting that "the first person that uses its freedom, so as to offend the restorer of liberty and destroyer of bondage, will be shot in a ditch at midnight").[117] Nor did Scott credit the sincerity of Napoleon's sudden conversion to the slave trade's abolition.[118] He read Napoleon's employing Benjamin Constant as an act of desperation, not liberalism.[119] Scott likened Napoleon's praise of liberty and peace to his earlier embrace of Islam—both were temporary and insincere.[120]

Napoleon's pernicious nature, however, was not sufficient in Scott's view to justify Britain's return to war. Indeed, if Britain's governors declared war simply because of the French people's choice of leader, then the present ministry "ought to be opposed as enemies to their country and to the principles of justice." If Napoleon reverted to his aggressive ways, as Scott seemed to think likely, then "a strenuous and immediate resistance" was in order—but not until then.[121] So Scott argued at the beginning of April. In a somber essay one month later, he seemed resigned to the prospect of war, but fearful of its consequences. A war against Napoleon would be, "more directly and avowedly than any other of modern date, a war in behalf of principle." Napoleon had neither encroached on foreign soil nor given any indications of planning to do so. The French people, Scott reiterated, supported Bonaparte. Destroying the nation's government by foreign arms would present a "fatal precedent," whose consequences for the world would be worse than those that would arise from Napoleon's continued rule.[122]

Despite the doubts of journalists like Scott and Lovell, and the voices of opposition members within its own Houses, Parliament approved the renewal of war late in May. Few thought a new war could end soon; indeed, the ruinous cost of extended warfare had been cited by critics as an additional argument for negotiating with Bonaparte.[123] That such a decisive victory as Waterloo could occur within weeks—it was fought on 18 June, and news reached London by the night of the 21st—was a shock. "How this Victory pursues my imagination!" the painter Benjamin Robert Haydon, a friend of John Scott, wrote in his diary on 23 June. After reading an account of the battle "four times without stopping," and then once more right before bed, Haydon "dreamt of it & was fighting and walking all night"—only to wake "in a steam of intense feeling" and devour the gazette yet again. Seeking further insight into the momentous battle, he went out and ordered a month's sub-scription to the *Courier* and "read all the Papers till my stomach aked." Soon, Haydon claimed to know the gazette by heart. He was not alone in finding "something . . . infinitely imposing, sublime, & overwhelming in the present degraded state of France & Napoleon."[124] A whole host of poets ("All our bards, . . . great and small, and of all sexes, ages, and professions") soon offered their hyperbolic accounts of Waterloo—leaving, one must agree with the *Edinburgh*, "scarcely a line to be remembered" until Byron offered his version in the third canto of *Childe Harold*.[125]

Not all were exhilarated by reports of the battle. Henry Crabb Robinson reported that several of his acquaintances (he named William Godwin, Capel Lofft, and the radical journalist William Hazlitt) "grieve[d]" at the British victory; they anticipated it would lead to the "revival of ancient despotism in France."[126] Hazlitt was reported by Haydon to be "prostrated in mind and body" by the news, "unwashed, unshaved, hardly sober by day, and always intoxicated by night, liter-ally, without exaggeration, for weeks."[127] Waterloo inspired, almost immediately, a counter-myth, in which the Bourbon restoration was por-trayed as a triumph of oppression over the people's will, a triumph made possible only by foreign interference and the sacrifice of untold numbers. "Myriads of people," the *Statesman* proclaimed in mid-August, had been "called from their peaceful occupations to perish in the field, . . . to drag their maimed bodies through the remains of a wretched exis-tence, and call this state of being glory." All this "to place a weak old man on a throne which he cannot keep, and give the British nation the honour of spurning from its shores a man who may yet hurl the thunder-bolt of implacable vengeance against them."[128] William Burdon pre-dicted that before the "imposed" Louis could "sit quietly on his Throne, one-third of France must be murdered, another must be silenced, and the last will rejoice at the degradation of their fellow-citizens."[129] In November, George Cruikshank engraved a chained France being force-fed the Bourbons at bayonet point. The next month, he showed a Bourbon throne resting on bloody and mangled corpses—with, in the distance, a banner ironically declaring, as British ministers had so often, that the Allies would not "interfere with the internal government of France." That Louis remained in power only through force was sug-gested by the caption's statement that Louis' throne was composed of cannon, pistols, and daggers—"the best supporters of the King."[130] Many British observers, in short, felt that Louis had been "restored, not by the affection of his subjects, but by the bayonets of foreigners."[131] That Britain had been foremost among these foreigners was a point the opposition would stress in the years to come. In its more forceful version, this would become the claim that Waterloo had been a scene of "*butchery*," where "Gallia's heroes fell" and where "freedom fell by Englishmen."[132]

While the British began their argument over Waterloo, Napoleon wended his path from power to captivity. After his defeat in Flanders he rushed to Paris, but found the assembly ready to give up their emperor for a peace settlement. Told to step down or be deposed, Napoleon abdicated and proclaimed his son emperor—a wishful gesture, as the boy was in Austrian hands. The boy's grandfather Francis I might have warmed to the idea, but the duke of Wellington would have none of it—and it was he, not Francis, who, approaching the gates of Paris, was in a position to determine who would occupy the throne. Napoleon made his way to the Atlantic coast. Though he considered attempting an escape to America, the imperial fugitive dismissed the risky proposition. Instead he decided to surrender to a British ship, the *Bellerophon*, named for a hero whose ambitious effort to scale the heavens had stirred up the gods' wrath. Dictating a letter to the Prince Regent, Napoleon compared himself with Themistocles who, ostracized by Athens, had thrown himself on the mercy of his long-time enemy Persia. Napoleon submitted himself, he wrote, to the British people and the protection of their laws. He added hopefully that the Regent was not only the most powerful and most constant, but also the most generous of his enemies.

After years of threatened invasion, Bonaparte finally came within sight of England's shore at the end of July 1815. The *Bellerophon* arrived at Torbay, and soon moved on to Plymouth harbor. Men and women who for years had feared Napoleon's arrival in British waters now rushed to spot him on the ship's deck; some boarded tiny harbor boats to get a better view ("like the natives of Otaheite about Captain Cook, or so many Lilliputians about Gulliver").[133] Newspapers reported every detail of his physical appearance, observing that he was "now very corpulent."[134] The painter Charles Eastlake, a native of Plymouth, sketched Napoleon from a boat and produced a full-length portrait (whose exhibition and sale earned him enough to support himself in Italy

for years).[135] The number who took to the waters to approach
Napoleon's ship, according to one correspondent in the *Monthly
Magazine*, "progressively increased daily, until they amounted to not
less than TEN THOUSAND" swarming the harbor, "on average of ten to
a boat."[136]

The *Monthly*'s correspondent portrayed the crowd as sympathetic to
the defeated emperor. In his eagerness to demonstrate this, the correspondent was driven to contradict himself: after first claiming that the
onlookers "considered it more respectful to preserve a profound silence,
lest plaudits might be considered as an insulting approval of his situation," he then attributed the ship's eventual "remov[al] to a greater
distance" to official annoyance at the crowd's "cheerings and accla-
mations" of the fallen emperor.[137] William Cobbett celebrated the spectators' offerings of "sorrow" and "respect" as a "glorious triumph" for
Napoleon. "Of all this matchless hero's victories this is the *greatest*,"
wrote Cobbett. "It is a victory over prejudice deep-rooted; prejudice,
the work of twenty years of calumnies, and of wars that have cost
sixteen hundred millions of pounds sterling to England." It was not idle
curiosity but political esteem that drew British spectators to Plymouth
harbor, Cobbett claimed. He emphasized the crowd's respectability and
affluence, contrasting their sober demeanor with "the noisy and drunken
mob" who had so recently celebrated the continental dynasts and "Old
Blucher" in London. This was no "*rabble*," Cobbett declared; they were
ready to rent boats that cost them "from 20 to 50 guineas a day."
Napoleon's visitors "were tradesmen, farmers, gentlemen; in short, a fair
specimen of the nation, whose sentiments they so honourably expressed,
and whose character they did their best to vindicate." Were the continental dynasts to assemble on the *Bellerophon*'s deck "for a year, with
their crowns and tiaras upon their heads," Cobbett declared, "so many
of the people of England would not have been attracted to the spot."[138]

Critics of Napoleon did not, for the most part, dispute the claim that
the throng had applauded Bonaparte (though the *Quarterly Review*
insisted that the people of Plymouth, courteous to a fault, had doffed
their hats to Napoleon only because he had tricked them by "walk[ing]
about the decks of the Bellerophon bareheaded").[139] The crowd had
hailed Bonaparte, critics allowed, but this was hardly something to celebrate. The ministerial *Courier* at first sought to brush off the public
interest as "silly curiosity" (Napoleon should recognize "that any object
out of nature, a calf with five legs or with only three, would excite a

similar curiosity in this country").[140] But soon even the *Courier* had to recognize, with regret, that the spectators had cheered and removed their hats, "*apparently with the view of soothing his fallen fortunes, and treating him with respect and consideration;*—him whose whole life has been a series of exultations in the calamities of others!"[141] Dorothy Wordsworth (not herself a witness to the scene) declared that she was "sick of the adulation, the folly, the idle Curiosity which was gathered together round the ship that help the dastardly spirit that has so long been the scourge of all whom he *could* injure." The British people, by their readiness "to bend—to bow—to take off our hats to him—and call him great," revealed themselves as "dull of perception" and "insensible to the distinctions between vice and virtue."[142]

Some observers suggested that by becoming a visible presence Bonaparte might open new rifts in the British social fabric. Benjamin Haydon's sister, writing from Plymouth, described to her brother the "disgrace" of the crowd's rising to applaud the harbor's visitor. Napoleon's allure was such, she suggested, that his very presence posed a threat to public order: "His person is so prepossessing that it is dangerous to the loyalty of the people . . . to keep him here long. They all are fascinated!"[143] The same fear of Napoleon's overpowering charisma was expressed by Lady Charlotte FitzGerald, who witnessed Napoleon's transfer from the *Bellerophon* to the *Northumberland*, the ship that would carry him to St. Helena. Lady Charlotte characterized Napoleon's arrival in English waters as a turning point for British perceptions of the fallen ruler. Allowing the people to see Napoleon for themselves—"shewing John Bull that Bonaparte had neither Horns nor Hoofs"—was "the most unwise step our government ever took," she wrote. No longer did "the Common People" attach to Napoleon's name "the Epithets Monsters [*sic*], 'Rascal,' or 'Roast him alive.'" Instead, they expressed their "pity" for the "'Poor Fellow,'" and marveled at his "'Air of grandeur . . . tho' he is so dejected.'" Lady Charlotte, by contrast with the common folk, found the sight of Bonaparte a sobering one: "I went to see him admiring him [despite] all his Crimes, Compassionating him as a prisoner & one whom I thought had been harshly treated since he gave himself up to British Clemency, but I came away with my heart Considerably Steeled against him, & with many fears lest the Lion again escape from his Cage!"[144] It may have been the sight not so much of Bonaparte himself as of the applauding crowds, the rank and file paying their respects to the nation's enemy, that so alarmed FitzGerald. A year and a half later, the *British Critic* would thank the government for having resisted displaying its catch on shore. This had been "the forbearance of no ordinary minds." Had Napoleon been brought to dry land, "even as the most abject prisoner," he would inevitably have "raised a ferment in the nation." His figure would have provided "a rallying point of conspiracy and treason" for all the nation's "turbulent," "factious," and "disaffected" members. Violence, the magazine suggested, would have been unavoidable: Napoleon's disembarkation would have necessitated the sacrifice of the country's "best blood."[145]

When the *Bellerophon* withdrew from the harbor, some blamed governmental disapproval or embarrassment at the accolade accorded Bonaparte. Others suggested alternative reasons. The *Courier* claimed a French spy had been "*detected hovering around the ship, with letters addressed to Bonaparte*" (a claim that Cobbett scoffed at: why, if such a spy existed, had he not been brought to trial?).[146] The most intriguing explanation given for the ship's movement out to sea may also have had a grain of truth in it. Capel Lofft had suggested, in a letter published in the *Morning Chronicle*, that Napoleon, now within the jurisdiction of British courts, might be subject to a writ of habeas corpus.[147] Were a writ granted, the government would have to produce Napoleon in court and explain why he had been detained. The letter inspired more than a hundred letters to the *Chronicle* (which could print only a few).[148] The newspaper supported Lofft's suggestion: it would have been "an inestimable proof of the superiority of our Constitution, if it had been shewn that the moment BONAPARTE touched the sacred soil of Britain, he would have been entitled to a fair trial according to the laws of the land." Trying Napoleon would have set a precedent in the "public law of nations" (and for that very reason, the *Chronicle* suggested, the Allies were avoiding this path).[149] One *Statesman* writer doubted that such a writ would actually help the imperial captive, but felt it would at least serve to ascertain the legal rationale for his detention.[150] Perhaps this correspondent underestimated the practical and symbolic power of habeas corpus—a symbolic power that had only been reinforced by the frequent suspensions of this ancient right during the years of war. Allowing a writ to be served would have amounted to setting in motion the wheels of British justice, with a trial or the prisoner's release the only possible results. The ministry well knew how outraged libertarians would be were a writ served, and the process *then* stopped. Hence, according to the *Statesman*, the sudden retreat from harbor. The radical duke of Bedford, word had it, bore a writ of habeas corpus for Napoleon. The Admiralty "telegraphed" Lord Keith "just in time" to get Napoleon's ship sufficiently far from shore to avoid being served with the writ.[151]

In fact, it seems to have been a subpoena, not a habeas corpus writ, that drove the *Bellerophon* away from Plymouth—though Capel Lofft's letter may still have provided the inspirational spark. One Anthony Mackenrot had the right to subpoena witnesses in a trial in the Court of King's Bench. Mackenrot's desire to cross-examine Napoleon seems to have stemmed not from the internal details of the court case but from the same impulse that made him boast of owning several Napoleonic busts.[152] The subpoena made it to Plymouth on the morning of the 4th, just as the *Bellerophon* was pulling out to sea.[153] Two attempts to pull Napoleon's case into the mechanism of British justice, Lofft's and Mackenrot's, had failed (though the *Monthly Magazine* promptly pronounced Lofft a "great man" whose protests would "be read with profound interest in ages when the very names of his enemies are forgotten").[154] The struggle to establish Napoleon's rights would have to continue in his absence; the *Northumberland* was bound for St. Helena.

CHAPTER 6

Radicals, "Legitimacy," and History

"Fine word, Legitimate!" We wonder where our English politicians picked it up. Is it an echo from the tomb of the martyred monarch, Charles the First? Or was it the last word which his son, James the Second, left behind him in his flight, and bequeathed with his *abdication*, to his legitimate successors? It is not written in our annals in the years 1688, in 1715, or 1745. It was not sterling then, which was only fifteen years before his present Majesty's accession to the throne. Has it become so since?

William Hazlitt, 7 March 1818[1]

Anthony Mackenrot was not the only proud British owner of a Napoleonic bust. In 1817, wishing to lull the suspicions of the would-be insurrectionists whose ranks he had infiltrated, the government informer William Oliver placed a bronze Napoleon on his mantelpiece. By doing so, he proved himself an astute student of radical semiotics. Oliver's talismanic Bonaparte would have served as a convincing shibboleth to his "fellow" radicals.[2]

The radical upheaval of the postwar years—characterized by an efflorescence of radical journalism, and by mass meetings advocating parliamentary reform and protesting against state corruption—roughly coincided with Napoleon's exile on St. Helena. But only rarely, in existing histories, does one turn up such tantalizing details regarding Bonaparte's role in radical discourse. The figure of Napoleon has not loomed large in the historiography of British radicalism. By over-emphasizing loyalist consensus during the Napoleonic wars—portraying radicalism as in a state of near-hibernation until Waterloo—historians may have helped obscure the extent to which Bonaparte retained

British admirers during his rule.[3] But even historians of "the heroic age of popular Radicalism," as E. P. Thompson christened the four years between Waterloo and Peterloo, have rarely suggested that Napoleon was a significant feature in the postwar political imagination.[4] The first goal of this chapter is to demonstrate that Napoleon did in fact play an important role in radical argument after Waterloo.

The loyalist laureate Robert Southey was guilty of caricature when, in late 1816, he called Napoleon "the Perfect Emperor of the Ultra-Whigs and Extra-Reformers," "this Perfect Emperor of the British *Liberales*," "their *beau idéal* of a philosophical sovereign."[5] Southey was one of many who, during and after the French wars, found that damning reformers as Jacobins or Bonapartists could save one the trouble of engaging with their arguments. But while the impulse to defend late Georgian radicals against arbitrary slurs is understandable, we must recognize that a good number, both plebeian and genteel, did respect and praise Bonaparte. Many of the radicals who had previously written off Napoleon as yet another dynast had second thoughts when confronted in 1814 by the reality of the newly ascendant reactionary monarchs. Percy Shelley, in a poem summing up the "Feelings of a Republican on the Fall of Bonaparte," bemoaned the return of "old Custom, Legal Crime, / And bloody Faith, the foulest birth of time."[6] The glee with which the dynasts' champions proclaimed the victory of hereditary monarchy over "usurpation" gave pause to many reformers—who had been under the impression that Britain was fighting to restore not a monarch but French liberties. Moreover, as we have seen, Napoleon's effort during the Hundred Days to craft a more liberal regime allowed many radicals to convince themselves that whatever his earlier faults, Napoleon had now established a republican government.[7]

This chapter considers Bonaparte's place in the historical arguments that radicals marshaled between Napoleon's first abdication in 1814 and his death in 1821. A number of important recent studies have illustrated how certain moments in British history (notably the Norman Conquest, Magna Carta, and the Glorious Revolution) served as magnets for political controversy in the eighteenth and nineteenth centuries.[8] H. T. Dickinson and Kathleen Wilson have shown how the revolution of 1688–89, in particular, was continually contested in the eighteenth century, as a subject for political theory and popular politics alike.[9] The case of Napoleon spurred radicals to examine yet again the Glorious Revolution, and the Hanoverian succession that was its

sequel—dropped stitches in the supposedly seamless tapestry of hereditary legitimacy.

By holding Bonaparte up to the mirror of British history, radicals and
reformers could scrutinize the circumstances by which the house of
Hanover had come to the British throne. Two contrasting attitudes
towards the past, and thus towards the constitutional underpinnings of
the British monarchy, informed post-Elba defenses of Napoleon. Some
praised Bonaparte by drawing parallels between his circumstances
and those of William of Orange (of sainted Whig memory). But others
defended France's ruler by defining his virtues *against* the political sins
evident in Britain's history. Napoleon, thus, could be used both by
constitutionalists, brandishing the banner of 1688, and by Paineite anti-
constitutionalists, for whom fetishizing the past was a blind, a false
scent. Napoleon could be absorbed into the ideology of British constitutionalism, or used as a weapon against it.

As this comment suggests, a secondary aim of this chapter is to re-
direct attention to the anti-constitutionalist nature of some post-Waterloo radical argument. Recent historical writing has rightly emphasized
the centrality to early nineteenth-century British radicalism of a "constitutionalist idiom," its rhetoric shaped by appeals to historical precedent, as opposed to natural rights.[10] James Epstein, in his important
study of radical argument and symbolism, has written that there was in
practice "little sense of incompatibility" between the constitutionalist
and the avowedly anti-historical Paineite idioms; and James Vernon has
seconded this, noting that contemporaries would have had little patience
with the neat intellectual-historical dichotomy by which rights are clas-
sified as either natural or customary.[11] Epstein and Vernon have usefully
complicated a distinction that can easily be drawn in too rigid a fashion;
they are right that individual radicals could offer self-contradictory
visions of rights and constitutions. But we should continue to differen-
tiate between these two ideological tendencies, even if they were not
always, in practice, mutually exclusive. The case of Napoleon demonstrates that there were two distinct ways in which radical admirers of
Bonaparte could draw connections between contemporary events and
the British past—and that these two readings involved countervailing
visions of the relevance of British history to constitutional reform. The
anti-constitutionalist idiom, in short, still had some life in it.

Historians of radicalism have investigated ways in which political
debate entailed struggles over language and symbols.[12] As Harling has

indicated in his account of Leigh Hunt's "linguistic appropriation" of loyalist keywords, radicals and reformers refused to allow ministerial apologists to control the language of politics.[13] Recognizing with William Cobbett that "*Words* have great power," radicals resisted and redefined the terms used against them.[14] The first part of this chapter shows how radicals working within the constitutionalist idiom used historical analogy to take apart the novel language of "legitimacy" employed by defenders of the restored Bourbon dynasty. Here I draw especially on *Cobbett's Weekly Political Register* and Daniel Lovell's *Statesman*. I then go on to examine Napoleon's treatment in two republican weeklies established in 1817, *Sherwin's Weekly Political Register* (edited by William Sherwin) and the *Black Dwarf* edited by T. J. Wooler. In these four sympathetic journals, Napoleon was sometimes assimilated into the narrative of British history, but at other times opposed to the pattern of British development.

The introduction of "legitimacy" into British political discourse was, as we have seen, a semantic innovation directly connected to events in France. A concerted radical assault on the assumptions implicit in the new usage began, significantly, around the time of Napoleon's 1815 return to power.[15] When Louis XVIII had come to the throne in 1814, his admirers had proclaimed the principle of "legitimacy" in justification of the Bourbon dynasty's restoration.[16] British writers of a radical or liberal cast—some generally unsympathetic to hereditary monarchy, others unready to support a theory of hereditary monarchy that brushed aside the question of popular support—viewed the "*misused* metaphor" with suspicion.[17] The *Edinburgh Review* used italics to place the "new-fangled phrase" at arm's length.[18] Leigh Hunt warned his readers never to pronounce "this new-fangled word" without its quotation marks ("There are inverted commas in tones as well as in types") lest they appear to be admitting the equation between hereditary and lawful rule.[19]

Different strategies presented themselves: some writers redefined the term "legitimacy" in order to apply it favorably to Napoleon, but others rejected it out of hand, hurling it back at the continent's hereditary monarchs as an imprecation. William Burdon—whose early ardor for Napoleon had blossomed again during the Hundred Days—employed the former strategy, refusing to let the term be hijacked by the lackeys of dynasticism. How, he asked in May 1815, after Parliament had determined on war against the reinstalled Napoleon, could Bonaparte possibly be "a rebel against the legitimate Government—Can that Government be legitimate which is against the will of the people?"[20] By contrast, Byron's friend John Cam Hobhouse, in his two-volume account of Napoleon's brief second reign—vetted for the press by Lord Holland and the future Lord Langdale, and lauded by Benjamin Constant and the *Edinburgh Review*—spurned the phrase.[21] He would use "the word *lawful*" instead, he announced, a term that plainly revealed the inadequate claim to rule of Louis XVIII, who had spurned a constitution, the one condition set by the senate calling him to the throne. The term "legitimate," by contrast, was effectively tainted, having, Hobhouse remarked, "been lately adopted to distinguish the bastard pretensions of election from that mysterious, hereditary, innate, unalienable, incorruptible right, which, mortal as to its birth, partakes of the godhead in its eternal duration— . . . which although not without a beginning, is yet sure, and promised, to last for ever and ever." Hobhouse rejected this new definition of "legitimacy," which apparently held it to be a "miraculous property and attribute of certain royal races."[22] (And by insinuating that "legitimate" dynasties had their basis in usurpation—note his reminder that legitimacy was "not without a beginning"—he raised an eyebrow at the certainty that they would "last for ever and ever.") He accurately, though ironically, captured the new sense in which "legitimacy" was being used. The term now referred to lineal, "regular," hereditary monarchical descent, or to the political doctrine upholding such descent.

As far as its critics were concerned, the virtue now trumpeted by continental dynasts amounted to nothing less than the "old doctrine of Divine Right, new-vamped up," as the radical journalist William Hazlitt put it.[23] "Legitimacy" seemed an anachronism to Hazlitt, a "mock-doctrine" dug up by "resurrection-men."[24] Thomas Babington Macaulay, in a similar spirit, would write in 1825 of "the doctrine of Divine Right" having "come back to us, like a thief from transportation, under the *alias* of Legitimacy."[25] To those who worried about the strength of the executive, the new term "legitimacy" seemed a bare-faced admission of a plot, on the Stuart model, against British liberties. Necessity had often been invoked, during the French wars, to justify infringements on traditional freedoms. Many now shared Hazlitt's foreboding, expressed as news of Napoleon's 1814 fall reached Britain, that "The restoration of the Bourbons in France will be the re-establishment of the principles of the Stuarts in this country."[26]

In articulating their critique of "this fiction of Legitimacy,"[27] opposition figures reflexively cited the revolution of 1688–89 and the Hanoverian succession of 1714 (effected by the 1701 Act of Settlement)—the political transactions that had allowed "legitimacy" to transfer from the Stuart to the Brunswick dynasty. In drawing parallels between events in France and the Glorious Revolution, the liberals and radicals of 1815 were not setting sail on uncharted waters. As we have seen, Richard Price had greeted France's revolution as a Gallic version of Britain's 1688: even if the French had not yet "cashiered" their king, Price celebrated Britons' having done so a century earlier.[28]

The extent to which the Whiggish exaltation of 1688 had become an unquestioned element of the national narrative is illustrated by the fact that Price's argument could only be countered by *denying* the parallel between 1688 and 1789, rather than by questioning the virtues of the revolution that had installed William III. Edmund Burke, in his 1790 response to Price's address, *Reflections on the Revolution in France*, emphasized the slightness of the deviation from hereditary succession, and the lawfulness of the process by which William and Mary had come to power. Mary, after all, was James' daughter: even if her claim was inferior to that of James' newborn Catholic son, Britain still had "an hereditary descent in the same blood, though an hereditary descent qualified with protestantism." For Burke, the revolution of 1688 did not unsettle but actually *confirmed* the rule of hereditary succession. He noted approvingly that the Whig engineers of 1688's dynastic shift "kept from the eye" the "depart[ure] from the strict order of inheritance," framing their exceptional actions in terms of well-established constitutional forms. The smooth process by which the helm of state was transferred from Stuart to Orange and then to Brunswick hands, could hardly be compared with the radical political transformation France was experiencing.[29]

Burke's refusal to recognize 1688 as a genuine revolution was famously addressed by James Mackintosh. In his *Vindiciæ Gallicæ* of 1791, Mackintosh played the complicated game of demonstrating that the Hanoverian claim was based on actions which, while not lawful in the everyday sense, had a higher legality—a tactic that would later be exploited by radicals extolling Napoleon's regime. The process by which William had become king, Mackintosh argued, lay outside the law. His title to the crown was not based on succession; the notables who offered him the throne had been "neither lawfully elected nor lawfully assembled"; the Parliament that later passed a nugatory Act to absolve this convention had itself been "without *legal* authority." The events of 1688–89, in short, conformed in no way to the orderly narrative of hereditary succession—even if the men who put William on the throne insisted on papering over the revolutionary nature of their enterprise with "legal phraseology." The year 1688 marked a true rift. But unlike the rifts that underlay Bourbon claims to power ("the usurpations of Pepin or Hugh Capet"), the elevation of William to the throne stood "as a *direct* emanation from the sovereignty of the people," and thus distinguished the English monarchy, uniquely, as a government "legitimate in its origin."[30] For Mackintosh, the revolution of 1688 could be at once extra-legal and *legitimate*. The Hanoverian claim rested on the rejection of simple hereditary succession—on a recognition of the *elective* nature of Britain's monarchy.

The relevance of 1688 to events across the Channel was thus promoted by the British left, and denied by the right, from an early moment in France's revolution. And since the claims to power of George III and the Prince Regent could be traced back to the claim of William III, the underpinnings of Hanoverian rule could be portrayed as intimately connected to the current struggle over France's throne.[31]

"Tories" were no longer Jacobites, defenders of Stuart pretenders.[32] Instead, they sought, as Burke had, to treat 1688 as having necessitated the most trivial of deviations from a hereditary line. In contrast, radical Whigs nearly erased James' daughter Mary from their analysis. By emphasizing William, and subsuming Mary, they exaggerated the extent to which hereditary succession had been defied in 1688. If one did not mention his wife, William's claim to the throne seemed to rely *only* on popular approval. Similarly, a central radical point was that James had never abdicated. Abdication would imply that the choice of a new ruler depended on the decision of the departed one. Radicals stressed that James had fled, and was *declared* to have abdicated: this left Parliament as the king-maker, the arbiter of lawful rule.[33] Thus, when the argument over 1688's relevance to contemporary France came to a head in 1815, British political discourse offered a paradox. It was now "Whigs" who stressed the ways in which 1688's revolution had broken the letter of the law, and "Tories" who desperately tried to demonstrate the revolution's orderly and constitutional nature.

Few if any conservative writers in 1815 actually praised "the divine right of kings" as such; defenders of dynastic "legitimacy" often sought to tone down the term's connotations of blind adherence to hereditary rule. Unease with the term was especially strong on the part of moderate Whigs who had held their noses when offering support to the Bourbons. "No one, surely, now-a-days," wrote the *Champion*'s editor John Scott, who had wavered on the question of a Bourbon restoration, "will be found in this country to maintain, that mere birth alone constitutes royal legitimacy."[34] In the House of Lords, Lord Grenville, the Whig leader who by supporting renewed warfare against Napoleon in 1815 helped open up a fissure between his faction and Earl Grey's Foxite Whigs, made a similar effort to argue himself out of the corner that radicals were trying to paint him into. Grenville insisted that when he described the new Bourbon government as "legitimate" he did not mean "mere legitimacy of birth," but rather "that legitimacy which was founded upon the principles of the constitution, upon the condition of the people, and upon a due regard to the various ranks and divisions of society"—the same legitimacy that had featured "in our own revolution, where the regular succession had been abandoned, for the sake of supplying a government legitimate by the laws and constitution of the country." Grenville ruled Napoleon's regime out of the running *ipso facto*, because it had been "a military usurpation, inconsistent with the rights of men."[35]

The discomfort of Scott and Grenville remind us that the new meaning of "legitimacy" was partly its critics' invention. "Legitimacy" was at once an actual vision of monarchy advanced by some advocates of hereditary rule, and a monolithic rhetorical adversary constructed by the dynasts' enemies. In their role as collaborators in the creation of "legitimacy," British radicals carved out a space for themselves in which they could praise Napoleon and criticize Britain's government and Regent— while at the same time ostentatiously offering their allegiance to Britain's constitution and the Hanoverian line.

In the spring and summer of 1815, Cobbett's *Political Register* and Lovell's *Statesman* led the effort to repudiate the new conservative definition of "legitimacy." The two editors, and their contributors, sought to wrest the term from the advocates of hereditary succession and claim it for the figure they now held to represent the antithesis of hereditary rule, Napoleon. The radical argument hinged on a democratic or elective definition of "legitimacy": Napoleon was *"legitimate,"* one *Statesman* contributor explained, because he had been called to the throne by "the universal voice, or consent, at least, of the people."[36] Unlike Louis, Napoleon did not rest his claim to power on descent.

The implications of this argument were not necessarily anti-monarchical, for one ruling family might be said to resemble Bonaparte in this regard. The Hanoverians were "not the descendents of the elder branch of the Stuarts"—a fact that should count in their favor, as Napoleon's common origin should in his. George III's claim to the throne, according to Cobbett, was "really *legitimate*" because it resulted from "*an act of Parliament.*"[37] But promoting Napoleon's legitimacy in this way also meant pointing out the *contingency* of Hanoverian rule. Subject to the will of Parliament, the British monarch's continued power depended on something other than ancestry.

In the spring of 1815, as a renewed war against Napoleon seemed ever more likely, many radicals pointed out how wrong it would be for Britain, of all nations, to side with hereditary "legitimacy" against Napoleon (or as one *Statesman* contributor put it, with "legitimate imbecility" against "legitimate talent"). Historically, England's liberties depended on "the doctrines of popular Election," not "the Divine right of Kings."[38] By joining a renewed crusade against Napoleon—by defending an unpopular hereditary monarch against a popular ruler—the Prince Regent would chip away at the very principle that had installed his own family on Britain's throne. A letter to the *Statesman* in early April—from "Verax" of Bath (very likely William Godwin, who a few weeks later used this pseudonym to defend Napoleon)—argued that Napoleon's right to power, resting as it did on parliamentary approval, was the same as the right of "the PRINCE REGENT, in the absence of his father" to rule Britain.[39]

Readers of the *Statesman* and the *Political Register* could not escape the argument that a Hanoverian war against Napoleonic "usurpation" was hypocritical to the core—"infamous in its principle, being contrary to our Constitution, [and] against the principles which placed the house of Brunswick on the English Throne."[40] A Brunswick embrace of divine-right "Tory principles" would amount to "madness, ingratitude, treachery," one writer noted. The Hanoverians' making "common cause" with the Bourbons, he added darkly, "might involve both in one common fate."[41]

Opposition writers often borrowed the logic and rhetoric of their political opponents in order to turn it against them: nothing made a radical happier than to assume, often half parodically, a posture more loyal than that of a loyalist. Thus radical journalists reveled in reversing the significations of the loyalist shibboleths "legitimacy" and "usurpation." The hereditary claims of the Bourbons became, in the hands of one *Political Register* contributor, "ancient and renovating usurpation"—while Napoleon's regime became "one of the grandest instances of legitimate government that ever was proposed and adopted for the welfare of a country."[42] It was in this spirit that the *Statesman* mischievously suggested it was treason to define legitimacy as hereditary rather than elective. *The Times*, its radical critic reported, was "enraged at the Declaration of NAPOLEON, that Kings are made for and by the People." Might not the *Times*' attack "on the principle which seated the House of BRUNSWICK on the Throne of these realms ... be deemed worthy of the attention of the ATTORNEY-GENERAL"?[43] Another instance of this rhetorical ploy—turning the self-described advocates of "legitimacy" into traitors—was employed by a *Political Register* contributor who argued that if Louis' flight and reliance on foreign armies did not amount to abdication, then James II had not abdicated either, which left the Hanoverians with "no better title to the sceptre of these realms than usurpation." From here, it was but a short step to the claim, presented in suitable tones of mock-outrage, that British critics of Napoleon were "miscreants" hoping to prove that the Hanoverians were "*usurpers.*"[44]

Making the legitimacy of the Hanoverians depend on that of Bonaparte was, then, a common stratagem.[45] One particular use of 1688 derived from the line of reasoning Mackintosh had employed a quarter-century earlier: demonstrating the murkiness of the process by which the Prince of Orange had become a British king. The purpose of such arguments was not to cast doubt on William's virtues, or to brand as "illegitimate" the revolution of 1688, but to demonstrate that no easy measure of legitimacy existed, that a leader who came to power by an extraordinary path could be more legitimate than one whose claim rested on heredity. Thus when one anti-Napoleonic correspondent in the monthly *Scourge* suggested, during the Hundred Days, that Napoleon, unlike William III, had not been invited by "the constituted authorities of the state" or called for by "the voice of the people,"[46] a second reader (while insisting he was "no advocate for Buonaparte") retorted that the messiness of William's arrival on English soil easily matched that of Napoleon's return from Elba. William had falsely presented the purpose of his expedition; at a crucial moment, he had received support from a high-ranking military figure; Parliament had waited months before even acknowledging the crown to be vacant; and many remained loyal to James long after he had vacated the throne.[47] The revolution that had breathed new life into the British constitution had not followed constitutional forms, or reflected the unquestioned unanimous sentiments of the nation. It followed that Napoleon's path to power should not by itself disqualify him from exercising that power. John Cam Hobhouse joined in pointing out the similarities between 1688 and 1815. It was true, Hobhouse wrote, that Louis' troops, by switching their allegiance to Napoleon as he marched toward Paris, had violated their oaths. But the English army under Marlborough had done the same thing on Hounslow Heath. Only the passage of time, and the entrenchment of a new regime, had determined the "final denomination" of 1688 to be one of "reformation" rather than "heresy."[48]

Hobhouse feared the rising foreign tide of "legitimacy" might drown Britain's more liberal monarchical principles. British admirers of the continental dynasties might wish "to abolish the tedious, embarrassing, discredited forms of our government, in favour of the more simple, vigorous, and now victorious institutions of pure monarchy." Regard for "the principles which placed the house of Brunswick on the throne ... might be lost in the delirium of a final triumph over these terrific monsters" of the Jacobins and Napoleon.[49] Failing to recognize the basis of William III's claim to power might mean losing British liberty.

Similar voices spoke up in Parliament (as well as in provincial meetings).[50] During the Hundred Days, Sir Francis Burdett proclaimed in the Commons that the principle of hereditary legitimacy was "reprehensible to maintain in a country, the sovereign of which held his throne alone by the will of the people"; embracing the principle by aiding Louis meant declaring Britain's monarch "a greater usurper than Buonaparté."[51] In early 1816, the Whig Lord John Russell reminded the Commons that if Britain had in 1688 been "the rallying point of legitimacy" (as some now wanted it to be), the current sovereign, "instead of an imperial throne, would have been the possessor of a petty electorate in Germany."[52]

Defenders of the government's anti-Napoleonic policy, recognizing the power of the left's rhetorical strategy, tried to appropriate 1688 and the Act of Succession in aid of their own positions. The prime minister Lord Liverpool insisted that the Hanoverian accession had been guaranteed by foreign powers against "internal conspiracy and sedition" (that is, against Jacobites) by the Treaty of Utrecht in 1713. Thus Britain's own dynasty had relied on the threat of foreign arms to cement its rule. British troops in France were doing no more than what continental arms had been pledged to do for the good House of Hanover.[53] Liverpool's redeployment of the opposition's favorite historical examples was taken up by Grenville, who declared the Glorious Revolution to have demonstrated that "an odious tyrant" (then James II, now Bonaparte) could, for the "safety of Europe," be removed by a "foreign army" (then Dutch, now British). Britain's foreign presence in France recapitulated the indisputably beneficial arrival of William of Orange on British soil.[54] By linking Napoleon to James rather than to William—by treating him as a despot rather than the people's choice—both Liverpool and Grenville hoped to snatch 1688 away from Bonaparte's defenders.

In turn, MPs hostile to the Bourbons criticized these ministerial analogies.[55] Prominent in this effort was James Mackintosh himself, who twenty-five years previously had helped blaze the rhetorical trail on which so many defenders of Napoleon now traveled. Mackintosh had famously renounced his revolutionary sympathies after the Terror, befriending the dying Burke and attacking Godwin. The advocate's change of heart had seemed certain by 1803, when, during the peace of Amiens, he had defended Peltier; the Addington ministry was sufficiently confident of his conversion to knight him and give him the splendid plum of recorder at Bombay. As it turned out, Mackintosh's metamorphosis was only partial, or only temporary. Approached by the government on his return from India in 1812, he had opted instead to sit on the opposition benches. In now rising to question the grounds for Bourbon rule, Mackintosh resumed his probing of the language of legitimacy.

"Legitimacy," Mackintosh announced, was "only another word for legal, or rather for lawful." If authority was "exercised for the people agreeably to the rules of justice and law," then that authority "was doubtless, in the highest and most sacred sense, legitimate." The term, however, was being used in "questionable and dangerous" manner in France. Legitimacy could not attach itself permanently to a government or family—this was a "pretended legitimacy." Even "the most legal title to authority might be forfeited by its abusive exercise," and, as British history revealed, there might "be a legitimate resistance as well as a legitimate authority." Having defined the word to his satisfaction, Mackintosh turned to Liverpool's historical analogy, in order to reverse its significance. When Britain's allies, earlier in the century, had upheld the Hanoverian regime, he declared, they were vowing "to resist the claims of pretended legitimacy," to resist, not uphold, Stuart principles.[56] The European powers had endorsed a popular dynasty over a hereditary one: such a precedent could not be used, as Liverpool wished it to be, to justify Britain's propping up an unwanted French dynasty. Mackintosh, who in the revolution's early days had claimed the word "legitimate" for the principle of popular election, refused to allow it to be filched now by pretenders.

One conclusion we can draw at this point is that William Hazlitt—whose adoration of Napoleon is often regarded as an eccentricity distinguishing him from his radical contemporaries—was not so unusual after all.[57] In championing Bonaparte as the alternative to "that old bawd, Legitimacy,"[58] as he did in his newspaper essays (and later in his biography of Napoleon), Hazlitt marked himself simply as one of the more diligent exploiters of a common rhetorical tactic. In 1818, Hazlitt noted the novelty of the word "Legitimate." It had not appeared "in our annals in the years 1688, in 1715, or 1745"—years in which the scales of hereditary right would have weighed against the House of Hanover. Did the term's use today mean that the revolution of 1688 was now seen as "a blot in the family escutcheon of the Prince of Orange or the Elector of Hanover?" Was the Hanoverian debt to the people now felt to be a "flaw in their title to the succession"? Hazlitt warned that the principle taking root in France, the principle that had put a Bourbon back on the throne, might "in time stretch out its feelers and strong suckers to this country; and present an altogether curious and novel aspect, by ingrafting the principles of the House of Stuart on the illustrious stock of the House of Brunswick."[59] The hybrid, oxymoronic product of this graft would be pernicious, Hazlitt warned. A Hanoverian king embracing Stuart principles was a "solecism": an English prince could not deny being the people's servant "without disclaiming his title to the crown."[60]

In 1819, Hazlitt collected his political articles together at the behest of the radical publisher William Hone. Hazlitt's preface to these *Political Essays* once again shows how the radical assault on "legitimacy" was tied to the radical celebration of Bonaparte. "Legitimacy" threatened to turn the people into mere "chattels," mere "live-stock" on its estate, Hazlitt wrote. Anyone who could save humanity from this debasement would be "not less than the God of my idolatry," he declared. And the man who had temporarily achieved this was Napoleon, who "put his foot upon the neck of kings, who would have put their yoke upon the necks of the people." Even if Bonaparte had been a tyrant—which Hazlitt denied—then at any rate "he was not, nor he could not become, a tyrant by right divine." His very *illegitimacy* meant that his tyranny could not be "sacred" or "eternal"—it would end "with the individual," Hazlitt wrote (forgetting for the moment Napoleon's son, the king of Rome).[61] Napoleon embodied the opposite principle to Legitimacy. And for this, the emperor was to be adored.[62]

The radical deployment of history against "legitimacy" was a canny tactic. Historical analogies between contemporary French events and the revolution of 1688—that critical moment in modern British constitutional history—allowed radicals to meet the perceived re-emergence of Stuart theory with a threatening reminder of the Stuarts' fate. Drawing such analogies allowed reformers to criticize the policy of the Regent's government while theatrically brandishing their own loyalty to the House of Hanover. By arguing that Napoleon's claim to power was no different from that which had entitled William III to the British crown, the opposition could defend Napoleon from within a framework that foregrounded the British constitution, rather than "foreign" Jacobinical principles. By continually reminding their opponents that the existing political establishment rested on a successful revolution, the opposition warned them that in embracing the continental advocates of "legitimacy," they were pulling the rug out from under the very feet of their own monarch. The British king, constitutional radicals argued, should have more in common with a foreign upstart than with any foreign dynast.

But not all radicals took this road. Some prominent representatives of the plebeian radicalism that blossomed after Waterloo chose to praise Napoleon without tying him to the Hanoverian settlement. Napoleon, in their rendition, recommended himself as a model precisely because he broke with precedent. These radicals felt no obligation to attribute elective qualities to the British monarchy. Celebrating Napoleon's popular mandate, they contrasted his system with the English constitution— advancing in the process their own reading of the British past and monarchy. Napoleon's enforced captivity on St. Helena allowed many radicals to portray British ministers as "arbitrary and cruel" jailers, who had transported a man without trial.[63] But his significance went beyond his victim status: contributors to new republican journals like *Sherwin's Weekly Political Register* and the *Black Dwarf* would defend Napoleon also for his past actions as ruler of France. These journalists punctuated their litany of British economic and political injustice with references to Napoleon's alternative regime, whose features threw into relief the flaws of British government.

In February 1817, William Sherwin, eighteen years of age, founded the weekly journal the *Republican*. A few weeks later—citing the recent disorders at Spa Fields, where a peaceful reform meeting had spiraled into an armed riot—Sherwin changed the periodical's name to *Sherwin's Weekly Political Register* (its former, unabashed title, he explained, might make even sympathetic readers feel conspicuous and vulnerable); the journal's title would revert to the *Republican* when Sherwin's publisher, the former tinsmith Richard Carlile, assumed the editorship in August 1819, after witnessing British troops mow down protesters at St. Peter's Fields in Manchester.[64] The newspaper's politics were Paineite (as a side project Carlile and Sherwin published Thomas Paine's political works both as cheap individual tracts and in a two-volume collected set).[65] And while it may be true that many Paineites treated the historicist idiom of constitutional precedent as a symbiotic partner to the language of ahistorical "natural rights," seeing no fundamental tension between Magna Carta and the Declaration of the Rights of Man, Sherwin's *Register* rejected the very notion that anything could be salvaged from Britain's constitutional heritage. For the *Register*'s contributors, political solutions were not to be found by searching through the British past. Instead, the historical example that Sherwin's paper repeatedly raised, and almost always in a positive light, was that of Napoleon Bonaparte.

Rather than criticizing governmental actions as departures from constitutional precedent, as the *Statesman* tended to, the *Register* dismissed out of hand the notion that constitutional precedent mattered at all. Studying the history of English government, Sherwin wrote in September 1818, one met with a set of "precedents which ought to be held in abhorrence." Rather than express constitutionalist nostalgia for bygone years when England's rulers lived within the law, Sherwin saw England's past as marked by unending strife between rulers and ruled. By its very nature—monarchical—and from its very beginning, the English government worked against the interests of the people: all that one should "reverence" in the English past was "the bravery of our ancestors in their attempts to shake off the cumbrous load of despotism." Even if some past moment could be found when the government had been acceptable, Sherwin was careful to add, "the difference between the circumstances and manners of the People of the present day, and those of a former period" made it useless to argue from precedent.[66]

Sherwin teasingly played with the opposition between history and theory, claiming that the conclusions he reached by tracing English political history "from the present period up to its source" were superior to "any that can be deduced from the best finished theory." Thus even as he rejected the claims of precedent, and insisted that "existing establishments" should be judged not by their age but by "the standard of reason," Sherwin recommended the study of history as a means of countering the conservative claim that Britain had "a system worthy of imitation." It was the precedent-citers, in short, not Sherwin's own republicans, who were proponents of the dread theories and systems that anti-Jacobins since Burke had railed against. Sherwin one-upped the writers who claimed they could prove the best government by "searching into antiquity." These validators of the status quo erred by "not going *far enough*," he declared, not going "to the origin at once, . . . the source from whence all their precedents have sprung." If they traced the English monarchy back to its roots, they would find it had been "established by the inhuman butchery of thousands of the People . . . and that the House of Commons was first convened as an instrument for plundering the Nation" on behalf of the monarch.[67] The nation's present governors were not abandoning the virtuous path of their predecessors, as radical Whigs might have it; they were speeding along the same vicious avenue. English government, poisoned at its very source, would not be repaired by appeals to an ancient constitution.

Like the *Statesman* contributors who pointed out that Britain, like France, had experienced rifts in its political development, Sherwin endeavored to portray English history as a tangle of discontinuity, not the orderly succession painted by conservatives. But while *Statesman* writers had dwelt on the redemptive potential of these rifts—painting William III's arrival in 1688 as a triumph of liberty—Sherwin emphasized the suffering that was involved in such disruptions. "What is the whole history of England," he asked, "but a continued scene of rapine and desolation with now and then a few solitary intervals of repose?"—intervals, moreover, that arose more from "exhaustion" than from "a wish for peace." Sherwin offered a table of English kings and queens since the Norman Conquest, the sequence of their names disturbed every few lines by an "Interruption"—a usurpation, deposition, or restoration of some stripe. He concluded that since the Conquest there had never been "more than *three reigns* in succession, without some violent interruption." Rift was the rule, not the exception, one of the "characteristic features" of monarchical rule. Whether the pattern remained true, Sherwin darkly hinted, would soon be seen. Certainly, Britain seemed due for another interruption after the reign of three successive Hanoverians. The final lines of Sherwin's article made it clear what form the interruption would be likely to take: if one wished to destroy "the popery of government"—the superstitious devotion to "relics of former devotion"—only "a thorough revolution" would do.[68] Establishing a republic would end the incessant interruptions inevitable under a monarchy. For Sherwin, then, the English constitution was not even steady and enduring: its only consistent feature was its jumpy unsettledness. The constitution offered itself not as a thing to be restored, but as a thing to be escaped.

In an 1818 letter to the *Register*'s editor, Allen Davenport, a frequent contributor, suggested a means by which this escape might be effected. Davenport was a sometime Methodist, a follower of Thomas Spence, and a shoemaker. In this last capacity, he practiced a trade marked by a vigorous radical tradition (associates of the would-be regicide Despard had made shoes, as did many of the men who conspired at Cato Street in 1820 to kill the Cabinet).[69] For Davenport, the constitution had been "huddled together in a dark age"—and had perhaps been laudable then, when no better alternative existed [...] constitution was at once too nebulous and too unchanging for [...] o constitution could "be a good one, [...] nd too unchanging, for no constitution sl [...] Magna Carta, Davenport maintained, s [...] "com-pelling all succeeding governmer [...] onstitu-tion of the country, to the sens [...] and, at certain given periods, suppose e [...] sion of every new king to the throne." Davenport had a particular model in mind when he presented this Jeffersonian objection to constitutional stasis. Napoleon, he wrote, had been elected emperor "by sending books through every parish, and hamlet in the empire in which every one was at liberty to sign their names for, or against." A majority had voted for him. And thus, wrote Davenport, Napoleon became "one of the most 'legitimate' monarchs that ever reigned."[70]

Note the quotation marks Davenport set around "legitimate." While postwar radicals could use the term in a positive sense (as when "Orator" Hunt proclaimed "That the only source of all legitimate power is the People"), the term more often figured pejoratively or ironically.[71] Sherwin, criticizing the hereditary dynasts' treatment of Napoleon, complained that "in an alliance of legitimates, ... the misfortunes of subdued greatness furnish matter for joy and exultation."[72] Both Davenport, by using quotation marks, and Sherwin, by omitting them, drew attention to the politically contested nature of the term. Napoleon, according to Davenport, was legitimate in the *true* sense of the word. Sherwin, for his part, was calling the dynasts by the name they wished to be called—but demonstrating through a contrast with Napoleon just how far short of the mark they fell. Napoleon, when he "might have crushed them," had instead "treated them with kindness"; the dynasts were capable neither of appreciating nor of emulating his "magnanimity." The "page of history" would reveal the true relative worth of Napoleon and the hereditary monarchs: Napoleon's name, wrote Sherwin, "will be placed in its proper station in the Temple of Fame, while theirs will serve as a by-word for infamy to future generations."[73] History itself, the present day viewed retrospectively from a later one, would legitimize Napoleon's reign.

As a republican, Davenport acknowledged that Napoleon, "by accepting of a crown himself," had checked the progress of the revolution "and held up tottering royalty for a season." This mistake had "lost him millions of friends, and was the chief cause of his final overthrow." But even in describing Bonaparte's fall from grace, Davenport highlighted the man's revolutionary potential. Had Napoleon "remained the citizen soldier, and retained the same principles that he professed when he was placed in the consular chair," Davenport declared, "there would not at this moment have remained one single crowned head in Europe!" After his imperial mistake, Napoleon had redeemed himself in 1815: his return from Elba was "a bloodless revolution, although a French one." The lack of resistance to his progress through France was a greater triumph than all his previous "splendid achievements, whether military or civil."[74]

The *Register* continually turned against Britain's governors the very rhetoric that wartime loyalism had used to indict France's emperor. One should read Sherwin's denunciation of "the usurpations of King Castlereagh" and "King Sidmouth" (the foreign and home secretaries) in light of the constant wartime skewering of Napoleon as a usurper.[75]

Similarly, when Sherwin compared Castlereagh's ministry to a band of robbers, he was echoing not only the epithets that had so often been used against Napoleon ("robber," "ruffian") but the logic that Goldsmith had employed to argue for assassinating Bonaparte. As a houseowner is justified in killing those that invade his house, Sherwin argued, so too would "death" be "a just punishment" for those who had suspended habeas corpus and thus "violated every principle of civilized society."[76]

Sherwin capped his defense of tyrannicide (a set of articles entitled "King Killing") by reprinting, shortly before the Peterloo massacre, the 1657 work *Killing No Murder*, which had advocated assassinating Cromwell. The pamphlet's lesson, he maintained, was "much more applicable" to "the tyrants of the present day" than it had been to Cromwell ("for *he* was a man of ability, courage and enterprize").[77] Once again, Sherwin was turning a loyalist weapon against its anti-Napoleonic wielders. Fifteen years earlier, as we have seen, the pamphlet had been reprinted and cited approvingly by loyalists seeking to justify Bonaparte's assassination.[78] Loyalists had failed to anticipate the ease with which these arguments could be redirected towards other rulers—despite Samuel Whitbread's wartime warning that foolhardy British advocacy of assassination would invite "retaliation."[79] The reckless loyalist argument was now indeed, as Whitbread had warned, coming home to roost.

The *Register*'s most important rhetorical borrowing from the anti-Napoleonic arsenal was the charge of "military despotism." While this complaint owed something to the standard radical fear of a standing army, the phrase itself was at this point identified specifically with Napoleon: political critics on the left and right alike had from an early point employed the term to describe his system.[80] To apply the term to the British government was, among other things, to accuse ministers of the most pernicious hypocrisy—of having proclaimed themselves opponents of the very system they hoped to establish.[81] Again and again, writers in Sherwin's *Register* suggested that a military despotism awaited the people of Britain. Thus one letter of June 1818 told the British people that the war their government had sent them to fight ("by which your brothers and sons have been butchered") had sought "*not* Bonaparte's overthrow, but the destruction of liberty in France, and the security of despotism at home." Allen Davenport, the same summer, denied that the 1815 war had been directed simply against Napoleon; in reality,

British arms had fought against "the laws of nature and the rights of mankind, in order to subject the whole world to a military despotism." Waterloo was "alike the grave of heroism, and of the liberties of Europe."[82]

The message of the *Register*'s contributors, in short, was that it was not Napoleon but the enemies of Napoleon who wished to clamp the shackles of a military system onto the people's liberties. Sherwin, a few weeks before the events that would come to be known as Peterloo, told the nation's soldiers "that your triumphs over the liberties of France, were but the prelude to the triumphs of your masters, the Borough-mongers, over the liberties of England." As if on cue, working men and women attending the radical meeting in Manchester were trampled down by the Manchester Yeomanry, and then by the regular troops who came to relieve the yeomanry; eleven were killed and hundreds injured. Carlile declared that the government had now become in fact what it already was in principle, "a MILITARY DESPOTISM."[83] For some Britons, the epithet that quickly attached itself to the Manchester horror, "Peterloo," may have offered an ironic contrast with the genuine glory of Waterloo: the army that had so recently conquered a tyrant had now managed to overcome a mass of peacefully assembled women and men. But the pages of Sherwin's *Register* remind us that even before the 1819 massacre, there were Britons for whom Waterloo itself signified not a glorious victory but the defeat of liberty.

Sherwin's was not alone in presenting this counter-myth of Waterloo. "Orator" Hunt had, seven months before Peterloo, denounced the "bloody butchers of Waterloo" to a crowd outside Manchester's Theatre Royal (whence a few nights before he had been ejected by hussars for refusing to sing "God Save the King").[84] Even Jeremy Bentham, a radical of a different stripe (if one equally scornful of historical precedent), had in his 1817 *Plan of Parliamentary Reform* proclaimed that "The plains, or heights, or whatsoever they are, of *Waterloo*" would "one day be pointed to by the historian as the grave—not only of French but of English liberties." Events in France (where "every idea of any thing better than the most absolute despotism" was being "thoroughly weeded out by the Bourbons, as ever it had been by Bonaparte") would be replayed in Britain, Bentham warned. Wellington would prove a "worthy vanquisher and successor to Bonaparte"—he would be "the conqueror of French and English liberties."[85] Bentham's *Plan* found an additional audience in an 1818 edition prepared for "the popular reader" by Thomas J. Wooler, publisher of the prominent radical organ the *Black Dwarf*.[86] And the *Black Dwarf*, while less sympathetic to Napoleon than some *Sherwin's* contributors were, shared the *Register's* readiness to use the fallen emperor as a bludgeon with which to beat the British government.

The *Black Dwarf's* relationship to the constitutionalist idiom was at best ambivalent. The journal's first article, in January 1817, presented the English constitution as an "enigma" so muddily defined as to be practically useless: "So many things opposite in themselves, have been constitutional in their turn, that the constitution is every thing, and nothing—a blessing, and a curse—the offspring of immaculate wisdom—the produce of the weakest intellect." There may have seemed to be a hint of constitutionalism in Wooler's acclamation of Magna Carta, and in his call to members of a "degenerate race" to "cleans[e] and repai[r] the edifice" built by their ancestors. But it was not a simple act of restoration for which Wooler called; he stressed the limits of the ancestral "state of knowledge" and emphasized that these earlier men were admirable precisely because they had not been "led by the dull interpretation of ancient precepts." To follow truly in their footsteps would mean pursuing "the light of liberty" wherever it might lead. In short, the constitution for Wooler was a thing of limited direct utility, "in fact nothing but the recorded merits of our ancestors." Rather than expecting "protection" to spring from it, one must engage in fresh struggles.[87] "We are continually told of the excellence of the English constitution," he wrote in 1820; "but a very slight reference to our history, will show that its excellence consists in its *non-existence*. In any fair understanding of the use of language *there is no such thing!*"[88]

The *Black Dwarf* was more ready than *Sherwin's* to acknowledge Napoleon's flaws. The journal chastised him for his "childish ambition . . . to be called an Emperor, when he might have had Emperors for his valets" (and additionally regretted his assumption of the consulship for life and "the fatal intermarriage with the house of Austria").[89] It recognized that "liberal opinions" had suffered under Napoleon's "military dominion." While "submission" to Napoleon was "better merited" than to Louis, the *Dwarf* noted, "yet servitude was required."[90] Still, Wooler presented his criticisms in a fashion that placed Britain's own government in the worst comparative light possible.

The Bonapartist regime, unlike France's earlier revolutionary governments, had indeed been a "tyranny," rife with police and government agents "at every man's elbow," Wooler wrote (and in this authoritarianism, he pointedly noted, Napoleon's regime "might have satisfied even the English administration"). But in other respects, Napoleon's government had stood as a reproof to Britain's governors. The arts had been encouraged; just and liberal laws had been established; bribery and entrapment were not, as in Castlereagh's Britain, endemic. Napoleon's system had not been ideal, but at least circumstances could be blamed: "In a time of danger and difficulty, of foreign war, multiplied in a thousand degrees, France was compelled to trust herself to the guidance of one great man:—in a time of profound peace and general repose, England is called upon to confide the powers of an absolute tyranny into the hands of a hundred little ones."[91] While rejoicing "that humanity is freed from one plague," Britons should remember that a more burdensome plague remained. Bonaparte's conduct, while "criminal," had been superior to that of any other sovereign: he had been "less abusive of the enormous power placed in his hands, than it is reasonable to expect any other person would have been."[92] Wooler's ambivalence about Napoleon was not so great as to prevent him publishing, in 1819, a poem that asked "protecting heaven" to bless Napoleon, and that declared his "valiant deeds" would "live for ever / Gallia's pride and Britain's shame."[93]

In the spring of 1817, Wooler found himself personally entangled in the convoluted web of logic with which loyalists hoped to bridge the rift of 1688. The editor was arrested, and charged in the Court of King's Bench with, amazingly, "a libel upon King John, King Charles the First, King James the second, and King William the Third: besides the commons house of Parliament, and *the whole people of England*, under the familiar appellation of *John Bull*." The mere notion that one might simultaneously libel James II and William III—let alone a national metonym—made the mind boggle. A few minutes before the charge was read in court, Wooler noted, "the customary oaths were administered, in which the descendants of that King James, are proscribed as rebels." And yet the court saw no contradiction between requiring allegiance to the House of Hanover and upholding James against a libel. The readiness to overlook this inconsistency was all too easily explicable, according to Wooler: the present ministry hoped to abandon Brunswick principles for Stuart ones.[94] The reality—a monarchy whose roots were elective—must be replaced in the public mind by a fictive monarchy true to Stuart political theory.

A curious footnote to the radical assault on "legitimacy," and one that illustrates yet again the delight that opposition members took in using loyalist logic to undercut loyalism, lies in the radical reaction to the death in childbirth of Princess Charlotte, the heiress presumptive to the throne. This sudden and unexpected hitch in the orderly narrative of Legitimacy allowed British radicals to stress the artificiality of that narrative. A remarkable genealogical coincidence allowed them to use Napoleon to make their point.[95]

The first reports of Charlotte's death, in November 1817, were received by Wooler with measured sympathy. It would have been too much to expect the *Black Dwarf* "to mourn merely for a *Princess*," but Wooler did offer condolences to her grieving husband. (Cobbett was more hard-hearted, pronouncing it "impossible . . . to feel either joy or sorrow at any event which affects any person of the Royal Family, unless such event also affect ourselves or our country"; the death of a young woman in childbirth, he declared, was too common an event to comment upon.)[96] The *Dwarf* praised Charlotte for having distanced herself from court pomp. If any member of the royal family might have ushered in reform, it would have been Charlotte, a "ray of hope" whose reign might have "healed our present sorrows." Her death had not only removed a good woman from the line of succession, but had restored the spirits of her father's despotic ministers.[97]

Charlotte's death left the royal succession looking distinctly grayer: rather than the Regent's youthful daughter, the country found itself awaiting the rule of his aging brothers. That the duke of York—the commander-in-chief and thus a potential *"military monarch"*—now stood first in the line of succession worried Wooler: the coming of Frederick Augustus to power "might totally annihilate even the semblance of liberty" (for a military ruler would necessarily bring with him "despotism").[98] Another question of succession seemed equally pressing. It was very likely that none of George III's sons would produce legitimate offspring. (One, the duke of Kent, soon did: Victoria, born in 1819.) Who would then succeed to the throne? The publisher William Hone, in a pamphlet produced soon after Charlotte's death, provided an answer. If George's sons died without issue, then the Princess Catherine, third cousin of Princess Charlotte and the wife of Napoleon's brother Jerome, would be third in line of succession to the British crown. If the continental princes first and second in line were to die childless, then Catherine's son (also named Jerome) could, on professing the Protestant religion, succeed to the throne on her death. Thus, Hone concluded, "unless Parliament interferes, the line of GUELPH failing, the British Throne may be filled in succession by the line of BUONAPARTE."[99]

Wooler practically rubbed his hands in glee at the ironies that this tortuous genealogical reasoning produced. Britain had spent a fortune in lives and money fighting "to preserve the crowns of all countries in a lineal descent, as a matter of right and a principle of religion." Hence the nation's crusade, fought with "the united arms of the *legitimate race*," against Napoleon, "who was only descended from his own parents." And the result of Britain's great war against political illegitimacy? "The NEPHEW of NAPOLEON is GREAT GRANDSON to the KING OF ENGLAND; and by lineal descent, may one day claim the throne of that country which now detains his uncle a prisoner as an illegitimate usurper!" Wooler lingered over the delicious thought of Castlereagh, Legitimacy's great defender, having at some future date to "unsay all his tirades against Napoleon, and compliment the virtues of the Bonapartean dynasty!" Legitimacy, to be consistent in its principles, would have to crown the nephew of the great usurper.[100]

While he reveled in the rhetorical ploy of being more legitimist than the legitimists, Wooler's ultimate goal was not to embrace hereditary principles. He had no desire "a second time to trouble Germany for a race of monarchs," nor to place a Bonaparte on the British throne. Should Britain be deprived of a Brunswick, "perhaps the good sense of the nation may be consulted," and a ruler found in Britain. The British people should not suffer a stranger to come and demand allegiance, as William the Conqueror had in an earlier day. They were still at liberty, Wooler reminded his readers, "to act as freely as our ancestors at the revolution of 1688."[101]

The energy that post-Waterloo radicals expended contemplating a deposed emperor may at first appear backward-looking or fanciful—a politically questionable tangent.[102] Rather than a marginal, easily discounted burst of inexplicable hero worship, however—mere static in the transmission of political culture—pro-Napoleonic sentiment was a seriously intended component of the radical critique of British government. When the radical weaver and poet Samuel Bamford, visiting the "Waterloo Museum" in London at the time of his Peterloo trial, doffed his hat to the hat of Napoleon on exhibition, and "reverently" touched the weapons of Napoleon's generals, the gestures were neither frivolous nor idiosyncratic.[103] Napoleon had come to stand for a set of arguments about British government. His case allowed the thorny matters of British history, the constitution, and the monarchy to be approached from new directions.

The radical reworking of loyalist language relating to Napoleon—such as the term "legitimacy"—reminds us that radical discourse was not an autonomous creation but something that adapted itself to the contours of loyalist argument. Nor was there a single radical discourse: Napoleon was used to different ends by radicals with sharply contrasting visions of history's relevance. For constitutionalists, historical analogies with Napoleon provided the means by which to distinguish elective from hereditary monarchy—and to insist that the Prince Regent stop sitting on the fence between these two and acknowledge his own resemblance to Napoleon. For republicans like Sherwin, Davenport, and Wooler, Napoleon helped make concrete the possibility of an alternative system of government, while allowing them the option of keeping some distance from the Terror. Skillful appropriation of anti-Napoleonic rhetoric allowed these radicals to portray Britain's ministers as hypocritical liberticides. The figure of Napoleon assisted republicans, moreover, in their critique of the constitutionalist idiom favored by some of their fellow radicals.

Somewhat like the people's princess Charlotte, whose death so young allowed her to become many things to many people—or like the Regent's estranged wife (and Charlotte's mother) Caroline, who in 1820–21 became the eye of a radical whirlwind[104]—Napoleon, once removed from power, functioned in British radical argument as a counter-monarch. His résumé was much fuller than that of either woman, of course. But like them, he posed a contrasting case that enabled the interrogation of monarchy. Measuring Napoleon against the yardstick of history, radicals were also measuring contemporary Britain against the Napoleonic France they imagined.

CHAPTER 7

The Politics of Exile

Hearts that were not so weak as to sigh at the murder of
the Duke d'Enghien ... will bleed for ... the culinary pri-
vations of the Great Napoleon.

Quarterly Review, January 1817[1]

Behold the grand result in yon lone isle,
And, as thy nature urges, weep or smile.
Sigh to behold the eagle's lofty rage
Reduced to nibble at his narrow cage;
Smile to survey the Queller of the Nations
Now daily squabbling o'er disputed rations;
. . .
Behold the scales in which his fortune hangs,
A surgeon's statement and an earl's harangues!
A bust delayed, a book refused, can shake
The sleep of him who kept the world awake.

Byron, "The Age of Bronze," 1823[2]

During the years of war, a number of British writers had rushed to
defend the sport of boxing, which was under siege from evangelical and
humanitarian reformers. William Cobbett had declared pugilism to be a
distinctively English popular pastime, a manly mode of terminating
quarrels which, depending as it did on "fair play," contrasted with more
cowardly continental practices. Sparring, moreover, honed the martial
mettle of both boxer and spectator.[3] If this peculiarly English activity
declined, Cobbett had warned, so too might the nation.

Given the importance of boxing to contemporary appraisals of the

11. C. Williams, "Boxiana, or, the Fancy," 1815 (Houghton Library, Harvard University)

nation's health, it is no surprise that the bout between Britain and Napoleon was figured in terms of "the Fancy."[4] A poem that surfaced in opposition newspapers, soon after Napoleon's deportation to St. Helena, admonished one party in a boxing match for his poor sportsmanship:

> WHAT! BEN, my big hero, is *this* thy renown?
> Is *this* the new go?—kick a man, when he's *down!*
> When the foe has knock'd under, to tread on him *then*—
> By the fist of my father, I blush for thee, BEN![5]

Kicking a prone opponent was most assuredly not fair play.

The poem only hinted at the identities of the fighters (Ben, it explained, displayed not a single cowardly white feather but "a whole PLUME"—a reference to the Prince of Wales' crest). An October 1815 caricature that borrowed the opening stanza was more explicit. The print depicted the result of a match between Napoleon and the Prince Regent.[6] Bonaparte lies on the ground, felled by George. Both men are shirtless; the Regent's gross bulk contrasts with Napoleon's handsome features. One observer, perhaps a referee, looks on in horror, raising his hands as if to stop the fight. He recites the familiar stanza admonishing Ben. Another onlooker cries, "Foul! Foul! by all the rules of honor!" But the Regent's ministers defend the conduct. One holds a manuscript reading, "Rules of the new Fancy. Kicking allowed."[7]

The poem and caricature accused the Regent and his government of a shocking breech of etiquette—and more than that, if one agreed with Cobbett that boxing was a key to the English national character. A later stanza of the poem, indeed, attributed the Regent's departure from fair play to his "cursed foreign notions," which had left in his body "hardly a drop . . . / Of pure English claret." The Regent's unmanly "wigs, . . . gold lace and lotions" contrasted with John Bull's traditional heartiness. The cruel deportation of Bonaparte was part and parcel of a general national disintegration, evident at the very pinnacle of society.

Napoleon's enforced exile and imprisonment, as this chapter will show, came under immediate fire from British radicals. They portrayed the government's policy as defying the English constitution. The opposition's great fear was that the Prince Regent wished to erase the distinction between Britain's monarchy and its continental counterparts. Lovell, writing in August 1815, after Napoleon had left Plymouth harbor, feared that George had "become surrounded with all the attributes of a Continental Sovereign, and has the power of dispensing with constitutional forms as much as any of the great Potentates who compose the Confederacy." With Bonaparte gone ("BONAPARTE, who was so impious as to affirm . . . that the approbation of a people was the most legitimate title which a Prince could have to the sovereignty of a nation") so too, felt Lovell, had disappeared a glorious instance of the elective principle. The threat to British liberties was clear. By sending Napoleon to "the distant prison house of St. Helena" without consulting Parliament, the Regent's ministers were simply flexing their muscles. The action demonstrated that the Regent could "act independent of any restraints springing from the Constitution of this country." He could now be as arbitrary as any continental dynast.[8] As the *Northumberland* set sail for St. Helena, many joined Lovell in suggesting that Napoleon's treatment was an ill portent for all British subjects. An enforced exile, they argued, defied the British constitution and the law of nations alike, and revealed the ministry's desire to eclipse Parliament and expunge basic liberties.

Napoleon did not vanish from British political discourse with the *Northumberland*'s disappearance over the horizon. Instead, his figure took on new meanings, as British observers put him to new political uses. By the time Napoleon had landed on St. Helena, a camp of ardent journalists and politicians was already protesting loudly against the conditions and the very fact of his imprisonment. They would use Napoleon to demonstrate the fragility of British liberties. In captivity, the man many had denounced as despotic would become instead a victim demonstrating the would-be despotism of British ministers. Reformers believed the very hallmarks of English liberty—habeas corpus, trial by jury, freedom of the press—were under fire. Habeas corpus had been repeatedly suspended during the wars; state use of "special juries," composed of men deemed reliable, had become habitual; one radical journalist after another had been tried for libel. Hence the desire to invoke each of these in discussions of Napoleon's captivity. Napoleon's treatment at the hands of his British jailers would be read as a test of the health of Britain's constitution and its national character.

None were more vocal in denouncing Bonaparte's detention than the radicals who were convinced by his recent declarations of republicanism. Thomas Wooler of the *Black Dwarf* decried the "petty and malignant" treatment of the exiled leader—persecution especially repellent because it was being meted out to Napoleon by "men more guilty than himself, . . . destitute of any virtue to relieve the dark page of their history." Napoleon's detention allowed Wooler to harp upon the ministry's neglect of domestic concerns: thousands were being spent per year, Wooler told his readers, "to torture one man abroad, while tens of thousands are starving at home to furnish the expense."[9] Other *Dwarf* contributors sympathized more directly with the detainee himself. In the words of one 1817 poem published in the weekly, St. Helena was "the prison of the brave"—and "the grave" of "England's honour."[10]

But even those uncertain about his merits as a leader could grieve for him as a victim of British persecution. Sympathy could be extended to Napoleon the long-suffering prisoner which might never have been granted to Napoleon the proud emperor. The British myth of Napoleon took on its richest poetic shadings, in the wake of Waterloo, in its portrayal of a man who had climbed to unprecedented heights only to fall precipitously. Napoleon's suffering under adversity on St. Helena— patient suffering, some claimed—added a human dimension to his public persona. Even in the eyes of some long-standing critics, Napoleon began to lose his demonic luster and to seem worthy of qualified elegy. He became a moral subject—indeed an aesthetic one, as posthumous poems, plays, and paintings on the lonely exile (considered in the chapter following this one) would reveal. The exile on St. Helena was a figure whose meaning would come to transcend the mundanely political. But the debate that made this transformation possible would be a partisan conflict rife with charges of intrigue and dark design, a cold war drama replete with claims of spying, coded messages, unlawful detention, and assassination.

Those sympathetic to Napoleon made much of his decision to surrender to Britain, rather than to his continental enemies. His preference (as it was characterized by writers willing to overlook his lack of alternatives) was interpreted as "perhaps one of the best and one of the most welcome compliments that could be paid" to England's "native independence."[11] Reading the surrender as an embrace of "English law and British generosity" fitted nicely with the claim that Napoleon's aim as emperor had been to adapt the principles of Britain's constitution to the French nation.[12] If his admiration for British principles had not revealed itself sufficiently in his constitutional reforms, surely it did so now in his readiness to place himself under British law. (John Wilson Croker would have none of this, refusing to be taken in by the "shallow and blundering flattery of the English fashions, manners, and laws" Napoleon suddenly undertook once aboard the *Bellerophon*.)[13] Napoleon's act, according to Lovell, was that of "a brave man" setting out "to make trial of the generosity of his rival."[14] If so, Napoleon's test of British magnanimity and the British constitution was yielding disappointing results.

Opposition writers dwelt on Napoleon's submission to British law in order to argue that the moment he had become "subject to" he had also come "under the protection of, *the laws of England*."[15] One *Statesman* correspondent saw the surrender as a "voluntary emigration" by which Napoleon had instantly become subject to British laws.[16] For Cobbett, the moment at which Napoleon "became as much subject to [Britain's] laws as if he had been born, bred, and had always resided there" came a little later, at the "moment the waters of the ocean bore him within the constitutional jurisdiction of the country."[17] British laws certainly applied to Bonaparte once he had reached Plymouth, wrote Cobbett: if Napoleon had murdered a fellow passenger aboard the *Bellerophon*, he would have been brought ashore and tried in Devon. Cobbett's conclusion was twofold. First, Napoleon could hardly have had time to commit a crime punishable by a British court, "because he never, till now, was within the dominions of England." And second, Napoleon, once under British jurisdiction, was entitled to enjoy the rights due him under British law, including habeas corpus and trial by jury. The fact that he was not going on trial showed the government's recognition that no jury would believe Bonaparte had committed a crime *"within the jurisdiction of the court."*[18]

Under British law, then, Napoleon should either be tried or freed. Under the law of nations, too, several opposition writers suggested, Britain had no right to hold onto Napoleon after his defeat.[19] Bonaparte had not been a rebel or a usurper but an independent Elban sovereign, wrote the tyrannicidally pen-named "Cassius" in an early August *Statesman*. In waging war on France, "the utmost he could lose would be his kingdom"; defeated, he was simply "an illustrious prisoner of war."[20] And as Lovell and Lofft added in the following days, citing Blackstone and Vattel respectively, once a war was over, a prisoner must be set free.[21] Napoleon was *"no subject of ours,"* Lofft insisted; "once forced from our island," the former emperor's movements could not be hindered by British power.[22] The law of nations, on which Goldsmith had rested his argument for assassination during the war, was now in peacetime used to agitate for Napoleon's release.

The ministry, it was all too evident, planned to transport Napoleon to St. Helena without a trial. The absence of a hearing, or even of "a distinct accusation" against Napoleon, prompted the *Statesman* to term the government's treatment of its prisoner "arbitrary and cruel."[23] The decision to exile the captive seemed all the more pernicious because it had been made without consulting Parliament.[24] The legislature had been prorogued in mid-July, and then its prorogation had been extended. By the time Parliament met again, as Capel Lofft pointed out, the *Northumberland* would have arrived at St. Helena and the chambers would have only a *fait accompli* to debate.[25] Opposition journalists were outraged at the "extra-judicial" nature of the government's policy.[26] Not that they would be any more forgiving once the banishment had retrospectively been given parliamentary sanction ("as if a parliament of Englishmen could abrogate the rights of all mankind, and justify an infringement of the prescriptive principles of humanity and civilization").[27] Cobbett, Burdon, and Lovell all condemned the ministry's actions as threatening the constitution; working outside of the written and customary law in this fashion, according to Cobbett, betokened "high treason against the *national sovereignty*."[28] Napoleon's expulsion, in sum, had ramifications extending far beyond his own personal fortunes. In the process by which he was being dispatched to a mid-Atlantic exile, the opposition read the ministry's general hostility to habeas corpus and trial by jury, and its desire to completely subordinate the legislature to an overreaching executive.

All Britons should fear this new turn in ministerial policy, opposition writers suggested. Napoleon's fate today might be that of any other British subject tomorrow. If Napoleon's transportation were effected "without remonstrance," the *Statesman* warned in August, a system might come into being that in future days "may be extended to any person who may become obnoxious to that Government."[29] Napoleon's particular identity did not signify, Cobbett wrote around the same time:

> He is the man who will give his name to the age in which he has lived. His renown will swallow up that of all other men. But that is no matter. In the eye of the law, he is a mere man, who was in the county of Devon, and, as the COURIER tells me, has been transported from that county beyond the seas, without a trial. Now, if *one* man can be thus transported from the County of Devon, why not another; why not any man? Why any more *trials*, previous to transportation?[30]

Napoleon's banishment set a precedent that should terrify all Britons; the wrong committed against him was "in *principle* committed against *every individual* in this country, and may, sooner or later, be practically visited accordingly."[31] The *Statesman*'s Timothy Trueman endorsed Cobbett's warning, maintaining that if ministers could dispense with trial by jury in this one case, then they were "as absolute masters of the lives and properties of the people of England as ever JAMES II. desired to be."[32] But Cobbett—even as he reiterated his fear that the "case of the great, the immortal, the resplendent Napoleon may, at any moment, become that of any subject of this nation"—suggested the possibility of a happier outcome as well. Napoleon had already advanced the cause of civil liberty more than any living man. Perhaps he might now, through his example as a victim of British injustice, become "the legal corrector of an outrage, involving . . . the constitutional integrity and protection of every one living within the legal jurisdiction of the British dominions."[33]

While opposition writers feared Napoleon's expulsion could be used to justify future abuses of power, they also warned that this "dreadful experiment" might prove a precedent just as dangerous to Europe's dynasts.[34] As the British editor of some letters of the count de Las Cases, one of Napoleon's companions in his exile, suggested, the St. Helena residence being constructed for Napoleon might some day find itself housing "some people, who are now exulting in Napoleon's humiliation and sufferings."[35] A work smuggled from St. Helena in late 1817 at Napoleon's behest (thought by some contemporaries to have been written by Bonaparte himself) imagined a future moment when "in the revolution of ages, a king of England shall be brought before the dread tribunal of the nation." At that time, the author warned, the imprisonment of an earlier "great sovereign," "twice the annointed [sic] of the Lord, twice consecrated by religion," might be cited in justification.[36]

Critics sought to set Napoleon's "*Ostracism*" in the most sweeping historical framework.[37] Cobbett claimed that the outrageous plan "would stink in the nostrils of the world for ages to come."[38] But while some damned the very decision to imprison Napoleon, others focused on criticizing the *nature* of his imprisonment. The two positions were not mutually exclusive: those who opposed exile in the first place stood foremost among those criticizing the terms of the captivity. But even some who had acknowledged the necessity of detention, or had tacitly acquiesced in the enterprise, came to challenge the fashion in which the captive emperor was treated. Periodical literature and parliamentary debate overflowed with minute details of Bonaparte's circumstances: price schedules of the foods provided to the emperor's retinue; anecdotal evidence of the climate's wholesome or enervating qualities; testimony regarding Napoleon's reading materials; and accounts of his miniature power struggle with the last of his antagonists, the island's governor, Sir Hudson Lowe. Even if Napoleon did indeed need to be kept under lock and key for the sake of Europe—many would conclude from this evidence—surely there were more humane ways of going about it.

The departure of Napoleon for St. Helena stirred up considerable curiosity about the island. British readers were now "epidemically overrun with accounts, plans, and views of St. Helena, most of which are borrowed and deteriorated from former publications."[39] The isolated and rocky island, ten by six miles in size and seven hundred miles removed from its nearest neighbor, seems to have been constructed with political controversy in mind: its tropical, windswept environment could easily be characterized in extreme terms, either as unusually salubrious or uniquely debilitating; its remoteness made it unlikely that such arguments would be easily settled. So while critics of Napoleon's captivity termed St. Helena "a desert island" or "the most lonely and desolate of deserted rocks," government supporters could portray it (as a skeptical *Edinburgh Review* put it) "as little less than a terrestrial paradise."[40]

Many painted the island's climate as "destructive to health," arguing that Napoleon's exile amounted to a death sentence. Reportedly, many British soldiers stationed on St. Helena had died; a tour of local cemeteries supposedly revealed few islanders to have lived past forty-five.[41] Some saw Napoleon's enforced exile as regicide in all but name: while Charles I and Louis XVI had been executed in a manner that was "prompt, and without agony!", Napoleon was consigned to "a death sufficiently slow to be apparently natural."[42] Ministerial writers insisted on the environment's healthful qualities (John Wilson Croker pronounced himself satisfied that the "alleged plague of rats" was imaginary).[43] But the ministry would find itself dogged by complaints about Napoleon's health, especially after the prisoner refused to continue his only form of exercise, horse riding, because of the new requirement, late in 1816, that an English officer accompany him. So ministerial supporters tried to emphasize Napoleon's continued heartiness—reporting, for example, that there was "nothing in the appearance of Bonaparte which in the least indicated ill health; on the contrary, he looked well, and less bloated than ordinary."[44]

Just as controversial as St. Helena's natural environment were the material goods with which Napoleon had been provided, and the social privileges he was allowed. The *Statesman* protested about the "cruel" attempt to limit Napoleon's entourage on St. Helena.[45] The size of his retinue decreased as members came severally back to Europe and published their harrowing accounts of St. Helena (his servant Santini reporting in 1817 the shortage of butter, the high price of meat, the scarcity of water, and in general the *"absolute want"* suffered by Napoleon).[46] Ministerial writers responded not simply by denying Napoleon's deprivation, but by condemning the indulgences provided for this "great criminal."[47] Croker's position at the Admiralty may have prompted him to deny the "absurd stories" that Napoleon's accommodation and furnishings were "extravagant"—but he gladly endorsed the sentiment that too much attention had been shown Bonaparte, "much more than is consistent with good morals or good policy."[48] The *Quarterly* mocked Santini's accounts of *"famine,"* and held that rather than relax "the already too loose custody" of Bonaparte, further restrictions should be imposed.[49] Lewis Goldsmith, writing in 1816, decried the "royal magnificence" enjoyed by the low-born prisoner. Napoleon deserved "to die a thousand deaths," but the vanity of his dynastic captors could not thus treat a man who once "cohabited with the daughter of an Emperor," and whose person they therefore perceived as "sacred."[50] (On rare occasions, Goldsmith the young Jacobin could peek out through the shell of the mature anti-Napoleonist.)

One advocate of Napoleon cited the high price of his captivity in order to argue that Bonaparte should instead be sent to Britain. A simple detention in England or Scotland would require a fraction of the sum currently being spent, the pamphleteer reasoned, and Napoleon and his followers would be happier and healthier. In English prisons, captives heard news of their relatives and had access to newspapers and books. Napoleon, by contrast, was starved for news of his wife and son, and of the world.[51] Anthony Mackenrot, whose race to the *Bellerophon* had proved so unfruitful, wrote to the *Statesman* and Cobbett's *Political Register* of his failed efforts to send issues of the two newspapers (and other works) to St. Helena. The government had informed him that periodicals and books were already being supplied to the prisoner and his retinue, and that the ones he had sent would not be passed on. Apparently, Mackenrot concluded, "Government has determined to imprison the intellects as well as the person of the Great Napoleon, and will most probably confine the Newspapers to be sent to him to the courtly columns of the *Herald, Post, Times,* and *Courier.*"[52]

Napoleon's access to reading matter would remain a point of controversy. Lady Holland sent boxes of books to Napoleon. Her husband, who had vociferously protested in the Lords against the captivity itself, further denounced the restrictions on reading matter.[53] Famously, Sir Hudson Lowe would refuse to let Napoleon have the volumes that John Cam Hobhouse sent to the island because Hobhouse had inscribed his work, not to General Bonaparte, but to the Emperor Napoleon.[54] (The policy of refusing to acknowledge Napoleon's desired title predated Lowe: in early November 1815, Admiral George Cockburn had feigned puzzlement at Count Bertrand's reference to an emperor, claiming to "have no cognizance of any Emperor, being actually upon this Island, or of any Person possessing such Dignity having (as stated by you) come hither with me in the Northumberland.")[55] The reformist MP and future lord chancellor Henry Brougham, writing anonymously in the

Edinburgh Review, condemned the restrictions on Napoleon's reading as stemming not from "any rational plan of security" but from a design to create "vexation and mere annoyance."[56] There was no reasonable justification for depriving him of the publications that criticized his confinement: "Let him read as much abuse of his keepers as he can find printed."[57]

Of such abuse there was much. Lowe's terror at the thought that his illustrious prisoner might escape—a terror no doubt sharpened by the criticism Campbell had received after his supposed laxity—made him devise ever more binding rules and restraints for Napoleon and his followers. Lowe made it difficult for Napoleon to receive visitors; directed that letters sent to or from Longwood, Napoleon's residence, be inspected at the governor's headquarters; mandated twice-daily sightings of Napoleon, lest the prisoner somehow escape. Napoleon, in response, withdrew from sight, sometimes refusing even to stroll in his garden if it meant submitting to the indignity of being watched. Relations between the prisoner and his jailer quickly broke down.

The tale of the mutual suspicion and animosity between Napoleon and Lowe resembles, at moments, an absurdist play. Theirs was a battle of two strong wills, fought at arm's length (for they met only a half-dozen times)—a battle scrutinized by distant political observers who feasted on every tidbit they could garner about the two men's affairs. It was a battle over the most petty-seeming of affairs, affairs taken by Napoleon's advocates to be matters of life and death. In a sense, the debate over Napoleon's conditions amounted to a continuation of the wartime debate over assassination. The exercise Napoleon was deprived of, the spoiled and meager foods he was said to have been provided with, the medical attention that Lowe was believed to have interfered with for political reasons: all these were seen as hurrying Napoleon, deliberately or no, to an early grave. Calling for an investigation of such charges, Brougham noted that if Napoleon died before the British government proved itself to have acted honorably, "we may rest assured that her justification will never be complete." Until the allegations were answered, "no man can pretend to deny that there is some colour for even the worst imputations which may be flung upon the character of the nation."[58] The *Black Dwarf* declared that only Napoleon's removal from St. Helena would "vindicate the national character" of Britain. If he should die on the island, his death would "be imputed to the agency, or to the silence of the nation."[59]

All Lowe's restrictions were criticized by the British opposition and by Napoleon. A pamphlet to which Napoleon attached his imprimatur lambasted Lowe for designing restrictions "according to his own fancy, precipitately, and in forms illegal and obscure." The "caprice" and "folly of a single man" was the law on St. Helena (there was "no council, no magistrate, no lawyer, no public opinion on this rock"). The "insidious, ignoble, and violent" Lowe was a dictator to rival the worst portraits of Bonaparte himself.[60] Lowe's greatest mistake, from the standpoint of public relations, was his handling of Barry O'Meara, the navy surgeon who served as Napoleon's doctor from 1815 to 1818. Lowe's attempts to limit the topics of conversation between O'Meara and Bonaparte, and his effort to have O'Meara report to him about Napoleon's feelings—essentially to recruit the doctor as a spy—backfired. O'Meara would become the most prolific reporter in the English language on Napoleon's captivity, anonymously at first, and then, once removed from St. Helena and drummed out of the navy, under his own name. No one did more to turn opinion against the island's governor. Even some who accepted the rationale for imprisoning Bonaparte came, after reading O'Meara, to feel a strong aversion to his oppressive jailer. By the time Benjamin Haydon bumped into Lowe on the street in 1832, the reputation of the "paltry jailer" (Byron's phrase) was set in stone.[61] Taking "a d—n good stare" at the man, Haydon concluded that a "meaner face no assassin ever had. He answered Napoleon's description to a Tee."[62]

The historian wishing to determine what really happened on St. Helena faces a labyrinth of sources.[63] Friends and enemies of Napoleon wrote works that contradicted one another and overflowed with mutual recriminations. Some writings were anonymous; the authorship of other works, with names attached, was sometimes thrown into question by contemporaries. Even ideological soulmates attacked each other's accounts. An 1816 book by William Warden, the *Northumberland*'s surgeon, was criticized not only by an anti-Napoleonic *Quarterly* reviewer (who termed Warden "the ignorant tool of the cabal" of St. Helena)[64] but also, anonymously, by a fellow Napoleonic advocate (who noted that Warden's ignorance of French and Italian made him dependent on members of Napoleon's camp as translators).[65] Why would one admirer of Napoleon—probably O'Meara, who would in 1819 claim credit for this critique—thus impugn the account of another?[66] John Wilson Croker suggested that Napoleon, by speaking through a series of mouthpieces, was engaged in a process of constantly revising his own *apologia*, allowing the testimony of one agent to be corrected by another. The beauty of this ventriloquistic "trickery," Croker wrote, was Napoleon's ability to disavow a tract which had not achieved all it might, in order to reiterate its claims "with greater care and skill."[67]

With even the question of authorship such a hall of mirrors, the historical reconstruction of events seems near-impossible; which side a historian chooses depends largely on the credibility he assigns to O'Meara, to Lowe, and to the various members of Napoleon's company who recorded for posterity their island experiences. Matters as basic as Napoleon's physical circumstances remain controversial to this day. A present-day French historian pronounces authoritatively that "Saint Helena has a healthful climate, and Napoleon's food was good, carefully prepared, and plentiful."[68] By contrast, a recent English student of Napoleon's years in exile, having herself visited the island, affirms nineteenth-century accounts of debilitating winds and ubiquitous rodents.[69]

For the historian of British opinion, what matters is not the actual conditions Napoleon faced, but the controversy itself. In the six years of the exile, a politically aware Briton, a reader of pamphlets and periodicals, would have been besieged by contradictory claims about the events on St. Helena. Even had one encountered only the *Quarterly Review*, or alternatively the *Edinburgh*, one would have become familiar with the accusations being made by the other side. No matter how one reacted to this debate—by assailing Lowe, applauding him, or throwing up one's hands in confusion—one would have been aware of the contentious dynamic at work. The debate took on a life of its own, requiring only occasional replenishment from the sources at St. Helena. The ideological and the anecdotal became intertwined to the point where the larger issues at stake seemed hostage to personal minutiae. The debate may have centered on foodstuffs and newspapers. This did not prevent its participants from using the rhetoric of grand political drama, in which each side could accuse the other of conspiracy and treachery.

For the anonymous author of one 1818 pamphlet, for example— *Letters from the Island of St. Helena, Exposing the Unnecessary Severity Exercised towards Napoleon*—the island was a prison, not only for the fallen emperor but for all its residents. Despite being British subjects, "the poor devils of islanders here are subjected to the most arbitrary

power which has ever been entrusted to an *English* Governor," the
pamphlet complained. Sir Hudson Lowe had set up an "odious system
of police, so contrary to our manners, laws, and customs." The belief
that one might without fear express one's opinion "openly and liberally,
as John Bull is accustomed to do," had been crippled by Lowe's restrictions. On arriving, the author claimed to have been warned not to voice
anything that might be construed as sympathy for Napoleon (" 'Don't
speak so loud; it is a crime here to call him Emperor, or even to say any
thing that is good of him' "). He responded that as an Englishman, he
would speak forthrightly: " 'Come, here is [Napoleon's] health in a
bumper. He is no longer our enemy!' " All others at the dinner table,
save two recent arrivals, kept silent, "and appeared like so many slaves,
in the presence of their masters."[70]

To explain Lowe's "obnoxious conduct," the pamphleteer trotted out
the trusty standby of national character. Lowe had spent many years
commanding "a foreign [in fact, a Corsican] regiment, chiefly composed
of deserters and expatriated fellons [*sic*] and assassins." He "had entirely
lost the national character, knew no longer our manners or customs, in
place of which he had contracted the characteristic traits of those with
whom he had been so long accustomed to associate."[71] He had become
a foreigner. But blame could not be confined to the island's governor.
The secretary for war and the colonies, Lord Bathurst, had (the pamphleteer declared) spoken a falsehood in Parliament when he claimed no
new restrictions had been placed on Napoleon since Lowe's arrival.[72]
Either Bathurst had "been grossly deceived himself," or he had
"deceived the public." The falsehood must be corrected, for "the dignity
of the national character" was "involved in every transaction which
takes place at St. Helena."[73]

Lowe had his defenders, in and out of Parliament. Perhaps the most
curious tract supporting Napoleon's warden was an anonymous 1819
pamphlet titled *Facts, Illustrative of the Treatment of Napoléon
Buonaparte in Saint Helena*. The work's nameless author had been able
to carry out "minute inquiries and personal research" into Napoleon's
circumstances because, he reported, "affairs, not 'germaine to the
matter,' and in themselves wholly unimportant and uninteresting to the
generality of readers," had landed him on St. Helena. The author portrayed himself as a natural Whig, initially inclined to feel "indignation"
towards Lowe and sympathy for Napoleon's defenders, Las Cases
and Lord Holland. He had begun his visit "prepossessed in favour of

insulted, fallen greatness, and pitying Napoléon," but against all expectations he left the island siding with Lowe, whom he now saw to have been unfairly "attacked, vilified, and traduced."[74]

The pamphlet declared the author's conversion to be the simple result of his prejudices having been dissipated by "the sun of truth." [75] But the circumstances of his visit to the island were more interesting than that. Theodore Edward Hook, a renowned wit in the Prince Regent's circle, had in 1813 been rewarded, despite a complete ignorance of financial matters, with the position of accountant-general and treasurer of Mauritius. When, four years later, it was discovered that an underling had pocketed £12,000, Hook found himself shipped back to England, there to cool his heels for several years waiting to be investigated (and, as luck would have it, imprisoned). St. Helena was a stop on his shameful voyage back from Mauritius.[76] At the time Hook wrote his pamphlet, then, he needed to work his way back into the government's good graces. *Facts* (and the Tory newspaper Hook founded the following year, *John Bull*) should be read in light of the treasurer's awkward personal situation.

Hook's pamphlet was a compendium of assertions contradicting the claims of anti-Lowe pamphlets. Where Santini had described scarcity, Hook defended the high quality of the wines, meats, and breads supplied to Napoleon's household.[77] Where others had painted the island's climate as "destructive to human life, especially to Europeans,"[78] Hook insisted that the "refreshing" wind made for a "healthy and temperate" climate and that the island's natives were uniformly robust, and the women often pregnant. As evidence of the island's beneficial qualities, Hook offered the "rosy cheeks and sparkling eyes" of the children ("little traitors," he called them) of Bertrand and Montholon, two members of Napoleon's camp. In sum, to the Napoleonist assertion that "'*The Great man is dying on a rock*,'" Hook countered "the evident fact, 'that the *little* man is *living* on a *fertile plain*.'"[79]

In defending the restrictions imposed on Napoleon's reading matter, Hook raised the spectre of conspiracy. He elaborated on a suggestion tossed out by Bathurst in the Lords: "that attempts had been made, through the medium of newspapers, to hold communication with Napoleon."[80] How better for Napoleon to communicate with "his continental confederates," Hook asked, than "through the medium of the public papers"? As evidence, Hook pointed to one particular advertisement in a British newspaper, "peculiar in its form, curious in its contents, and pointedly, and purposely placed in a most conspicuous part of a Journal, not, as I believe, ordinarily admitting advertisements." The advertisement, Hook suggested, "will be seen on a reference, (which it is really worth while to make,) to be in cypher—the key is the Letter X. which stands amongst the figures, and the cypher was discovered several months afterwards at VIENNA!" If Napoleon's associates were at work even within the offices of the British press, how could one deny the need to limit his contact with printed material? Hook's trump card was the name of the newspaper in which the suspicious advertisement had appeared: "the *Anti-Gallican! Monitor*, of ALL papers."[81] If a coded message to Napoleon could be slipped under the nose of Lewis Goldsmith—or if, as Hook seemed to insinuate, Goldsmith himself could be a Napoleonic operative—surely some sort of restriction was needed.[82]

A reader of Hook's tract, turning to the pages of the *Antigallican* (which, contrary to Hook's claim, printed advertisements in every issue), would be disappointed: all one finds is sixteen lines of numbers, colons, and commas—possibly a coded message, but possibly nonsense.[83] Hook's claim that the letter X was "the key" seems meaningless (though a single X does indeed appear amidst the numbers). When John Wilson Croker echoed Hook's charge three years later, claiming in the *Quarterly Review* that Napoleon's "partizans" had communicated through "what appeared only an ordinary advertisement," he clearly did not expect many of his readers actually to have seen (or to remember) the paragraph in question, which was far from ordinary in appearance.[84] Whoever placed the advertisement took no pains to hide the fact that it should be read as—or as if—a coded message.

Goldsmith took Hook's charges as a personal affront.[85] He quickly asked the prime minister, Lord Liverpool, for an interview to explain the advertisement's publication. Hook's charge—coming as it did "in a publication which it is said has been published by order of His Majesty's Government"—amounted, as Goldsmith wrote to Liverpool, to a suggestion that the journalist had "play'd the part of an Hypocrite for the last 10 years & should be totally unworthy of the good Opinion which I know your Lordship is pleased to entertain of me."[86] In the *British Monitor* (the new title of Goldsmith's paper), Goldsmith denounced *Facts* as "a miserable rancorous rhapsody," "replete with falsehood." He was particularly incensed by the pamphlet's "barbarous" abuse of the Bertrand children, which showed the author to be a "fiend." Explaining his acceptance of the coded advertisement, Goldsmith noted that he had consulted not only other newspaper editors but the under-secretary of state for home affairs as to the propriety of its publication, and had been told to proceed. But Goldsmith went beyond merely defending himself against Hook's insinuations. He hinted that he was ready to re-evaluate the nature of the British government's treatment of Napoleon. If Hook's pamphlet reflected the sentiments of Sir Hudson Lowe, Goldsmith suggested, then the tract served to confirm rather than refute the charges of Las Cases and others.[87] The next week's *Monitor* featured a letter denouncing the anonymous pamphleteer ("the Governor's apologist") in terms that might easily have been lifted wholesale from a radical periodical.[88]

Goldsmith did not challenge the suggested provenance of the coded advertisement: it was indeed, he believed, a communication with Bonaparte. But Napoleon's sympathizers questioned the claim. Barry O'Meara, freshly returned from St. Helena and deprived of his position in the navy, suggested not only that Napoleon had very little contact with publications of any stripe, but also that the circumstances surrounding the *Antigallican*'s advertisement were even more peculiar than Goldsmith was ready to suggest. All issues of "interesting works," O'Meara claimed, "particularly any numbers of the *Edinburgh Review*," were "bought up by Sir Hudson Lowe and Sir Thomas Reade, pretending, sometimes, that they are purchased for the use of Napoleon, but in reality to deprive him of any possibility of procuring them." So it was, in the first place, highly unlikely that Bonaparte would see any suspicious publication. Even loyalist journals were rarely delivered. "Not a single number of the Antigallican," O'Meara reported, "except *one*, ever arrived at Longwood." That one issue, O'Meara continued, "was sent there by Sir Hudson Lowe's directions," under "circumstances, then inexplicable." O'Meara himself had been handed a copy of the *Antigallican* in July 1817, "WITH DIRECTIONS TO DELIVER IT TO NAPOLEON." (Though this may have been a different issue from that containing the coded advertisement, it did feature, according to O'Meara, "a letter addressed to 'General Bonaparte.'") The surgeon thought it reasonable to conclude that the British government had itself planted the coded message "as a pretext to excuse the system which had been adopted towards Napoleon, of withdrawing from him every number of the TIMES and other newspapers, in which there appeared any article, that might be supposed calculated to afford him some consolation." Certainly if the message originated with the government, it would explain why the author of the *Facts* should claim acquaintance with the mysterious "key" to the coded message. As circumstances making more likely his theory of an anti- rather than pro-Napoleonic conspiracy, O'Meara pointed out that a few months before the advertisement's placement, the comte de Montholon, one of Napoleon's island entourage, had officially complained to Lowe about the paucity of newspapers sent to Longwood—and that a few months after the advertisement, the home secretary had in a parliamentary defense of the existing restrictions "made a point of alluding to this *important* discovery" of the coded message.[89]

O'Meara would become one of the most controversial figures in the debate over St. Helena, his expulsion from the navy itself becoming a bone of contention for the British political audience. Brougham, in the *Edinburgh*, gladly embraced O'Meara's account of abuses at St. Helena, and joined him in condemning Hook's anonymous *Facts*.[90] O'Meara reached the apex of his notoriety after Napoleon's death, when in 1822 he published his magnum opus, *Napoleon in Exile; or, A Voice from St Helena*. Dedicated to Lady Holland, the two-volume work (which went through five British editions in a few months' time) provided a detailed daily account of the surgeon's tenure on the island, relating his conversations with Napoleon and laying out the case against Lowe.[91] Croker, naturally, saw the book as an "immense and complicated tissue of calumny and falsehood"—a further illustration of Napoleon's "peculiar . . . knack at discovering persons who were fit to be made his tools." Croker took advantage of his dual position, as first secretary to the Admiralty and anonymous reviewer in the *Quarterly*, to leak to himself—quoting from his own official correspondence while professing ignorance as to how such material "got into the public papers" (though concluding that "Mr. Croker's letter" bore "all the marks of official authority" and seemed authentic). Croker aimed to discredit O'Meara by claiming the surgeon had initially been eager to spy for Lowe: O'Meara had "*volunteered*" this duty, "*forcing*" gossip on the uninterested governor. Lowe's subordinates had tolerated such "tittle-tattle," little realizing the "double treachery" O'Meara had in mind.[92]

Among O'Meara's champions were many long-time congregants of the Napoleonic church (Lady Holland wrote to tell Count Bertrand that O'Meara's book had "revived & Strengthened" her attachment to Napoleon).[93] But O'Meara's evangelism brought others into the fold as well. Thomas Macaulay, not yet twenty-two, wrote to his father that the recently published *Napoleon in Exile* had "made me Buonapartiste." The

young man hastened to qualify this remark: he was speaking "comparatively, with reference to my former opinion of the man"; undoubtedly
Napoleon was "wicked," like "all conquerors, and almost all kings." But
he had "destroyed such immense and ancient abuses," and provided his
people with such an "admirable" system of jurisprudence. "When prejudices have subsided," Macaulay concluded, Napoleon would be "ranked
with the great mixed Characters of ancient and modern times."[94]

O'Meara's work was powerful enough to convert another budding
historian as well, at least for a time. A year after Napoleon's death, the
26-year-old Thomas Carlyle allowed the human drama of St. Helena, as
reported by O'Meara, to increase his "respect" for Napoleon and his
"indignation" at Lowe. Writing to his future wife Jane Welsh, Carlyle
noted that he had been especially affected by Napoleon's "touches of
human affection," which "enhance the respect of meaner mortals by
uniting it with their love."[95] Carlyle's letter should be read as part of his
arduous wooing of Jane, a far less critical observer of Napoleon than
he. The two wrote poems on Napoleon to one another, and Jane pretended to bristle at Thomas' suggestion that an acquaintance might conceivably "love and admire" Napoleon more than she herself did.[96] Still,
Carlyle's, like Macaulay's, letter testifies to the surgeon's persuasive
powers.

In a later decade, Carlyle would suggest that Napoleon had been
seduced by ambition and "the fatal charlatan-element"—by the "Sem-
blances" of dynasties and "old false Feudalities which he once saw
clearly to be false." Carlyle's 1840 lectures on hero worship picked up
the sartorial trope present in British criticism of Napoleon since the consulate, in order to denounce the "paltry patchwork of theatrical paper-
mantles, tinsel and mummery" that Napoleon had "wrapt his own great
reality in, thinking to make it more real thereby!"[97] But at this earlier
point, it was sincerity, not semblance, that Carlyle saw in the exile of St.
Helena.

On 5 May 1821, Napoleon Bonaparte died on St. Helena. When news
reached Britain in midsummer, the critics of his unhealthy confinement
felt vindicated. Capel Lofft, writing to Lord Holland, attributed the
captive's stomach cancer to the combined effects of an insalubrious
climate, an inadequate diet, and the "want of sufficient air which the
system of jealous & vindictive surveillance carried with it." That
Napoleon had been allowed to remain in such conditions, even as his

health worsened, was "inexcusable."[98] Another Holland House correspondent—one Arthur Armstrong, writing to Lady Holland—suggested
that "the Govt. cancer story" would probably be doubted. There would
inevitably be "suspicions of his confinement having hastened his death."
Though "no Bptist myself" (he abbreviated), Armstrong admitted
to being "much hurt" by the exile's death. Others were as well, he
claimed: the news "seemed to make people gloomy."[99] When, soon after
Bonaparte's death, another enemy of the newly crowned George IV—
his estranged wife Caroline—died "equally *suddenly*," the *Black Dwarf*
saw sinister forces at work, "a pestilence *walking unseen* amongst us,
and selecting its victims with such a nicety of *discrimination!*" Napoleon
had conveniently, and suspiciously, died just as political unrest on the
continent was beginning to make it likely (according to the *Dwarf*)
that he might be "rescued from the cowardly keeping of the English
boroughmongers," and again lead a conquering army fighting for "more
liberal principles."[100]

Lady Holland, bequeathed a snuffbox in Napoleon's will, found
herself a magnet for the attentions of his British admirers. One wrote to
hail her for having "felt that appeal of our modern Themistocles which
the British Court was too courtly to acknowledge," and sighed over
"how much happier a state of political existence" England might enjoy
were Napoleon alive and an ally.[101] Another unsolicited correspondent
was William Henry Ireland, who had gained notoriety as a teenager in
the late 1790s by convincing literary London that the ludicrously
antique-seeming plays he had written were newly found works of
Shakespeare.[102] Ireland published Napoleon's will in 1821, exclaiming
in his preface that there was a "sacred association appertaining to every
thing connected with that wonderful being, who, for so many years,
decided the fate of kingdoms, and rode like a Colossus over the destinies
of prostrate Europe."[103] Sending Lady Holland a copy of his 1822 book
on Restoration France, he proclaimed that her "generous and humane
sentiments" for Napoleon had "not only excited the warmest interest in
the public mind, but an admiration bordering on reverence in the souls
of his ardent admirers."[104]

Critics of Napoleon wrote to Lady Holland as well. The Earl of
Carlisle sent verses asking that she reject the snuffbox "tinged with
gore!" It was a Pandora's box filled with "Discord, and Slaughter, and
relentless War," and its recipient would find her dreams disturbed by
"Spectres of myriads slain, a ghastly band!"[105] Lord Holland did not

pass the poem on to his wife, knowing it would upset her. He privately vented his spleen at Carlisle's "base lines" in seven stanzas of his own; Byron and others would also defend Lady Holland in verse.[106]

In his prose response to Carlisle, Holland explained that Lady Holland felt "both flattered & affected by so unexpected & feeling a testimony of regard from a man of such great & transcendent qualities in his last moments of disease exile & affliction." His wife's admiration for Napoleon, Holland admitted, was "more unqualified & more enthusiastick than mine," but he too would be "proud of receiving a memorial" from the late emperor. And here, despite the gout that had led him to dictate the earlier part of the letter, Holland took over the pen to write words too inflammatory to entrust to another. Napoleon's death he considered to be "a legal or political murder, a species of crime which tho' not uncommon in our age is in my eyes one of the blackest dye & most odious nature."[107] The assassination urged by Goldsmith had, in Holland's reading, finally been carried out.

CHAPTER 8

Fallen Greatness

Though fallen from thy high estate,
By fatal errors—seen too late;
Thy brilliant race of glory run,
Yet how resplendent is thy setting sun;
Transported to a living tomb,
By those who seal'd, unjustly seal'd thy doom;
By those who once thy gen'rous bounty prais'd,
When by thy pow'r their fallen thrones were rais'd:
Though now thou bear'st Oppression's yoke,
Thy great, thy manly spirit is not broke,
Still unsubdu'd—the free-born mind,
The chains of Tyrants ne'er can bind;
And though Injustice bids thee now depart,
Thy fame still lives in every Freeman's heart.

"Ode to Napoleon Bonaparte,"
Cobbett's Weekly Political Register, September 1815[1]

The myth of Napoleon was constructed in many stages. His lasting political and cultural significance in Britain, as elsewhere, would not have been the same without his nigh-incredible return to power in 1815, nor without his donning of republican garb during the Hundred Days, which allowed many to insist he had mended his ways.[2] The years on St. Helena proved just as critical a component in the Napoleonic myth. It was less Napoleon's victories that won him a place in the Romantic pantheon, than his tragic reversal of fortune.

Common wisdom holds that Napoleon was a "Romantic hero," and certainly his rise from the ranks to the very peak of military achievement and political power thrilled many hearts, even British ones. Still,

Napoleon's appeal derived less from his victories as general and emperor than from his defeat and exile. Sympathy for Napoleon, though an unbroken strand in British radical thought during the years of his rule, took on new overtones in the wake of Waterloo. He became a tragic figure, a melancholy hero, a child as much of misfortune as of fortune. It was Napoleon's suffering rather than his triumphs that spoke to the temper of the age: "adversity alone," as Benjamin Robert Haydon wrote in 1831, "reconcile[d] him again to the world."[3]

The meteoric fall of Napoleon, more than his meteoric rise, recommended him to the Romantic imagination. British sympathizers called attention to the incredible turn of fate he had suffered, and to his stalwart bearing through it all. They ascribed to Napoleon a dignity in adversity that attested to his strength of character as no act of state could. In the hands of some, we have seen, he became (remarkably) something of an everyman: if even this mighty conqueror must suffer at the hands of British tyranny, then no one could be free of its grasp, and radical reform was truly necessary. The St. Helena years generated accounts of Napoleon's mundane, quotidian concerns, turning the superhuman figure into a weak and vulnerable human, whose appeal reached beyond the limited ranks of radicalism. As Haydon noted, when the world found a "genius . . . liable to the same infirmities as themselves, it is extraordinary how fear and hatred change into sympathy and reconcilement; they can afford to pity, and pity inplies [sic] equality at least."[4]

To some, the laundry-list of complaints circulated by the emperor's advocates seemed trifling, insignificant. Croker, looking back after Napoleon's death, felt that a captive "of true dignity of mind," placed in Napoleon's position, would have submitted to even the most arbitrary regulations "with a calm contempt, and that resignation under such reverses, which is the true mark of a noble soul." Instead, Napoleon revealed his low nature: "we find him kicking like a froward child; scolding with all the violence and grossness of Billingsgate; and playing off every kind of evasive trick and subterfuge, like the clown of a pantomime."[5]

But others saw grandeur, drama of tragic proportions, in the severe circumstances to which Napoleon submitted. They echoed the early opinion expressed by one *Statesman* reader that Napoleon had—by weathering "a transition so sudden, so tremendous," from emperor to captive—displayed an "invincible fortitude of soul which rises superior to all the vicissitudes of fate and fortune, and sets at defiance the most cruel persecutions of adversity."[6] What Croker mocked, others found a sublime instance of "fallen greatness"—a phrase that littered the prose and poetry of the day.[7] "To suffer well is the highest praise that man can earn," one observer commented after Napoleon's death; as a prisoner, Napoleon had demonstrated "greatness of soul."[8] Byron portrayed the beached emperor as a subject hovering between tragedy and comedy, prompting some to amusement, others to grief. St Helena's prisoner had suffered a terrible decline best captured in terms of pathetic juxtaposition: he was an eagle "Reduced to nibble at his narrow cage," a former "Queller of the Nations / Now daily squabbling o'er disputed rations."[9] The ambivalent lines suggest anger at a hero's reduction to undignified whining, and yet sympathy for the fragile humanity of a world-shaker now sleepless for lack of a bust of his son.[10]

The image that many chose to express Napoleon's terrible fall and cruel punishment was that of Prometheus, who for giving fire to humanity had been condemned to eternal suffering, vultures gnawing each night at his liver. Napoleon had been figured, somewhat haphazardly, as the Titan as early as 1803, but his downfall provoked a burst of more coherent Promethean descriptions.[11] George Cruikshank's 1814 print, "The Modern Prometheus, or Downfall of Tyranny" showed a vulture already tearing at a shackled Napoleon's innards; Justice, crushing underfoot an imperial eagle and crown, brandishes scales that tilt towards a Bourbon crown (as tiny imperial emblems and a *bonnet rouge* tumble to the ground).[12] Byron, in his censorious *Ode* of 1814 asked whether, "like the thief of fire from heaven," Napoleon would submit to the "vulture" and the "rock." Such a fate, noble when suffered by an immortal, signaled, in Napoleon's case, timidity. Bonaparte had shrunk from death; his prototype (and here Byron elided the Titan with Satan) had "in his fall preserv'd his pride, / And, if a mortal, had as proudly died!" Napoleon was simultaneously victim and vulture, doomed to perpetual auto-consumption: "thou must eat thy heart away!" Byron declaimed (much as Cruikshank tagged his vulture with the label "Conscience").[13] Byron's 1823 vision of the "fettered Eagle" nibbling at his cage marked a return to this vision of the fallen emperor as psychological self-devourer.[14] Others similarly invoked a Promethean Napoleon, "by vulture-conscience slow devoured."[15] Even when Prometheus was not explicitly invoked, the term "chain," and even the term "rock" (used so frequently in descriptions of St. Helena), may have summoned up the

THE MODERN PROMETHEUS, OR DOWNFALL OF TYRANNY.
This Print Presented gratis to every Purchaser of a Ticket or Share at Martins Lottery Office & Cornhill.

12. George Cruikshank, "The Modern Prometheus, or Downfall of Tyranny," 1814 (British Museum).

Titan's image in readers' minds. When the Irish novelist Lady Morgan, in her 1817 work *France*, portrayed Napoleon (the unfortunate "victim of the caprice of petty delegated power; harassed by every-day oppression") as "chained to a solitary and inaccessible rock," she did not need to mention Prometheus by name.[16]

The fascination for Prometheus of the age (think of the Shelleys' *Prometheus Unbound* and *Frankenstein, or, The Modern Prometheus*) had a significance that reached beyond Napoleon; most references to the Titan had little or nothing to do with St. Helena's captive.[17] Still, Napoleon seems to lurk in the background of Macaulay's 1825 description of Prometheus as seeming "hardly superhuman enough. He talks too much of his chains and his uneasy posture: he is rather too much depressed and agitated. His resolution seems to depend on the knowledge which he possesses that he holds the fate of the torturer in his hands, and that the hour of his release will surely come."[18] Napoleon did indeed (like Macaulay's Prometheus) seem a smaller, more human subject by the end of his captivity. His restive complaints signaled his impotence. And yet, as Macaulay suggested, a powerless captive can hold the strange power of shaping his own reputation and that of his captors.

Robert Bloomfield—a humble shoemaker who, discovered by Capel Lofft, had become a bestselling poet on rustic themes—made this point in an oddly affecting poem he published soon after Napoleon's death.[19] In the poem, a dozing shepherd sees the Napoleonic wars acted out by thousands of tiny fairies. The dreamer witnesses the burning of Moscow, the Bourbon restoration, Waterloo, and a fairy-hero's final captivity on an island whose rulers "mock'd fallen greatness, and left him to die." Some disapprove of the hero's treatment, the dreamer senses: they "bewail'd him that fell, / And liked not his victors so gallant, so clever." Just before he wakes, the shepherd is provided with a moral meant to soothe the suffering hero. "Bear misfortune with firmness," one fairy reassures the captive, "you'll triumph for ever."[20]

Bloomfield was not alone in feeling that Napoleon had faced fortune's arrows with fortitude and dignity, and that the very weakness of his final role had paradoxically allowed him to triumph. Carlyle, writing to Jane in the first flush of reading O'Meara, applauded Napoleon for standing up to the abuse of his captors:

> Since the days of *Prometheus vinctus*, I recollect of no spectacle more moving and sublime, than that of this great man in his dreary prison-house; given over to the very scum of the species to be tormented by every sort of indignity, which the heart most revolts against;—captive, sick, despised, forsaken;—yet rising above it all, by the stern force of his own unconquerable spirit, and hurling back on his mean oppressors the ignominy they strove to load him with.[21]

In Carlyle's treatment, Napoleon's moral victory stood in direct proportion to his suffering; it was precisely the torment he endured that revealed his heroic nature and the baseness of his oppressors. Carlyle's Promethean Napoleon, tortured by the lowest scum but transcending all, was a Napoleon beyond politics, a Napoleon whose interest arose not from great deeds of state but from strength of character. Whether or not he had served as a giver of fire ceased to matter very much; it was his behavior while in shackles, his brave weathering of misfortune, that demonstrated his mythic status. Carlyle described O'Meara's Napoleon in terms he might have used to describe a work of art (the "spectacle" of the tormented prisoner was "sublime"). With exile and death, Napoleon took on a new status in the British imagination. He still posed political questions, and could serve as a focal point for political discontent. But he now began to function as a moral and aesthetic problem as well.

To achieve the "sublime" sensation of communing with the absent Napoleon, many Britons sought out objects once owned by Napoleon, or connected in some more distant way to the fallen emperor.[22] William Cobbett regarded it as a tribute to the hero that respectable British citizens, during Bonaparte's stay in Plymouth harbor, had sought "the honour to put on, for a moment, a shirt, a waistcoat, a neck-cloth, of Napoleon."[23] Relics could serve as private tokens of political affiliation: thus, Barry O'Meara sent his fellow Napoleonist Lady Holland a lock of Napoleonic hair after the emperor's death, and Lady Holland distributed prints of her inherited snuffbox to fellow acolytes.[24] Public exhibitions of Napoleonic objects helped ensure that the "ex-emperor" (as some derisively called him) remained a prominent figure in British popular culture. Bonaparte's carriage was exhibited in London in 1816, alongside his personal wardrobe, his horses, and his Dutch coachman, Jean Hornn—and moved on to Bristol, Dublin, and Edinburgh (through whose streets Hornn drove the coach triumphantly). William Bullock, the impresario of this traveling show, claimed the exhibition had received 110,000 visitors, and explained that proximity to the carriage would "bring the spectator into an almost immediate contact" with Napoleon.[25] This possibility of grasping an elusive history by means of an encounter with its tangible traces would haunt and frustrate postwar British encounters with Napoleonic detritus, not least after his death placed him still further out of reach.

No Napoleonic sympathizer took the enterprise of relic-collecting as seriously as John Sainsbury. A desire to respond to the "unmeasured abuse" that so many Britons had heaped on "the Greatest Hero of both Ancient and Modern times" motivated Sainsbury, in the early 1820s, to start assembling a collection of "every thing worth notice in a portable form relating to Napoleon"—from bronzes and cameos to paintings and autograph letters. Though financial worries prompted him to try selling his ever-growing collection for £6,000 to Sir John Soane in 1835 (Sainsbury hoped it might be absorbed into the architect's home-museum), Sainsbury still possessed the goods in 1843—by which point the collection's reported value had risen to £50,000 and the printed catalogue had

expanded from 90 to 700 pages. Sainsbury now opened his massive collection to the public as the Napoleon Museum, an exhibition housed in
the London Museum (or "Egyptian Hall") on Piccadilly. One hundred
thousand people, including Wellington and Sir Robert Peel, were
reported to have visited the exhibition, paying a half-crown each for
admission.[26] No doubt many visitors proved resistant to Sainsbury's
professed goal of demonstrating Napoleon's "wonderful character and
uncommon genius," his "general superiority over his species."[27] After
all, one could relish these emblems of a lost cause as reflecting glory on
the nation that had defeated it: Napoleonic relics could be viewed as
martial trophies, as signs of British triumph. Even so, the museum's phenomenal success indicates a widely shared hunger for things Napoleonic,
a hunger that Sainsbury's collection fueled further.

Contemporary songs and plays confirm this hunger, and show the surprisingly positive role that the late emperor played in the popular imagination in the decades following his death. The songs—sold in broadside
form by publishers based largely in Seven Dials or Soho—are difficult
to pinpoint in time: many that were published in the 1840s and 1850s
may have originated earlier, and may have been reprinted for decades to
follow. Songs frequently portrayed Napoleon as a victim of deception
and persecution. Waterloo, one lyric suggested, had been "bought for
English gold": the British army had won the battle because the French
marshal Grouchy had betrayed France and "sold" Napoleon.[28] Another
song recalled that England had on St. Helena "persecute[d] that hero
bold," and noted darkly that his son had "followed to the tomb, it was
an awful plot."[29] While one ballad mocked the warrior Napoleon, who
"dropt his wings and turned his tail to us at Waterloo," another recalled
him as "valiant and brave," and "lamented" by thousands.[30]

St. Helena was the scene of several songs.[31] One lyric imagined
Napoleon's soliloquies on this "desert island where the rats the devil
would affright." It reminded listeners that Bonaparte "drove Kings from
their throne" and at Waterloo "stood the plain, liberty's cause for to
maintain."[32] Another, recounting a dream of St. Helena, contrasted the
fallen emperor (betrayed "by dark deeds of treachery") with monarchs
who "their stations demean," spitting "venom and spleen" like "scorpions." Again, Napoleon was identified with freedom, with the imminent dawn of "liberty . . . o'er the world."[33]

In 1840, Louis-Philippe's regime, hoping to hitch its cart to
Napoleon's popularity, brought the former emperor's body—the

ultimate Napoleonic relic—back from St. Helena to Paris, to be buried
in the Invalides that Bonaparte had constructed for veterans of his wars.
British songs treated the event respectfully, even movingly. One
exclaimed:

> So beg the bones of Bonaparte! the frenchmans [*sic*] pride.
> Oh! bring him back again 'twill ease the Frenchman's pain
> And in a tomb of marble we will lay him with his son,
> We will decorate his tomb, with the glories he has won,
> And in letters of bright gold inscribe Napoleon.[34]

Another song for the occasion, "The Removal of Napoleon Bonaparte's
Ashes," hailed the "valiant Corsican" of "noble" heart who "struggled
hard for liberty." One remarkable verse reiterated the array of heroic
British names so often invoked in the broadsides of 1803—but now
added Napoleon to their ranks:

> We read of gallant Marlborough, we read of valiant Nelson,
> We read of noble Jarvis, brave Howe, and gallant Blake,
> Of Wolf, and Abercrombie, great men who fought by
>   land and sea,
> Back from the days of Wellington, unto Sir Francis Drake;
> They were all men of courage [t]rue, and fought like Britons
>   of true blue
> Always was undaunted, so noble was each heart,
> But Europe we must understand, could not boast of late
>   of such a man,
> As the valiant little Corsican, Napoleon Bonaparte.[35]

Having performed his noble deeds against British troops did not, apparently, count as a mark against the Corsican upstart. He could hold his
own in this British pantheon.

  Plays on Napoleonic themes, like songs, appeared regularly in the
decades following Bonaparte's death. In 1824 and 1825, two "equestrian spectacles" by J. H. Amherst, *The Battle of Waterloo* and *Napoleon
Buonaparte's Invasion of Russia*, staged sensational battle scenes complete with horses and cannon fire (and in the latter case the Muscovite
conflagration, presented though projected transparencies).[36] The 1830
revolution, the 1840 reburial of Napoleon, and the 1848 election and
1851 coup of Napoleon's nephew Louis-Napoleon each prompted new
theatricals about the late emperor.

While some plays on Napoleonic themes were published, the manuscripts of others survive in the papers of the lord chamberlain, to whom they were submitted for vetting.[37] As interesting as the lines delivered in one 1830 play performed at Covent Garden were the lines apparently censored. The Lord Chamberlain's Office penciled out the lament, voiced in the St. Helena scene by one "true staunch Englishman," at the "cruel policy which coops up within this narrow circle, the Man who once filled one of the first Thrones in the World! It will be an ever-lasting stain on the bright page of our history." A reference to Napoleon's "odious new Governor," the still-living Sir Hudson Lowe, was also struck out, as was much (though not all) of a passage comparing Napoleon's right to rule with that of Britain's Prince Regent.[38]

Many lines sympathetic to Napoleon, however, survived the cut. This drama's Napoleon declares that "the power that raised *me* to the Throne, was only the choice of the people!" He laments the "petty tyranny" which has deprived him of reading material. And his companion in exile, Marshal Bertrand, denounces the surveillance that leads Napoleon to seclude himself and thus invite "a slow and certain death." If these phrases recall the words of radical journalists, then a pronouncement by Bertrand in the final act (in fact a paraphrase of Seneca) could have been made by the young Carlyle, or one of the many others who romanticized the imperial exile: "the most sublime of all sights is a great Man struggling with adversity."[39]

This play's gentle, humanizing treatment of Napoleon was surprisingly typical. A theme in several plays was Napoleon's attention to the common people, as revealed in his concern for the individuals he encounters. In Amherst's *Battle of Waterloo*, Napoleon's voice breaks when a Fleming speaks to him about family. "All the world is taught to believe me a monster," Bonaparte says in an aside, "incapable of understanding these soft words."[40] In more than one play, Napoleon travels among the people unrecognized, like Shakespeare's Henry V on the eve of Agincourt or like a Greek god in human guise.[41] Napoleon and Fouché, entering a café incognito in an 1852 drama, learn that the lovely Louise is about to marry a man she does not love; to save her from this fate, the emperor promotes her true love to captain and "orders" the marriage of the now-happy couple.[42]

Significantly, in light of the wartime debate over killing Bonaparte, assassination featured in several plays. One story told frequently— but with a different historical locale each time—involved a would-be assassin whom Napoleon mercifully frees, or who is won over by the emperor's virtues. In Amherst's *Invasion of Russia*, for example, Napoleon forgives and releases the Russian who has tried to kill him. The nobility of this act converts the failed killer, who now declares that "Napoleon himself has taught me the distinction between a soldier and a murderer." When commanded to fire on the emperor's sledge, he deliberately misses.[43] In an 1830 play, similarly, Napoleon seeks to spare the life of the Austrian who has tried to kill him, but the hothead assures him he will try again if freed. Awaiting execution, and even as he reiterates his desire to kill Bonaparte, the man tells his French executioner to defend the emperor, "for he is a great man!—It is glorious to die for him" (though he makes sure to add that "it is more glorious to die for one's own Country!"). Napoleon ultimately succumbs to the gentle voice of a woman, letting the assassin's wife convince him to free the man.[44] Yet again, in George Dibdin Pitt's 1850 play *Napoleon the Star of France*, an aspiring assassin, captured and now interrogated by Napoleon, insists that a pardon will simply hand him the opportunity for a repeat attempt. He escapes, only to show up years later on St. Helena, filled with "a sincere zeal to serve [Napoleon], to rescue him from the hands of those who have made him a prisoner for life." He offers to trade clothes and places with Napoleon, and admonishes a British officer to "act as becomes a noble foe" and set Napoleon free.[45]

Through this extraordinary motif of the reformed assassin, British playwrights first of all sought to convey Napoleon's charisma, which during his reign had been a controversial matter for those who denied the French people or army to be willing participants in the Napoleonic enterprise. Bonaparte's power to compel led one female character in Amherst's *Invasion of Russia* to wish she "might have followed Napoleon through life—have bled for him—perhaps have died for him! ecstatic thought."[46] The assassination subplot also fitted into the broader effort by playwrights to portray Napoleon as merciful and noble. In one play, Napoleon's mercy is revealed first when he forgives a man who has stolen his watch. A greater demonstration follows, when the robber, about to be shot, condemns the emperor—whom he believes absent—as a tyrant and usurper. Having heard the denunciation, Napoleon reveals his identity and intervenes to save the man.[47]

Praise for Napoleon did not imply denigration of Britain (nor of Wellington, who stood bravely as bullets whizzed past him in Amherst's *Waterloo*).[48] But it did necessitate certain peculiar compromises. One refrain was the natural affinity between Britain and France. In a one-act piece from the 1840s, an Englishman and a Frenchman agree that "it's a great pity that two nations, the best informed in Europe, should ever be set to loggerheads, when, by their union, no people could be happier; and then they might defy the world."[49] An 1840 one-act "burletta" (or comic opera) had Napoleon's ghost, seeing the French ships arrive in St. Helena to bear his remains back to Paris, observe approvingly that "The French nation, England and the world appear resolved to do my memory justice." An English sentry in the play, grateful to Napoleon for having once saved his life in Egypt, now swears to the imperial shade that he would "do anything to serve you, and yours;—not injuring the Country I serve!"[50] In an 1850 play, Napoleon denies being a bellicose tyrant: he fights only "to curb the overweening tyranny of despots—and to give law and liberty to other nations as I have to France." When the exiled hero dies, an English captain prophesies that "in after Times his name shall live, and Englishmen be the first to give the meed of praise to Napoleon the great" (an accurate enough prediction, to judge from the theater of these years).[51] And an 1852 "spectacle" allowed British characters in Egypt a bizarre loophole: they actually join the French army, once they have been assured that they need not battle against England, only against "this rascally Pacha."[52]

The songs and plays of the decades following Napoleon's fall from power suggest that he had become, to a degree that would have been unthinkable to a previous generation, *domesticated* in the British imagination. He could be listed in song alongside British heroes, and hailed on the stage by British soldiers. The notion that a British patriot might admire Napoleon, once voiced only by radicals, had become a commonplace.

In the 1816 caricature "The British Atlas," a world-weary John Bull—though in tatters and with unpaid bills poking out of his pockets—supports an "extravagant" standing army that in turn supports and protects a gouty Louis XVIII. One prominent bill, at John's feet, is for "keeping Bonaparte in St Helena." In the background, the British army's rifles are trained on Napoleon's island, which is ringed by British ships. Napoleon stands with arms akimbo and legs apart, towering over his island prison—so gigantic in stature that a ship might navigate, if it dared, the space beneath his legs. His stance and size indicate that he remains, in exile as in power, a Colossus.[53]

13. C. Williams, "The British Atlas, or John Bull Supporting the Peace Establishment," 1816 (Houghton Library, Harvard University).

More now portrayed him as ruin, scarred and fallen, than as intact Colossus. The orator James Henry Lewis, sketching the sublimely terrible St. Helena, portrayed the fallen hero as a landmark bearing a lesson: "there must stand, 'midst nature's horrors, through all his wintry days, a mighty ruin of fallen greatness, to be the warning beacon to ambition."[54] But in an age that cherished the beauty of the relic and the fragment, a ruin could seem poetically grander than an undamaged object. Byron compared the memory of Napoleon with the "colossal statue" of

Amenhotep III, which possessed greater powers in its broken state than when intact: "though cast down from its seat of honour," it still bore "the ineffaceable traces of grandeur and sublimity to astonish future ages."[55] Time's wounds could make a spectacle more grand and imposing, not less. Indeed, Percy Shelley's sonnet about another torso-less Egyptian titan, the 1817 "Ozymandias," can be read as a meditation on Napoleon's fall. Read with an eye to contemporary politics, the poem offers the same picture as that Shelley gave in an 1815 sonnet that described "time" sweeping the "pomp" of Bonaparte's empire "in fragments towards oblivion."[56] The ostensible Egyptian subject served as a device for gaining historical distance—it allowed Shelley to speak about Napoleon's fall at one remove.[57]

Napoleon's fate was taken to be a proper object for poetic and moral contemplation. Napoleon was himself often figured as an active party in such contemplation. "Here lonely musing fills my pensive soul!" Bonaparte declared in an anonymous British poem of November 1815.[58] The exiled Napoleon's role in the British imagination was not simply as the victim of fortune but as a *meditator* on fortune. The man of action had become, of necessity, a man in thoughtful repose. After his death, poets and artists would represent him as a solitary figure musing on recent history while surrounded by an almost inhuman and ahistoric nature, St. Helena's "barren and blasted rock."[59] He was a lone communicant with both history and nature.

This ruminative figure, with all the time in the world, appeared repeatedly in posthumous renderings of Napoleon on St. Helena. Consider the frontispiece for William Hamilton Reid's 1826 life of Napoleon: the exile on the island's shore, wide- and innocent-eyed, his cloak blowing in the breeze, his hat and a book casually perched upon a rock—practically the hero as poet.[60] Or Napoleon in the young John Ruskin's 1838 poem: "A lonely figure gaz[ing] on the deep," wrestling with "memory"; a noble figure in "a dark quiet of serene despair."[61] Or, again, Napoleon as he appears in J. M. W. Turner's 1842 painting, *War. The Exile, and the Rock Limpet*. In a surreally blazing sunset beachscape, with one solitary guard positioned a respectful distance away to signal the prisoner's captivity, the exile looks down into the water to consider both his own reflection and a limpet—a fragile mollusk which, clinging to life amidst the overpowering elements, still possesses liberty.

Turner's sublime painting was probably inspired by a mediocre one, Benjamin Robert Haydon's *Napoleon Musing at St. Helena*. This painting foregrounds a uniformed Napoleon, facing away from us with arms folded; he stands atop a rocky cliff, perched above the Atlantic, and looks out toward a distant sunset. Haydon's first version of the image, in 1829, was quickly followed by an engraved version, and then by a second, larger painting commissioned by the future prime minister Robert Peel and placed on public exhibition.[62] Haydon considered including a broken column in the picture, but decided against it, apparently judging that the scene would tell the story of decline and ruination well enough without the device: "Napoleon, the Sea, & the Sun should tell their own story."[63]

One narrative of Haydon's life might pin the decline of the painter's fortune and emotional stability on his attachment to this image of Napoleon musing. Haydon felt a strange connection to Napoleon.[64] Beginning work on the painting for Peel, he had tried on Bonaparte's hat to discover that it "fitted me exactly" and "excited associations as powerful as the helmet of Alexander." Napoleon appeared to him in a dream in 1831 "and presented me with a golden key": Haydon believed this indicated that "something grand in my destiny is coming on, for all the spirits of the illustrious dead are hovering about me." But the painter was highly ambivalent about his subject. He identified with Napoleon, but rued the similarity he saw between his character and Bonaparte's. His colleague David Wilkie, Haydon recognized, followed "the Wellington System—principle & prudence," "caution & integrity." Haydon felt himself to be, by contrast, "of the *Napoleon* species," displaying "audacity, with a defiance of principle, if principle was in the way." The diverging characters produced opposite fortunes, sending Napoleon to St. Helena and Haydon to debtors' prison while Wellington and Wilkie were fêted and prosperous.[65] Haydon's opinion of Wellington rose and fell as well, like the crashing waves in the "sublime dream" Haydon later had about the duke. His respect for Napoleon's subduer was sometimes excited, but often grudging.[66]

Given his peculiar fascination with Napoleon, Haydon might have done well to avoid painting him quite so often. Constantly plagued by financial troubles, the history painter decided the solution lay in turning away from large canvases on new subjects, which demanded large investments of time and were uncertain to sell. Haydon "resolved to paint cheap & small" to pay his bills, and so started producing endless repetitions of the same, practiced Napoleonic image. Soon he could turn one out in four hours; then in two and a half. " 'Haydon's patent for

14. Benjamin Robert Haydon, "Napoleon Musing at St. Helena," 1830 (National Portrait Gallery).

rapid manufacture of Napoleons musing,'" he termed the practice on the completion of his eighth version. The Dukes of Sutherland and Devonshire bought Napoleons from Haydon; so did the King of Hanover. Little more than a year after the seventh Napoleon at St. Helena, Haydon was on number twenty-three (not including his "other musings" of Napoleon in Egypt, Napoleon on the eve of abdication, and "Napoleon Contemplating his Future Grave").[67]

All this, given Haydon's long-standing identification with Bonaparte, was a dangerous dive into solipsistic self-regard (not sufficiently offset by his five versions of Wellington musing at Waterloo and two more of Wellington visiting Waterloo with George IV). His near-mechanical revisiting of the same scene, though it helped keep creditors at bay, frustrated his desire to tackle new subjects. Waning public interest in those new projects that he did attempt sapped the self-confidence he had felt as a younger man. After Waterloo, he now claimed, he had despised Napoleon "for not trying the 18th Brumaire" again; now he recognized Bonaparte had been right, that "You can't do anything twice in daring with the same effect on the World." The day his final public exhibition closed (it had lost Haydon more than one hundred pounds), the painter again took solace from Napoleon's example. A second triumphant coup could not be effected—not because Haydon had changed, but because his audience had, just as the French nation had been transformed by 1815: "I have not decayed, but the people have been corrupted. I am the same, they are not, & I have suffered in consequence."[68]

One month later, 18 June 1846, was the thirty-first anniversary of Waterloo. Haydon had habitually noted and celebrated the day with a loyal "huzza." This year he did not remark on the day's significance. He noted in his diary entry for the day the failure of several friends and patrons to respond to his plea for financial support, and wrote that he had sent several paintings and the manuscript of his autobiography to his friend Elizabeth Barrett, the poet, "to protect." He killed himself four days later, as he had more than once maintained Napoleon should have done ("the Romans were right; surely it is not cowardice to brave the sublime uncertainties of another World, rather than to creep through a wretched existence in this when one has outlived his honor").[69] In his last moments, Haydon's failure to hew to Wellington's path weighed heavily on his mind. His suicide note lamented the evils he had committed with good ends in mind: "Wellington never used evil, if the good was not certain; Napoleon had no such scruples & I fear the Glitter of his Genius rather dazzled me."[70]

Haydon, a man who often felt alone and embattled in the world of art, must, for all his reservations about Napoleon, have felt a special sympathy for the "genius in captivity" as he portrayed him, "enveloped" in "solitude," facing an "endlessly extensive" Atlantic. Haydon saw Napoleon as a poetic soul, "peculiarly alive to poetical association as produced by scenery or sound." He could only picture him (he wrote in the pamphlet for his 1831 exhibition of Peel's painting) "musing" or "melancholy": "Napoleon never appeared to me but at those moments of silence and twylght [*sic*], when nature seems to sympathise with the fallen."[71] Napoleon himself, in Haydon's painting, embodied the Romantic trope of the ruin in a landscape; he was a man out of time. But he was also the poet reflecting on that ruin.

Haydon's image replicated itself, not only within, but also beyond the confines of his studio. Napoleon's posture in the painting was imitated by General Tom Thumb in an 1844 performance at London's Egyptian Hall, to Haydon's displeasure.[72] Thackeray parodied Haydon's image of Napoleon in an illustration of Becky Sharp, the anti-heroine of his 1847–48 novel *Vanity Fair*.[73] The final act of George Dibdin Pitt's 1850 play *Napoleon the Star of France* opened with a *tableau vivant* of Haydon's painting.[74]

Most memorably, the painting inspired an 1831 sonnet by his friend William Wordsworth. The poet dwelled on the landscape framing the exile's musings:

> That unencumbered whole of blank and still,
> Sky without cloud—ocean without a wave;
> And the one Man that laboured to enslave
> The World, sole-standing high on the bare hill—
> Back turned, arms folded, the unapparent face
> Tinged, we may fancy, in this dreary place
> With light reflected from the invisible sun
> Set, like his fortunes.[75]

Wordsworth's "unencumbered" St. Helena is a space defined by absence: "blank" sky, "bare hill," "invisible sun." His human subject seems equally evasive. The only speculation the poet dares offer about Napoleon's unseen face has to do not with the face's features but with the light that might make that face visible, light reflecting from a source equally unseen. All is elusive, removed. In Wordsworth's eyes, Haydon's painting is sublimely empty. We are left with the exile musing on his own career, the historical figure considering himself *as* historical.

This book has pursued Napoleon as a thread in the fabric of political culture, a figure over whom antagonists in a larger discourse struggled. No sharp line marks the end of that story, but it did come to an end. British authors never stopped writing about Napoleon. But at some point about a generation after his death—even as a new Bonaparte came to the fore in French government—Napoleon gradually ceased to be the subject of broad cultural contention, as opposed to independent analysis or obsession. He would continue to be a subject of historical controversy, about whom radically contradictory things could be written, and would continue to inspire artistic production (and mass production, as the six busts of Napoleon in a Sherlock Holmes short story suggest).[76] But later British treatments of Napoleon were, increasingly, independent salvoes, fired at a distance from one another, rather than thrusts and parries in an ongoing battle.

Some British intellectuals would question the stark opposition that had been drawn between Britain and Napoleon's France. For Matthew Arnold, writing in the flush of 1848's French revolution, England had missed a great opportunity to learn from Napoleon: the nation had crushed Bonaparte despite his commendably advanced ideas "on government and the *future of Europe.*"[77] Arnold saluted Napoleon's "noble" innovations in education, administration, and the law, and praised the Legion of Honor as "the justest system of public recompenses ever founded," one which rescued from the egalitarian excess "those distinctions of rank which are salutary and necessary to society."[78] Walter Bagehot, for his part, diminished the contrast between Britain and France by suggesting that British contemporaries had misidentified as a Jacobin someone who in fact had been no less a representative of "conservative reaction" than the British ministries of the day.[79] The two writers, each in his own way, contradicted the conventional narrative of the two nations at odds. But in the popular imagination, the contrast held.

The threat of a Napoleonic invasion retained its hold on the British imagination. There may have been some truth in the common notion that naughty nineteenth-century children were threatened with the bogeyman of Boney (and that Napoleon, as a result, played just as terrifying a role in British child-rearing as that described in the pamphlet that prophesied compulsory French lessons for the children of a conquered England).[80] The historical precedent of Napoleon would provide later generations with a pool of nightmare images to mine whenever invasion seemed imminent. Many feared Napoleon III might wish to complete the work his uncle had begun.[81] Others, to be sure, marveled at the miraculous new harmony of Anglo-French relations evident when the first Napoleon's nephew visited London in 1855, during the Crimean war. One poet imagined the spirits of Nelson and Wellington in the vaults of St. Paul's, initially incredulous that England could "mingle hands with one / Kin to the hated Corsican."[82]

Later still, the prospect of a Nazi invasion of Britain stirred up a flurry of historical interest, both British and American, in the invasion threat of 1803.[83] Much as late Georgian writers had recalled earlier struggles against the French in order to put Napoleon into context, so the title of one 1943 work reminded its readers that their "forefathers" (that word so often invoked in 1803 broadsides) had "been through it all before," and had "laughed at Boney."[84] Napoleon has yet to recover fully from the wartime parallels drawn between him and Hitler.[85] The desire to paint the rising Führer as a latter-day Napoleon, in order to emphasize the threat that Germany posed, had the unintended consequence of tarring Napoleon as a proto-Hitler.[86] Such is the nature of historical analogy.

So Napoleon was not forgotten as an enemy. But the six years on St. Helena saw to it that he was lastingly remembered, in addition, as a victim. Napoleon was fortunate, in that sense, to have died in exile and captivity. His posthumous reputation in Britain would undoubtedly have been less positive had he expired at the peak of his glory. His treatment at the hands of the European Allies, and in particular of the British state, became, as we have seen, one of the central exhibits in positive accounts of his character and career. Even the more critical and ambivalent accounts of his life would extend some sympathy to "the Recluse of St Helena."[87] But with the growing feeling for Napoleon the prisoner came the waning of his power as a figure of divisive radical force in British political culture. The posthumous goodwill proffered him was more humane than partisan. It had become possible to treat Napoleon not simply as a political subject, but as a human one.

Epilogue: The Historical Napoleon

You desire me to give you a sketch of the character of this extraordinary personage; but who at present can well acquit themselves of such a task?—We must leave him to posterity—Time will place his figure in the point of view, and at the proper distance, to become a study for mankind.

Helen Maria Williams, 1815[1]

As time advances the impression of the evils he inflicted will wear out; posterity will never be able properly to estimate the intensity of our feelings who lived during his career; and will be more alive to the Genius of his Battles, than the despotism of his Government; more disposed to wonder at his daring attempts, than lament his efforts to debase the generation he ruled, into humble instruments of his military will, that he might slake a burning and feverish thirst for dominion and war.

Benjamin Robert Haydon, 1831[2]

And I, entranced,—with the wide sense of gods
Confronting Time—receive the equal touch
Of Past and Present. . . .
. . . Collapsing to a point
In Time, I see thee, O red Waterloo,
A deadly wound now healed.

Sydney Thompson Dobell, "To a Cathedral Tower, on the Evening of the Thirty-Fifth Anniversary of Waterloo," 1850[3]

As early as July 1815, when Bonaparte surrendered himself, his former advocate Helen Maria Williams could describe him as having "bid a last farewel [*sic*] to the present generation"; he "may be said to belong already to history," she wrote.[4] With his death at St. Helena, Napoleon's life could, in a new sense, be viewed historically. In 1831, Benjamin Robert Haydon noted that the "poetry" of Bonaparte's "melancholy conclusion" (that is, his St. Helena exile) had "rendered him already as much a character of history as Mithridates or Hannibal."[5] Haydon's classical references arguably indicated as much a mythic as a historical approach. Certainly that characterization applies to the young Benjamin Disraeli's 1834 *Revolutionary Epick*, a never-completed verse drama inspired by the future prime minister's realization that the French revolution was as important as the siege of Troy, and Napoleon as interesting as Achilles.[6]

That a proper historical distance had been reached, and thereby a certain objectivity, was a common claim in the years following Napoleon's death. (Indeed, even at the height of Napoleon's powers, Leigh Hunt had insisted on the importance of viewing the emperor *as if* historically: "It is in calm domestic circles only, . . . where the present times are regarded as nothing but a portion of future history, that the talents and vices of [Napoleon] are properly appreciated.")[7] William Henry Ireland, in the 1823 preface to what would become a four-volume biography of Bonaparte, described history as bringing balance. "The unerring march of time," Ireland wrote, "while levelling every sublunary object, dispels our past prejudices as it unveils truths long concealed." The "lapse of a few years," Ireland claimed, had effected a tremendous change in British public opinion. Napoleon's severe turn of fortune had "softened the spirit of his most implacable foes."[8] William Hamilton Reid (the radical who two decades earlier had praised, through a veil of biblical exegesis, Napoleonic France as the New Jerusalem) would make similar claims about historical distance in the 1827 edition of his biography of Napoleon. Censuring the pre-existing literature on Napoleon as a "chaos of exaggeration, enthusiasm, and calumny," Reid announced the "period of recriminations" and "libels"—and likewise of inconsistent "apologies"—to be over. "The time is at length arrived when, irritation having subsided, praise and reprehension enter the sage limits prescribed, and faithful History in turn assumes her wonted mastery."[9]

These claims about historical distance were accompanied by a general mellowing of antagonism to Bonaparte in the wake of his death. Writers announced their desire to reach a moderate middle position. Simply because "Napoleon's name alternately has been / A theme for indiscriminate applause / And fiercest censure, must we blindly lean / To either?" asked the poet Bernard Barton in 1822. "Truth is, surely, found between." (That truth, he added, would be that "Napoleon's lasting charm" must "be consider'd GREAT.")[10] Barclay de Mounteney—a former *détenu* in France and future gentleman of the privy chamber to William IV—proclaimed in 1824 his desire "to see Napoleon placed on his just level amongst the mighty of the earth,—neither to be unfairly depressed, nor inconsiderately elevated."[11] Sir Walter Scott pointed out that the passage of little more than a decade had erased the opinion once widely held that Napoleon should have been handed over to the Bourbon government "to be treated as he himself had treated the Duke d'Enghien"; even Napoleon's critics, the Tory novelist wrote, no longer needed to be convinced that he had been "at least entitled to security of life, by his surrender to the British flag."[12]

But those critics, unambivalent ones at any rate, were becoming harder to find. Scott's own nine-volume biography, published in 1827, no doubt surprised a good many readers by its even-handedness. He proclaimed himself "no enemy to the person of Napoleon," and applauded "his splendid personal qualities—his great military actions and political services to France." Though Napoleon's system of government "comprehended the slavery of France, and aimed at the subjugation of the world," he also, Scott allowed, had enriched French society through the institutions and legal code he had crafted. In a true sign that times had changed, Scott went so far as to apologize for his printer having spelled Buonaparte with a "u." Scott's own critical view of the Enghien affair—which marked an "indelible blot" on Napoleon's character—was tempered by his ethnographic observation that Corsicans, "ruthless and indiscriminate in their feuds," were in this respect like Scottish Highlanders: Napoleon had instinctively revenged himself on the nearest member of his rival clan, the Bourbons. Remarkably, this remark seems almost to cast Napoleon as the hero of one of Scott's novels—caught between a waning feudal age, romantic but doomed, and a rising modern one.[13]

Hazlitt, who had in 1825 described Scott as a champion of Legitimacy and the Bourbons, must have feared the worst from the author of *Waverley*.[14] Early reports of Scott's project inspired Hazlitt to write his

own rather worshipful four-volume study of Bonaparte, published
between 1828 and 1830, in which he hailed this *"thorn in the side of
kings."*[15] While Scott presented even his more controversial opinions in
a measured air of cool Olympian dispassion—his judicious criticism
seemed stripped of the rage that had fueled so many wartime diatribes—
Hazlitt's *Life of Napoleon* blazed with an ardor undiminished by the
passage of years. The *Life* extended the interrogation of Legitimacy that
Hazlitt had undertaken in the previous decade's essays. As in his earlier
pieces, Hazlitt criticized the inconsistency of Britain's Hanoverian king
for now upholding the Legitimacy that his own ancestors had denied by
taking the British throne ("Thus," Hazlitt wrote, "the centuries stammer
and contradict each other"). In this biography, even Napoleon's flaws
indicted hereditary monarchs rather than the emperor himself: while
many radicals had never forgiven Napoleon for accepting an imperial
crown, for Hazlitt "even his abuse of power and aping the style and title
of the imaginary Gods of the earth only laughed their pretensions the
more to scorn."[16]

The additional theme of national character colored the biography. For,
as much as he hailed the heroic leader of France, Hazlitt despised the
French. Evidently, Napoleonic adulation did not have to abandon the
verities of national stereotype; in its Francophobia, Hazlitt's radicalism
could be indistinguishable from loyalism. Hazlitt joined the many broadside writers who had described a gap between the emperor's character
and that of the people he ruled: Napoleon, he wrote, was "the only man
in a nation of grasshoppers." The French were complacent and vain.
Their mercurial volatility endangered any regime, irrespective of its
virtues. Even branding them ferocious was giving them too much credit:
the Terror's excesses had sprung not from natural fierceness but from
effeminacy pushed beyond its bounds.[17]

The French, in short, did not deserve liberty: they were "the least
worthy of it of any people on the face of the earth." Indeed, they did
not deserve Napoleon, as they had demonstrated in giving him insuffi-
cient support during his Hundred Days. Hazlitt did allow that it was
possible for an individual like Napoleon to transform the character of
the people he ruled ("these things it is in the power of man to do and
to undo"). But Bonaparte had evidently failed in the case of the French—
as well as the case of the Italians, who might have been raised "out of
the very dregs of sloth, of effeminacy, and superstition."[18] Interestingly,
Scott's biography had actually been more sympathetic to Napoleon than

Hazlitt's was on this score: Scott credited Bonaparte with having made Italians more masculine through encouraging the use of arms.[19]

Hazlitt turned the lens of national character onto the English as well, praising their "plain, grave, straight-forward, sturdy character," even attributing the superiority of their naval tactics over the French to English "honesty or sincerity of feeling . . . accompanied with a steadiness of purpose." But he faulted his compatriots for their natural "spleen, distrust, and haughtiness," their "headstrong self-will, and insensibility to others." These characteristics crystallized in the figure of Sir Hudson Lowe, whose insensitive treatment of Napoleon did not, in Hazlitt's eyes, derive from personal cruelty but rather from the national character. In England's bull-headed stubbornness, however, lay the nation's security. For Napoleon to have conquered England, "he must have covered the face of the country with heaps and *tumuli* of the slain, before this mixed breed of Norman and Saxon blood would have submitted to a second Norman conquest." What a contrast with France, which had arrived at such a fine point of "politeness and effeminacy" as to receive its invasion by the forces of reaction "as a visit of courtesy."[20]

Perhaps, then, it was only a half-truth that, as yet another biographer of Napoleon remarked a decade after Hazlitt's *Life*, "The violent feelings of the English public having now passed away, a period has already commenced for the exercise of a temperate judgment."[21] Napoleon's critics had grown more temperate, but some of his defenders remained warmly partisan. Two sympathetic biographies were published in 1840, the year of Napoleon's reburial in Paris.

George Moir Bussey's work, dedicated to Lord Holland, painted a sympathetic portrait of Napoleon's sufferings in exile and defended the killing of the duc d'Enghien as an act of self-defense.[22] Richard Henry Horne—a playwright and journalist who had participated in the Mexican war of liberation—offered an equally favorable reading of Bonaparte's life. Horne praised the emperor's public works, Civil Code, and struggle against "divine right," while defending Napoleon's less palatable deeds as Anne Plumptre had, by comparing them with the actions of his enemies. It did not, he told his readers, "become an English biographer to accuse Napoleon of the horrors of war, when we recollect how prominent a part our government took in the proceedings which called him into action."[23]

In so many of these retrospective considerations of Napoleon, time was invoked as a force whose passage effected epistemological change. Ireland's certainty that time had unveiled truths was of a piece with Helen Maria Williams' assurance in 1815 (quoted in one of this epilogue's epigraphs) that historical distance would bring to future observers a wisdom that contemporaries lacked. We might contrast Williams' optimism about future understanding with Haydon's suggestion (also quoted above) that future historians would fail to comprehend Napoleon precisely because of time's passage. But the attitudes of Williams and Haydon, each of whom spoke confidently about "posterity," were flip sides of a single coin. The two writers shared a recognition of the epistemological difference between contemporary and historical viewpoints. For both, historical understanding functioned differently depending upon the position of the observer. Each writer saw the path between past and present as clouded by mist—though for Williams, the mist cleared rather than thickened as one proceeded away from the moment one wished to grasp.

Stephen Bann has argued that the early nineteenth century saw the rise of a new "historical-mindedness," a new recognition of the inevitable incompleteness of historical representation and understanding. Bann sees the age as newly cognizant of the complexities of the historical enterprise—newly aware of the epistemological leakage and loss that occurs in explaining the past to the present.[24] Sometimes this sense of the necessary flaws in historical knowledge was haunted by a utopian dream of ideal historical understanding—a dream nicely expressed in this epilogue's third epigraph, in which the poet "with the wide sense of gods / Confronting Time—receive[s] the equal touch / Of Past and Present." But the mystic, absolute terms in which this vision was phrased suggest a recognition of the dream's impossibility. Speaking for the past had become a more difficult proposition. The mindset of one age could not, it was increasingly felt, be easily mapped onto that of another age, even a recent one.

It is in this light that we should read Lady Morgan's impressions on visiting France in 1816. To convey the historical wrongness of the Bourbon restoration, Morgan drew on the language of anachronism. The returning Bourbons, "suddenly recalled from their suspended animation," arrived "covered by the mould of centuries" in a France "strewn with relics of remote time," she wrote. "The remains of a worn-out race, the mouldering relics of ancient errors" had been "brought back, to throw their chilling influence over awakened energy." Morgan likened Louis XVIII to an "antiquarian, who rises from the depths of Herculaneum or of Portici, encumbered with relics, and accompanied with the remains of other times."[25] In short, the restored monarchy stood in defiance of a natural historical progression. Time was out of joint. Louis did not belong; he scratched against the grain of history.

Perhaps the most sophisticated reading of Napoleon from a self-consciously historical perspective—a perspective, that is to say, which viewed the passage of time as itself a problem to reckon with—was offered by Thomas Babington Macaulay. In the immediate wake of the French revolution of 1830, Macaulay—twenty-nine, and just elected to Parliament—began a history of France's Bourbon restoration and the recent revolution. He wrote the opening sections on the first restoration and the Hundred Days, but abandoned the project as the demands of government grew. The surviving fragment, not published in his lifetime, presented a largely unsympathetic picture of Napoleon as a creature of "depraved ambition," prone to "bursts of senseless fury." Though "great," Bonaparte had been selfish; having inspired the love of the French people, he had then taken advantage of them. If his rule had not been cut short, "He would have renewed, perhaps for centuries, the expiring lease of tyranny," imposing an oriental despotism, "the equality of the Turks."[26]

Though Macaulay's criticisms of Napoleon echoed loyalist ones, his was a liberal indictment. He held that Napoleon's greatest sin lay in having abused the legacy that the revolution had handed him. This "artful tyrant" sought to harness the energy of the revolution—"the most tremendous convulsion ever produced by the spirit of liberty"—for his own ends, cribbing from it "hints which might enable him to construct an impregnable system of arbitrary power."[27] To explain Napoleon's relationship to the revolution and the Bourbon monarchy, Macaulay returned to the question of legitimacy that had been so important for postwar radicals. The middle position he staked out—based on a recognition of historical contingency—offered legitimacy to Napoleon, but in a manner that would have displeased as many radical democrats as it did advocates of hereditary rule.

Macaulay made the familiar radical point that the Bourbon monarchy could itself be traced to Hugh Capet's usurpation, and ultimately to Pepin's.[28] The logic of legitimacy, strictly followed, did seem to demand the return of the Merovingians. But rather than conclude from this absurdity, as most postwar radicals had, that "legitimacy" itself must be discarded—that power had no tenure, and must yield to the people's will—Macaulay was ready to consider the inherent claims of the status quo. In a pragmatic move that brought the term "legitimacy" closer to its present-day meaning, Macaulay in effect shifted its definition from *hereditary* rule to *existing* rule. Where some radicals had claimed that true legitimacy must be democratic rather than hereditary, Macaulay offered a reading quite agnostic on the structure of government. In a Europe of ancient hereditary monarchies, most established governments happened to share certain features, but Macaulay put these to one side. Macaulay read the legitimists' argument as an anti-revolutionary one—irrespective of the content of that revolution—and approved.

It was quite true, he decided, that any revolution, even one that substituted a good government for a bad one, brought misery with it. Usually, this misery was greater than any that might have existed under the previous regime. Revolution was "in itself an evil," he wrote, so the "burden of proof" lay on revolutionaries to prove that they would improve matters, and not just marginally. Following this reasoning, Macaulay concluded that the Bourbons had had legitimacy on their side in 1789. Even if a Frenchman of that day could have accurately forecast the advances of the coming quarter-century, he would have been wise to accept the concessions offered by the monarch, and "trust the rest to time and the progress of the human mind" rather than suffer the consequences of "effecting a complete purification in a few years."[29] Significantly, we see, Macaulay's counter-historical reformist scenario trusted to an abstractly defined Whiggish history ("time and the progress of the human mind") to effect the changes that an all-too-concrete history, violent and calamitous, had accomplished in the real world.

But the revolution *had* taken place. By 1814, "The purification had been accomplished," and could not be reversed without a second upheaval just as overwhelming as the first. The price paid had been "tremendous; but it had been paid." And so any reckoning of legitimacy must be made on the basis of the new circumstances. The case of Pepin showed that power, even if "unlawful in its origin," could "by lapse of time become lawful." The only question, then, was how much time was necessary. As with property, there must be a statute of limitations—"a time after which a title, however illegally acquired, cannot be legally set aside." One could not dictate a precise time that must elapse before a government became legitimate; the period would "vary according to the

violence of the revolution and the movement of the public mind."[30] So
Macaulay set out to determine whether, in this case, such a period had
elapsed by 1814.

Here he picked up on a conceit quite common to British writers on
the revolutionary and Napoleonic years: the *density* of lived experience
in an ever-changing France. The French had undergone enormous historical changes in a few short years, James Mackintosh had suggested
in his 1803 defense of Peltier. Moving from monarchy to anarchy to
military despotism, "France, in a few years, described the whole circle
of human society."[31] Around the same time, Henry Redhead Yorke wrote
that France had lived, "during the short space of ten years, the history
of man for ages."[32] Such remarks were especially common during and
after the tumultuous events of 1814–15. After the first Bourbon restoration, Francis Jeffrey of the *Edinburgh Review* suggested that history had
been compressed even for British observers: "We have lived ages in these
twenty years; and have seen condensed, into the period of one short life,
the experience of eventful centuries." A mere twenty-five years had seen
"exhausted . . . all the problems that can be supplied by the whole
science of politics."[33] As the historian Edward Baines put it, "If time
were measured by events instead of years, centuries might be said to
have passed during the age in which we live."[34]

In Macaulay's rendering, the fact that "the events of ages had been
compressed" into twenty-five years—the fact that "Men had lived years
in every month"—meant that the French "no more resembled their
fathers, than their fathers resembled the burghers of the League, or the
peasants of the Jacquerie." In short (and as many earlier British commentators had suggested), the national character of France had been
transformed: "A new people—new in their opinions, their prejudices,
and their social relations,—had sprung into existence." The France to
which Louis returned "was not that France which he had formerly
known." And so enough time had passed, since time had been so
packed with events, to legitimize the Napoleonic regime. "Legitimacy,
in the rational sense of the word, had crossed over to the side of the
revolution."[35]

Macaulay did not conclude that the Allies had been wrong in 1815
to seek Napoleon's removal by force. They properly regarded him as "a
most powerful, most crafty, and most obstinate enemy of the independence of all nations." But the young historian's reasoning denied the
specific validity of the argument from legitimacy. Where the Jacobins

had destroyed the old order, Napoleon had built a new one on the ruins, Macaulay wrote, "and had thus rendered it impossible to restore the ancient fabric without a second demolition. In his person the revolution had assumed the character of legitimacy." Those who attacked the revolution had become "the real revolutionists."[36]

Macaulay's limited defense of Napoleon depended on the passage of time, but so too did his denunciation of the ruler. Shadowing Macaulay's Whiggish sense of an orderly historical development was a recognition that history's stately pace could be tripped up. History was not tamper-proof; it could be manhandled, as Napoleon wished it to be. "Too selfish to govern in conformity with the liberal principles of the age," according to Macaulay, Napoleon had "attempted to compress the spirit of the age into conformity with his maxims of government. Political science was to be forced backwards."[37]

History itself, the passage of time, is the legitimizing force in Macaulay's scheme: not bloodline, not the favor of God, not even historical analogy, which seems a weaker tool after reading his analysis. For if history can speed up, slow down, or even be wrenched backwards—and if legitimacy depends on the prevailing historical momentum—then it is not enough to draw a simple parallel between Napoleon and Pepin, or between Napoleon and William. Similar figures may have different meanings at different times. An individual's significance depends upon his relationship to the climate of his day.

History may have legitimized Napoleon, but Napoleon, in Macaulay's estimate, was working against the liberal "spirit of the age." We have already encountered this phrase in the unsympathetic writing of Henry Redhead Yorke, who saw it as "a wicked and perverse spirit" moving the people of Britain. With its variant, "the spirit of the times," the novel phrase had figured in contemporary discussions of Napoleon. Both critics and admirers had associated France's ruler with such a *Zeitgeist.*[38] Doing so did not mean that resisting Napoleon was pointless, any more than acknowledging Napoleon as the scourge of God necessitated surrendering to him. But linking Napoleon to the spirit of the age did suggest a pessimism parallel to this apocalyptic view. Loyalist fears of British degeneracy—of a present less pristine than the past—met their complement in the apprehension that Napoleon, for good or ill, marched in step with the times.

Yorke felt Napoleon posed a special threat because, unlike despotic hereditary kings, he came unencumbered with historical baggage:

There have been lawful, hereditary monarchs, who, regardless of the rights of their subjects, have trampled them under their feet, and destroyed those who were bold enough to resist their pretensions. But even in these cases, the rigour of despotism was more or less chastened by ancient establishments and habits, which the despot himself could not demolish.[39]

Others, too, attributed the strength of Napoleon's despotism to its lack of historical trammel. Leigh Hunt, we have seen, felt Napoleon owed his strength to the fact that he had sharpened his blade on "the temper of the age."[40] John Scott believed that because of its modernity Napoleon's system of government posed a greater danger to Britain than the anachronistic and corroded shackles of Bourbon rule.[41] Napoleon was feared as a creature of the historical moment.

Posing the question of Napoleon's relationship to the spirit of the age was one more way of asking, as British observers had on first encountering this figure of uncertain identity, how and whether he belonged. And while Macaulay, looking back a generation, was ready to offer Bonaparte legitimacy—and ready to enlist national character in the service of this cause (in his claim that France was now a different nation from before)—he stopped short of allying Napoleon completely with the spirit of the times. By suggesting that Napoleon wished to squeeze the day's liberal spirit into a form more useful to him, Macaulay echoed Leigh Hunt's implication that for Bonaparte, the spirit of the age was simply a grindstone on which to sharpen his own blade. The young historian was also demonstrating, as so many other British observers had, that the Corsican usurper could serve as an instrument with which to hone one's own arguments and categories. In the British imagination, Napoleon became a tool put to uses he himself never contemplated.

Notes

Abbreviations

Periodical Publications

AGM	*The Antigallican Monitor* (begins 27 January 1811; after 30 June 1811, *The Antigallican Monitor, and Anti-Corsican Chronicle*; after 5 January 1818, *The British Monitor*)
CAR, CWPR	*Cobbett's Annual Register* (until 1803); *Cobbett's Weekly Political Register* (from 1804)
ER	*Edinburgh Review*
MM	*Monthly Magazine*
QR	*Quarterly Review*
RYWPR	*Mr. Redhead Yorke's Weekly Political Review*

Other Sources

Add. MSS	Additional Manuscripts (British Library Manuscript Room)
DNB	*Dictionary of National Biography*
MDG	indicates catalogue number of caricatures listed in M. Dorothy George, *Catalogue of Political and Personal Satires Preserved in the Department of Prints and Drawings in the British Museum* (London, 1870–1954). The relevant volumes are VII (1793–1800; cat. nos. 8284–9692), VIII (1801–10; cat. nos. 9693–11703), and IX (1811–19; cat. nos. 11704–13500).
OED	*Oxford English Dictionary*, 2nd ed. (1989)
PD	1803–12: *Cobbett's Parliamentary Debates. During the ... Session of the ... Parliament of the United Kingdom of Great Britain and Ireland* (London, 1804–12) from 1812: *The Parliamentary Debates from the Year 1803 to the Present Time* (London, 1812–)
PH	*The Parliamentary History of England from the Earliest Period to the Year 1803* (London, 1806–20)

Locations

BL	British Library, London
Houghton	Houghton Library, Harvard University

NYPL   New York Public Library
Penn   Rare Book Room, University of Pennsylvania
PRO   Public Record Office, Kew

In the following notes, a title given in quotation marks, with a library's name or
initials after it—e.g. "Who is Bonaparte?" (BL)—is the title of a broadside or song.
The library at which the individual piece was studied is indicated parenthetically.
Nearly all of the broadsides cited are products of the year 1803.

Epigraphs on p. vii

Benjamin Robert Haydon, *The Diary of Benjamin Robert Haydon*, ed. Willard
  Bissell Pope, 5 vols. (Cambridge, Mass., 1960–63), 1: 182 (9 September 1810).
Hazlitt, *The Life of Napoleon Buonaparte* (orig. 1828–30), vols. 13–15 of *The
  Complete Works of William Hazlitt*, ed. P. P. Howe, 21 vols. (London, 1930–34),
  2: 187.

Introduction

   1. *Description of Haydon's Picture of Napoleon Musing at St. Helena* (London,
      1831), 8.
   2. *The Military Carriage of Napoleon Buonaparte, Taken after the Battle of
      Waterloo ... Now Exhibiting at the Bazaar, Baker Street, Portman Square*
      (London, 1843), 24.
   3. William Hone published the title as a handbill in 1815; I quote from a later
      octavo edition: *Buonapartephobia. The Origin of Dr. Slop's Name*, 10th ed.
      (London, 1820), 7.
   4. William Hunter, *A Vindication of the Cause of Great Britain*, 3rd ed. (London,
      1803), 40.
   5. *Substance of the Speech of the Earl of Selkirk, in the House of Lords, Monday,
      August 10, 1807* (London, 1807), 5.
   6. *The Scourge* 10 (Aug. 1815): 84.
   7. See Rory Muir, *Britain and the Defeat of Napoleon, 1807–1815* (New Haven
      and London, 1996).
   8. Richard Whately, *Historic Doubts Relative to Napoleon Bonaparte*, ed. Ralph
      S. Pomeroy (orig. 1819; Berkeley, 1985), 35.
   9. William Wordsworth, "November, 1806," in *William Wordsworth: The
      Poems*, ed. John O. Hayden, 2 vols. (New Haven and London, 1981), 1: 725.
  10. Wordsworth to Captain Pasley, Royal Engineers, 28 March 1811, *The Letters
      of William and Dorothy Wordsworth*, 2nd ed., ed. Ernest de Selingcourt,
      8 vols. (Oxford, 1967–93), 2, pt. 1: 480.
  11. On France as a critical component in Britain's (or England's) thinking about
      itself, see Gerald Newman, *The Rise of English Nationalism: A Cultural
      History, 1740–1830* (New York, 1987); Linda Colley, *Britons: Forging the
      Nation, 1707–1837* (New Haven and London, 1992); and Michael Duffy, *The
      Englishman and the Foreigner* (Cambridge, 1986), esp. 31–9. For balance,
      one book that emphasizes British sympathy with France is Robin Eagles,

Francophilia in English Society, 1748–1815 (Manchester, 2000). Eagles criticizes Newman for relying on the "tiny minority" who were part of "literate and theatrical England" (p. 45), but his own emphasis on travelers to France seems rather more limited than Newman's. The corresponding problem of French attitudes toward England is treated in Norman Hampson, *The Perfidy of Albion: French Perceptions of England during the French Revolution* (Basingstoke, 1998). On the eighteenth-century backdrop, also see Jeremy Black, *Natural and Necessary Enemies: Anglo-French Relations in the Eighteenth Century* (London, 1986).

12. On sincerity, see Newman, *Rise*, 127–39; on transparency, see Jean Starobinski, *Jean-Jacques Rousseau, Transparency and Obstruction* (Chicago, 1988).

13. Whately, *Historic Doubts*, 13–15, 22–3.

14. Indeed, participants in the historiographical debate can find their arguments attributed to contemporary political motive—as when J. C. D. Clark suggests that Linda Colley's "present purpose" must be recommending "devolution or dissolution." Clark, "Protestantism, Nationalism, and National Identity, 1660–1832," *Historical Journal* 43 (2000): 249–76, pp. 264–5.

15. See Marianne Elliot, *Partners in Revolution: The United Irishmen and France* (New Haven and London, 1982).

16. Newman, *Rise*. A similar criticism of Newman is offered in Krishan Kumar's wide-ranging critical study, *The Making of English National Identity* (Cambridge, 2003).

17. Colley, *Britons*, 1, 5. Of necessity, perhaps, given the broad scope of her work, Colley takes English national sentiment as a given, concentrating instead on the way in which this sentiment was woven together with other allegiances into a new national consciousness. As a result, her work may—by implicitly suggesting a static, already developed English national character—inadvertently risk understating the similarly constructed nature of "Englishness."

18. Gerald Newman, "Nationalism Revisited" (review article), in *Journal of British Studies*, 35 (Jan. 1996): 118–27. But see Eric Evans, "Englishness and Britishness: National Identities, c. 1790–c. 1870," in Alexander Grant and Keith J. Stringer, eds., *Uniting the Kingdom? The Making of British History* (London, 1995), 234. J. C. D. Clark has gone further, claiming that "no very powerful sense of shared Britishness" and no "cultural homogeneity" resulted from the union of crowns and kingdoms. But surely Clark is here setting the bar too high: could England alone qualify as "culturally homogeneous"? Clark, *English Society, 1660–1832: Religion, Ideology, and Politics during the Ancien Regime*, 2nd ed. (Cambridge, 2000), 40.

19. Adrian Hastings, *The Construction of Nationhood: Ethnicity, Religion and Nationalism* (Cambridge, 1997), 62–3. The more one downplays *British* identity, the earlier one is tempted to date the birth of *English* national consciousness. Hastings posits an early medieval origin for English national identity. Liah Greenfeld, in *Nationalism: Five Roads to Modernity* (Cambridge, Mass., 1992), sees Tudor England as the first state to enjoy a nationalism.

20. Needless to say, this list omits additional vectors of identity: ones of gender, class, political affiliation, religion, trade, profession, and so on.

21. See Rebecca Langlands' acute "Britishness or Englishness? The Historical Problem of National Identity in Britain," *Nations and Nationalism* 5:1 (1999): 53–69. As Langlands writes, "the ethnic populations of the British state have

dual (or even multiple) political sentiments and historical memories." The "fluid or 'fuzzy' relationship between Englishness and Britishness" (a result of the "English core" having become "Britonised") does not, Langlands suggests, have a parallel in the other British nations, "where a sharper distinction with Britain tends to be drawn" (pp. 63–4). "Ukanian" is the adjective coined by Tom Nairn to describe the United Kingdom. Nairn, *The Enchanted Glass: Britain and its Monarchy* (London, 1988).

22. I agree with Marcus Collins' suggestion (made about a later period) that "any clear distinction between [Englishness and Britishness] is bound to be artificial" when so many authors "used the terms in almost interchangeable fashion." Marcus Collins, "The Fall of the English Gentleman: The National Character in Decline, *c*.1918–1970," *Historical Research* 187 (Feb. 2002): 90–111.

23. Paul Langford has warned that while many contemporaries did describe stereotypically English qualities as "British," we should not, when describing their beliefs, take their practice as license to do the same. "It is difficult to discover any alleged British characteristic that does not in practice coincide with an alleged English characteristic," Langford reasons. "Nor is it easy to find any supposed characteristic of one of the so-called Celtic nations that was not specifically contrasted with an English characteristic." (Indeed, he suggests that one defining feature of Englishness may have been the "tendency to elide the distinction between England and Britain"—"while preserving the strong sense of identity of the former," he adds, "and permitting alternative cultures to flourish even in mainland Britain.") Without rejecting Langford's logic, this book respects the fact that many late Georgian writers did attribute the same characteristics sometimes to the English and sometimes to the British. Paul Langford, *Englishness Identified: Manners and Character, 1650–1850* (Oxford, 2000), 14, 319.

24. When cultural historians speak of the invention or construction of national identity, they do not generally mean to imply, as Clark fears, the back-room schemings of a well-placed coterie, but rather a collaborative and ongoing process, characterized by both conscious and unconscious elements and occurring over the course of generations—a process that unfolded in several dimensions at once, with some aspects at odds with others. Few, I think, would cavil at Clark's own description of British national identity as having been constructed as a result of "the often unintended result of actions by men and women in many walks of life, often, too, the result of conflicts and cross-purposes." But such a description should not remove individual agency as one constructive factor. Clark suspects Linda Colley of viewing nationalism as false consciousness, but "invented" does not mean false. "Protestantism, Nationalism, and National Identity," 275, 262.

25. Newman, *Rise*, 227. On the question of dating national consciousness, see Walker Connor, "When is a Nation?", *Ethnic and Racial Studies* 13 (1990): 92–100. Connor usefully insists that "nation-formation is a process, not an occurrence" (in other words, that we should resist claiming that a national identity is ever "set").

26. H. T. Dickinson and Eirwen E. C. Nicholson have cautioned against over-estimating the reach of political prints. While crowds gathered outside printsellers' windows to enjoy caricatures they could not afford, Dickinson

reminds us that fewer than ten such shops existed, all in central London. (Moreover, that any pedestrian *could* study a window display does not mean he or she *did*—as a glance at the unrepresentative crowd in Gillray's "Very Slippy-Weather" (MDG 11100; 10 Feb. 1808) will suggest.) H. T. Dickinson, *Caricatures and the Constitution 1760–1832* (Cambridge, 1986), 15. Nicholson incisively dissects the tendency to claim too wide an audience for political prints; he sees the audience as narrow, elite, and "Westminster-oriented." Caricatures were pricier and scarcer than newspapers: Nicholson estimates initial print runs of merely 100–600. In this reading, political prints are still important—but as instances of high political culture, not popular politics. Nicholson, "Consumers and Spectators: The Public of the Political Print in Eighteenth-Century England," *History* 81 (Jan. 1996): 5–21, pp. 11, 19. But see Diana Donald's contention that some graphic prints did have a wide social and geographic circulation—just not the more erudite ones like James Gillray's, which, collected and preserved by genteel cognoscenti, have survived in greater numbers. Donald, *The Age of Caricature: Satirical Prints in the Reign of George III* (New Haven and London, 1996), 19–21. The classic work on British prints about Bonaparte is A. M. Broadley, *Napoleon in Caricature, 1795–1821*, 2 vols. (London, 1911).

27. Even Cobbett's many students have neglected his preoccupation with, and shifting view of, Napoleon. But see George Spater, *William Cobbett: The Poor Man's Friend*, 2 vols. (Cambridge, 1982), 2: 333–4; Daniel Green, *Great Cobbett: The Noblest Agitator* (London, 1983), 373–4. On the press, see Hannah Barker, *Newspapers, Politics, and Public Opinion in Late Eighteenth-Century England* (Oxford, 1998); Jeremy Black, *The English Press in the Eighteenth Century* (London, 1987); and Stuart Andrews, *The British Periodical Press and the French Revolution, 1789–99* (Basingstoke, 2000). Two important works on radical print culture are Kevin Gilmartin, *Print Politics: The Press and Radical Opposition in Early Nineteenth-Century England* (Cambridge, 1996) and Marcus Wood, *Radical Satire and Print Culture, 1790–1822* (Oxford, 1994).

28. E. P. Thompson, *Making of the English Working Class*, rev. ed. (Harmondsworth, 1968), 820.

29. *Argus*, 15 Nov. 1802, 35.

30. Haydon, *Diary*, 3: 42 (1 Sept. 1825).

31. On the economic viability of late eighteenth-century newspapers, see Barker, *Newspapers, Politics, and Public Opinion*, 48–9.

32. "For pamphlets, a standard first print run was 500 copies, with subsequent editions of the more celebrated or controversial reaching total figures of 1,500–5,000." Nicholson, "Consumers and Spectators," 9.

33. On literacy, see David Vincent, *Literacy and Popular Culture: England, 1750–1914* (Cambridge, 1989). For a critical view of some common assumptions about "elite" and "popular" literary culture, see Jonathan Rose, "Rereading the English Common Reader: A Preface to a History of Audiences," *Journal of the History of Ideas* 53 (1992): 47–70, as well as Rose's *The Intellectual Life of the British Working Classes* (New Haven and London, 2001).

34. Richard Altick, *The English Common Reader: A Social History of the Mass Reading Public, 1800–1900* (Chicago, 1957), 392.

35. The British population, excluding Ireland, amounted to twelve million in 1811. Doing the same arithmetic for *Cobbett's Weekly Political Register,* which reportedly sold 40,000–50,000 copies, suggests comparisons with a present-day British magazine selling between 190,000 and 240,000, or an American magazine selling between 930,000 and 1.1 million.

36. This paragraph draws on Altick, *English Common Reader,* 322–6.

37. "Fingal," *Truth: Containing the Cast of the Seven Princes of Britain* (London, 1812), 11. On newspapers in taverns, see also *CWPR,* 11 April 1807, quoted in Arthur Aspinall, *Politics and the Press, 1780–1850* (1949; reprint, Brighton, 1973), 11.

38. Aspinall, *Politics and the Press,* 25.

39. *Monthly Magazine (MM)* 51 (1821): 397–8, cited in Altick, *English Common Reader,* 323.

40. The radical tinsmith Richard Carlile was here describing the blackened state of his own copies of the *Black Dwarf,* which he circulated among his "fellow-workmen." *Black Dwarf,* 8 April 1818, quoted in R. K. Webb, *The British Working Class Reader, 1790–1848: Literacy and Social Tension* (London, 1955; reprint, New York, 1971), 47.

41. "Effects of the Register" (1803) in *Selections from Cobbett's Political Works,* ed. John M. and James P. Cobbett, 6 vols. (London, [1835?]), 1: 321.

42. The figure of 12,000 (reported in Webb, *British Working Class Reader,* 48, and Altick, *English Common Reader,* 326) comes from the *Black Dwarf* of 8 April 1818, and should be handled with some caution.

43. Altick, *English Common Reader,* 322.

44. On the period preceding Napoleon's coup, see Albert Goodwin's *The Friends of Liberty: The English Democratic Movement in the Age of the French Revolution* (Cambridge, Mass., 1979); Mark Philp, ed., *The French Revolution and British Popular Politics* (Cambridge, 1991); Marilyn Morris, *The British Monarchy and the French Revolution* (New Haven and London, 1998); David Bindman, et al., *The Shadow of the Guillotine: Britain and the French Revolution* (London, 1989). Emma Macleod's thoughtful *A War of Ideas: British Attitudes to the Wars against Revolutionary France, 1792–1802* (Aldershot, 1998) ends with the Peace of Amiens. For the broader period, see H. T. Dickinson, ed., *Britain and the French Revolution, 1789–1815* (Basingstoke, 1989); Seamus Deane, *The French Revolution and Enlightenment in England, 1789–1832* (Cambridge, Mass., 1988). On the still more long-term reverberations of the revolution, see J. R. Dinwiddy, "English Radicals and the French Revolution, 1800–1850," in *Radicalism and Reform in Britain, 1780–1850* (London, 1992), 207–28.

45. Clive Emsley, *British Society and the French Wars, 1793–1815* (London, 1979); J. E. Cookson, *The Friends of Peace: Anti-War Liberalism in England, 1793–1815* (Cambridge, 1982). Neither work devotes much attention to British opinion of Napoleon himself. H. T. Dickinson, *British Radicalism and the French Revolution, 1789–1815* (Oxford, 1985) is another work that usefully covers the period, though again without special attention to Napoleon.

46. Thompson's *Making of the English Working Class* was itself concerned with bridging this gap. See also Dickinson, *British Radicalism*; J. Ann Hone, *For the Cause of Truth: Radicalism in London, 1796–1821* (Oxford, 1982); and Dinwiddy, *Radicalism and Reform.*

47. Perhaps the most outspoken advocate of this thesis is Roger Wells, in *Insurrection: The British Experience, 1795–1803* (Gloucester, 1983).

48. Colley, *Britons*. See also Ian R. Christie, *Stress and Stability in Late Eighteenth-Century Britain: Reflections on the British Avoidance of Revolution* (Oxford, 1984); Thomas Philip Schofield, "Conservative Political Thought in Britain in Response to the French Revolution," *Historical Journal* 29 (1986): 601–22; H. T. Dickinson, "Popular Loyalism in Britain in the 1790s," in Eckhart Hellmuth, ed., *The Transformation of Political Culture: England and Germany in the Late Eighteenth Century* (Oxford, 1990), 503–34; Robert Dozier, *For King, Constitution, and Country: The English Loyalists and the French Revolution* (Lexington, Ky, 1983); Dickinson, "Popular Conservatism and Militant Loyalism, 1789–1815," in Dickinson, ed., *Britain and the French Revolution, 1789–1815* (Basingstoke, 1989), 103–26 (but note that this essay, despite its title, concerns itself chiefly with the 1790s).

49. Important responses to the new loyalist consensus include John Dinwiddy, "Interpretations of Anti-Jacobinism," in Mark Philp, ed., *The French Revolution and British Popular Politics* (Cambridge, 1991), 38–49; Philip Harling, "Leigh Hunt's *Examiner* and the Language of Patriotism," *English Historical Review* 111 (1996): 1159–81; Harling, "The Duke of York Affair (1809) and the Complexities of War-Time Patriotism," *Historical Journal* 39 (1996): 963–84; A. V. Beedell, "John Reeves's Prosecution for a Seditious Libel, 1795–96: A Study in Political Cynicism," *Historical Journal* 36 (1993): 799–824; and Mark Philp, "Vulgar Conservatism, 1792–3," *English Historical Review* 435 (Feb. 1995): 42–69. On the limits of loyalism as a unifying force, also see Timothy Jenks, "Contesting the Hero: The Funeral of Admiral Lord Nelson," *Journal of British Studies* 39 (2000): 422–53.

50. J. E. Cookson, *The British Armed Nation, 1793–1815* (Oxford, 1997). Emma Macleod draws a rather different distinction between "loyalists" ("the broad mass of conservative activists who by and large supported government policy") and "crusaders" ("the smaller group who campaigned for a more hardline, Burkean strategy in the war"). *War of Ideas*, 66.

51. Clark, *English Society*, 1. Clark rejects, for example, use of the word "radicalism"; contemporaries, he tells us, would have said "Jacobinism" (p. 8). But surely many to whom this term was applied would have objected that it was misapplied, and that they in fact did not embrace the policies of France's revolutionaries. Clark's logic seems especially unhelpful when the term he proffers, as in this case, was used largely as a slur.

52. Sack, *From Jacobite to Conservative: Reaction and Orthodoxy in Britain c.1760–1832* (Cambridge, 1993), 1–7. Sack finds this term "both politically meaningful and politically neutral": external to Hanoverian debates, yet helpful because it serves to establish the continuity of developing ideas, irrespective of shifting terminology over the long period he studies.

53. Yet another approach to the question of terminology is to trace the history of a political word and tendency over an extended period, and thus to acknowledge (and usefully explore) the diversity of the term's meanings. On the various and shifting meanings of "republican," see Frank Prochaska's rich *The Republic of Britain, 1760–2000* (Harmondsworth, 2000).

54. According to Clark, "The noun 'radical' . . . was established by 1802, but

seems to have gone into abeyance until after 1810, and was not common until 1819." *English Society*, 8.

55. One contemporary alternative would be "Friend of Peace." See Macleod, *War of Ideas*, 126–34, and Cookson, *Friends of Peace*.

56. One early twentieth-century effort, F. J. Maccunn's *The Contemporary English View of Napoleon* (London, 1914), dismissed newspapers, pamphlets, and caricatures, key sources for the present book, as "worthless" and "deplorable" (pp. 5–6). But see the excellent exhibition catalogue by Alexandra Franklin and Mark Philp, *Napoleon and the Invasion of Britain* (Oxford, 2003). For assessments of Napoleon's reception beyond British shores, see Pieter Geyl's classic *Napoleon: For and Against*, trans. Olive Renier (New Haven and London, 1949), a close study of nineteenth-century French historical writing; Jean Tulard, *Napoleon: The Myth of the Saviour*, trans. Teresa Waugh (London, 1984); Barbara Ann Day-Hickman, *Napoleonic Art: Nationalism and the Spirit of Rebellion in France (1815–1848)* (Newark, Delaware, 1999); and R. S. Alexander's wide-ranging consideration of Napoleon's European reputation in the nineteenth and twentieth centuries, *Napoleon* (London, 2001). Sudhir Hazareesingh's forthcoming study *The Legend of Napoleon* offers an important demonstration of the continued significance of Napoleon to nineteenth-century French politics.

57. A notable exception is Simon Bainbridge's fine *Napoleon and English Romanticism* (Cambridge, 1995), which explores how canonical Romantic poets (and William Hazlitt) used Napoleon to characterize the imaginative and creative process. In a similar vein, see the Columbia Ph.D. thesis of Christina Root, "Representations of Napoleon in English Romantic Literature" (1991).

58. Thus E. Tangye Lean's *The Napoleonists: A Study in Political Disaffection, 1760–1960* (London, 1970), while offering a lively anecdotal account of the radical Holland House circle, does not treat its subjects' opinions of Napoleon as a problem to be investigated. Lean's chief analytical energy is devoted to providing a psychological profile (liked pets, tendency towards dandyism) of the "Napoleonist," loosely defined, in Bonaparte's day and in the twentieth century. For a perceptive account of Lord and Lady Holland's attitudes toward Napoleon, see Leslie Mitchell, *Holland House* (London, 1980), 250–63.

59. The exceptions to this are chapter 1, introducing the subject, and chapter 5, which discusses the period between Napoleon's first abdication in April 1814 and his August 1815 transportation to the island of St. Helena—a period of terrific instability for French politics, and of equally dramatic shifts in British political opinion of Napoleon.

60. Even Jeremy Bentham, surprisingly, does not seem to have much pursued the Code's details. See Bentham to Alexander I (June 1815), 8: 485, in *The Correspondence of Jeremy Bentham*, ed. Timothy L. S. Sprigge et al. (London, 1968–). Also see, e.g., Bentham to Sir Frederick Morton Eden (4 Sept. 1802), and Bentham to William Plumer Jnr. (Dec. 1818), 7: 123–25, 9: 309.

61. By *history*, I mean something more than simply the formal writing of historical works. Napoleon played an important role in the broader British historical imagination—what Stephen Bann has referred to as "historical consciousness" or "historical-mindedness." See Stephen Bann, *Romanticism and the Rise of History* (New York, 1995), xi. Also see Hedva Ben-Israel, *English Historians on the French Revolution* (Cambridge, 1968); J. W. Burrow,

A Liberal Descent: Victorian Historians and the English Past (Cambridge, 1981); Timothy Lang, *The Victorians and the Stuart Heritage: Interpretations of a Discordant Past* (Cambridge, 1995).

62. James A. Epstein, *Radical Expression: Political Language, Ritual, and Symbol in England, 1790–1850* (New York, 1994), chap. 1.

63. Haydon, *Diary*, 2: 248, 251 (4 Dec. 1819).

1 *Classifying Napoleon*

1. "Harlequin's Invasion," in *The Anti-Gallican; or Standard of British Loyalty, Religion and Liberty* (London, 1803), 70.

2. For opinions on Napoleon's likely destination, see Add. MS 39891 (Warren Hastings Papers, Supplement), f. 138; Eyles Irwin, *An Enquiry into the Feasibility of the Supposed Expedition of Buonaparté to the East* (London, 1798); "An Officer in the Service of the East India Company," *Reply to Irwin* (London, 1798).

3. *The Piozzi Letters. Correspondence of Hester Lynch Piozzi, 1784–1821 (formerly Mrs. Thrale)*, ed. Edward A. Bloom and Lillian D. Bloom (Newark, Delaware, 1989–), 2: 508 (to Rev. Daniel Lysons, 9 July 1798).

4. On Napoleon's death, see the one-penny chapbook *Egypt Delivered; or, The Conqueror Conquered* (BL); *British Critic* 12 (Dec. 1798), 614–15; *European Magazine* 34 (Dec. 1798), 428–9.

5. On Enghien, see chapter 4.

6. Letter from Q. R., *MM*, 4 (Sept. 1797): 165–6. Such arguments would continue in later years: see William Burdon, *The Life and Character of Bonaparte, from his Birth to the 15th of August, 1804* (Newcastle upon Tyne, 1804), 34–5; [Archibald Alison, et al.], *Travels in France, During the Years 1814–15*, 2nd ed., 2 vols (Edinburgh, 1816), 1: 125.

7. Vivant Denon, *Travels in Upper and Lower Egypt, During the Campaigns of General Bonaparte*, trans. E. A. Kendal, 2 vols. (London, 1802).

8. W. Craig, *Anecdotes of General Buonaparte, Compiled from Original and Authentic Papers* [1799].

9. *MM* 3 (May 1797): 374, 376–7.

10. *British Critic*, 12 (Dec. 1798): 615.

11. *PH*, 34: 1206 (28 Jan. 1800).

12. *PH*, 34: 1470 (13 Feb. 1800). See also William Sturges' speech in *PH*, 34: 1475 (19 Feb. 1800).

13. *PH*, 34: 1473 (19 Feb. 1800).

14. *PH*, 34: 1259 (3 Feb. 1800). See also George Tierney's speech, *PH*, 34: 1442 (17 Feb. 1800).

15. *PH*, 34: 1449 (17 Feb. 1800). See also speech by Thomas Jones, *PH*, 35: 216 (8 May 1800).

16. *PH*, 34: 1340 (3 Feb. 1800).

17. *PH*, 34: 1443 (17 Feb. 1800).

18. From the *Morning Post*, 2 Oct. 1800, in *Essays on His Times in the Morning Post and the Courier*, ed. David V. Erdman; Vol. III (in three parts) of *The Collected Works of Samuel Taylor Coleridge*, ed. Kathleen Coburn (Princeton, 1969–), 1: 334.

19. *PH*, 34: 1485 (27 Feb. 1800).
20. *PH*, 35: 1132 (25 March 1801).
21. *PH*, 34: 1457 (17 Feb. 1800).
22. *PH*, 34: 1451 (17 Feb. 1800).
23. Letter to Samuel Taylor Coleridge, 23 Dec. 1799, in *New Letters of Robert Southey*, ed. Kenneth Curry, 2 vols. (New York, 1965), 1: 211.
24. Letter to Coleridge, 16 Jan. 1800, ibid., 1: 214.
25. Letter to John Rickman, 9 Jan. 1800, in *The Life and Correspondence of Robert Southey*, ed. Charles Cuthbert Southey, 6 vols. (London, 1849–50), 2: 46; Coleridge to Southey, 28 Dec. 1799, in *Collected Letters of Samuel Taylor Coleridge*, ed. Leslie Griggs, 6 vols. (Oxford, 1956–71), 1: 553.
26. Letter to Thomas Southey, 2 Feb. 1800, in *New Letters*, 1: 221–2.
27. Burdon republished these letters in his *Various Thoughts on Politics, Morality, and Literature* (Newcastle upon Tyne, 1800); citations are from this volume. Biographical information on Burdon is drawn from the *Dictionary of National Biography*, 7: 299, and from the chief source for the *DNB*'s essay, the "Memoir of William Burdon" appended to the fifth, posthumous edition of Burdon's *Materials for Thinking*, 2 vols. (London, 1820), 3–11. The "Memoir" has been attributed to the political writer George Ensor. The author of the "Memoir" describes himself as having had only a "short personal acquaintance" with Burdon (p. 4).
28. [Ensor], "Memoir," in Burdon, *Materials*, 4–5.
29. Burdon, *Various Thoughts*, 154–6 (letter of 9 March 1800).
30. Ibid., 156 (9 March 1800); 166 (9 April 1800).
31. Ibid., 155–6 (9 March 1800).
32. Ibid., 163 (9 April 1800). Burdon would have had in mind, most particularly, the *coup d'état* of Floréal VI, May 1798, when many defeated candidates were given office over elected ones.
33. Lewis Goldsmith, *The Crimes of Cabinets; or, a Review of their Plans and Agressions* [sic] *for the Annihilation of the Liberties of France and the Dismemberment of her Territories* (London, 1801).
34. Letter from "An Enemy to all Sedition, Private Conspiracy and Rebellion," in William Cobbett's *Porcupine*, 8 Sept. 1801. The letter may well have been from Cobbett himself, given the journalist's signature anti-Semitism.
35. Goldsmith, *Crimes*, 149–51, 129, 240.
36. Ibid., 45, 46n, 160, 217, 227.
37. Thomas Robinson to Henry Crabb Robinson, 20 Oct. 1801, in *Diary, Reminiscences, and Correspondence of Henry Crabb Robinson*, 3rd ed., ed. Thomas Sadler, 2 vols. (London, 1872; New York, 1967), 1: 57.
38. *Oracle*, 3 Oct. 1801.
39. *Oracle*, 12 Oct. 1801.
40. Add. MS 37853 (Windham Papers), f. 12 (Cobbett to Windham, 7 Oct. 1801).
41. *Porcupine*, 12 Oct. 1801.
42. Add. MS 37853, f. 14 (Cobbett to Windham, 10 Oct. 1801).
43. Ibid., f. 13 (Cobbett to Windham, 7 Oct. 1801).
44. William Cobbett, *Letters to the Right Honourable Lord Hawkesbury, and to the Right Honourable Henry Addington, on the Peace with Buonaparté*, 2nd ed. (London, 1802), 26 (orig. letter 16 Oct. 1801).
45. Ibid., 15 (orig. 16 Oct. 1801).

46. Ibid., 26 (orig. 16 Oct. 1801).
47. *Courier*, 12 Oct. 1801. The *Oracle* reported the monarchical initials "G. R." to be "among the mottos most used on the occasion." 12 Oct. 1801.
48. Cobbett, *Letters to . . . Hawkesbury*, 27–8 (orig. 16 Oct. 1801).
49. *Porcupine*, 15 Oct. 1801. Cobbett, *Letters to . . . Hawkesbury*, 19 (orig. 16 Oct. 1801). Cobbett also used the phrase a few days earlier in a letter to William Windham: Add. MS 37853 (Windham Papers), f. 13 (7 Oct. 1801).
50. Cobbett, *Letters to . . . Hawkesbury*, 19n.
51. *Porcupine*, 15 Oct. 1801.
52. Add. MS 37853, f. 16 (Cobbett to Windham, 20 Oct. 1801).
53. Cobbett, *Letters to . . . Hawkesbury*, 9–10 (orig. 14 Oct. 1801).
54. And see "General FitzPatrick's Journal" (copy), Holland House Papers, Add. MS 51455, f. 3, for Lord and Lady Holland's visit.
55. "Calais, August, 1802," in *Wordsworth: Poems*, 1: 575–6.
56. Smithson to Holland (3 Dec. 1801), Add. MS 51799 (Holland House Papers), ff. 54–5.
57. *CAR*, 14 Aug. 1802, 213. Not that Cobbett had been delighted with the criticism of Bonaparte that had formerly appeared: most of it, he noted (in an apparent dig at "Jacobin" critics of Napoleon), had been "levelled against his good, and not against his evil, deeds; and, if it has any rational object, it is to create a thousand tyrants in France by the destruction of one despot."
58. *CAR*, 21 Aug. 1802, 255.
59. *The Trial of John Peltier, Esq. for a Libel against Napoléon Buonaparté, First Consul of the French Republic, at the Court of King's Bench, Middlesex* (London, 1803), xviii, 205, 208.
60. John Carr, *The Stranger in France: or, a Tour from Devonshire to Paris* (London, 1803), 253–6.
61. Benedict Anderson, *Imagined Communities*, rev. ed. (London, 1991), 201.
62. See Christopher Hill, "The Norman Yoke," in *Puritanism and Revolution: Studies in Interpretation of the English Revolution of the 17th Century* (1958; New York, 1964), 50–122. And see chapter 6 of the present book on the divide between constitutionalist and anti-constitutionalist readings.
63. "The Little Island. A New Song" (BL). Note the song's transformation of Harold from a merely English king to monarch of the whole island.
64. Advertised in "To the United Kingdom" (BL).
65. Martin Arthur Shee, "A Patriotic Song, on the Present Crisis," in *Anti-Gallican*, 206. See also William Wordsworth, "To the Men of Kent. In October, 1803," in *Wordsworth: Poems*, 1: 594–5.
66. "Epitaph Underneath a Gibbet over a Dunghill, near Hastings" (BL).
67. E.g., Eyles Irwin, *Buonaparte in Egypt* (Dublin; London, 1798), 16.
68. *The Atrocities of the Corsican Demon; or a Glance at Buonaparte* (London, 1803), 6; *Porcupine*, 28 Jan. 1801; William Hunter, *A Vindication of the Cause of Great Britain*, 3rd ed. (London, 1803), 39 (also see "Ring the Alarum Bell!", 27; *Atrocities of the Corsican Demon*, 25); "On the military talents of Buonaparte," in *The Loyalist: Containing Original and Select Papers; Intended to Rouse and Animate the British Nation* (London, 1803), 278 (also see a "Parallel between Bonaparte and Augustus Cæsar," *MM* 14 (Oct. 1802): 222–6).
69. *Porcupine*, 8 Jan. 1801.

70. E.g., *The Genius of France; or, the Consular Vision* (London, [1801?]), 5. Hester Lynch Piozzi and William Cobbett questioned this parallel, thinking that it underestimated Napoleon's ambition: *Piozzi Letters*, 3: 154 (to Chappelow, 12 Dec. 1799); *Porcupine*, 8 July 1801.

71. *PH*, 34: 1526 (28 Feb. 1800). *The Speech of the Honourable Charles James Fox, in the House of Commons*, new ed. (London, 1800), 41; see also *PH*, 34: 1391 (3 Feb. 1800). George Mackereth, *An Historical Account of the Transactions of Napoleone Buonaparte* (London, [1801]), 88.

72. "The Lion Sleeps" (BL). See also, on Washington, *MM* 14 (Oct. 1802): 269, and Burdon, *Life and Character of Bonaparte*, 203, 269, 285.

73. David Rivers, *A Discourse on Patriotism, or the Love of our Country*, 4th ed. (London, 1804), 11; *Porcupine*, 1 Jan. 1801, 3.

74. "Galgacus" [Henry Redhead Yorke], *The Anti-Corsican; or, War of Liberty* (London, 1804), 135 (letter originally published 18 Jan. 1804).

75. *Rassurez Vous; or the Improbability of an Invasion* (Edinburgh, 1803), 8.

76. *The Exposé; or, Napoleone Buonaparte Unmasked* (London, 1809), 199–203.

77. *MM* 3 (May 1797): 374.

78. One exception, the poet and novelist John Scott Byerley, prefaced his translation of Machiavelli's *The Prince* with the claim that Napoleon's success reflected simply the studious attention he had paid to the crafty Florentine: Napoleon fought "with Machiavelli in one hand, and his sword in the other, the one performing the dictates of the other." J. Scott Byerley, *The Prince: . . . To Which is Prefixed an Introduction, Shewing the Close Analogy between the Principles of Machiavelli and the Actions of Buonaparte* (London, 1810), vii.

79. "Address of the Rev. Gerrard Andrewes, Rector, to the Inhabitants of the Parish of St. James, Westminster . . . the 10th August 1803" (BL).

80. Henry Redhead Yorke, *Letters from France, in 1802*, 2 vols. (London, 1804), 1: 124.

81. E.g., "The Sailor to his Messmates" (BL); "Victorious Englishmen" (Houghton); "John Bull Turned into a Galley Slave" (NYPL); "Buonaparte's Confession of the Massacre of Jaffa" (BL); "The True Briton" (BL).

82. Publicola, "Navy of Britain, Terror of your Foes" (BL); George Colman, *Epilogue to the New Play of The Maid of Bristol* [1803].

83. *Morning Post*, 1 Feb. 1803, quoted in Vincent Cronin, *Napoleon* (1971; London, 1990), 231.

84. *Exposé*, 144n.

85. *Thoughts on the Relative State of Great Britain and of France* (London, 1806), 26–7.

86. See chapter 4.

87. "Invasion. Scene of a Play" (BL). Rivers, *Discourse*, 12.

88. "Harlequin's Invasion," in *Anti-Gallican*, 70.

89. William Hunter, *A Sketch of the Political State of Europe, at the Beginning of February, 1805* (London, 1805), 191. See also *Exposé*, 227.

90. Coleridge, from the *Morning Post*, 10 Jan. 1800, in *Essays on His Times*, 1: 91; Burdon, *Life and Character*, 276–7. Also see the broadsides "Harlequin's Invasion" (in *Anti-Gallican*, 70) and "In Rehearsal. Theatre Royal of the United Kingdoms" (Houghton), and the caricature "Harlequin's Last Skip" (MDG 10270; 20 Aug. 1803).

91. Charles Maclean, *An Excursion in France, and Other Parts of the Continent of Europe* (London, 1804), 51, 49–50, 47.

92. *Atrocities of the Corsican Demon*, 4.

93. Rivers, *Discourse on Patriotism*, 11–12. Hunter, *A Sketch of the Political State*, 84. Also see Burdon, *Life and Character*, iii, 58.

94. Burdon, *Life and Character*, 223–4. For more on Napoleon's "theatrical arts," see *Times*, 1 Jan. 1801.

95. Hunter, *A Sketch of the Political State*, 184.

96. *Exposé*, *95–*96, [sic], 150-1.

97. Ibid., 189.

98. "Twenty Thousand Pounds Reward" (BL); *Morning Post*, 1 Feb. 1803, quoted in Cronin, *Napoleon*, 231; "An Address to those Brave, Gallant, and Loyal Hearts" (BL). Also see "No Change for the Worse, a Mistaken Notion" (BL); "History of Buonaparte" (BL); *Atrocities of the Corsican Demon*, 6; *Buonaparte's Pedigree*, 4th ed. (London, 1814), 25.

99. William Barré, *History of the French Consulate, under Napoleon Buonaparte* (London, 1804), 473, 451; "A Peep into Hanover; or, A Faint Description of the Atrocities Committed by the French in that City" (BL).

100. Hunter, *A Sketch of the Political State*, 84; "To the Inhabitants of the British Isles" (BL).

101. *PH*, 34: 1340 (3 Feb. 1800).

102. *Thraliana: The Diary of Mrs. Hester Lynch Thrale (Later Mrs. Piozzi), 1776–1809*, 2nd ed., ed. Katharine C. Balderston, 2 vols. (Oxford, 1951), 2: 1031–2 (5 Oct. 1801).

103. *Porcupine*, 2 Jan. 1801, 2.

104. Hunter, *Vindication*, 46, 55.

105. *Thoughts on the Relative State*, 14–15.

106. Burdon, *Life and Character*, 6, 114.

107. *An English Taylor Equal to Two French Grenadiers* (London, [1803?]), 7–8. See also "An Address to the French Soldiers, circulated near certain parts of the coast of France, by the French Emigrants" (Houghton).

108. Hester Piozzi's anti-Gallican animus was so great that in 1804 she declared herself "truly glad" to see the regicide French now at the command of "this devouring Despot and his Dame": "in every Act of Oppression in this new home I wish him Success." Letter to the Rev. Leonard Chappelow, 18 June 1804, in *Piozzi Letters*, 3: 469.

109. *An Address to the People of the United Kingdom of Great Britain and Ireland on the Threatened Invasion* (Edinburgh, 1803), 7.

110. *Exposé*, 20–1n.

111. See chapter 6.

2 National Character and National Anxiety

1. To Thomas Poole, in *Collected Letters of Samuel Taylor Coleridge*, 2: 524.

2. Robinson, *Diary, Reminiscences, and Correspondence*, 1: 45.

3. *Courier*, 2 Jan. 1801.

4. James Rodger Miller, *The History of Great Britain, from the Death of George II to the Coronation of George IV* (Philadelphia, 1844), 470.

5. *Courier*, 1 Jan. 1801. On the French demand, at the Lille negotiations in 1796, see Miller, *History*, 429.

6. According to Cobbett, Pitt had used the phrase in a Commons debate of 10 Nov. 1797. See *CWPR*, 17 Nov. 1804, 737.

7. *CAR*, 27 Oct. 1804, 614–18. In 1814, much more sympathetic to Napoleon's now tottering regime than he had been a decade before, the journalist reported having heard that the king's shedding of his title had derived from his feeling that it had "become *a disgrace to be king of such a people*" as the French. *CWPR*, 5 Feb. 1814, 185.

8. *Courier*, 1 Jan. 1801.

9. Colley, *Britons*; Dickinson, "Popular Loyalism"; Dickinson, "Popular Conservatism"; Schofield, "Conservative Political Thought."

10. Wordsworth, "Anticipation. October, 1803," in *Wordsworth: Poems*, 1: 595; "London, 1802," 1: 579–80.

11. Quoted in J. E. Cookson's important reconsideration of the movement, "The English Volunteer Movement of the French Wars, 1793–1815: Some Contexts," *Historical Journal* 32 (1989): 867–91, p. 886. See also Cookson's *British Armed Nation*; Linda Colley, "The Reach of the State, the Appeal of the Nation: Mass Arming and Political Culture in the Napoleonic Wars," in Lawrence Stone, ed., *An Imperial State at War: Britain from 1689 to 1815* (London, 1994), 165–84. For Volunteer organizations earlier in the French wars, see Dozier, *For King, Constitution, and Country*, 138–71. Arthur Bryant clearly summarizes the 1803 politics of mobilization in *Years of Victory, 1802–1812* (London, 1944), 53–5.

12. William Burdon, *Unanimity Recommended* (Newcastle upon Tyne, 1803). The following year, Burdon published a hostile biography: *The Life and Character of Bonaparte* (Newcastle upon Tyne, 1804).

13. These works receive close attention in Stella Cottrell's "The Devil on Two Sticks: Franco-phobia in 1803," in Raphael Samuel, ed., *Patriotism: The Making and Unmaking of British National Identity*, 3 vols. (London, 1989), 1: 259–74, which derives from her 1990 Oxford D.Phil. thesis, "English Views of France and the French, 1789–1815." Cottrell gives special attention to the function of gender and animality in portrayals of the French, and looks closely at how atrocities, most importantly the Jaffa massacres, figured in British accounts.

14. In raw numbers, as many political prints are listed in the BL catalogue for 1803 as for 1801, 1802, and 1804 together. The great majority of these 178 titles—and nearly all of the 130 after 10 June, which saw the first print directly speaking to the question of invasion—treat Napoleon.

15. [Cobbett], *Important Considerations for the People of this Kingdom* (July 1803); [Piozzi], "Old England to her Daughters" (Houghton).

16. *CAR*, 12 Nov. 1803, 710.

17. *Buonaparte in Britain!... Addressed to all Ranks* (London, [1803?]), xvi.

18. *European Magazine* 44 (Dec. 1803): 455.

19. The commentator was Mrs. R. C. Biggs, who claimed she had been consulted to proofread Cobbett's manuscript ("& indeed some of the facts were supply'd & some alterations made by myself"). Add. MSS 31234, ff. 23–4, Biggs to Nicholas Vansittart 4 December 1812. I am currently engaged in a separate research project on Mrs. Biggs.

20. "Circular to the officiating ministers of the several parishes in England and Wales," in *Selections from Cobbett's Political Works*, 1: 304.

21. Add. MS 31234, ff. 23–4.

22. "John Bull Turned into a Galley Slave; or, the Corsican Bonaparte" (BL).

23. Cox and Baylis, publishers of "The Alarum Bell," were the reported benefactors. See *The Loyalist: Containing Original and Select Papers; Intended to Rouse and Animate the British Nation* (London, 1803), 134.

24. See "Who is Bonaparte?" (BL) and many other broadsides.

25. *Loyalist*, title page. Another miscellany was *The Anti-Gallican; or Standard of British Loyalty, Religion and Liberty*.

26. "A Full, True and Particular Account of the Birth, Parentage, and Education, Life, Character, and Behaviour, and Notorious Conduct of NAPOLEONE BUONAPARTE, the CORSICAN MONSTER" (Houghton).

27. E.g., "Who is Bonaparte?" (BL); "To the People of the United Kingdoms" (BL). "An Address to those Brave, Gallant, and Loyal Hearts, the Commanders, Officers, Seamen, and Marines, of the British Navy" (BL) asked those "residing near the Coast" to distribute the broadside "amongst the Sailors."

28. "John Bull Turned into a Galley Slave; or, the Corsican Bonaparte" (BL).

29. *European Magazine* 44 (Aug. 1803): 131.

30. "Ring the Alarum Bell" (Houghton).

31. "The Corsican Assassin's Progress" (NYPL).

32. *European Magazine* 44 (Aug. 1803): 130–1.

33. "The Genius of Britain" (BL).

34. E.g., "Boney and Talley. The Corsican Carcase-Butcher's Reckoning Day" (BL); "Bonaparte and Talleyrand; or the French Invasion" (BL); "Plain Answers to Plain Questions, in a Dialogue between John Bull and Bonaparte, Met Half-Seas over between Dover and Calais" (BL); "A Second Dialogue between Buonaparte and John Bull" (BL).

35. Handbills for imaginary plays titled "Harlequin's Invasion" (Houghton); "The Invasion of England" (BL); "Buonaparte; or, the Free-Booter Running Away" (BL).

36. "Address of the Rev. Charles Edward Stewart, Rector of Wakes-Colne, in Essex" (BL); "Address of the Rev. Gerrard Andrewes, Rector, to the Inhabitants of the Parish of St. James, Westminster" (Houghton).

37. "Buonaparte's Confession of the Massacre of Jaffa" (BL); "History of the Conduct of the French Armies in Suabia" (BL); "Horrors upon Hororrs [*sic*]" (BL).

38. "Substance of the Corsican Bonaparte's Hand-bills; or, a Charming Prospect for John Bull and his Family" (BL).

39. E.g., "War Address" (NYPL); "To the United Kingdom" (BL); "The Declaration of the Merchants, Bankers, Traders, and other Inhabitants of London and its Neighbourhood" (BL).

40. "John Bull Turned into a Galley Slave" (BL); "A Solemn Appeal to the British Nation" (Houghton); "To the United Kingdom" (BL).

41. "A Full, True and Particular Account" (Houghton).

42. "Caution to John Bull" (BL).

43. *CAR*, 12 Nov. 1803, 705–6.

44. E.g., "Britons Ever the Same. A New Song" (NYPL); John Mason Good, "The

Triumph of Britain, an Ode" (BL); "Ring the Alarum Bell!" (Houghton); "A Word of Advice to the Self-Created Consul" (Houghton). See chapter 4.

45. *An English Taylor*, 13–15n.

46. "No Change for the Worse, a Mistaken Notion" (BL). Legitimacy and national character (indeed race) played a part in this broadside, for George's resemblance to Englishmen was noted by way of a contrast with the difference of the "little, swarthy, sullen, down-looking, Corsican Adventurer, sprung from Nobody knows whom."

47. Linda Colley, "The Apotheosis of George III: Loyalty, Royalty and the British Nation, 1760–1820," *Past and Present* 102 (Feb. 1984): 94–129.

48. "A King or a Consul? A New Song to the Tune of *Derry Down*" (BL); "A Full, True and Particular Account ..." (Houghton); "Address of the Rev. Gerrard Andrewes" (Houghton).

49. Colley, *Britons*, 210.

50. E.g., "Union and Watchfulness, Britain's True and Only Security" (Houghton); "Relish for Old Nick. Song, on the Threatened Invasion" (BL); "The Devil and the Consul. A New Song" (BL); I.H., "A New Song" (BL); *Appeal from the Passions*, 11–12.

51. E.g., "Ring the Alarum Bell!" (Houghton); "Buonaparte's Confession of the Massacre of Jaffa" (BL); "The Corsican Assassin's Progress" (NYPL).

52. E.g., John Mason Good, "The Triumph of Britain" (BL).

53. "Britons, the period is now arrived" (BL); see also "Publicola's Postscript to the People of England" (BL).

54. "The Invasion of England" (BL); see also [Yorke], *Anti-Corsican*, 11 (letter orig. pub. 9 Aug. 1803); and the play by "John Scott Ripon" [John Scott Byerley], *Buonaparte; or, The Free-Booter* (London, 1803).

55. "A Word of Advice to the Self-Created Consul" (Houghton).

56. "An Address to the French Soldiers" (Houghton). See also "John Bull Turned into a Galley Slave" (BL); "Buonaparte and Talleyrand" (BL).

57. "Victorious Englishmen" (Houghton); see also Maclean, *Excursion in France*, 46; "Britons, the period is now arrived" (BL); "SUCH IS BUONAPARTE!" (BL); "Encouraging Thoughts on the Threatened Invasion" (BL).

58. [Cobbett] *Important Considerations*, 7–9. "SUCH IS BUONAPARTE!" (BL); [Jacob] Sarratt, *Life of Buonaparte* (London, [1803]).

59. "A Full, True and Particular Account" (Houghton). See also the 14 Sept. 1803 letter of "Galgacus" [Yorke], in *The Anti-Corsican*, 51.

60. "Britons Triumph or Bonapartes Knell" (BL); "Buonaparte's Confession of the Massacre of Jaffa" (BL); Publicola, "Brave Soldiers, Defenders of Your Country" (BL); "Britons Unconquerable! A New Song" (BL); "Ring the Alarum Bell!" (BL); "The Corsican Assassin's Progress" (NYPL); "A Word of Advice to the Self-Created Consul" (Houghton); also see the opening of [Byerley], *Buonaparte; or, The Free-Booter*; "Bony's Visions or a Great Little Man's Night Comforts" (MDG 11736; 1 Sept. 1811). For a later example of the haunted Napoleon, see *The Vision of Napoleon, a Poem* (Edinburgh, 1813), 5–8; also see *Diary of Benjamin Robert Haydon*, 1: 66 (16 June 1809).

61. "A Song of Pity on Bonaparte" (BL); "The Despairing Hero" (BL).

62. W. J. Denison, "Address to the People of England" (BL); Publicola, "Navy of Britain, Terror of Your Foes" (BL); *An English Taylor*, 15; see also Sarratt, *Life*, 247–8.

63. "On the military talents of Buonaparte," in *Loyalist*, 274–8. On Napoleon's cowardice, see Publicola, "Brave Soldiers, Defenders of Your Country" (BL). See also Sarratt, *Life*, 26, 29, 165.
64. "A Peep into Hanover" (BL).
65. "Victorious Englishmen" (Houghton); "People of England!" (BL). See also Sarratt, *Life*, iii–iv.
66. "People of England!" (BL).
67. William Hunter, *A Vindication of the Cause of Great Britain*, 3rd ed. (London, 1803), 40.
68. "An Address to those Brave, Gallant, and Loyal Hearts, the Commanders, Officers, Seamen, and Marines, of the British Navy" (BL).
69. [Richard Arthur Davenport], "Sonnet. To France" (1809; orig. *Poetical Register and Repository of Fugitive Poetry* VI [1811]), in Betty T. Bennett, ed., *British War Poetry in the Age of Romanticism, 1793–1815* (New York, 1976), 444.
70. Publicola, "Navy of Britain, Terror of Your Foes" (BL).
71. *Escape from France* (London, 1811), 96–7.
72. William Playfair, *Political Portraits, in this New Æra*, 2 vols. (London, 1813), 1: 176.
73. Henry Redhead Yorke, *Letters from France, in 1802*, 2 vols. (London, 1804), 1: 123–4.
74. J. King, *Letters from France . . . In the Months of August, September, and October, 1802* (London, 1803), 165.
75. Carr, *Stranger in France*, 252.
76. [Yorke], *The Anti-Corsican*, 4–5 (orig. 2 Aug. 1803).
77. Yorke, *Letters from France*, 1: 113–14.
78. Hunter, *A Sketch of the Political State*, 75.
79. *MM* 25 (March 1808): 97.
80. "The Phantasmagoria—or a Review of Old Times" (MDG 9971; 9 March 1803). See also "John Bull at the Sign, the Case is Altered" (MDG 9714; 2 March 1801).
81. "An Address to those Brave, Gallant, and Loyal Hearts, the Commanders, Officers, Seamen, and Marines, of the British Navy" (BL); see also "Harlequin's Invasion" (Houghton).
82. Burdon, *Life and Character*, 271.
83. *A Sketch of the Present State of France. By an English Gentleman, who Escaped from Paris in the Month of May Last* (London, 1805), v–vii.
84. "Buonaparte; A Song, Printed by Order of the Stanmore Association" (BL); "The Menaces of Bonaparte" (BL). See also "The Invasion of England" (BL).
85. E.g., [Yorke], *Anti-Corsican*, 6 (orig. 2 Aug. 1803); George Colman, "Patriotic Epilogue to the Maid of Bristol," in *Anti-Gallican*, 174; "Song. The Invasion" (BL); T. Strange, *A Hint to Britain's Arch Enemy Buonaparte, an Effusion, Appropriate to Existing Circumstances*, 2nd ed. (London, 1804), 8.
86. This is the ratio given in "A Relish for Old Nick" (BL).
87. "Ode" (BL); "Epitaph Underneath a Gibbet over a Dunghill, near Hastings" (BL).
88. G. M. Woodward, "A Dialogue between John Stump and Giles Hobson, about Invasion" (BL).
89. *Porcupine*, 8 July 1801.

90. *Rassurez Vous*, 2–3.

91. "We must continue to be vigorous *alarmists*" (Burke, 1793). *OED*.

92. "John Bull and the Alarmist" (MDG 10088; 1 Sept. 1803).

93. "An Original Letter to the People of England, on the Threatened Invasion," in *Anti-Gallican*, 157.

94. "Address of Jacob Bonsanquet, Esq. On Tuesday the 26th of July, 1803, at the Royal Exchange, as Chairman of a Numerous and Respectable Meeting of Merchants, &c. of the City of London" (BL).

95. *Publicola's Addresses. To the People of England; to the Soldiers; and to the Sailors* (London, 1803), 18. For an earlier warning, see "An Officer," *Reply to Irwin*, 24–5.

96. "A Letter to the Volunteers" (BL).

97. "Britannia Correcting an Unruly Boy" (MDG 10012; 13 June 1803); "The Save-All and the Extinguisher!!" (MDG 10013; 13 June 1803).

98. "The King of Brobdingnag, and Gulliver" (MDG 10019; 26 July 1803); "The King of Brobdingnag and Gulliver. (Plate 2d.)" (MDG 10227; 10 Feb. 1804). Also see "The Little Princess and Gulliver" (MDG 10112; 21 Oct. 1803); "The Brodignag [*sic*] Watchman Preventing Gullivers Landing" (MDG 10130; Dec. 1803). See also the tiny Bonapartes in, e.g., "Britannia Repremanding [sic] a Naughty Boy!!" (MDG 9987; 3 May 1803); "The Lion and the Frog!!" (Houghton caricature; 30 July 1803); "A Peep at the Corsican Fairy" (MDG 10032; [July 1803]); "Amusement after Dinner, or The Corsican Fairy Displaying His Prowess!" (MDG 10034; July 1803); "John Bull Sounding his Bugle" (Houghton caricature; Nov. 1803).

99. For Napoleon bestriding the world, see "Fighting for the Dunghill; or, Jack Tar Settling Buonaparte" (MDG 9268; 20 Nov. 1798).

100. "The Plumb-Pudding in Danger:—Or—State Epicures Taking Un Petit Souper" (MDG 10371; 26 Feb. 1803).

101. E.g., "Conversation across the Water" (16 April 1803; reproduced in Franklin and Philp, *Napoleon and the Invasion of Britain*, 58); "A French Alarmist,—Or John Bull Looking out for the Grand Flotilla!!" (MDG 10231; March 1804).

102. E.g., "A Home Stroke for Little Boney, or John Bull Half Seas O'er" (Houghton caricature; 24 Aug. 1803).

103. "Buonaparté, 48 Hours after Landing" (MDG 10041; 26 July 1803).

104. "How to Invade England" (6 June 1803; reproduced in Franklin and Philp, *Napoleon and the Invasion of Britain*, 70).

105. "St. George and the Dragon—a Design for an Equestrian Statue, from the Original in Windsor Castle" (MDG 10424; 2 Aug. 1805). Unlike most of Gillray's political prints, which he both conceived and executed, this design was the work of Col. James Bradyll, who also conceived Gillray's "King of Brobdingnag." See also "Britannia Weighing the Fate of Europe; or John Bull too Heavy for Buonaparte" (Houghton caricature; Dec. 1803) in which the two figures are being weighed by a giant, though presumably not neutral, Britannia.

106. "A Lesson for Labourers" (BL). The argument was famously made in Gilbert Wakefield's 1798 *Reply to Some Parts of the Address of the Bishop of Llandaff to the People of Great Britain*.

107. "No Change for the Worse, a Mistaken Notion" (BL).

108. "Dialogue the Third. Stranger and John Bull Meeting" (BL).

109. "An Original Letter to the People of England," in *Loyalist*, 58.
110. "To the United Kingdom" (BL); "Freedom and Loyalty: With a New Song" (BL). See also "The Fate of Labouring Men, and the Poor, in Case of Invasion" (BL).
111. "Address of the Rev. Gerrard Andrewes" (Houghton).
112. "A King or a Consul? A New Song" (BL); "A Second Dialogue between Buonaparte and John Bull" (BL).
113. "Valerius's Address to the People of England" (BL).
114. "The Fate of Labouring Men, and the Poor, in Case of Invasion" (BL).
115. "A Peep into Hanover" (BL).
116. *Atrocities of the Corsican Demon*, 52.
117. *An Address to the Mechanics, Artificers, Manufacturers, and Labourers of England*, 2nd ed. (London, [1803]), 6, 9. On similar arguments that the poor depended on the rich, see Dickinson, "Popular Loyalism," 508–9.
118. "George and Tim" (Houghton).
119. "The Fate of Labouring Men, and the Poor, in Case of Invasion" (BL); "A Lesson for Labourers" (BL).
120. "Address of Jacob Bonsanquet, Esq. On Tuesday the 26th of July, 1803, at the Royal Exchange" (BL).
121. "George and Tim" (Houghton). See also "The Fate of Labouring Men, and the Poor, in Case of Invasion" (BL).
122. *An English Taylor*, 7–9.
123. T[homas] Newenham, *The Warning Drum, a Call to the People of England to Resist Invaders* (London, 1803), 12.
124. "Countrymen, The Whole Plot's Discover'd!!" (Houghton). See also *Atrocities of the Corsican Demon*, 58; *An English Taylor*, 7–9.
125. "A Peep into Hanover" (BL).
126. "Invasion. Scene II. of a Play" (BL). All four national types also appear in "Thoughts on the Invasion, Both Sides the Water" (MDG 10109; 11 Oct. 1803).
127. "John Bull to Brother Patrick in Ireland" (BL). For other images of a loyal and fraternal Pat, see "The Scare Crows Arrival, or Honest Pat Giving them an Irish Welcome" (MDG 10009; 10 June 1803); "The Corsican Beggar Rideing [*sic*] to the Devil" (MDG 10011; 13 June 1803). Also see the play "National Pantomime. The Magic of British Liberty; or, the Disintegration of Bonaparte" (performed in York in Dec. 1803), which describes an English and Irish sailor as "two British Bull-dogs" (p. 13). John Larpent Plays (Huntington Library), number 1397.
128. "Address to Irishmen Residing in England" (BL). See also Charles Butler, *A Letter to a Roman Catholic Gentleman of Ireland, on the Chief Consul Buonaparte's Projected Invasion* (London, 1803).
129. "Men of England!" (BL); "The Patriot-Briton; or, England's Invasion" (song, BL); Sarratt, *Life*, 285–6.
130. "Orders of Bonaparte to the Army of England," in *Anti-Gallican*, 243; "A Word of Advice to the Self-Created Consul" (Houghton). See also "Horrors upon Hororrs [*sic*]" (BL).
131. "People of the British Isles" (BL).
132. "This Day was published, An Address to the People of the United Kingdom of Great Britain and Ireland, on the Threatened Invasion" (BL). This

broadside summarized and advertised a pamphlet that was itself bulk-priced at a shilling a dozen, *An Address to the People of the United Kingdom of Great Britain and Ireland on the Threatened Invasion* (Edinburgh, 1803).

133. "Proclamation, made to every man in the United Kingdom of Great Britain and Ireland" (BL).

134. "A Peep into Hanover" (BL). See also "The Consequences of Buonaparte's Succeeding in his Designs against this Country" (BL).

135. On the role of women during the French wars, see Colley, *Britons*, 254–62.

136. *Buonaparte in Britain!*, xvi, 201–2.

137. "The Female Association for Preserving Liberty and Property" (Houghton).

138. *Buonaparte in Britain!*, 201–2.

139. "The Female Association" (Houghton).

140. *Invasion Defeated*, 2nd ed. (London, 1803), 20. See also "Old England to her Daughters" (Houghton).

141. *Buonaparte in Britain!*, 202.

142. G. M. Woodward, "A Female Meeting, on the Subject of Invasion! Mrs. Bull in the Chair" (BL).

143. "To the Women of England" (BL); "The Female Association" (Houghton).

144. "The Female Association" (Houghton).

145. "Old England to her Daughters" (Houghton).

146. The demolition of these markers of political liberty was frequently augured; see, e.g., "People of the British Isles" (BL), "A Full, True and Particular Account" (Houghton).

147. "No Change for the Worse, a Mistaken Notion" (BL). See the print "John Bull Transported; or the Case Alter'd" and the accompanying verse "Epigram. John Bull to his Countrymen," in *The Anti-Gallican*, 169 and opp.

148. "No Change for the Worse, a Mistaken Notion" (BL). See also "Countrymen, The Whole Plot's Discover'd!!" (Houghton) and the song "A Relish for Old Nick" (BL).

149. "A Fig for the Grand Buonaparte" (BL).

150. Roy Porter, *English Society in the Eighteenth Century*, rev. ed. (Harmondsworth, 1990), 21.

151. "No Change for the Worse, a Mistaken Notion" (BL).

152. *CWPR*, 4 Dec. 1813, 708.

153. *An English Taylor*, 7–9.

154. "No Change for the Worse, a Mistaken Notion" (BL).

155. Ibid.

156. *Atrocities of the Corsican Demon*, 57–9. Much of this warning was recycled in "A Farmer's Letter on the Invasion," in *Loyalist*, 65–7. See also "No Change for the Worse, a Mistaken Notion" (BL).

157. [Cobbett], *Important Considerations*, 15.

158. *An Appeal from the Passions to the Sense of the Country* (London, 1803), 5. See also "An Original Letter to the People of England," in *Loyalist*, 57–8; "Proclamation, Made to Every Man in the United Kingdom of Great Britain and Ireland" (BL).

159. "An Invasion Sketch" (BL).

160. *Appeal from the Passions*, 16; "A Dialogue between British Tar Just Landed at Portsmouth, and Brave Soldier Lately Returned from Egypt" (BL); "An

Address to those Brave, Gallant, and Loyal Hearts" (BL); "An Original Letter to the People of England," in *Loyalist*, 57–8.

161. A "contemporary periodical writer," quoted in *Examiner*, 24 Jan. 1808, 50.
162. *Examiner*, 27 March 1808, 194.
163. [James Stephen], *The Dangers of the Country* (London, 1807), 16, 48–50, 67–8.
164. "Bonaparte Answered; or, the Briton's War Song" (BL); "A Song for the Times. By Quintus Quoz, Esq." (BL). See also "Invasion. Scene of a Play" (BL); Publicola's "People of England!" (BL); Publicola's "Brave Soldiers, Defenders of Your Country" (BL).
165. "The Ghost of Queen Elizabeth" (Houghton caricature; 20 July 1803).
166. See, e.g., W. T. Fitzgerald, "Britons! To Arms!!!" (BL); "The Patriot-Briton; or, England's Invasion" (song, BL); "Invasion. A New Song" (BL).
167. Cottrell, "Devil," 263. Cottrell is right to detect "an idealization of continuity" in the broadsides—but "idealization of" does not necessarily equal "faith in."
168. "The Triumph of Britain, an Ode" (BL). See also the references to Sydney and Hamden in "Britons Strike Home! A New Song" (BL).
169. Wordsworth, "Lines on the Expected Invasion 1803," in *Wordsworth: Poems*, 1: 596.
170. "Substance of the Corsican Bonaparte's Hand-Bills" (BL). On anti-Gallican radical sentiment in the eighteenth century, see Linda Colley, "Radical Patriotism in Eighteenth-Century England," in Samuel, *Patriotism*, 1: 169–87.
171. Rivers, *Discourse on Patriotism*, 16.
172. "Queen Elizabeth's Speech to her People, When Threatened by the Spanish Armada" (BL); "Citizens of London!" (BL).
173. E.g., "An Address to those Brave, Gallant, and Loyal Hearts, the Commanders, Officers, Seamen, and Marines, of the British Navy" (BL).
174. "A Solemn Appeal to the British Nation" (Houghton).
175. "The Declaration of the Merchants, Bankers, Traders, and Other Inhabitants of London and its Neighbourhood" (BL). In a similarly Burkean phrase, a contemporary play spoke of the "honours which our ancestors have bequeathed to us, which they purchased with their blood, and devised in tail to their heirs." [Byerley], *Buonaparte; or, The Free-Booter*, 10.
176. Rivers, *Discourse*, 16. See, likewise, "Citizens of London!" (BL).
177. "The Antigallican Club" (Houghton).
178. "Men of England!" (BL).
179. "Victorious Englishmen" (Houghton). See also "Dialogue the Third. Stranger and John Bull Meeting" (BL).
180. E.g., "A Letter to the Volunteers" (BL).
181. "The Grand Privilege, Duty, & Defence of Britons" (BL).
182. "An Original Letter to the People of England, on the Threatened Invasion," in *Loyalist*, 56.
183. [Cobbett] *Important Considerations*, 16.
184. "Victorious Englishmen" (Houghton).
185. "The Duke of Shoreditch; or, Barlow's Ghost" (BL).
186. Rivers, *Discourse*, 10–11. Rivers did stress that patriotism, though "enfeebled," had not disappeared. Indeed, in his fourth edition, Rivers could announce that in the period since his first publication (though he was too

modest to take all the credit for himself) "the Nation has been roused from that *unnatural torpor*, that disgraceful apathy, which for some time pervaded it."

187. "The Patriot-Briton; or, England's Invasion" (song, BL).

188. "On the Extinction of the Venetian Republic," in *Wordsworth: Poems*, 1: 571–2. On Venice as a mirror for Britain, see John Eglin, *Venice Transfigured: The Myth of Venice in British Culture, 1660–1797* (Basingstoke, 2001).

189. "Declaration of the Parish of Ealing, Middlesex, at a Meeting Held for Forming a Volunteer Corps," in *Anti-Gallican*, 181; "Advice Suggested by the State of the Times" (Houghton).

190. On the funding of *RYWPR*, see Lord Sidmouth, quoted in Aspinall, *Politics and the Press*, 88. That Sidmouth, the former prime minister Henry Addington, could wish "hanged" those who might authorize any further government "encouragement" of Yorke suggests the perceived outrageousness of the journalist's views. Previously, Yorke had succeeded Cobbett as editor of the *Porcupine* in November 1801—much to his predecessor's disapproval, as Cobbett had heard "that Yorke has *an allowance from the* [Addington] *Ministry*," and feared that the paper would be too much in favor of peace with Napoleon. Add. MS 37853 (Windham Papers), f. 17 (Cobbett to Windham, 24 Nov. 1801). The prospectus for *RYWPR* (BL) declared that he had formerly been "confidentially employed" by the government.

191. *RYWPR*, 10 June 1809, 442. For earlier demonizations of the French, see, e.g., [Yorke], *Anti-Corsican*, 148–9 (orig. 15 Jan. 1804); *RYWPR*, 12 July 1806, 529; 30 Aug. 1806, 635; 26 April 1806, 321.

192. *RYWPR*, 27 June 1809, 472.

193. *RYWPR*, 11 Feb. 1809, 95.

194. See Newman, *Rise*, 80–4.

195. *RYWPR*, 11 Feb. 1809, 95; 26 April 1806, 325.

196. *RYWPR*, 11 Feb. 1809, 93–5 (emphasis added). Yorke's usage predates the earliest English instances given by the *OED*: 1820 for the phrase "spirit of the age" (Percy Shelley) and 1824 for "spirit of the times" (Walter Savage Landor). For an even earlier example of the latter phrase, see Burdon, *Life and Character*, 176.

197. *RYWPR*, 17 June 1809, 451. We see in concerns about emasculation, as in the ambivalence about the unleashing of women's martial energies, some evidence of what Dror Wahrman has termed the "gender panic" of late Georgian Britain. "*Percy's* Prologue: From Gender Play to Gender Panic in Eighteenth-Century England," *Past and Present* 159 (May 1998): 113–61. On the eighteenth-century transformation of sexual categories, see Randolph Trumbach, *Sex and the Gender Revolution, Volume One: Heterosexuality and the Third Gender in Enlightenment London* (Chicago, 1998). On the increasingly brittle qualities of identity in the late eighteenth century, also see Wahrman's "The English Problem of Identity in the American Revolution," *American Historical Review* 106 (Oct. 2001): 1236–62, and "On Queen Bees and Being Queens: A Late-Eighteenth-Century 'Cultural Revolution?'" in Colin Jones and Dror Wahrman, eds., *The Age of Cultural Revolutions: Britain and France, 1750–1820* (Berkeley and Los Angeles, 2002), 251–80.

198. *CAR*, 12 Nov. 1803, 710–11.

199. From Cobbett's descriptions, it is clear that he had in mind the broadside

"Invasion. Scene II. of a Play" (BL), and the engravings "After the Invasion. The Levéé [*sic*] en Masse, or Britons Strike Home" (MDG 10052; 6 Aug. 1803), "The Consequence of Invasion or the Hero's Reward. None but the Brave deserve the Fair" (MDG 10047; 4 Aug. 1803), and "Buonaparté, 48 Hours after Landing" (MDG 10041; 26 July 1803).

200. *CAR*, 12 Nov. 1803, 710–12, 717.

3 *The Pious Proteus and the Nation's Destiny*

1. BL.
2. John Cam Hobhouse, *The Substance of Some Letters, Written by an Englishman Resident at Paris* (London, 1816), 1: 4–5.
3. On Brothers and Southcott, see J. F. C. Harrison, *The Second Coming: Popular Millenarianism, 1780–1850* (London, 1979), 57–134; James K. Hopkins, *A Woman to Deliver Her People: Joanna Southcott and English Millenarianism in an Era of Revolution* (Austin, 1982); John Barrell, *Imagining the King's Death: Figurative Treason, Fantasies of Regicide, 1793–1796* (Oxford, 2000), 504–47.
4. Historians of British chiliasm in the period of the French revolution have given little attention to Napoleon. Harrison's excellent *The Second Coming* does not mention him. Clarke Garrett's *Respectable Folly: Millenarians and the French Revolution in France and England* (Baltimore, 1975) doubts that Napoleon "inspired, after 1799, the same sorts of millenarian hopes and fears . . . that the Jacobins had aroused in 1794" (p. 211). See also W. H. Oliver's *Prophets and Millennialists: The Uses of Biblical Prophecy in England from the 1790s to the 1840s* (Auckland, 1978).
5. See Harrison, *Second Coming*; Deborah M. Valenze, *Prophetic Sons and Daughters: Female Preaching and Popular Religion in Industrial England* (Princeton, 1985).
6. Roger Wells, "English Society and Revolutionary Politics in the 1790s: The Case for Insurrection," in Philp, ed., *French Revolution and British Popular Politics*, 188–225, p. 202.
7. The centrality of theology to eighteenth- and nineteenth-century political thought is argued in Clark, *English Society*, and Boyd Hilton, *The Age of Atonement: The Influence of Evangelicalism on Social and Economic Thought, 1785–1865* (Oxford, 1988). See also Iain McCalman's important *Radical Underworld: Prophets, Revolutionaries, and Pornographers in London, 1795–1840* (Cambridge, 1988; Oxford, 1993), and Jon Mee, *Dangerous Enthusiasm: William Blake and the Culture of Radicalism in the 1790s* (Oxford, 1992). On two of the most prominent exegetes, see Jack Fruchtman, "The Apocalyptic Politics of Richard Price and Joseph Priestley," *Transactions of the American Philosophical Society*, 73: 4 (1983), 1–121.
8. I will not dwell on the distinction drawn by historians of eschatology between "millenarian" and "millennial" sentiment (indeed, I will use the terms interchangeably). The former term is sometimes used to refer to pre-millennialism, the notion that Christ's advent will precede the millennium, and the latter to post-millennialism, the belief that Christ will return only on the heels of an earthly chiliad. But this distinction was not central to the arguments of the

writers I discuss (though see note 70, below, on Lewis Mayer's response to Joanna Southcott). Pre-millennialism is associated with a more conservative attitude toward social institutions (as the millennium, in this schema, does not depend on prior reform).

9. For an overreaching (but thought-provoking) consideration of the connection between religion and nationalism, see Hastings, *Construction of Nationhood.*

10. On British Protestant Francophobia, see the first chapter ("Protestants") of Colley, *Britons.*

11. E.g., "Sawney's Defence against the Beast, Whore, Pope, and Devil" (MDG 5534; 1 April 1779); "The Times" (MDG 5643 26 Feb. 1780).

12. *MM* 3 (May 1797): 374, 376–7; W. Craig, *Anecdotes of General Buonaparte, Compiled from Original and Authentic Papers* [1799].

13. "Conquest or Death" (poem), in *Anti-Gallican,* 132.

14. "A King or a Consul? A New Song" (BL). See also "A Fig for the Grand Buonaparte" (BL); "Boney Attacking the English Hives" (MDG 10079; [Aug. 1803]).

15. George Colman, Jr., "Epilogue to the New Play of *The Maid of Bristol,*" reproduced with varying punctuation in *European Magazine* 44 (Aug. 1803): 133, and (the version here quoted) in *Anti-Gallican,* 174. See also "Harlequin's Invasion," *Anti-Gallican,* 70; *A Concise History of the Origin, Progress and Effects of the Papal Supremacy* (Dublin, 1810; London, 1810), 109–10.

16. "An English Israelite," *A Letter to the Parisian Sanhedrin* (London, 1808), 44. One writer suggested that Napoleon had once claimed to accept the Jewish faith: letter from "Sica," *Gentleman's Magazine* 69, pt. 2 (July 1799): 568.

17. Lord Minto, *The Speech of the Right Honourable Lord Minto, at a General Meeting of the County of Roxburgh* (Kelso, 1803), 18. See also, e.g., letter from "Sica," *Gentleman's Magazine* 69, pt. 2 (July 1799): 568; Byerley, *The Prince,* lxxxvi; Barré, *History of the French Consulate,* 443; *British Critic* 35 (April 1810): 333.

18. *MM* 11 (May 1801): 351.

19. *Annual Review* 6 (1807): 318–19.

20. Thus Joseph Priestley maintained that toleration would encourage Catholic conversion to Protestantism, by replacing Protestantism's stern visage with a welcoming one. *A Free Address to Those Who Have Petitioned for the Repeal of the Late Act of Parliament* (London, 1780). Pamphlets defending the Catholic Relief Act of 1778 argued that religious toleration would encourage Catholics to convert. See, for example, Thomas Lloyd, *An Essay on the Toleration of Papists* (London, 1779); *Thoughts on the Present State of the Roman Catholics in England* (London, 1779); *A Reply to an Appeal from the Protestant Association* (London, 1780).

21. E.g., *Vox Stellarum* (1803): 42.

22. "A Kentish Clergyman" [Edward Hankin], *Thoughts on the Preliminary Articles of Peace* (London, 1801), 12. [Hankin], *The Civil and Religious Advantages Resulting from the Late War* (London, 1802), 24–5. Two years later, when Hankin gave up on peace with Napoleon, he became more sympathetic to France's Catholic clergy. The group he had formerly seen as an "intolerant priesthood" became a sympathetic "Clergy," victims of a government that "plundered, crucified, and despised" them. [Hankin], *Civil and*

Religious, 24; [Hankin], *The Independence of Great Britain, as the First of Maritime Powers, Essential to . . . the Prosperity and Preservation of all European Nations* (London, 1804), 37.

23. E.g., Hester Lynch Piozzi to Hester Maria Thrale (21 Aug. 1796), *Piozzi Letters* 2: 374; Joseph Priestley to Rev. T. Lindsey (1 Nov. 1798), *Life and Correspondence of Joseph Priestley*, ed. John Towill Rutt, 2 vols. (London, 1831–2), 2: 410.

24. E.g., *Concise History of the Origin*, 109–10.

25. "A Protestant Spectator," *The Territories of Popery Invaded, Exemplified in the Conduct of Napoleon Buonaparte towards the Church of Rome* (London, 1814), 37.

26. Lewis Mayer, *The Important Period, and Long Wished for Revolution, Shewn to be at Hand*, 3rd ed. (London, 1806), 37; Mayer, *The Emperor of the Gauls Considered as the Lucifer and Gog of Isaiah and Ezekiel*, 3rd ed. (London, 1804), frontispiece.

27. See William Barré, *The Rise, Progress, Decline and Fall, of Buonaparte's Empire in France* (London, 1805), 88, 561. Augustus Markett, a student of prophecy who favored Lord Liverpool with a series of letters, believed that Napoleon's desire for universal empire would lead him to "make himself Pope, or give it to one of his own Creatures," perhaps his infant son, born in 1811 (who already held the title of king of Rome). Add MS 38251, f. 318 (20–21 Feb. 1813). Bonaparte's uncle, Cardinal Fesch, was also thought to be a potential pope. See, e.g., "The Imperial Coronation" (MDG 10262; 31 July 1804); *RYWPR*, 5 July 1809, 20.

28. *AGM*, 1 Dec. 1811, 357.

29. *AGM*, 15 Dec. 1811, 376.

30. *PD*, 20: 380, 376–7 (31 May 1811).

31. *PD*, 20: 423 (31 May 1811).

32. *PD*, 20: 411 (31 May 1811). In his fifteen years at Westminster, Duigenan spoke on few matters besides restrictions on Catholics; see R. G. Thorne, ed., *The History of Parliament: The House of Commons, 1790–1820* (London, 1986), 3: 629–31.

33. For a similar argument, see *A Concise History of the Origin*, 111–12.

34. For a critical presentation, see Simon Schwarzfuchs, *Napoleon, the Jews and the Sanhedrin* (London, 1979). A more balanced account, which emphasizes the inner tensions of Napoleon's Jewish policies, can be found in chapter 3 of Paula E. Hyman's *The Jews of Modern France* (Berkeley and Los Angeles, 1998), 37–52.

35. R[alph] Wedgwood, *The Book of Remembrance: The Outline of an Almanack Constructed on the Ancient Cycles of Time* (London, 1814), lviii. See also *Annual Review* (1807): 346–50, which hailed the Sanhedrin as betokening the rise of a rational Unitarianism; and "Eben-Ezer" [Ebenezer Aldred], *The Little Book; (See the Tenth Chapter of Revelations)* (London, 1811), xxxvi–xxxvii, according to which the Sanhedrin showed Napoleon to be "not like some others"—Aldred had in mind Britain's own king—"a religious bigot and an intolerant persecutor."

36. Letter from W. Hamilton Reid, *Gentleman's Magazine* 80, pt. 2 (July 1810): 12, criticizing Robert Atkins' *A Compendious History of the Israelites*, which had been reviewed in *Gentleman's* 80, pt. 1 (June 1810): 557. This is the letter

in which Reid acknowledged his identity as the "Advocate for the House of Israel" (see p. 95).

37. Letter from Atkins, *Gentleman's Magazine* 80, pt. 2 (Sept. 1810): 237-8.

38. F. D. Kirwan, preface to *Transactions of the Parisian Sanhedrim [sic]* (London, 1807), iv-xi.

39. Ibid., xiv-xv.

40. *Gentleman's Magazine* 80, pt. 2 (July 1810): 12.

41. "English Israelite," *Letter.* See also *MM* 24 (Aug. 1807), 35.

42. "English Israelite," *Letter,* vi-vii, 24-5.

43. Ibid., 21-2.

44. For a similar accusation of "apostacy from Judaism," see *MM* 24 (Aug. 1807): 35.

45. "English Israelite," *Letter,* v, vii, title.

46. Letter from "C——" [E. Clarkson], *AGM,* 20 Oct. 1811, 314.

47. Rev. 13: 18.

48. Mayer, *A Hint to England; or, A Prophetic Mirror* (London, 1803), 18. See Mayer, *Death of Bonaparte, and Universal Peace,* 2nd ed. (London, 1809), 87-97 for a detailed table of his calculations.

49. *British Press,* 12 Jan. 1805. (U = V = 5.)

50. "A Royal Arch Mason," *The Corsican's Downfall. The Rise, Name, Reign, and Final Downfall of Napolean, Alias Nicolais Buonaparte* (Mansfield, [1814]), 7, 7-8n. Another student of prophecy, John Dale, provided four different ways in which "Napoleon Bonaparte," or some variant thereupon, added up to 666: *The Restoration of All Things; or, the State of a New World,* 4th ed. (London, 1808), ii. See also Ralph Wedgwood's mathematical calculations, involving among other phrases "le croix d'honneur," the Napoleonic honor that Wedgwood claimed to be the mark of the beast. *Book of Remembrance,* 10n., 110, xix (in the book's "Explanation of the Figures").

51. *Monthly Review* 63 (Oct. 1810): 208-9 (review of G. R. Hioan, *Thoughts on Prophecy*).

52. The letters were to be read as Roman numerals (ignoring S, and counting O as zero). James Bicheno, *The Signs of the Times, in Three Parts,* 5th ed. (London, 1799), 24; Bicheno, *The Fulfilment of Prophecy Farther Illustrated* (London, 1817), 81; Aldred, *Little Book,* 18. Even writers unfriendly to Napoleon were ready to cite this correspondence, for Louis was hardly the darling of all anti-Napoleonists: Augustus Markett to Lord Liverpool (20 Feb. 1813), Add. MS 38251 (Liverpool Papers), f. 317. Nor did a desire to target Bonaparte erase the traditional antipathy of scriptural interpreters to the Catholic Church: see Faber, *Dissertation,* 2: 226, 280.

53. Letter from "Senex," *The Scourge* 6 (July 1813): 10. "Senex" also objected to the numerologists' reliance on the misspelling "Napolean" (Bonaparte, according to believers, "spelt his name Napoleon to baffle enquiry and defeat the end of revelation"). A similar misspelling was used in *European Magazine* 53 (June 1808): 430. See also "The Beast as Described in the Revelations, Chap. 13. Resembling Napolean Buonaparte" (MDG 11004; 22 July 1808).

54. Thomas Witherby, *Observations on Mr. Bicheno's Book, Entitled The Restoration of the Jews the Crisis of all Nations* (London, 1800), 153.

55. Hobhouse, *Substance,* 5. "The Pope was formerly [John Bull's] great aversion," William Hazlitt similarly wrote in 1816. "But since other people took to

imitating his example, John has taken it into his head to hinder them; . . . [he] has become sworn brother to the Pope, and stands by the Inquisition." "Character of John Bull" (orig. *The Examiner*, 19 May 1816), *The Round Table*; in *Complete Works of William Hazlitt*, ed. P. P. Howe, 21 vols. (London, 1930–34), 4: 99.

56. Witherby, *Observations*, 157–66.

57. Mayer, *A Hint to England; or, A Prophetic Mirror* (London, 1803), 28, 34; *Bonaparte the Emperor of the French*, 3rd ed. (London, 1806), 7, 9, 12, 16–17; *Death of Bonaparte, and Universal Peace*, 2nd ed. (London, 1809), 68. Augustus Markett, correspondent of Lord Liverpool, also interpreted the mark of the Beast (Rev. 13: 16) as the revolutionary cockade. Add. MS 38251 (Liverpool Papers), f. 317 (20 Feb. 1813).

58. Mayer first made this charge in his 1803 *Hint* (p. 17), several years before the official formulation (in 1806) of Napoleon's "Continental System," and repeated it in his 1809 *Death of Bonaparte* (p. 82). A later pamphlet would also link the Beast's mark to the Continental System, claiming that under Napoleon's regime, those who had been caught importing English goods had been branded on the head. See "A Royal Arch Mason," *The Corsican's Downfall*, 18, 143.

59. Mayer, *Important Period*, iv.

60. As one recent scholar has remarked: "All religions are one, which in Faber's case speaks with the voice of angels (that is to say the Book of Common Prayer) and sings to the tune of the Anglican hymnal." Stuart Curran, "The Political Prometheus," *Studies in Romanticism* 25 (Fall 1986): 430. Faber's syncretic approach can be perceived in the title of an early work, *Horæ Mosaicæ; or, A View of the Mosaical Records, with Respect to their Coincidence with Profane Antiquity; Their Internal Credibility; and Their Connection with Christianity* (Oxford, 1801).

61. *British Critic* 35 (April 1810): 322. The *Annual Review* had devoted nine pages to a careful summary of the *Dissertation* on its initial publication, albeit one that closed on a note of skepticism: *Annual Review* (1806): 99–107.

62. *DNB*, xviii, 111. Faber, *Dissertation*, "Postscript."

63. G. S. Faber, *The Revival of the French Emperorship Anticipated from the Necessity of Prophecy*, 5th ed. (orig. 1852; London, 1859). Others who joined Faber in believing that Napoleon III should be read through the lens of prophecy included W. Meynell Whittemore, *The Seventh Head: or, Louis Napoleon Foreshadowed by Prophecy* (London, 1853); M. [Michael Paget] Baxter, *Louis Napoleon the Infidel Antichrist Predicted in Prophecy* (Toronto, 1861); and G. B. Hildebrand, *The Application of Prophecy to the Crimean War* (London, 1864).

64. Faber, *Dissertation*, 1: xix, 100, 102; Faber, *Remarks on the Effusion of the Fifth Apocalyptic Vial*, 2nd ed. (London, 1815), 5.

65. Faber, *Remarks on the Effusion*, 5, 14; *Revival*, 41.

66. Faber, *Dissertation*, 1: 103n, 330.

67. Ibid., 1: 349, 349n, 346–7, 161n.

68. Ibid., 2: 399, 1: xxiii. See also Faber, *A General and Connected View of the Prophecies*, 2 vols. (London, 1808), 2: 10.

69. Henry Kett, *History the Interpreter of Prophecy* (orig. 1799; 4th ed., 2 vols., London, 1801), 2: 291–2n.

70. Mayer, *Peace with France, and Catholic Emancipation, Repugnant to the Command of God*, 3rd ed. (London, 1806), 30 (Isaiah 2: 2); Mayer, *Hint*, 36; *The Woman in the Wilderness, or, The Wonderful Woman, with her Wonderful Seal, Wonderful Spirit, and Wonderful Child*, 2nd ed. (London, 1806), 6n. (See also, e.g., Mayer, *Important Period*, iv and *Emperor*, 20.) Mayer was non-committal as to whether Britain's victory would bring Christ's advent: he distinguished himself, in this matter, from the visionary Joanna Southcott (claiming that she had asserted "that the kingdom of Christ will be established by the destruction of Bonaparte"). Thus Mayer did not take a side in the nascent debate between pre-millennialists and post-millennialists.

71. Witherby, *Observations*, title page.

72. Faber, *General*, 10–11, 14.

73. James Hatley Frere, *A Combined View of the Prophecies of Daniel, Esdras, and St. John* (London, 1815), 466–7, 468.

74. *Remarks on Some Parts of Mr. Faber's Dissertation on the Prophecies* (London, 1809), 48.

75. Wedgwood, *Book of Remembrance*, 54, iii, xlvii, 201, xlvii, 12–13, 62, 46. The world, according to Wedgwood, was divided between Britain and Rome— "Brit and anti-Brit"—Rome acting "against the covenant ... with deadly enmity" and opposing its "mystery and darkness" to "the light of Brit." Richard Brothers and William Blake had also drawn links between Britain and the Jews; see Harrison, *Second Coming*, 80–1.

76. Markett to Liverpool, 20 Feb. 1813. Add MS 38251 (Liverpool Papers), f. 321.

77. Frere, *Combined View*, 287, 93n, 114, 128, 294–5.

78. Letter to Hester Maria Thrale, 21 Aug. 1796, *Piozzi Letters*, 2: 374–5. See also *Thraliana*, 2: 990 (20 Nov. 1798).

79. William Ettrick, *The Season and Time: Or, an Exposition of the Prophecies* (London, 1816), 79. See also, e.g., "Theourgos," *Plain Arguments Advanced to Convince the Nation of the Impropriety of the Restrictions at Present Imposed on the Royal Family* (London, 1812), 21; Frere, *Combined View*, 387; Wedgwood, *Book of Remembrance*, xlvii; *Eclectic Review*, n.s., 1 (May 1814): 516, 518.

80. *Remarks on Some Parts*, vii, 44–8. The second woe is described in Rev. 11.

81. Joanna Southcott, *The Long-Wished-For Revolution Announced to be at Hand in a Book Lately Published, by L. Mayer* (London, 1806), 17.

82. Mayer, *Hint*, iv.

83. Conor Cruise O'Brien, *God Land: Reflections on Religion and Nationalism* (Cambridge, Mass., 1987), 41. O'Brien adds to his categorization the caveat that "within the two first [milder] categories of holy nationalism there is, I think, always at least a little deified nation, screaming to be let out" (p. 42).

84. E.g., Mayer, *Hint*, 35; Frere, *Combined View*, 294–5, 379; Faber, *Dissertation*, 1: xxiii; Witherby, *Observations*, 85; Rev. James Ivory Holmes, *The Fulfilment of the Revelation of St. John Displayed* (London, 1819), 368.

85. On the relation between radical and millenarian discourses, see J. F. C. Harrison, "Thomas Paine and Millenarian Radicalism," in Ian Dyck, ed., *Citizen of the World: Essays on Thomas Paine* (New York, 1988), 73–85; Jon Mee, "'The Doom of Tyrants': William Blake, Richard 'Citizen' Lee, and the Millenarian Public Sphere," in Jackie DiSalvo, G. A. Rosso, and Christopher Z. Hobson, *Blake, Politics, and History* (New York, 1998), 97–114; Jack Fruchtman, "Apocalyptic Politics"; and McCalman, *Radical Underworld*.

86. James Bicheno, *The Destiny of the German Empire* (London, 1801), 10, 11.

87. Bicheno, *The Restoration of the Jews the Crisis of all Nations*, 2nd ed. (London, 1807), 158. The opinions offered in the *Restoration* may reasonably be claimed for two dates. The pamphlet was initially published in 1799; Bicheno added footnotes and a prefatory "Address" in 1807, leaving the original text unchanged. All citations are to the 1807 edition.

88. Mayer, *Important Period*, 37.

89. Bicheno, *Restoration*, 158n.

90. On Aldred, see Thompson, *Making*, 420. On Reid's religion, see note 105, below.

91. Bicheno, *A Supplement to the Signs of the Times; Containing a Reply to the Objections of the Rev. G. S. Faber* (London, [1807]), 7.

92. Bicheno (specifically criticizing Frere), *Fulfilment*, 171–2.

93. Bicheno, *Signs*; *Supplement*, 6–7; *Restoration*, 232; *Fulfilment*, 167–8.

94. Bicheno, *Restoration*, 232; *Signs*, 7.

95. Bicheno, *Supplement*, 59–60; *Restoration*, 157.

96. Bicheno, *Preparation for the Coming of Christ; Inculcated: in a Discourse, Delivered at Newbury, October 19, 1803* (London, 1803), 20–1, 23–4. See also *Restoration* (1807 "Address"), 67.

97. Bicheno, *Signs*, 5th ed., iv–v; *Restoration*, 230.

98. Bicheno, *Restoration*, 156–8, 165–6, 203n, 208.

99. Aldred, *Little Book*, 3.

100. Rev. 9: 11. Apollyon is the Greek name for the character whose Hebrew name is Abaddon: "How peculiar that the comparison should be in the English dialect," Aldred remarked, in a passage one can only hope to have been puckish: Napoleon "has been generally stigmatized as A-bad-on [a bad 'un] by the inhabitants of this island, perhaps there never was a human being ever more so." Aldred, *Little Book*, xlii–xliii.

101. Ibid., 51n., *l*, 9, 43n. In an unpaginated afterword, printed after the rest of the pamphlet, Aldred told his readers that *The Little Book* was ready for release in February 1811, when the Prince Regent opened Parliament in lieu of his father, but that distribution was delayed until 12 January 1812, when Parliament granted the Regent, "the sixth king," all George III's powers.

102. Aldred, *Little Book*, 16.

103. Ibid., 6–7.

104. Ibid., 39–40.

105. "An Advocate for the House of Israel" [William Hamilton Reid], *Sanhedrin Chadasha* [New Sanhedrin] *and Causes and Consequences of the French Emperor's Conduct towards the Jews* (London, 1807). For Reid's acknowledgment of his authorship, see *Gentleman's Magazine* 80, pt. 2 (July 1810): 13. On an earlier moment in Reid's career, when Reid "informed on his colleagues out of combined political and commercial motives" in an 1800 exposé of tavern debating clubs, see McCalman, *Radical Underworld*, 1, 238n2. Reid soon reverted to his original radicalism. Elsewhere, McCalman describes him as a buckle-maker turned hack writer, and (in the early 1790s) a member of the radical London Corresponding Society. McCalman, "The Infidel as Prophet: William Reid and Blakean Radicalism," in Steve Clark and David Worrall, eds., *Historicizing Blake* (New York, 1994), 24–42. Reid also figures in McCalman's fine article on "radical restorationism or Dissenting

philosemitism" (the restoration in question being the return of the Jews, once converted, to Palestine). McCalman, "New Jerusalems: Prophecy, Dissent and Radical Culture in England, 1786–1830," in Knud Haakonssen, ed., *Enlightenment and Religion: Rational Dissent in Eighteenth-Century Britain* (Cambridge, 1996), 312–35 (see esp. 329–33, on reactions to Napoleon).

106. William Hamilton Reid, *Memoirs of the Public Life of John Horne Tooke, Esq.* (London, 1812), 191; *Memoirs of the Life of Colonel Wardle; Including Thoughts on the State of the Nation* (London, 1809), 2, 241–2, 228–9.

107. Reid, *Memoirs of . . . Wardle,* 221–2, 234–6.

108. Ibid., 2, 215–16.

109. Ibid., 224.

110. See [Reid], *Sanhedrin Chadasha,* 125. Reid had earlier flirted with Swedenborgians and Muggletonians; Belsham's congregation, too, would prove only a temporary home. McCalman, "Infidel as Prophet."

111. [Reid], *Sanhedrin Chadasha,* 181, 170–1, 174. The "new Jerusalem" is mentioned in Rev. 3: 12 and Rev. 21: 2.

112. [Reid], *Sanhedrin Chadasha,* 169–74.

113. Ibid., 75, 173, 154.

114. Ibid., 102.

115. Ibid., 179. The seven vials are spoken of in Rev. 16.

116. [Reid], *Sanhedrin Chadasha,* 180. Rev. 18: 17.

117. Wedgwood, *Book of Remembrance,* xlix, lvi.

118. Ibid., xiii, liv, lv.

119. Ibid., xlvii.

120. *Estimate of the Peace* (London, 1802); *Preparation for the Coming of Christ; The Consequences of Unjust War* (London, 1810).

121. Rev. G. J. Skeeles, *The Recent Events in France Considered* (Bury St. Edmunds, [1814]), 5–6.

122. Rev. Charles Edward Stewart, *Obedience to Government, Reverence to the Constitution, and Resistance to Bonaparte* (Bury St. Edmunds, 1803). This was also reprinted in part as a one-penny broadsheet ("Address of the Rev. Charles Edward Stewart" [BL]). See Robert Hole, "English Sermons and Tracts as Media of Debate on the French Revolution, 1789–99," in Philp, *French Revolution and British Popular Politics,* 18–37.

123. *Annual Review* (1803): 175.

124. Rev. D. MacIndoe, *Our Sin, Danger, & Duty. A Sermon, Occasioned by the Present War with France* (Newcastle upon Tyne, 1804), 21. According to John Barrell, analogies between Nebuchadnezzar and George III were a staple of radical discourse: see Barrell, *Imagining,* 546.

125. Harrison, *Second Coming,* 50–2; Colley, *Britons,* 20–2.

126. Bernard Capp, *Astrology and the Popular Press: English Almanacs 1500–1800* (London, 1979), 239, 263–4. The *Vox Stellarum* would reach its peak circulation, of 560,000, in 1839.

127. Another almanac, the *Merlinus Liberatus* of "John Partridge," offered occasional consideration of the war, sometimes in language almost identical to the *Vox Stellarum* (cf., e.g., *Merlinus* 1815: 44–5, 47, with *Vox* 1815: 45, 48). Both titles, like all almanacs, were published by the Company of Stationers, which retained an effective hold on almanac production (though their actual monopoly had been overturned by the Court of Common Pleas in 1775). See

Cyprian Blagden, *The Stationers' Company: A History, 1403–1959* (Stanford, 1960), 234–42.

128. *CWPR*, 8 July 1815, 6.

129. E.g. *Vox Stellarum* (1803): 41; *Vox Stellarum* (1811): 44.

130. [Thomas Orger], *The Nativity of Napoleon Bonaparte, Emperor of All the French, Calculated by a Professor* (High Wycombe, 1805), 48. Another astrological pamphlet concluded by praising God: John Worsdale, *The Nativity of Napoleon Bonaparte, Emperor of France; Calculated According to the Genuine Rules and Precepts of the Learned Claudius Ptolemy* (Stockport, 1805), 106.

131. [Orger], *Nativity*, 37–8.

132. Worsdale, *Nativity*, 82, 67–8.

133. Ibid., 80, 78, 91. [Orger], *Nativity*, 40.

134. William Horner, *The Nativity of Napoleon Bonaparte, Wherein is Predicted the Downfall of the Murdering Despot*, 2nd ed. (Leeds, 1809); [John Corfield], *Destiny of Europe!!! The Nativity of Napoleone Buonaparte, Emperor of France* (London, [1812]); but the quotations are from Corfield's *The Urania; or, the Philosophical and Scientific Magazine* 1: 1 (June 1814): 31. Corfield, after razoring out the printed authorial initials and publisher's name on his 1812 nativity, wrote his own name on the title page of the copy now in the British Library. I date it on the basis of his letter to the *Antijacobin Review* (July 1813): 92—attached to the BL's pamphlet—which described the pamphlet as having appeared in Sept. 1812. Here he criticized (without acknowledging authorship of) the previous year's nativity. The horoscope he published the following year treated Napoleon as the first in a "Series of Depraved Minds"—but Corfield later crossed out "Depraved" in his copy (BL) so as to superscribe his new belief that Napoleon's mind was "Intrepid." This revised opinion may have been a reaction to the escape from Elba; another factor may have been the chastening monetary loss Corfield recorded on the title page of his failed magazine: "By this Magazine & Naps nativity I lost above £500. John Corfield." *Urania* (June 1814): 4; the nativity appears on pages 29–34.

135. *Vox Stellarum* (1797): 44.

136. Bernard Capp is mistaken to claim (*Astrology*, 266) that the rise of Napoleon led Andrews to embrace the loyalist cause.

137. *Vox Stellarum* (1799): 43; see also *Vox Stellarum* (1810): 41.

138. Ibid. (1803): 42; (1810): 41, 44; also see (1811): 2.

139. Ibid. (1806): 47; (1808): 43.

140. Ibid. (1809): 43; (1813): 17.

141. Ibid. (1809): 43.

142. Ibid. (1808): 47; (1809): 46.

143. Ibid. (1812): 43. For similar complaints, see ibid. (1808): 43 and (1813): 42.

144. Ibid. (1811): 44.

145. Ibid. (1808): 47; (1815): 45.

146. Ibid. (1811): 21; (1815): 45.

147. E.g., *Porcupine*, 24 April 1801; "Job Nott," *The Lion Sleeps* (Birmingham, 1803), 2; Sarratt, *Life*, 198; "SUCH IS BUONAPARTE" (BL); "A Solemn Appeal to the British Nation" (Houghton); "Part of the Speech of James Mackintosh . . . Aug. 8, 1803," in *Loyalist*, 71–2; *An Address to the People*,

1803, 16; letter from "C.C." in *RYWPR*, 25 Oct. 1806, 779–80; William Hunter, *Reasons for Not Making Peace with Buonaparté*, 2nd ed. (London, 1807), 5; "On Bonaparte's Abuse of England in the Moniteur" (poem), *Morning Herald* (30 Jan. 1809), reprinted in *Spirit of the Public Journals* 13 (1809): 41–2. For a series of eschatological characterizations of Napoleon from the *Gentleman's Magazine*, 1812–16, see Bernard Semmel, *The Methodist Revolution* (New York, 1973), 155–6.

148. [Reid], *Sanhedrin Chadasha*, 183–9.

149. *MM* 21 (June 1806): 408–9. Young turns out to have been an admiring correspondent of G. S. Faber. Add. MS 35130 (Arthur Young Papers), f. 285, Faber to Young (27 July 1809).

150. Report of recent parliamentary debate, *AGM*, 7 July 1811, 192.

151. *AGM*, 7 July 1811, 192. On Goldsmith's proposal, see chapter 4.

152. *CWPR*, 15 Jan. 1814, 68–9; 26 Feb. 1814, 258; see also, e.g., *CWPR*, 7 Nov. 1812, 581. John Scott and Leigh Hunt were similarly skeptical: see *Champion*, 9 April 1815, 113; *Examiner*, 26 March 1815, 194.

153. Byerley, *The Prince*, v, vi. See also the American pamphlet *Bonaparte No Universal Monarch, and Not Proved to be Favourably Noticed in Prophecy* (Boston, 1809), 3; and letter from "B." in *Satirist* 1 (Dec. 1807), 283.

154. Letters from "C.", *AGM*, 13 Oct. and 20 Oct., 1811, 306–7, 314. The later letters appear in *AGM*, 16 April 1815, 4172, and 7 May 1815, 4195. "C" is almost certainly E. Clarkson of Upper George Street, the identity given in later letters about Methodists and Napoleon.

155. Frere's explanation of how Napoleon's motives were "over-ruled and made subservient to the accomplishment of the will of God" (*Combined View*, 387) may put one in mind of Hegel's "cunning of reason." (In Hegel's scheme, particular interests, obeying their individual passions, contend with one another and allow the universal to emerge: the world-historical individuals Caesar and Napoleon "fall aside like empty husks" once the universal end has been attained. G. W. F. Hegel, *Lectures on the Philosophy of World History, Introduction*, trans. H. B. Nisbet (Cambridge, 1975), 89, 85. Providential determinism bears a strong resemblance to nineteenth-century historical determinism. When, in later decades, Thomas Carlyle—once a close friend of Frere's acolyte Edward Irving—approached Napoleon, he deliberately used language that drew connections between exegesis and historiography. In *Sartor Resartus*, Carlyle's *alter ego* Teufelsdröckh describes Napoleon as "a Divine Missionary, though unconscious of it"—essentially the unwitting scourge described by exegetes. "Great Men" like Napoleon, Teufelsdröckh goes on, "are the inspired (speaking and acting) Texts of that divine BOOK OF REVELATIONS, whereof a Chapter is completed from epoch to epoch, and by some named HISTORY." Thomas Carlyle, *Sartor Resartus* (1833–34), in *A Carlyle Reader: Selections from the Writings of Thomas Carlyle*, ed. G. B. Tennyson (Cambridge, 1984), 247–8.

4 *The Imperial Sans-culotte*

1. Jernensis, "Parallel between Bonaparte and Augustus Cæsar," *MM* 14 (Oct. 1802): 225–6.

2. [Matthew Rolleston], *The Anti-Corsican, a Poem, in Three Cantos* (Exeter, 1805), 8.

3. "Tiddy-Doll, the Great French-Gingerbread-Baker; Drawing out a New Batch of Kings" (MDG 10518; 23 Jan. 1806).

4. "The New Dynasty:—or—The Little Corsican Gardiner [*sic*] Planting a Royal-Pippin-Tree.—'All the Talents,' busy, in Clearing the Ground of Old Timber" (MDG 10744; 25 June 1807).

5. "Paris Fashions" (orig. *London Chronicle*, 24 Aug. 1802), in Bennett, *British War Poetry*, 279. Wordsworth, *The Prelude* (1805–06 version, book X, lines 934–6), ed. J. C. Maxwell (Harmondsworth, 1971), 454.

6. See, e.g., *Porcupine*, 8 Aug. 1801; "A Word of Advice to the Self-Created Consul" (Houghton); "Union and Watchfulness, Britain's True and Only Security" (Houghton); "A Solemn Appeal to the British Nation" (Houghton).

7. "The Triumph of Britain, an Ode" (BL); Faber, *Dissertation*, 1: 129–30; *True Briton*, 8 Jan. 1801.

8. Charles Colton, *Napoleon: A Poem; in Which that Arch Apostate from the Cause of Liberty is Held up to the Just Indignation of an Injured People* (London, 1812), vi, 15. See the 1803 engraving "The Oak and the Mushroom" (MDG 9990; *c.* May 1803), which contrasts the British oak with the Napoleonic fungus.

9. [Edward Hankin], *Independence of Great Britain*, 36. *Buonaparte's Pedigree, Including his Collateral Branches, and Great Military and State Officers*, 4th ed. (London, 1814), 5–6. "No Change for the Worse, a Mistaken Notion" (BL). See also William Hunter, *A Sketch of the Political State of Europe, at the Beginning of February, 1805* (London, 1805), 43.

10. *Exposé*, 240, 229.

11. From the *Courier*, 26 June 1811, in Coleridge, *Essays on His Times*, 2: 195. See Cobbett's response to this (anonymous) piece: *CWPR*, 4 May 1811, 1099–1103.

12. *AGM*, 24 April 1814, 3062; 3 March 1816, 4531. See also *The Crisis*, 3rd ed. (London, 1807), 17–18.

13. Hence, e.g., a 1691 reference to "A virulent libell . . . endeavouring to prove the legitimacy of the prince of Wales." Narcissus Luttrell, *A Brief Historical Relation of State Affairs from September 1678 to April 1714*, 6 vols. (Oxford, 1857), 2: 207; cited in *OED*, 8: 811.

14. *OED*, 8: 811–12. An electronic search of the *OED*'s full text, while turning up many seventeenth- and eighteenth-century instances of the words "legitimate" and "legitimacy," reveals none signifying the principle of hereditary right. An unscientific survey of materials relating to Jacobitism appears to confirm that the term was not yet used in this sense. (But see Samuel Taylor Coleridge: "Legitimate is too vague a word to be understood without a definition: the Jacobites were indefatigable in bandying it against the House of Brunswick." *Morning Post*, 28 Jan. 1800, in *Essays on His Times*, 1: 36.) One slightly pre-Napoleonic instance that *verged* on the new meaning was Edmund Burke's reference to "the true principles of legitimate Government in opposition to Jacobinism." *Remarks on the Policy of the Allies* (1793), in *The Writings and Speeches of Edmund Burke*, ed. Paul Langford (Oxford, 1980—), 8: 455.

15. *True Briton*, 8 Jan. 1801. The earliest instances the *OED* cites of this usage

come from 1812, and from America. Significantly, in each cited case, the author distinguished his own use from a "straight" usage of the term by quotation marks, an inflection suggesting a reaction to uncritical political uses of the word.

16. "To the United Kingdom" (BL). See also, e.g., King, *Letters from France*, 162; William Cobbett, *Important Considerations*, 6; *Morning Post*, 22 Feb. 1804, reprinted in *Cobbett's Spirit of the Public Journals*, 1: 146; *Exposé*, 231n.

17. Lewis Goldsmith, *The Secret History of the Cabinet of Bonaparte*, 4th ed. (London, 1810), 428; see also, among many instances, Goldsmith's *AGM*, 19 Jan. 1812, 414; 22 March 1812, 490.

18. E.g., letter from "Anth. Pasquin, A. J.," *Statesman*, 8 July 1815.

19. E.g., "No Change for the Worse, a Mistaken Notion" (BL); [Hankin], *Independence of Great Britain*, 36; *Buonaparte's Pedigree*, 5–6.

20. "Feelings of a French Royalist, on the Disinterment of the Remains of the Duke D'Enghien" (1816), in *Wordsworth: Poems*, 2: 341.

21. References to Palm and Wright would be a staple, e.g., for Lewis Goldsmith; see *AGM*, 3 March 1811, 45; 5 May 1811, 121; 3 May 1812, 537.

22. Burdon, *Life and Character*, 242, 244. See also the poem of the Midhurst schoolboy Matthew Rolleston, *The Anti-Corsican*, 44–5.

23. *The Revolutionary Plutarch: Exhibiting the Most Distinguished Characters, Literary, Military, and Political, in the Recent Annals of the French Republic*, 3 vols (London, 1804), 3: 51.

24. *Annual Review* for 1803 (pub. 1804): 335.

25. *Oracle*, 20 Aug. 1804, in *Cobbett's Spirit*, 1: 859.

26. *The Times*, 21 Dec. 1804, in *Cobbett's Spirit*, 1: 1281.

27. Burdon, *Life and Character*, 259.

28. *Morning Post*, 6 Sept. 1804, in *Cobbett's Spirit*, 1: 981, 983.

29. *Morning Chronicle*, 6 Sept. 1804, in *Cobbett's Spirit*, 1: 979–80. The *Courier*, two days later, priggishly construed this comment of its Whig antagonist as "little less than an indirect attack upon the whole volunteer system," likely to "dishearten" Britain's defenders. *Courier*, 8 Sept. 1804, in *Cobbett's Spirit*, 1: 983–4.

30. *Morning Chronicle*, 6 Sept. 1804, in *Cobbett's Spirit*, 1: 979–80. In a similar spirit, a few years later, John Scott Byerley would remark on the ancient dynasties' cerebral failings: "One ray of intellect might have saved them, but even that was wanting, and they fell." Byerley, *The Prince*, xxxii.

31. *Thoughts on the Relative State*, 16–17.

32. For the grafting metaphor, see, e.g., Coleridge, *Courier*, 8 Jan. 1814, in *Essays on His Times*, 2: 371.

33. On the new couple's sex life, see "The Arch Dutchess [*sic*] Maria Louisa going to take her Nap" (Houghton caricature; 12 April 1810); "Boney and his New Wife, or a Quarrell [*sic*] about Nothing!!" (Houghton caricature; 16 Aug. 1810); "The Devil and his Protegée or another Separation in Contemplation" (MDG 11566; June 1810).

34. *RYWPR*, 30 March 1811, 225–7. Among other caricatures mocking the baby Bonaparte, see "Boney the Second or the Little Babboon [*sic*] Created to Devour French Monkies" (MDG 11719; 9 April 1811) and "Nursing the Spawn of a Tyrant" (MDG 11721; 14 April 1811).

35. *An Inquiry into the Justice of the Pretensions of Napoleon Bonaparte to the Appellation of "Great"* (London, 1812), 66.

36. *CWPR*, 25 Sept. 1813, 386–7: see also *CWPR*, 16 April 1814, 481.

37. *CWPR*, 23 Oct. 1813, 515.

38. Richard Price, *A Discourse on the Love of our Country, Delivered on Nov. 4, 1789* (London, 1789), 25, 34–5.

39. *CWPR*, 28 July 1804, 152; 29 Sept. 1804, 461.

40. On the public scandal over York, see Harling, "The Duke of York Affair."

41. *RYWPR*, 8 April 1809, 257–8. For Yorke's criticisms of the duke, see *RYWPR*, 25 Feb. 1809, 135.

42. Alternative spellings included Garratt and Garrett; these spellings go uncorrected in my quotations.

43. John Brewer, "Theater and Counter-Theater in Georgian Politics: The Mock Elections at Garrat," *Radical History Review* 22 (Winter 1979–80): 7–40, pp. 8, 34–7.

44. *General Evening Post*, 16 Oct. 1804. Reprinted in *Spirit of the Public Journals*, 8: 55. (This is a distinct publication from *Cobbett's Spirit of the Public Journals*, cited in note 16, above.) Dimsdale was, according to an 1831 history of Garrat, the last of the constituency's mayors, installed in 1796. The 1831 chronicler made no reference to the 1804 ceremony that had raised Dimsdale to a higher position than mayor. "History of the Mock Election of Garrett," preface to a reprint of Samuel Foote's 1764 play *The Mayor of Garratt: A Comedy, in Two Acts* (London, 1831), x–xi.

45. *Morning Chronicle*, 13 Oct. 1804. *General Evening Post*, 16 Oct. 1804, in *Spirit of the Public Journals*, 8: 56. The *Spirit* also contains commentary on the coronation from the *Times*, the *Oracle*, and the *Morning Post*, 8: 53–5, 59–60, 353–4. On Dimsdale's physical condition, see "History of the Mock Election," viii; James Peller Malcolm, *Anecdotes of the Manners and Customs of London during the Eighteenth Century* (London, 1808), 224.

46. Quoted in *CWPR*, 15 Dec. 1804, 945–6n.

47. A question asked of two 1803 engravings by Linda Colley, *Britons*, 283.

48. *Morning Chronicle*, 16 Oct. 1804.

49. *General Evening Post*, 16 Oct. 1804, in *Spirit of the Public Journals*, 8: 57.

50. *CWPR*, 15 Dec. 1804, 944–6.

51. *CWPR*, 15 Dec. 1804, 945–6n.

52. *A Sketch of the Present State of France*, 61.

53. [Alison], *Travels in France*, 140–1.

54. *Trial of John Peltier*, 266.

55. Lewis Goldsmith, *Secret History*, xiii. Goldsmith's claim was in keeping with one detainee's report of rapid turnover among the paper's English and Irish émigré staff. Maclean, *Excursion*, 129.

56. *Argus*, 14 Sept. 1803, 566–7; 26 Sept. 1803, 584.

57. *Argus*, 30 Oct. 1802, 7.

58. *Argus*, 27 Oct. 1802, 2.

59. British readers could order subscriptions from a Mr. Bishop of Sherborne Lane, and the Paineite Clio Rickman accepted advertisements and communications for the *Argus*. 27 Oct. 1802, 2.

60. "Maniac-Raving's—Or—Little Boney in a Strong Fit—" (MDG 9998; 24 May 1803); "Pacific-Overtures,—Or—A Flight from St. Cloud's— 'Over the Water

to Charley.'—A New Dramatic Piece Now Rehearsing" (MDG 10549; 5 April 1806).

61. Goldsmith, *Secret History*, xvi–xvii.

62. Ibid., xxvi, xxvii, xxviin., xiiin.

63. Ibid., 74.

64. *AGM*, 30 Jan. 1814, "20065" (my quotation marks around page numbers indicate Goldsmith's incorrect pagination).

65. *AGM*, 15 Sept. 1811, 272.

66. Goldsmith, *Secret History*, and *An Exposition of the Conduct of France towards America*, 2nd ed. (London, 1810).

67. Goldsmith, *Secret History*, 180, 74, 107–8, 111n., 172, 110, iii, 436.

68. Add. MS 38257 (Liverpool Papers), f. 356. Goldsmith offered this account of the newspaper's origins in a May 1814 letter that he intended to be forwarded to Lord Liverpool. See Add. MS 45045 (Supplementary Hardwicke Papers), ff. 108–9 (to C. P. Yorke). On the statutory limits on press subsidy, see Aspinall, *Politics and the Press*, 66–7; Aspinall usefully discusses Goldsmith's paper at 91–3.

69. Letter to Cumberland, 21 Sept. 1812, in *The Letters of King George IV 1812–1830*, ed. A. Aspinall, 3 vols. (Cambridge, 1938), 1: 152.

70. *AGM*, 27 Jan. 1811, 4–5.

71. *AGM*, 12 May 1811, 125.

72. *AGM*, 19 May 1811, 133.

73. *AGM*, 24 Nov. 1811, 353; 24 May 1812, 563; 31 May 1812, 575.

74. *AGM*, 26 May 1811, 141; 7 June 1812, 578.

75. *AGM*, 17 May 1812, 554.

76. *AGM*, 3 March 1811, 41.

77. For partial transcripts of the trial, see *Satirist* 10 (May 1812): 460–80, and *AGM*, 24 May 1812, 564–6. On Lovell, see chapter 5.

78. *AGM*, 3 March 1811, 45. For Cobbett's defense of his conversion (in which he proclaimed his consistency of principle), see *CWPR*, 6 Oct. 1804, 513–30.

79. *AGM*, 17 March 1811, 58.

80. *AGM*, 6 Oct. 1811, 299; 3 Nov. 1811, 329. According to Goldsmith, Peltier was too cowardly to accept his challenge to a duel. See *AGM*, 24 Nov. 1811, 353.

81. *AGM*, 10 Feb. 1811, 21; 24 March 1811, 67.

82. *AGM*, 18 Aug. 1811, 242.

83. *AGM*, 17 May 1812, 553.

84. See, e.g., *AGM*, 2 Jan. 1814, "20033."

85. *AGM*, 2 Feb. 1812, 429.

86. E.g., *AGM*, 31 March 1811, 79.

87. *RYWPR*, 30 March 1811, 227.

88. Add. MS 38257 (Liverpool Papers), f. 358 (Liverpool to C. P. Yorke, 27 May 1814 (copy)).

89. For the phrase, see, e.g., *AGM*, 12 Jan. 1812, 406. Also "his *sans culotte Majesty*"; *AGM*, 12 May 1811, 131.

90. See John Barrell's remarkable study, *Imagining the King's Death*.

91. These included two in Paris in 1800, and another in Austria in 1809. See Byerley's consideration of the attempts on George and Napoleon's lives: *The Prince*, lvi–lvii.

92. Thompson, *Making*, 527. On Despard's ties, see Marianne Elliott, "The 'Despard Conspiracy' Reconsidered," *Past and Present* 75 (May 1977): 46–61.

93. George Ensor, *The Independent Man*, 2 vols. (London, 1806), 1: 422–3.

94. *Courier*, 17 Jan. 1801. For later arguments for assassination, see chapter 6.

95. *Trial of John Peltier*, v–vi.

96. Ibid., x.

97. Ibid., 61.

98. Ibid., 81, 131.

99. *Revolutionary Plutarch*, 2: appendix. Since this work has been so often ascribed to Lewis Goldsmith, it should be stated that this attribution makes no sense at all; Goldsmith would not return from France for several years, and was still in Napoleon's service. Others have attributed the work to a certain "Stewarton."

100. *Revolutionary Plutarch*, 2: appendix, i.

101. [Yorke], *Anti-Corsican*, 129 (letter orig. pub. 18 Jan. 1804); *RYWPR*, 10 June 1809, 442. On this article, see chapter 1.

102. *European Magazine* 45 (Jan. 1804): 56.

103. *Annual Review* (1803): 510. On the elder Aikin, see Cookson, *Friends of Peace*, 99–100.

104. For the tale of the would-be assassin, see William Roscoe, *Considerations on the Causes, Objects and Consequences of the Present War* (London, 1808), 41. CWPR, 20 Feb. 1808, 257, 260; 27 Feb. 1808, 321, 333–5. Friends of Fox were disturbed by the letter to Cobbett: see Add. MS 51799 (Holland House Papers), f. 104 (Sir Francis Vincent, Bt. to H. W. Brooke, Admiralty Office, 29 Feb. 1808).

105. *Examiner*, 10 Jan. 1808, 21.

106. *Exposé*, 194.

107. *Courier*, 17 Jan. 1801.

108. *Argus*, 27 Nov. 1802, 54.

109. Goldsmith, *Secret History*, 373.

110. AGM, 17 March 1811, 64. The letter was signed "Anti-Tyrannus," but Goldsmith's later boast "that I was the *first* projector" of this society suggests that he himself wrote this letter. *AGM*, 2 June 1811, 149–50.

111. AGM, 31 March 1811, 79. Goldsmith habitually quoted this passage, eventually adding it to the weekly masthead of his paper.

112. See chapter 1. Goldsmith had specifically cited Vattel against Britain's supposed counterfeiting of *assignats*. *Crimes*, 151.

113. AGM, 28 April 1811, 109; "to kill him would be a meritorious act" (*AGM*, 5 May 1811, 121).

114. AGM, 19 May 1811, 138.

115. AGM, 2 June 1811, 149–50.

116. Grey confessed that he had only encountered Goldsmith's writing at one remove, translated into French in a royalist newspaper "published in this country, and which he understood had considerable circulation on the continent." *PD*, 20: 738–40 (24 June 1811).

117. PD, 20: 738–40 (24 June 1811).

118. AGM, 30 June 1811, 181.

119. AGM, 2 June 1811, 149–50; 30 June 1811, 181.

120. *Courier*, 29 June 1811, in Coleridge, *Essays on His Times*, 2: 200.

121. *Courier*, 27 June 1811, ibid., 199.
122. *Courier*, 9 July 1811, ibid., 220.
123. *Courier*, 2 July 1811, ibid., 210.
124. *Courier*, 4 July 1811, ibid., 212.
125. *Scourge* 2 (1 July 1811): 73.
126. *PD*, 20: 777–82 (2 July 1811).
127. *Scourge* 2 (Aug. 1811): 133–6.
128. *AGM*, 12 Jan. 1812, 405.
129. *AGM*, 19 Jan. 1812, 414; 22 March 1812, 490. In an 1813 pamphlet, directed to the people of Germany, Goldsmith declared "that assassination is lawful in some particular instances" and that it was "lawful and justifiable to kill the tyrant Napoleon in any way you can." *Buonaparte, an Outlaw!!! An Appeal to the Germans, on the Necessity of Outlawing Buonaparte* (London, 1813), 8.
130. Goldsmith to Cumberland, 21 Sept. 1812, in *Letters . . . George IV*, 1: 153.
131. See, e.g., *AGM*, 2 Jan. 1814, "20033."
132. Add. MS 38257 (Liverpool Papers), f. 355.
133. Goldsmith to George Canning, 20 Feb. [1824], at PRO FO 97/169. Goldsmith had written a pamphlet in praise of Canning a year and a half earlier, *Observations on the Appointment of the Right Hon. Geo. Canning to the Foreign Department* (London, 1822).
134. Goldsmith to Planta [6 Dec. 1824], and memorandum of 10 Dec. 1824, and notes on backs of these, at PRO FO 97/169.
135. Goldsmith to Robert Peel, 8 March 1835, Add. MS 40416 (Peel Papers), f. 280.
136. Mayer, *Bonaparte the Emperor*, i.
137. *Thoughts on the Relative State*, 29.
138. Cookson, *Friends of Peace*, 180–1.
139. Hone, *For the Cause of Truth*, 137–8, 168, 230.
140. On Burdon's later return to the Napoleonic camp, see chapter 5.
141. Letter from "An Oxonian" to Earl Grey, *AGM*, 30 June 1811, 187.
142. Anne Plumptre, *A Narrative of a Three Years' Residence in France*, 3 vols. (London, 1810), 3: 270.
143. *Examiner*, 24 Jan. 1808, 49–50.
144. *Examiner*, 11 Sept. 1808, 577.
145. *Examiner*, 19 June 1808, 386.
146. *Examiner*, 13 March 1808, 161.
147. *Examiner*, 10 July 1808, 434.
148. *Examiner*, 24 Sept. 1809, 609–10.
149. *Examiner*, 30 Sept. 1810, 609–10.
150. Robinson, *Diary, Reminiscences, and Correspondence*, 1: 156.
151. Plumptre, *Narrative*, 3: 272, 399, 289.
152. Ibid., 3: 372–3. Plumptre also equated the killing with Britain's bombardment of neutral Denmark's capital Copenhagen in 1807.
153. Ibid., 3: 383, 384, 388. On Napoleon as patron, cf. Byerley, *The Prince*, lxxxix.
154. *Statesman*, 22 Oct. 1811, 2–3. For a fuller introduction to the *Statesman*, see chapter 5.
155. *MM* 32 (Sept. 1811), 158, 169, 170n.
156. See Mitchell, *Holland House*, 217–39, 255–6.

157. *A Letter from Mr. Whitbread to Lord Holland* (London, 1808).

158. *PD*, 20: 777–82 (2 July 1811).

159. *Examiner*, 5 June 1808, 362. Hunt's attitude was that of William Wordsworth's landlord Mr. Crump: see Wordsworth to Thomas de Quincey, 29 March 1809, in *Letters of . . . Wordsworth*, 2, pt. 1: 306.

160. Plumptre, *Narrative*, 3: 346.

161. Byerley, *The Prince*, lxxxi–lxxxiii.

162. Ibid., lxxxiii–lxxxiv.

163. *Trial of John Peltier*, 112.

164. Plumptre, *Narrative*, 3: 247–8.

165. *Examiner*, 11 Sept. 1808, 577.

166. *Examiner*, 28 Aug. 1808, 482.

167. Plumptre, *Narrative*, 3: 394.

168. *Independent Whig*, 3 Sept. 1809, 1143.

169. *CWPR*, 15 Dec. 1804, 949.

170. Ibid., 941.

171. The article on flogging appeared in *CWPR*, 1 July 1809; for later discussion of this article in *CWPR* see, e.g., 14 July 1810.

172. Cobbett switched from the Italian to the French spelling suddenly and without comment: see *CWPR*, 12 March 1814.

173. *CWPR*, 29 May 1813, 777.

174. *CWPR*, 2 March 1811, 513.

175. *CWPR*, 12 Feb. 1814, 203.

176. *CWPR*, 9 May 1812, 593.

177. *CWPR*, 4 May 1811, 1099; 6 Oct. 1810, 554. Cobbett had argued in similar terms long before his own libel trial; see *CWPR*, 21 Dec. 1805, 978–80. For further discussion of Peltier, see, e.g., 2 March 1811, 513; 7 Nov. 1812, 584; 29 May 1813, 777; 7 Aug. 1813, 166.

178. *CWPR*, 4 May 1811, 1099.

179. *CWPR*, 4 May 1811, 1103.

180. See, e.g., *CAR*, 12 Nov. 1803, 705–6, discussed in chapter 2.

181. *CWPR*, 22 Aug. 1812, 236.

182. *CWPR*, 31 Dec. 1808, 995.

183. *CWPR*, 19 May 1810, p. 745.

184. *CWPR*, 23 Jan. 1811, 169.

185. *CWPR*, 22 Aug. 1812, 232.

186. *CWPR*, 12 Feb. 1814, 203. For Cobbett's criticisms of such matters as information *ex officio*, see, e.g., *CWPR*, 6 April 1811.

187. *CWPR*, 31 March 1810, 481–6.

188. *CWPR*, 21 Dec. 1811, 769–79.

189. *CWPR*, 15 Sept. 1810, 365.

190. "Fingal," *Truth*, 52; see esp. 55–6, 86–8, 104–7.

191. "The Life of William Cobbett—written by himself. No. 7" of 8 (29 Sept. 1809; MDG 11378).

192. On the Jubilee, see Colley, *Britons*, 217–25, and "Apotheosis," 111–12, 116–17, and 122–4 (where she discusses Cobbett). I am currently pursuing further research on the creation and criticism of the Jubilee. The woman who conceived the event, Mrs. R. C. Biggs, had proof-read Cobbett's *Important Considerations* in 1803—but Cobbett would not have been aware of her

current role as remote impresario of the Jubilee, nor perhaps of her earlier efforts as his copy-editor. For Mrs Biggs' other activities in the loyalist cause, see Add. MS 31234 (letters to Nicholas Vansittart).

193. *CWPR*, 23 Sept. 1809, 394.
194. *CWPR*, 14 Oct. 1809, 515.
195. *CWPR*, 28 Oct. 1809, 640.
196. *CWPR*, 27 Oct. 1804, 616, quoted in 10 Nov. 1810, 865–6.

5 From Elba to St. Helena

1. In *The Collected Letters of Thomas and Jane Welsh Carlyle*, ed. Charles Richard Sanders (Durham, NC, 1970—), 1: 6–7.
2. Ibid., 1: 44.
3. *Champion*, 26 March 1815, 97.
4. On the Yarmouth feast, see *MM* 37 (June 1814): 480, and "A Royal Arch Mason," *The Corsican's Downfall*, 145–7. According to the *Monthly*, nearly 10,000 pounds of beef, 1,300 plum puddings, and eighty barrels of beer were served.
5. *CWPR*, 23 July 1814, 101. An apparent typesetting error turns "Bolton" into "Boston" in all but the first of Cobbett's references—but Cobbett clearly identifies the town in question as "a manufacturing town in Lancashire."
6. See *England's Triumph* (London, 1814).
7. Byron to Thomas Moore, 20 April 1814, in *Byron's Letters and Journals*, ed. Leslie A. Marchand, 12 vols. (Cambridge, 1973–82), 4: 100–1.
8. For descriptions of the three nights of illuminations, see *Statesman*, 12–14 April 1814.
9. William Wordsworth regretted not being able to join the London throngs. Wordsworth to Samuel Rogers, 5 May 1814, in *Letters . . . Wordsworth*, 2, pt. 2: 148.
10. *MM* 37 (July 1814): 560–1, 574–5. The absent Francis I was also made a KG.
11. *MM* 37 (July 1814): 561. See *The Christian Conqueror; or, Moscow Burnt, and Paris Saved* (London, 1814), and the caricaturist William Heath's twin allegorical portraits of "Alexander" (Houghton; 4 March 1814) and "Buonaparte" (MDG 12195; 6 March 1814).
12. Dorothy Wordsworth, Letter to Catherine Clarkson, 24 Apr. 1814, *Letters . . . Wordsworth*, 2, pt. 2: 142.
13. "Calvus" [Walter Savage Landor], *Letters Addressed to Lord Liverpool, and the Parliament, on the Preliminaries of Peace* (London, 1814), 6, 67.
14. *AGM*, 23 Jan. 1814, "20057."
15. *AGM*, 27 March 1814, 3033.
16. *AGM*, 10 April 1814, 3045.
17. *AGM*, 17 April 1814, 3054.
18. *AGM*, 1 May 1814, 3069.
19. *AGM*, 24 July 1814, 3189.
20. *AGM*, 17 April 1814, 3053.
21. "Little Boney Gone to Pot" (MDG 12261; 12 May 1814).
22. *QR* 12 (Oct. 1814): 241. Also see William Dickenson, "A Poetical Address to the Usurper Bonaparte; by a British Veteran" (1814 Houghton broadside).

23. As a pupil at Harrow, he had "defended [a] bust of him . . . when the war broke out in 1803." Recalled in Byron, journal, 17 Nov. 1813, in *Byron's Letters and Journals*, 3: 210.

24. Byron, journal, 9 April 1814, ibid., 3: 256.

25. Byron to Thomas Moore, 9 April 1814; to Annabella Milbanke, 20 April 1814. Ibid., 4: 93, 101.

26. *Ode to Napoleon Buonaparte* (London, 1814). I refer to the 3rd edition, to which Byron added an extra stanza. An 11th edition was published in 1815, a 12th in 1816, and a 13th in 1818.

27. [Byron], *Ode*, 9, 12.

28. *Scourge* 7 (May 1814): 417.

29. [Byron], *Ode*, 7.

30. *CWPR*, 20 Aug. 1814, 230-1.

31. *CWPR*, 16 April 1814, 488, 490, 492.

32. *CWPR*, 16 April 1814, 487; 23 April 1814, 517-22 (Cobbett reprints the *Times* article at 518-22). Cobbett may have overread in claiming that *The Times* was actually calling for the "re-occupation, and *re-colonization*" of Britain's former colonies in America. On Andrews, see Chapter 3.

33. Letter from Aristides, *CWPR*, 16 April 1814, 493-5. *CWPR*, 7 May 1814, 587.

34. *Edinburgh Review* (ER) 23 (April 1814): 2-7, 14. Attributions of *Edinburgh* reviews are given in *The Wellesley Index to Victorian Periodicals, 1824-1900*, ed. Walter E. Houghton et al., 5 vols. (Toronto, 1966-89).

35. *ER* 23 (April 1814): 13, 16, 24.

36. Ibid.: 18, 21.

37. For Samuel Whitbread's description of Lovell's troubles, see *PD*, 29: 450-62 (23 Nov. 1814). The 1811 libel conviction was for copying a critical account of Sir Francis Burdett's arrest from another newspaper (an account whose original composers suffered much lighter penalties); a second 1812 conviction was for a piece Lovell claimed not to have seen due to his incarceration. Unable to pay the additional fine for this second libel, Lovell remained in jail beyond the term of sentence. The *Satirist* scoffed at Lovell's suggestion that he had not seen the piece at issue in the 1812 action; the *Statesman*'s offices, it pointed out, were but 200 yards from Newgate. *Satirist* 10 (May 1812): 349. The biographer of Edwin Chadwick has suggested that Chadwick's father James "stepped into" Lovell's position during the Newgate years. S. E. Finer, *The Life and Times of Sir Edwin Chadwick* (London, 1952), 7. This would appear to overstate things, as Lovell remained, during his imprisonment, a more visible presence in the newspaper's pages than Chadwick. Certainly Lovell remained the paper's public face (e.g., 17 June 1814; 1 July 1814). Lovell was capable of carrying on from Newgate a libel action against Lewis Goldsmith (see chapter 4). Responding to Whitbread's Commons motion to release Lovell, the attorney-general noted that Lovell "not only was . . . able to conduct this paper while in prison, but he had set up a new weekly one" (reported in *Statesman*, 24 Nov. 1814). Chadwick may have been an important assistant to Lovell, but he does not seem to have usurped his place as editor. A similar confinement did not interfere with Cobbett's editing his *Political Register*.

38. Arthur Aspinall's classic work on politics and the press mentions Lovell only in a footnote, as the defendant in an 1817 libel suit brought by Daniel Stuart of the *Courier*. Aspinall, *Politics and the Press*, 88-89n. There are some

references to the newspaper in Dinwiddy, *Radicalism and Reform*, and Hone, *For the Cause of Truth*. But Lovell lacks an entry in the *Biographical Dictionary of Modern British Radicals*, vol. 1 (1770–1830), ed. Joseph O. Baylen and Norbert J. Gossman (Sussex, 1979).

39. *Statesman*, 24 Nov. 1814. *PD*, 29: 450–62 (23 Nov. 1814).
40. For the announcement of Lovell's release, see *Statesman*, 20 May 1815. For the list of those who came to Lovell's financial assistance, see the 4 Oct. 1815 *Statesman*, which mentions a meeting 8 Aug. of "the Friends of the Liberty of the Press," at the Crown and Anchor Tavern on the Strand, and lists the first batch of contributors. Whitbread gave a hundred pounds to the cause, as did Bedford; Burdett donated fifty pounds; Grey twenty; Cartwright, Holland, Tavistock, and Burdon each gave ten. Further donors were noted on 19 Oct. and 1 Nov. Some listed contributions must have been solicited earlier (Whitbread could not have made it to the August meeting, having died the previous month); we can assume that some donations preceded, and made possible, Lovell's release. Contributions may have arrived as early as June 1814; it was then that Lovell acknowledged the efforts of "several Friends (some of them unknown to him) who have liberally proposed to join in a Subscription, with a view to remove the obstacles to his liberation" (*Statesman*, 17 June 1814).
41. *Statesman*, 4 Oct. 1815; 19 Oct. 1815; 1 Nov. 1815.
42. See descriptions of meetings at Ashton-under-Lyne, near Manchester, and Oldham, Lancashire: *Sherwin's Political Register*, 6 June 1818, 61–3; 25 July 1818, 189–91.
43. *Statesman*, 13 April 1814.
44. *Statesman*, 14 April 1814.
45. Letter from "Equal Laws" of Russell Square, *Statesman*, 2 May 1814.
46. *Statesman*, 12 April 1814.
47. *Statesman*, 9 April 1814.
48. *Statesman*, 13 April 1814.
49. *MM* 37 (May 1814): 364.
50. *MM* 37 (June 1814): 457.
51. *MM* 37 (July 1814): 553.
52. *MM* 38 (Aug. 1814): 60.
53. Eyles Irwin, *Napoleon: Or, the Vanity of Human Wishes. Part II* (London, 1814), v.
54. *AGM*, 1 May 1814, 3075.
55. Scott may have been describing "The Sorrows of Boney, or Meditations in the Island of Elba!!!" (MDG 12223; 15 April 1814), which shows Napoleon with long streams of tears falling from his eyes. (Ironically, this illustration was lifted wholesale from an 1803 broadside, "Crocodiles Tears" [MDG 10119; *c.* Oct. 1803] and was intended to depict him sitting not on an island but on the French coast.) But Scott may have had another piece in mind. For caricaturists who habitually shrank the political map to tiny proportions—showing Napoleon bestriding Europe or John Bull conversing with him across the Channel—portraying Elba as tiny was second nature. See, e.g., George Cruikshank's "Boney's Elba Chair" (MDG 12258; 5 May 1814), "Little Boney Gone to Pot" (MDG 12261; 12 May 1814).
56. *Champion*, 7 May 1814, 145.

57. *ER* 23 (April 1814): 4.
58. E.g., *Statesman*, 1 April 1815.
59. *QR* 12 (Oct. 1814): 265.
60. See, e.g. [Alison et al.], *Travels in France*, 2: 70, 73.
61. *ER* 24 (Feb. 1815): 517, 508.
62. Marginalia in Walter Savage Landor's copy (BL) of *Letters Addressed to Lord Liverpool*, 6. Landor's marginal comments seem to have been intended for a second edition, which never materialized.
63. *Examiner*, 19 March 1815, 177.
64. *A Letter, &c. An Account of the Conspiracy and Conspirators of Napoleon Buonaparte* (London, 1815), 5–6, 11. But see Lord Castlereagh's defense of Campbell, in *PD*, 30: 427 (7 April 1815). In 1819, Campbell was still concerned with clearing his name; a privately printed memoir he gave to friends (asking that its contents be kept confidential) defended his behavior and referred them to Castlereagh's speech. See Add. MS 43350 (Aberdeen Papers).
65. Thomas Carlyle to Robert Mitchell, 25 March 1815, in *Collected Letters . . . Carlyle*, 1: 44. The image of the phoenix was also used in Cruikshank's "The Phenix [*sic*] of Elba Resuscitated by Treason" (MDG 12537; 1 May 1815).
66. Wordsworth to Miss M. Malcolm, [mid-March 1815], in *Letters . . . Wordsworth*, 2, pt. 2: 215.
67. *Champion*, 19 March 1815, 93.
68. E.g., *Statesman*, 27 March 1815; Add. MS 36456 (Broughton Correspondence), f. 225 (Henry Bickersteth to Hobhouse, 17 March 1815).
69. Macaulay to Selina Mills Macaulay, 22 March 1815, in *The Letters of Thomas Babington Macaulay*, ed. Thomas Pinney, 6 vols. (Cambridge, 1974–81), 1: 59.
70. Byron to Thomas Moore, 27 March 1815, in *Byron's Letters and Journals*, 4: 284.
71. Faber, *Remarks on the Effusion*, 15–16. See chapter 3.
72. Letter from "C." [E. Clarkson], *AGM*, 16 April 1815, 4172.
73. *CWPR*, 1 April 1815, 392.
74. *AGM*, 16 April 1815, 4170.
75. *AGM*, 4 June 1815, 4221–2.
76. *AGM*, 30 April 1815, 4182. The sight of the old "odious" restrictions against Protestants and Jews being reimposed by continental dynasts now led Goldsmith, who had just a year before called for the extirpation of every last trace of Jacobinism, to allow that the revolution had done "some good as well as much mischief." *AGM*, 30 April 1815, 4181–2.
77. *Statesman*, 1 May 1815. On Burdon's earlier writings, see chapters 1 and 2.
78. *MM* 23 (1807): index. In one letter of Oct. 1812, Lofft had urged peace with France, but had not actively praised Napoleon (*MM* 34: 207–8). Biographical information on Lofft is drawn from the *DNB* and from the *Biographical Dictionary of Modern British Radicals*.
79. Numerous letters of Lofft can be found in the Holland House Papers (BL); see Add. MSS 51528–9. For a contemporary reference to his handwriting, which postponed publication of at least one of his letters, see *Morning Chronicle*, 10 Aug. 1815.
80. *MM* 39 (May 1815): 308.
81. *CWPR*, 18 March 1815, 327–8. See *Statesman*, 1 April 1815 for similar complaints.

82. *CWPR*, 1 April 1815, 393.
83. *CWPR*, 25 March 1815, 359–61.
84. William Godwin, *Letters of Verax, to the Editor of the Morning Chronicle, on the Question of a War* (London, 1815), 7.
85. *Statesman*, 24 March 1815; 28 March 1815.
86. Letter to *MM* 39 (May 1815): 308.
87. *Courier*, 10 May 1815.
88. *Statesman*, 3 April 1815. See also letter from "Regulus," *Statesman*, 10 April 1815.
89. *Statesman*, 5 May 1815.
90. *CWPR*, 1 April 1815, 393–4.
91. *Statesman*, 31 March 1815.
92. *Statesman*, 24 March 1815.
93. Letter to the *Statesman*, 1 May 1815. See also letter from "A. B.," *Statesman*, 4 April 1815; letter from "Regulus," *Statesman*, 10 April 1815.
94. Letter to the *Statesman*, 24 April 1815.
95. Letter to the *Statesman*, 1 May 1815.
96. The declaration appeared in many contemporary British sources; I quote from Edmund Boyce, *The Second Usurpation of Buonaparte*, 2 vols. (London, 1816), 1: 175–6.
97. Letter from "Peter Quilt," *Statesman*, 4 April 1815.
98. *PD*, 30: 444–5 (7 April 1815).
99. Godwin, *Verax*, 7, 9, 4.
100. Godwin claimed to have been "contented" with the restoration of 1814, having then been "sufficiently disgusted with the character of Bonaparte, as it had been displayed up to his exile to Elba" (ibid., 12).
101. Ibid., 13, 15–16.
102. *PD*, 30: 444–5 (7 April 1815).
103. *Scourge* 9 (May 1815): 346.
104. *AGM*, 23 Jan. 1814, "20057"; 10 April 1814, 3045; 8 May 1814, 3077.
105. *AGM*, 13 March 1814, "30013."
106. On Hankin's earlier pamphlets, see chapter 1.
107. While Hankin cited the relatively limited figure of "half a million of men, who had never known any other pursuit than that of war," and who would have trouble "submit[ting] to the tranquil occupations of civil life," his pamphlet tended to portray the entire French population in these terms: "The profession of arms is the only one known in France; to it her citizens are trained from their infancy, they are compelled to embrace it, and the pursuit of it is sweetened by the hope of plunder." Hankin, *Political Reflections, Addressed to the Allied Sovereigns, on the Re-entry of Napoleon Buonaparte into France* (London, 1815), 1, 33–34. Hankin's dedication is dated 16 April 1815.
108. Ibid., 34–6, v.
109. *A Letter, &c. An Account of the Conspiracy*, 33.
110. John Chetwode Eustace, *A Letter from Paris, to George Petre, Esq.*, 4th ed. (London, 1814), 61–2, 96.
111. *PD*, 31: 446 (25 May 1815).
112. Godwin, *Verax*, 6–7.
113. *Champion*, 13 March 1814, 80; 3 April 1814; see also the leading articles of 12 Feb. and 10 April.

114. *Champion*, 2 April 1815, 105.
115. Ibid., 105–6.
116. Ibid.; *Champion*, 9 April 1815, 114n.
117. *Champion*, 2 April 1815, 106.
118. *Champion*, 7 May 1815, 145.
119. *Champion*, 16 April 1815, 124.
120. *Champion*, 2 April 1815, 106.
121. Ibid.
122. *Champion*, 7 May 1815, 145.
123. See, e.g., George Tierney's speech in *PD*, 31: 446 (25 May 1815).
124. *Diary of Benjamin Robert Haydon*, 1: 456 (23 June 1815), 1: 458 (25 June 1815), 1: 462–3 (11 July 1815). On Haydon, see chapters 7 and 8, and Stuart Semmel, "Reading the Tangible Past: British Tourism, Collecting, and Memory after Waterloo," *Representations* 69 (Winter 2000): 9–37.
125. [Francis Jeffrey], *ER* 27 (Dec. 1816): 295. Among the scores of poems about Waterloo published in the years immediately after the battle, the best-remembered are Walter Scott, *The Field of Waterloo; A Poem* (Edinburgh, 1815), and Robert Southey, *The Poet's Pilgrimage to Waterloo* (London, 1816). On these and other Waterloo poems, see Bainbridge, *Napoleon and English Romanticism*; on the mythologizing of Waterloo, see Semmel, "Reading the Tangible Past."
126. Robinson, *Diary, Reminiscences, and Correspondence*, diary, 30 June 1815, 1: 257.
127. Quoted in Stanley Jones, *Hazlitt: A Life, from Winterslow to Frith Street* (Oxford, 1989), 179.
128. *Statesman*, 16 Aug. 1815.
129. Letter to the *Statesman*, 15 July 1815.
130. "The Afterpiece to the Tragedy of Waterloo—or—Madame Françoise & her Managers!!!" (MDG 12620; 9 Nov. 1815); "The Present State of France Exemplified, in the First Chapter of the Second Book of the Restoration of Kings" (MDG 12623; Dec. 1815).
131. Boyce, *Second Usurpation of Buonaparte*, 2: 352.
132. "Napoleon" (poem by "Jeffrey"), in *Black Dwarf*, 17 Dec. 1817, 781–2. For more on the counter-myth of Waterloo, see chapter 6.
133. *Examiner*, 30 July 1815, 490.
134. *Courier*, 31 July 1815.
135. *DNB*, 6: 330–3. And see Eastlake's 25 Aug. 1815 letter to B. R. Haydon, in Haydon Papers (Shelfmark MS Eng 1331 (9); VII, f. 95).
136. Letter from "O. S. T." (dated 17 Aug.), in *MM* 40 (Sept. 1815): 173.
137. Ibid.
138. *CWPR*, 12 Aug. 1815, 173, 175–6.
139. *QR* 16 (Jan. 1817): 494.
140. *Courier*, 28 July 1815.
141. Quoted in *CWPR*, 12 Aug. 1815, 172–3.
142. Letter to Catherine Clarkson (15 Aug. 1815), in *Letters . . . Wordsworth*, 2, pt. 2: 244.
143. For her own part, she wished she had had a better view. Mrs Haviland to Haydon, 31 July 1815, in Haydon Papers (shelfmark MS Eng 1331 (9); VII, f. 92). A garbled version of this letter appears in *Benjamin Robert Haydon: Correspondence and Table-Talk* (London, 1876), 1: 288.

144. Letter from Lady Charlotte FitzGerald to "my dear Charles" (copy), 11 Aug. 1815, at Add. MSS (Warren Hastings Papers, second supplement), ff. 71–2. See also a sermon from near Torbay: *The Parallel: Nebuchadnezzar and N. Buonaparte* (London, [1816]).

145. *British Critic*, 2nd ser., 6 (Dec. 1816): 602–3.

146. CWPR, 12 Aug. 1815, 172–3 (*Courier* passage quoted from CWPR).

147. *Morning Chronicle*, 2 Aug. 1815. The *Chronicle* also reported that a Mr. Waddington planned to raise the question in the City of London's Court of Common Council. For the *Courier*'s response to Lofft, see 2 Aug. 1815. For Goldsmith's response, see his letter to the *Morning Chronicle*, 4 Aug. 1815. Lofft further elaborated his argument in other letters to the *Chronicle*, most notably that of 10 Aug. 1815.

148. *Morning Chronicle*, 10 Aug. 1815. Lofft's criticisms of Napoleon's detention would be further circulated in William Hone's *Interesting Particulars of Napoleon's Deportation for Life* (London, 1816). Also see Leigh Hunt's interest in Lofft's proposal: *Examiner*, 6 Aug. 1815, 497.

149. *Morning Chronicle*, 8 Aug. 1815.

150. Letter from "A Lover of My Country," *Statesman*, 8 Aug. 1815. For more on the legal critique of Napoleon's treatment, see chapter 7.

151. *Statesman*, 10 Aug. 1815.

152. For Mackenrot's busts, see *Statesman*, 18 Sept. 1815.

153. *Morning Chronicle*, 11 Aug. 1815. For a vivid description of Mackenrot's fruitless mission to Plymouth, and the identification of Mackenrot as a former West Indies judge, see Lean, *Napoleonists*, 164–5. Unfortunately, Lean does not cite his sources. Also see Gilbert Martineau, *Nappleon Surrenders*, trans. Frances Partridge (London: John Murray, 1971), 178–83; Martineau appears to be drawing on the papers of Lord Keith.

154. *MM* 40 (Sept. 1815): 170.

6 Radicals, "Legitimacy," and History

1. William Hazlitt, "What is the People?", in *Political Essays* (London, 1819), 308 (orig. pub. in the *Champion*). The opening quotation is from *King Lear*, I.ii.18. On Hazlitt's use of the bastard Edmund's speech, see Jonathan Bate, *Shakespearean Constitutions: Politics, Theatre, Criticism 1730–1830* (Oxford, 1989), 190.

2. This is Thompson's one mention of Napoleon after Waterloo. *Making*, 716. Though my point obviously extends beyond the question of whether Oliver's Napoleon would have seemed convincing, busts and statuettes did figure in many contemporary accounts. Hester Lynch Piozzi and Robert Southey complained about Napoleonic busts; the painter Benjamin Robert Haydon's wife Mary and Thomas Carlyle both treasured their domestic bronzes of the emperor. A Napoleonic statue plays a key role in William Hazlitt's novel *Liber Amoris*. *Piozzi Letters*, 3: 358 (letter to P. S. Pennington, 2 June 1802); [Southey], *Letters from England*, ed. with intro. Jack Simmons (orig. 1807; London, 1951), 26; *Diary of Benjamin Robert Haydon*, 2: 416 (19 June 1815); *Collected Letters of . . . Carlyle*, 6: 425n. (27 Aug. 1833); *Liber Amoris, or the New Pygmalion* (London, 1823).

3. See Philip Harling's cogent criticisms of recent portrayals of a stable and quiescent political culture in "Leigh Hunt's *Examiner*" and "The Duke of York Affair." Harling sees recent works—most notably, Colley's *Britons*—as suggesting erroneously that loyalists had "a virtual monopoly over the language of war-time patriotism" ("Leigh Hunt's *Examiner*," 1160).

4. Thompson, *Making*, 660.

5. *QR* 16 (Oct. 1816): 240–1. Southey is identified as the author in Hill and Helen Chadwick Shine, *The Quarterly Review under Gifford: Identification of Contributors, 1809–1824* (Chapel Hill, 1949).

6. "Feelings of a Republican on the Fall of Bonaparte," in *The Complete Poetical Works of Percy Bysshe Shelley*, ed. George Edward Woodberry, 4 vols. (Boston, 1898), 3: 171–2. For Shelley's earlier description of Napoleon as "hateful & despicable," see letter to Thomas Jefferson Hogg (27 Dec. 1812), *Letters*, ed. Frederick L. Jones, 2 vols. (Oxford, 1964), 1: 218.

7. *CWPR*, 1 April 1815, 393–4.

8. See esp. Burrow, *A Liberal Descent*; R. J. Smith, *The Gothic Bequest: Medieval Institutions in British Thought, 1688–1863* (Cambridge, 1987); Lang, *The Victorians and the Stuart Heritage*.

9. H. T. Dickinson, "The Eighteenth-Century Debate on the 'Glorious Revolution,'" *History* 61 (1976): 28–45; Kathleen Wilson, "Inventing Revolution: 1688 and Eighteenth-Century Popular Politics," *Journal of British Studies* 28 (1989): 349–86.

10. The phrase is James Epstein's; see chap. 1 ("The Constitutionalist Idiom") of *Radical Expression*. On the constitution as "the meta-narrative of nineteenth-century politics" (p. 12), see James Vernon, ed., *Re-reading the Constitution: New Narratives in the Political History of England's Long Nineteenth Century* (Cambridge, 1996); esp. the introduction by Vernon ("Notes towards an Introduction," 1–21) and, for its focus on the period covered by this chapter, Jonathan Fulcher, "The English People and their Constitution after Waterloo: Parliamentary Reform, 1815–1817," 52–82.

11. Epstein, *Radical Expression*, 11; James Vernon, *Politics and the People: A Study in English Political Culture, c. 1815–1867* (Cambridge, 1993), esp. 296–7, 305–9; Vernon, "Notes," 9.

12. E.g., "Understanding the Cap of Liberty: Symbolic Practice and Social Conflict in Early-Nineteenth-Century England," in Epstein, *Radical Expression*, 70–99; Olivia Smith, *The Politics of Language, 1791–1819* (Oxford, 1984).

13. Harling, "Leigh Hunt's *Examiner*."

14. *CWPR*, 29 April 1815, 515–16. Cobbett was specifically referring to the words "legitimate" and "usurper."

15. But also see, e.g., Leigh Hunt's earlier "On Certain Terms Magnanimously Applied to the French Ruler," *Examiner*, 30 Sept. 1810.

16. Consulting the ARTFL database (American and French Research on the Treasury of the French Language, University of Chicago, http://humanities.uchicago.edu/ARTFL) suggests that the term "légitimité" entered French political discourse only in the period of the revolution, when it was used by Sieyès, Marat, and Robespierre to define a lawful society, right, or institution. Joseph de Maistre used the term in 1810 in reference to hereditary kingship: *Des Constitutions politiques* (Paris, 1959), 10, 54. Employing the term to signify the principle of hereditary sovereignty seems to be a product of the final

years of Napoleon's empire. Germaine de Staël and Adolphe Thiers both attributed the usage to Talleyrand. De Staël, *Considérations sur la révolution française*, 2 vols. (orig. 1818; Paris, 1862), 2: 185; Thiers, *Histoire du consulat et de l'empire* (Paris, 1874), 18: 445. While *Le Grand Robert de la langue française* attributes the first usage of "légitimité" in the sense of hereditary right to Chateaubriand in 1797, this is a mistake; Chateaubriand did employ "légitimité" in his preface to the 1797 *Essai historique, politique et moral, sur les révolutions anciennes et modernes*, but this preface was not written until his works were collected decades later (*Oeuvres complètes*, ed. Ladvocat, 28 vols. [Paris, 1826]).

17. Letter from "L.," *Examiner*, 23 July 1815, 475.

18. *ER* 30 (Sept. 1818): 448.

19. *Examiner*, 10 Sept. 1815, 577.

20. *Statesman*, 29 May 1815.

21. Holland to Hobhouse, Holland House Papers, Add. MS 47224, ff. 48–9 ([early 1816]); Henry Bickersteth (later Lord Langdale) to Hobhouse, Add. MS 36456, f. 299 (11 Jan. 1816); 36456, f. 305 (23 Jan. 1816) and ff. 307–8 (24 Jan. 1816); Constant to Hobhouse, Add. MS 36456, ff. 340–1 (undated), 348 (17 June 1816); *ER* 26 (Feb. 1816): 215–16.

22. [Hobhouse], *The Substance of Some Letters, Written by an Englishman Resident at Paris During the Last Reign of the Emperor Napoleon*, 2 vols. (London, 1816), 1: 72–3 (from a letter purportedly written in April 1815).

23. "What is the People?" in Hazlitt, *Political Essays*, 308.

24. "The Times Newspaper. On the Connexion between Toad-Eaters and Tyrants" (orig. *Examiner*, 12 Jan. 1817), in Hazlitt, *Political Essays*, 167.

25. Thomas Babingon Macaulay, "Milton" (orig. *ER*, Aug. 1825), in *Critical and Historical Essays*, 2 vols. (London, 1907), 1: 173.

26. "On the Late War" (orig. *Champion*, 3 April 1814), in Hazlitt, *Political Essays*, 71.

27. The phrase is Hazlitt's (he also spoke of "the new law-fiction of legitimacy"): see "The Times Newspaper," 166.

28. Richard Price, *A Discourse on the Love of our Country* (London, 1789), 25, 34–5. See chapter 4.

29. Edmund Burke, *Reflections on the Revolution in France*, ed. and intro. Conor Cruise O'Brien (orig. 1790; Harmondsworth, 1968), 106, 102, 99–110. But cf. R. J. Smith, who sees Burke's treatment of the breach of 1688 as "cavalier" (*Gothic Bequest*, 122).

30. James Mackintosh, *Vindiciæ Gallicæ: Defence of the French Revolution and its English Admirers* (orig. 1791; Oxford, 1989), 296–7, 323–4, 314.

31. An interesting treatment, from a different perspective, of the Brunswick problem in the 1790s is David Womersley, "Gibbon's Unfinished History: The French Revolution and English Political Vocabularies," *Historical Journal* 35 (1992): 63–89.

32. On the shifting content of "conservative" ideas, and the terminological difficulties posed by "right-wing" thought, see Sack, *From Jacobite to Conservative*.

33. Hence the distancing italics that Hazlitt applied to the word "abdication" in this chapter's epigraph.

34. John Scott, *Paris Revisited, in 1815, by Way of Brussels* (Boston, 1816), 138.

35. *PD*, 32: 653 (19 Feb. 1816). On the split between Grenville's and Grey's followers, see Peter Jupp, *Lord Grenville, 1759–1834* (Oxford, 1985), 443–4.

36. *Statesman*, 4 April 1815.

37. *CWPR*, 29 April 1815, 515–16. See also letter from "N.," *European Magazine* 68 (Sept. 1815): 216–17.

38. Letter from "Draco," *Statesman*, 30 March 1815. See also *Statesman*, 30 March 1815.

39. *Statesman*, 1 April 1815. On Godwin's *Morning Chronicle* letters, republished as *Letters of Verax*, see Chapter 5.

40. Letter from "Hampden," *CWPR*, 8 April 1815, 443–4.

41. Letter from "Timothy Trueman," *Statesman*, 31 March 1815. See also Trueman's letters in *Statesman*, 15 April 1814, and 25 Aug. 1815; and letter from "Peter Quilt," *Statesman*, 4 April 1815.

42. Letter from "A True Briton," *CWPR*, 12 Aug. 1815, 189–90. See also *Examiner*, 23 July 1815, 475; letter from "Peter Quilt," *Statesman*, 4 April 1815; *CWPR*, 29 April 1815, 515–16; letter from Honestas, *CWPR*, 23 Sept. 1815, 389; and letter from "Anth. Pasquin, A. J.," *Statesman*, 8 July 1815.

43. *Statesman*, 1 April 1815. The remark bore a special piquancy coming from Lovell, who had twice been incarcerated because of the attorney-general's scrutiny.

44. Letter from Hortator, *CWPR*, 12 Aug. 1815, 182, 179.

45. Some went further, suggesting that Napoleon's claim to power was not equal to but greater than that of the Hanoverians—for had he not been made emperor "by suffrages incomparably more numerous than were ever given to establish any individual on any throne"? Letter from Capel Lofft, *Statesman*, 22 Aug. 1815. See also letter from "Justitia," treating Napoleon's throne as "the first in intrinsic worth on the face of the globe" (*CWPR*, 13 May 1815, 389–91), and one *Statesman* correspondent's warning that Britons had a history of looking abroad "to seek for Kings, who would pay to their laws that respect which their own British-born Princes did not pay. I wonder where they would now go. . . . What has given a legitimate title to the House of Hanover would, I presume, give a legitimate title to another man, under similar circumstances, even though he were a *Frenchman*." Letter from "Timothy Trueman," *Statesman*, 25 Aug. 1815.

46. "M.W.", in *Scourge* 9 (May 1815): 452.

47. "H.W.", in *Scourge* 10 (July 1815): 53–7. See also Cobbett's argument in *CWPR*, 28 Oct. 1815, 403–4.

48. [Hobhouse], *Substance*, 1: 132–3 (April 1815), 137n.

49. Ibid., 1: 136 (April 1815); 1: 318, 346, 348 (May 1815).

50. The *Statesman*, 9 Nov. 1815, described the Isle of Wight meeting of the "Society of Friends to the British Constitution" (where one member noted that the doctrine of Legitimacy would place Sardinia's king, descended from James II, on the British throne); *CWPR*, 4 May 1816, 373, described the meeting of "the *County of Cornwall*, legally assembled, with the High Sheriff at its head, and all the principal persons of the County being present" (where it was decreed that forcing the French "*to submit to a Government not chosen by themselves*" amounted to "*denying the justice of our own glorious Revolution*, and impeaching the *title of the House of Brunswick* to the Throne of these Realms").

51. *PD*, 30: 436 (7 April 1815). For other comparisons between Napoleon and

William III, see Earl Stanhope's speech, *PD*, 30: 347 (6 April 1815); Burdett's speech, *PD*, 31: 430 (25 May 1815); and the 26 May exchange between Sir John Newport and Stuart Wortley, reported in *Courier*, 27 May 1815, and in *PD*, 31: 472–3 (26 May 1815).

52. *PD*, 32: 33–4 (1 Feb. 1816). See also Lord Holland's protest, *PD*, 32: 670 (19 Feb. 1816).

53. *PD*, 32: 645–6 (19 Feb. 1816).

54. *PD*, 32: 653–4 (19 Feb. 1816). Grenville, as a Whig, felt no qualms about emphasizing, in the tradition of Mackintosh, the extra-constitutional nature of William's arrival: though Britain's "great deliverer," William had arrived in Britain "with no vested right, and no claim to the Crown but the people's will."

55. See the speech of Francis Horner, political economist and *Edinburgh* reviewer, *PD*, 32: 776 (20 Feb. 1816).

56. *PD*, 32: 714–16 (19 Feb. 1816).

57. Philip Harling persuasively argues that Hazlitt was not a "freakish iconoclast" out of step with his radical contemporaries—but even Harling portrays Hazlitt's sympathy for Napoleon as practically unique. Harling, "William Hazlitt and Radical Journalism," *Romanticism* 3 (1997): 53–65, esp. pp. 54, 56–7, 63.

58. "Illustrations of the Times Newspaper. On Modern Apostates" (orig. *Examiner*, 15 Dec. 1816), in Hazlitt, *Political Essays*, 143.

59. "What is the People?," ibid., 308–9.

60. "Preface," ibid., viii–ix.

61. Ibid., xii–xiv, xvi.

62. Hazlitt, *Life of Napoleon Buonaparte*. On the *Life*, see Barton R. Friedman, *Fabricating History: English Writers on the French Revolution* (Princeton, 1988), 67–108; John Kinnaird, *William Hazlitt: Critic of Power* (New York, 1978), 325–31.

63. *Statesman*, 1 Aug. 1815; 2 Aug. 1815. See chapter 7.

64. On Carlile, see Epstein, *Radical Expression*, 100–46; Joel Wiener, *Radicalism and Freethought in Nineteenth-Century Britain: The Life of Richard Carlile* (Westport, Conn., 1983).

65. Epstein, *Radical Expression*, 102.

66. *Sherwin's*, 5 Sept. 1818, 277–8.

67. Ibid.

68. *Sherwin's*, 12 Dec. 1818, 81–5.

69. On Davenport, see *The Life and Literary Pursuits of Allen Davenport* (London, 1845), and David Worrall, *Radical Culture: Discourse, Resistance, and Surveillance, 1790–1820* (London, 1992), 81–9. On shoemakers, see Thompson, *Making*, 771n. and E. J. Hobsbawm and Joan Wallach Scott, "Political Shoemakers," *Past and Present* 89 (Nov. 1980): 86–114.

70. *Sherwin's*, 12 Dec. 1818, 89–90.

71. For Hunt's declaration, see *Sherwin's*, 12 Sept. 1818, 294.

72. *Sherwin's*, 10 Oct. 1818, 359–60.

73. Ibid.

74. *Sherwin's*, 17 Oct. 1818, 376, 380. Davenport presented a similar picture in his verse dialogue, *The Kings, or, Legitimacy Unmasked, A Satirical Poem* (London, 1819), 10.

75. *Sherwin's*, 31 July 1819, 194.

76. *Sherwin's*, 24 Oct. 1818, 386.

77. Ibid., 386, 389. An advertisement for Sherwin's quarto edition of *Killing No Murder* appears in *Sherwin's*, 31 July 1819, 198. Sherwin's arguments in support of killing tyrants appeared in 20 June 1818, 102–3, and 22 May 1819, 29–36. The titles of Sherwin's articles and reprint also called to mind Richard Lee's notorious 1795 handbill, *King Killing*. See Barrell, *Imagining*, 607, 615–20.

78. *Revolutionary Plutarch*, 2: appendix; [Yorke], *Anti-Corsican*, 129 (letter orig. pub. 18 Jan. 1804); *European Magazine* 45 (Jan. 1804): 56. See chapter 4.

79. *PD*, 20: 777–82 (2 July 1811). See chapter 4.

80. See, e.g., *Speech of the Right Honourable William Pitt* [3 Feb. 1800], 97; *The Speech of the Honourable Charles James Fox* [3 Feb. 1800], new ed. (London: J. Debrett), 32; Mackintosh in *Trial of John Peltier*, 110; Horner to J. A. Murray, 31 Dec. 1805, in *The Horner Papers: Selections from the Letters and Miscellaneous Writings of Francis Horner, M.P. 1795–1817*, ed. Kenneth Bourne and William Banks Taylor (Edinburgh, 1994), 395; *AGM*, 21 May 1815, 4265; Southey, *Poet's Pilgrimage*, "Argument," n.p.

81. As 1815 opened, the *Statesman* warned that the reinvigoration of the Order of the Bath was designed "to humble and mortify the gentry of the kingdom, and to dispose the whole mass of the people to look to the military service as to be the most favoured profession." Leigh Hunt, similarly, feared a "military mania" that threatened to replace English "simplicity" with French "foppery." Both writers compared the new decoration to Napoleon's Legion of Honor. *Statesman*, 7 Jan. 1815, 3. *Examiner*, 15 Jan. 1815, 35; 22 Jan. 1815, 50; 29 Jan. 1815, 65. On the Bath and other military honors, see Cookson, *British Armed Nation*, 221–3.

82. *Sherwin's*, 20 June 1818, 110; 15 Aug. 1818, 236.

83. *Sherwin's*, 31 July 1819, 191–2; 21 Aug. 1819, 237.

84. Epstein, *Radical Expression*, 85. For Hunt's earlier (spring 1815) invocation of 1688, and opposition to renewed warfare, see John Belchem, *"Orator" Hunt: Henry Hunt and English Working-Class Radicalism* (Oxford, 1985), 46–7.

85. Jeremy Bentham, *Plan of Parliamentary Reform, in the Form of a Catechism* (London, 1817), iv–v.

86. Bentham, *Plan of Parliamentary Reform* (London, 1818).

87. *Black Dwarf*, 29 Jan. 1817, 1–2. Lest this statement seem to imply a positive view of the British past, see Wooler's comment three years later: "If some few instances of bravery and love of freedom gleam through a few pages of our history, what shall we say to the barren waste besides?" *Black Dwarf*, 26 Jan. 1820, 88.

88. *Black Dwarf*, 26 Jan. 1820, 83.

89. *Black Dwarf*, 21 March 1821, 403; 19 July 1821, 72.

90. *Black Dwarf*, 26 July 1820, 136.

91. *Black Dwarf*, 25 June 1817, 340–1.

92. *Black Dwarf*, 16 July 1817, 389; 29 Jan. 1817, 10.

93. J. D. Newman, "To Napoleon Buonaparte," *Black Dwarf*, 21 April 1819, 256. For a debate between *Dwarf* correspondents over Napoleon's vices and virtues, see letters from Deptfordiensis and Brutus, 28 April 1819, 270–1; 12 May 1819, 301–2; 19 May 1819, 318–20; 2 June 1819, 342.

94. *Black Dwarf*, 7 May 1817, 226–9. For a discerning reading of Wooler's trials for libel, see Epstein, *Radical Expression*, chap. 2 ("Narrating Liberty's Defense: T. J. Wooler and the Law").

95. On Charlotte's death, see Colley, *Britons*, 220–1, 270–3; Stephen C. Behrendt, *Royal Mourning and Regency Culture: Elegies and Memorials of Princess Charlotte* (New York, 1997); Esther Schor, *Bearing the Dead: The British Culture of Mourning from the Enlightenment to Victoria* (Princeton, 1994), chap. 6 ("Mourning Princess Charlotte").

96. *CWPR*, 7 March 1818, 293; 2 May 1818, 505.

97. *Black Dwarf*, 12 Nov. 1817, 691; 19 Nov. 1817, 703, 706. See, similarly, the *Champion and Sunday Review*, 9 Nov. 1817, 356. Barry O'Meara, Napoleon's physician on St. Helena, claimed that Napoleon himself had high hopes for Charlotte, thinking her accession might produce a more liberal policy towards himself. O'Meara, *Napoleon in Exile; or, A Voice from St. Helena*, 4th ed., 2 vols. (London, 1822), 2: 367.

98. *Black Dwarf*, 10 Dec. 1817, 752, 754.

99. *Authentic Memoirs of the Life of the Late Lamented Princess Charlotte* (London, 1817), 16.

100. *Black Dwarf*, 12 Nov. 1817, 693–4.

101. *Black Dwarf*, 19 Nov. 1817, 707.

102. When noticed, pro-Napoleonic sentiment does tend to be dismissed in such terms. See, e.g., Thompson's passing reference to "that slender band, which included Hazlitt, who took refuge in a truculent Bonapartism." E. P. Thompson, "Hunting the Jacobin Fox," *Past and Present* 142 (Feb. 1994): 94–140, p. 138.

103. Samuel Bamford, *Bamford's Passages in the Life of a Radical and Early Days*, 2 vols. (London, 1893), 1: 299. On British attitudes toward Napoleonic mementoes, see Semmel, "Reading the Tangible Past."

104. See suggestive remarks in Thomas W. Laqueur, "The Queen Caroline Affair: Politics as Art in the Reign of George IV," *Journal of Modern History* 54 (1982): 417–66, pp. 461–3.

7 The Politics of Exile

1. [John Wilson Croker or Robert Southey], *QR* 16 (Jan. 1817): 511.

2. Lines 53–8, 63–6. In *The Complete Poetical Works: Lord Byron*, ed. Jerome J. McGann, 7 vols. (Oxford, 1980–93), 7: 3.

3. See, e.g., *CWPR*, 10 Aug. 1805, 195–202; 7 Sept. 1805, 369. Also see Langford, *Englishness Identified*, 149. On the broad question of Cobbett's relationship to traditional country life, see Ian Dyck's important *William Cobbett and Rural Popular Culture* (Cambridge, 1992).

4. See, earlier, "John-Bull Offering Little Boney Fair Play" (MDG 10048; 2 Aug. 1803).

5. Version quoted is from the *Statesman*, 9 Sept. 1815; the ditty also appeared in the *Morning Chronicle*, 31 Aug. 1815, and was reprinted in *Napoleon and the Bourbons* (London, 1816), 16. The poem, titled "Epistle from Tom Crib to Big Ben," was written by Byron's friend Thomas Moore: see *The Poetical Works of Thomas Moore*, 10 vols. (London, 1840–41), 7: 83–5. Bennett repro-

duces it in *British War Poetry*, 490–1. The real Tom Cribb was a champion bareknuckle boxer, recently retired.

6. "One of the Fancy" [Pierce Egan], *Boxiana; or, Sketches of Antient & Modern Pugilism* (London, 1812).

7. "Boxiana, or, the Fancy" (MDG 12613; 1 Oct. 1815).

8. *Statesman*, 14 Aug. 1815.

9. *Black Dwarf*, 19 March 1817, 119.

10. "Napoleon" (by "Jeffrey"), in *Black Dwarf*, 17 Dec. 1817, 781–2.

11. *Scourge* 10 (Aug. 1815): 84.

12. *Statesman*, 10 Aug. 1815; and see 7 Aug. 1815.

13. *QR* 14 (Oct. 1815): 86.

14. *Statesman*, 14 Aug. 1815.

15. *CWPR*, 12 Aug. 1815, 168.

16. Letter from Antigonus, *Statesman*, 21 Sept. 1815.

17. *CWPR*, 16 Sept. 1815, 334.

18. *CWPR*, 12 Aug. 1815, 168.

19. For references to the law of nations, see, e.g., letter from "A Practicing Barrister," *Statesman*, 8 Aug. 1815; *CWPR*, 12 Aug. 1815, 166; letter from Lofft, *Statesman*, 22 Aug. 1815. Hobhouse, *Substance*, 2nd ed., 2: 283n.

20. Letter from "Cassius," *Statesman*, 1 Aug. 1815.

21. *Statesman*, 2 Aug. 1815; letter from Lofft, *Statesman*, 7 Aug. 1815.

22. *Statesman*, 22 Aug. 1815.

23. *Statesman*, 1 Aug. 1815.

24. See, e.g., Cobbett's complaint in *CWPR*, 12 Aug. 1815, 168.

25. Letter from Lofft, *Statesman*, 9 Sept. 1815.

26. *Statesman*, 2 Aug. 1815.

27. [Hobhouse], *Substance*, 2nd ed., 2: 283n.

28. *CWPR*, 16 Sept. 1815, 333. Burdon, letter to the *Statesman*, 19 Aug. 1815; *Statesman*, 7 Aug. 1815.

29. *Statesman*, 10 Aug. 1815.

30. *CWPR*, 12 Aug. 1815, 168.

31. *CWPR*, 16 Sept. 1815, 335.

32. Letter from "Timothy Trueman," *Statesman*, 25 Aug. 1815.

33. *CWPR*, 16 Sept. 1815, 333, 335.

34. Letter from Lofft, *Statesman*, 9 Sept. 1815.

35. *Letters from the Count de Las Casas* (London, 1819), xvii. Similarly, see *Statesman*, 2 Aug. 1815, 2.

36. *Observations on Lord Bathurst's Speech in the House of Peers, on March 18, 1817*, 2nd ed. (London, 1818), 49–50. For an attribution to Napoleon, see the review in *European Magazine* 74 (Oct. 1818): 349.

37. E.g., *MM* 40 (Sept. 1815): 170, which compared the exile to "that of Aristides in Athenian history, or as the fate of Regulus in Carthaginian history."

38. *CWPR*, 12 Aug. 1815, 170.

39. *QR* 14 (Oct. 1815): 146. See also, e.g., *European Magazine* 68 (Aug. 1815): 135–40; Capt. John Barnes, *A Tour through the Island of St. Helena* (London, 1817).

40. *Statesman*, 2 Aug. 1815; letter from Capel Lofft, *Statesman*, 1 Aug. 1815; [Henry Brougham], *ER* 32 (July 1819): 158.

41. *Letters from the Cape of Good Hope, in Reply to Mr. Warden*, 3rd ed.

(London, 1817), 203; *Letters from the Island of St. Helena, Exposing the Unnecessary Severity Exercised towards Napoleon* (London, 1818), 78.

42. *Observations*, 2, 3. See also Napoleon's letter in the appendix, 57.

43. *QR* 14 (Oct. 1815): 147.

44. *Blackwood's Edinburgh Magazine* 1 (Sept. 1817): 651–2.

45. *Statesman*, 28 July 1815.

46. Santine [Jean Noel Santini], *An Appeal to the British Nation on the Treatment Experienced by Napoleon Buonaparte in the Island of St. Helena* (London, 1817), 13–15.

47. Southey, *Poet's Pilgrimage*, 218.

48. *QR* 14 (Oct. 1815): 151.

49. [Southey or Croker] *QR* 16 (Jan. 1817): 506–7, 482.

50. *AGM*, 7 April 1816, 4571–2.

51. *Letters from the Cape of Good Hope*, 202–3. On the authorship of this work, see p. 214.

52. *Statesman*, 3 Oct. 1815; *CWPR*, 30 Sept. 1815, 412–13. The sequel to Mackenrot's tale is a peculiar one. He was admitted to the criminal lunatic department of Bethlem Hospital in 1816, having been tried for forgery and found not guilty by reason of insanity. (An early hospital report claimed that he tended to "aggravat[e] every groundless trifle into mighty evils.") In 1825, his wife published a pamphlet claiming that asylum staff were "conspiring" to keep him captive. If his writings ("on backs of letters, or margins of books") were responsible for his continued imprisonment, she noted, "he is the first British subject ever so treated." Frances Mackenrot, *A Letter to the Rt. Hon. Robert Peel, M. P., His Majesty's Secretary of State for the Home Department, upon the Detention of Anthony Mackenrot in New Bethlem Hospital, St. George's Fields* (Southwark, [1825]), 4, 8. In 1825, he was discharged by royal warrant on condition that he leave the country within a fortnight and not return. See communications between the asylum and the Home Office, volume CSA–01. I am very grateful to Patricia Allderidge and Colin Gale, archivists of the Bethlem Royal Hospital Archives and Museum, for this information about Mackenrot's release.

53. *PD*, 35: 1142 (18 March 1817). For an earlier protest of Holland, see *PD*, 30: 1011–20 (8 April 1816).

54. See, e.g., *Letters from the Island of St. Helena*, 25–6; Barry E. O'Meara, *Napoleon in Exile; or, A Voice from St. Helena*, 4th ed., 2 vols. (London, 1822), 1: 85.

55. PRO CO 247/4, Cockburn to Bertrand (copy), 6 Nov. 1815.

56. *ER* 32 (July 1819): 162.

57. Ibid., 169.

58. *ER* 30 (Sept. 1818): 462–3.

59. *Black Dwarf*, 5 Aug. 1818, 491.

60. *Observations*, 7, 47.

61. Byron, "The Age of Bronze" (1823), line 69. In *Complete Poetical Works*, 7: 3.

62. Haydon, *Diary*, 3: 648 (15 Oct. 1832).

63. Among the many British efforts to piece together the events of Napoleon's exile, the classic account is that by the former Liberal prime minister Lord Rosebery, *Napoleon: The Last Phase* (London, 1900). One of Rosebery's particular

charms is his forthright acknowledgment of the questionable nature of all St. Helena sources, combined with a readiness to pursue nonetheless the elusive events. Rosebery characterizes Santini's book as "pure fabrication," sees O'Meara's 1822 *magnum opus* as "worthless," feels the "unreliability" of Las Cases' work "make[s] it impossible to accept any of his statements, when he has any object in making them," and warns in addition that about the last three years of Napoleon's exile "we know nothing or next to nothing." Yet he is still ready to characterize Lowe as "a narrow, ignorant, irritable man, without a vestige of tact or sympathy" (pp. 31, 20, 21, 7, 66).

64. William Warden, *Letters Written on Board His Majesty's Ship the Northumberland, and at Saint Helena* (London, [1816/17]); [Croker or Southey,] *QR* 16 (Jan. 1817): 486–7. Positive reviews of Warden appeared in *ER* 27 (Dec. 1816): 459–61 and *British Critic*, 2nd ser., 6 (Dec. 1816): 593; an earlier negative review by Croker appeared in *QR* 16 (Oct. 1816): 210–11.

65. *Letters from the Cape of Good Hope*, 1–2.

66. Barry E. O'Meara, *An Exposition of Some of the Transactions, that have Taken Place at St. Helena.*, 2nd ed. (London, 1819), 39. According to Rosebery, the official editors of Napoleon's correspondence attributed the *Exposition* to Napoleon himself; Rosebery believed Napoleon had personally dictated the work, adding that a copy of its proofs existed with handwritten corrections by Napoleon. *Napoleon: The Last Phase*, 29.

67. *QR* 17 (July 1817): 509.

68. Jacques Godechot, "Napoleon I," *Encyclopædia Britannica*, 15th ed. (1990); 24: 748.

69. Longwood (or rather, the replica Longwood constructed on the same site) reportedly has "had to be repainted every year because the wind and the rain made it like being on a ship out at sea." Julia Blackburn, *The Emperor's Last Island: A Journey to St. Helena* (London, 1991), 186.

70. *Letters from the Island of St. Helena*, 47, 4, 21, 3.

71. Ibid., 29–30.

72. The *Letters* here referred to Bathurst's response to Lord Holland's protest; this same speech prompted the Napoleon-authorized *Observations*. See *PD*, 35: 1137–66 (18 March 1817).

73. *Letters from the Island of St. Helena*, 27, 100, v.

74. [Theodore Edward Hook], *Facts, Illustrative of the Treatment of Napoléon Buonaparte in Saint Helena* (London, 1819), 2, 4, 5, 53–4.

75. Ibid., 54.

76. R. H. Dalton Barham, *The Life and Remains of Theodore Edward Hook*, new ed. (London, 1853), mentions the stop at St. Helena (105n.), but not the resulting pamphlet. On Hook's disgrace (though not on the pamphlet), also see *Encyclopædia Britannica*, 11th ed. (1910–11), xiii, 670; *DNB*, xxvii, 274.

77. [Hook], *Facts*, 6–9.

78. *Letters from the Island of St. Helena*, 78.

79. [Hook], *Facts*, 12–13, 89, 20, 10. *Observations*, 3.

80. *PD*, 35: 1151 (18 March 1817).

81. [Hook], *Facts*, 18.

82. Hook intimated a dark connection between Lewis Goldsmith and a "Mr. *Lewis* Solomon" of St. Helena ("whose name, by the way, I believe not to be Solomon"), who had purportedly provided newspapers to O'Meara. The

coincidence of their identical first names (and, tacitly, their Jewish last names) was enough to prompt Hook to suggest Solomon was "an acquaintance" or "for all I know, . . . a relation of Mr. *Lewis* Goldsmith." *Facts*, 62.

83. *AGM*, 3 Nov. 1816, 4824.

84. *QR* 28 (Oct. 1822): 228 (review of O'Meara, *A Voice from St. Helena*).

85. *British Monitor*, 4 April 1819, 6729–30. Goldsmith had initially missed the insinuations against him; he now had to apologize for having praised the book the previous week.

86. Lewis Goldsmith to Liverpool (29 March 1819), Add. MS 38276 (Liverpool Papers), f. 101.

87. *British Monitor*, 4 April 1819, 6729–30. In 1822, Croker would take care to note that the newspaper editor facilitating the communication had taken part "quite innocently" in the operation. *QR* 28 (Oct. 1822): 228.

88. Letter from "Philopatriæ," *British Monitor*, 11 April 1819, 6742–3.

89. O'Meara, *Exposition*, 148, 36–8. O'Meara strongly hinted that he knew the author's identity when he suggested that the public was "indifferent" to whether the writer was "a greedy expectant, working his way into place, or some ruined profligate, who, after having betrayed his trust, endeavours to evade the offended majesty of the laws, by an attempt to bolster up the views of imbecility and oppression." Ibid., 6, 192.

90. *ER* 32 (Aug. 1819): 150–5. Brougham denied that the anonymous author could possibly have arrived well-disposed towards Bonaparte, as he claimed, given that so many of his criticisms targeted Napoleon's earlier life, on which recent events had no bearing.

91. The work quickly found American publishers as well, and was promptly translated into Swedish, German, and French. A sixth British edition was published in 1829.

92. *QR* 28 (Oct. 1822): 221, 222, 227–8, 236–8.

93. Add. MS 51529 (Holland House Papers), f. 123 (undated).

94. To Zachary Macaulay, 5 Oct. 1822, *Letters . . . Macaulay*, 1: 180.

95. To Jane Welsh, [c. 1 Aug. 1822], in *Collected Letters . . . Carlyle*, 2: 154.

96. About the poems, see Jane Welsh to Thomas Carlyle, 3 March [20? Feb.] 1822, in *Collected Letters . . . Carlyle*, 2: 52; Carlyle to Welsh, [c. 17 May 1822], 2: 109; Welsh to Carlyle, 29 [25? May] 1822, 2: 114. For Jane's bristling, see Welsh to Carlyle [24 Oct. 1822], 2: 178.

97. Thomas Carlyle, *On Heroes, Hero-Worship and the Heroic*, ed. Carl Niemeyer (1841; Lincoln, 1966), 241.

98. Letter to Lord Holland (date unclear). Add. MS 51529 (Holland House Papers), f. 143.

99. Letter to Lady Holland, 6 July 1821. Add. MS 51848 (Holland House Papers), f. 246.

100. *Black Dwarf*, 15 Aug. 1821, 217–18; see also 19 July 1821, 68. The *Examiner* shared Wooler's skepticism about "the notion of 'hereditary cancer'" and the attribution of Caroline's death to "a disproportionate dose of magnesia." *Examiner*, 15 July 1821, 433; 12 Aug. 1821, 498.

101. Samuel Gower to Lady Holland, 6 Nov. 1821. Add. MS 51848 (Holland House Papers), f. 17 (Samuel Gower to Lady Holland, 6 Nov. 1821).

102. On Ireland's forgeries, see S. Schoenbaum, *Shakespeare's Lives*, 2nd ed. (Oxford, 1991), 132–67.

103. W. H. Ireland, *The Last Will and Testament of Napoleon Bonaparte, Late Emperor of the French* (London, [1821]), 3.
104. Add. MS 51848 (Holland House Papers), f. 33 (letter of 1 Nov. 1822). See W. H. Ireland, *France for the Last Seven Years; or, The Bourbons* (London, 1822). According to one report, the custom house officer who examined the snuffbox when Count Bertrand landed in England exempted it from duty. Maria Edgeworth to Mrs. Edgeworth, 11 Feb. 1822, in *Letters from England, 1813–1844*, ed. Christina Colvin (Oxford, 1971), 350.
105. Add. MS 51529 (Holland House Papers), f. 127. "To Lady Holland, on the Legacy of a Snuff box, left to her by Bounaparte [*sic*]" (accompanying letter is dated 6 Oct. 1821).
106. Add. MS 51529 (Holland House Papers), ff. 132–3, 135–9, 141; Byron's, at f. 137, is reproduced in *Complete Poetical Works*, 6: 512.
107. Add. MS 51529 (Holland House Papers), ff. 129–30.

8 *Fallen Greatness*

1. *CWPR*, 30 Sept. 1815, 414.
2. On the importance of the Hundred Days for the French legend of Napoleon, see Sudhir Hazareesingh's forthcoming *The Legend of Napoleon*.
3. *Description of Haydon's Picture*, 4.
4. Ibid., 5.
5. *QR* 28 (Oct. 1822): 224.
6. Letter from "Bellerophon," *Statesman*, 17 Aug. 1815.
7. The trope was applied to Napoleon's case, rather than coined for it. It predated his fall and had been applied to politically opposite subjects as well: e.g., the American Unitarian William Ellery Channing's pro-Bourbon call to his parishioners "to sympathize with fallen greatness, with descendants of ancient sovereigns, hurled from their thrones." *A Sermon, Preached in Boston, April 5, 1810, the Day of the Publick Fast* (Boston, 1810), 10.
8. *New Monthly Magazine and Literary Journal*, n.s., 2 (1821): 183.
9. Byron, "The Age of Bronze," lines 54–8, in *Complete Poetical Works*, ed. McGann, 7: 3.
10. Lowe was said to have delayed, or perhaps refused, the delivery to Napoleon of a bust of the king of Rome.
11. [Yorke], *Anti-Corsican*, 113 (letter orig. pub. 14 Dec. 1803).
12. "The Modern Prometheus, or Downfall of Tyranny" (MDG 12299; [July 1814]).
13. [Byron], *Ode to Napoleon Buonaparte*, 3rd ed. (London, 1814), 10, 15. Here, Prometheus entered through elision, as the stanza's primary subject was the Greek athlete Milo, devoured by wolves. Byron also wrote a brief 1814 contrast between Bonaparte and the Titan, printed (as "[Prometheus and Napoleon]") in *Complete Poetical Works*, ed. McGann, 3: 269, and an 1816 poem "Prometheus" that does not directly mention Napoleon (and may, as a result, seem all the more to equate rather than contrast the two figures). Ibid., 4: 31–3.
14. Byron, "The Age of Bronze," lines 87, 56; in *Complete Poetical Works*, ed. McGann, pp. 4, 3; Prometheus is also invoked in lines 226–40; p. 8.

15. Rev. C. Colton, *The Conflagration of Moscow: A Poem*, 4th ed. (London, 1822), 28. Also see Ettrick, *Season and Time*, xxxvi, 524n; John Cam Hobhouse to Jeremy Bentham, 5 Nov. 1820, in *Correspondence of Jeremy Bentham*, 10: 141; *New Monthly Magazine and Literary Journal*, n.s., 2 (1821): 182.

16. Lady Morgan, *France*, 2nd ed., 2 vols. (London, 1817), 2: 313.

17. See Curran, "Political Prometheus," which sets out to identify sources for Shelley's *Prometheus Unbound*. Curran notes the attachment of Promethean imagery to George Washington, and rightly characterizes Napoleon-Prometheus (in contrast to Washington-Prometheus) as "more an allegorical icon of despair than an avatar of liberation" (p. 445).

18. Macaulay, "Milton," in *Critical and Historical Essays*, 1: 168. Macaulay contrasted Aeschylus' Prometheus with Milton's Satan, but allowed that both shared some characteristics: "the same impatience of control, the same ferocity, the same unconquerable pride," as well as, "in very different proportions, some kind and generous feelings." On Napoleon as Milton's Satan, see Bainbridge, *Napoleon and English Romanticism*. One might similarly see Napoleon the usurper as an implied presence in Leigh Hunt's declaration, to Percy Shelley, that he had considered "writing a poem myself, entitled *Prometheus Throned*; in which I intended to have described him as having lately taken possession of Jupiter's seat." *The Correspondence of Leigh Hunt*, ed. Thornton Leigh Hunt, 2 vols. (London, 1862), 1: 132 (July 1819).

19. Bloomfield's first and most successful work, *The Farmer's Boy* (1800), ushered to press by Lofft and illustrated by Thomas Bewick, sold tens of thousands of copies and was translated into French, Italian, and (by one over-zealous admirer) Latin.

20. Robert Bloomfield, "The Shepherd's Dream: Or, Fairies' Masquerade," in *May Day with the Muses* (London, 1822), 49-53.

21. Carlyle to Welsh [*c.* 1 Aug. 1822], in *Collected Letters . . . Carlyle*, 2: 154.

22. This and the following paragraph draw on Semmel, "Reading the Tangible Past."

23. *CWPR*, 12 Aug. 1815, 176-7.

24. The lock survives in the British Library's Holland House Papers: Add. MS 51529, f. 197 (i). On other hair clippings, see Clementine, Lady Malcolm to Hester, Lady Keith (4 July 1816), in *The First Napoleon. Some Unpublished Documents from the Bowood Papers*, ed. Earl of Kerry (London, 1925), 189. On Lady Holland's snuffbox prints, see Add. MS 51848, f. 45 and f. 51.

25. Jean Hornn, *The Narrative of Jean Hornn, Military Coachman to the Emperor Napoleon*, 3rd ed. (Newcastle, 1818), 67. *Description of the Series of Pictures, Painted by Order of the Late Emperor of France . . . Now Exhibiting at the London Museum, Piccadilly* (London, 1816), 3, 4. For the coach's itinerary, see Joseph Farington, *The Farington Diary*, ed. James Greig, 8 vols. (London, 1922-28), 8: 88 (24 Aug. 1816). On the carriage's arrival in Edinburgh, see *Blackwood's Edinburgh Magazine* 2 (March 1818): 711.

26. Sainsbury privately produced several works describing his collection, including *Catalogue of a Collection . . . Collected on the Continent and in England, during the Last Fifteen Years* (1834), *Supplement to the Catalogue of a Collection of Works* (n.d.), *Sketch of the Napoleon Museum* (1840), and *Particulars of the Exhibition Now Open at the Egyptian Hall* (1843), but the

fullest version of his catalogue was *The Napoleon Museum. The History of France Illustrated* (London, 1845). Citations from *Napoleon Museum*, i; letter of John Sainsbury to Sir John Soane, 9 Dec. 1835, bound with Soane's copy of *Catalogue of a Collection* (John Soane Museum, London); untitled promotional pamphlet (at BL 10659.bb.30), 1, 2, 12; Christie and Mason notice for auction of Napoleon Museum, 23 June 1845 (at BL 10601.e.21 (2)).

27. Untitled promotional pamphlet (at BL 10659.bb.30), 1; Sainsbury, *Sketch*, 5.

28. "The Removal of Napoleon Bonaparte's Ashes. I Would be a Soldier Still" (BL). This song, like those following, is undated. But according to Leslie Shepard, this song's publisher, E. M. Hodges, lived at the address listed on the songsheet from 1855 to 1861. Leslie Shepard, *John Pitts: Ballad Printer of Seven Dials, London, 1765–1844* (London, 1969), 85.

29. "The Grand Conversation on Napoleon" (BL).

30. "Plains of Waterloo" (Penn); "Oh, what a Stagnation in Trade" (Penn).

31. Including "The Grand Conversation on Napoleon" (BL).

32. "Napoleon's Farewell to Paris" (Penn). Again, the song is undated—but the publisher H. P. Such's business began in 1849. Leslie Shepard, *The History of Street Literature* (Newton Abbot, 1973), 76.

33. "A Dream of Napolean [*sic*]" (BL). Hodges is again the publisher, but the address listed indicates an earlier period, according to Shepard. Shepard, *John Pitts*, 85.

34. "Deeds of Napoleon" (BL).

35. "The Removal of Napoleon Bonaparte's Ashes. I Would be a Soldier Still" (BL).

36. J. H. Amherst, *The Battle of Waterloo: A Grand Military Melo-Drama in Three Acts* (London, [1824]); J. H. Amherst, *Napoleon Buonaparte's Invasion of Russia, or, The Conflagration of Moscow: A Grand Military and Equestrian Spectacle in Three Acts* (London, [1825]). On Amherst's productions, see Martin Meisel, *Realizations: Narrative, Pictorial, and Theatrical Arts in Nineteenth-Century England* (Princeton, 1983), 214–16; see also Louis James, "Inverted Emblems for Albion: Wellington and Napoleon on Stage," in Raphael Samuel, ed., *Patriotism* 3: 243–51.

37. Those in the British Library's collection (part of the collection formed by John Larpent, the lord chamberlain's inspector of plays; the earlier plays, to 1824, are housed at the Huntington Library) include *Napoleon* (entered 21 Dec. 1830), at Add. MS 42905, which was soon published as M. Rophino Lacy, *Programme of the New Grand Historical Military Spectacle, (in Seven Parts), called Napoleon Buonaparte, Captain of Artillery, General and First Consul, Emperor and Exile* (London, 1831); *The Little Corporal, or, Bonaparte at the Military School at Brienne* (1831), Add. MS 42910, ff. 590–604; *Napoleon. A Drama* (1852), Add. MS 52931 (B); *Bonaparte in Egypt. A Grand Millitary* [*sic*] *Spectacle* (1852), Add. MS 52931 (C); *Wellington and Waterloo* (1852), Add. MS 52936 (I). For a play banned by the licencing office, see *The Duke's Coat; Or, the Night after Waterloo: A Dramatick Anecdote . . . Interdicted by the Licenser of Plays* (London, 1815). The Lord Chamberlain's Office rejected this light piece despite the eponymous duke of Wellington's absence from the stage.

38. *Napoleon* (entered 21 Dec. 1830), at Add. MS 42905, ff. 445, 447 (published as *Programme of the New Grand Historical Military Spectacle*).

39. Lacy, *Napoleon*, ff. 455, 466. Napoleon's humbling prompted others also to

cite the line from Seneca. E.g., "A Midshipman of the Bellerophon" [George Home], *Memoirs of an Aristocrat and Reminiscences of the Emperor* (Edinburgh, 1837), quoted in Maccunn, *Contemporary English View*, 187.

40. Amherst, *Battle of Waterloo*, 33. Amherst's Napoleon, surprised by the burning of Moscow in the following year's sequel, offers a reward "to those who save the lives and property of the innocent inhabitants." *Invasion of Russia*, 38.

41. E.g., John Walker, *Napoleon! Or, The Emperor and the Soldier! A Petite Drama, in One Act* (London, [184–?]).

42. *Napoleon. A Drama* (1852).

43. Amherst, *Invasion of Russia*, 32, 42–3.

44. Lacy, *Napoleon*, ff. 401–2, 405–6.

45. George Dibdin Pitt, *Napoleon the Star of France* (1850), Add. MS 43025, ff. 753–4, 779–80. For yet another example of this motif, see the "juvenile drama" in which a Frenchman, offered riches for assassinating Napoleon, refuses: *Napoleon Buonaparte; General, Consul and Emperor: A Drama, in Two Acts* (London, [18–?]), 7.

46. Amherst, *Invasion of Russia*, 7. In Amherst's rendition of Waterloo, Napoleon wears no "coat of steel; no ruler chosen by the people need wear such a breast-work." *Battle of Waterloo*, 29–30.

47. Walker, *Napoleon!*, 11, 16. Other plays, too, made Napoleon a sympathetic listener to critics. See, e.g., Napoleon's mercy towards a fanatic enemy in *Bonaparte in Egypt*, 49.

48. Amherst, *Battle of Waterloo*, 35. On British comparisons of Wellington with Napoleon (specifically, how the two were seen as representatives of their respective nations), see Iain Pears, "The Gentleman and the Hero: Wellington and Napoleon in the Nineteenth Century," in Roy Porter, ed., *Myths of the English* (Cambridge, 1992), 216–36. On the two generals' opinions of one another, see Andrew Roberts, *Napoleon and Wellington* (London, 2001).

49. Walker, *Napoleon!*, 7.

50. *Napoleon's Glory, or, Wonders in Saint Helena* (1840), Add. MS 42957, f. 815.

51. Pitt, *Napoleon the Star of France*, Add. MS 43025, ff. 746, 786.

52. *Bonaparte in Egypt*, 72.

53. "The British Atlas, or John Bull Supporting the Peace Establishment" (MDG 12786; c. June 1816).

54. James Henry Lewis, *The Rise and Fall of Buonaparte*, in *Lewis's Orations, on the Battle of Waterloo, and on the Rise and Fall of Buonaparte* (London, 1815), 44. This paragraph and the following one draw on Semmel, "Reading the Tangible Past."

55. *Lady Blessington's Conversations of Lord Byron*, ed. and intro. Ernest J. Lovell, Jr. (orig. pub. in *New Monthly Magazine*, 1832–33, then in book form 1834; Princeton, 1969), 120.

56. "Feelings of a Republican on the Fall of Bonaparte," in *The Complete Poetical Works of Percy Bysshe Shelley*, ed. George Edward Woodberry, 4 vols. (Boston, 1898), 3: 171–2.

57. Looking backwards on the ruin of Ozymandias allowed Shelley to view Napoleon through the lens he elsewhere claimed to seek when "considering the political events of the day": it allowed him, that is, "to divest my mind of temporary sensations, to consider them as *already historical*." Shelley to T. J. Hogg, quoted in Richard Holmes, *Shelley: The Pursuit* (orig. 1974; London, 1987), 290 (emphasis added).

58. "Napoleon's Soliloquy in the Island of St Helena," in CWPR, 4 Nov. 1815, 154-5.
59. *Description of Haydon's Picture*, 4.
60. W. Hamilton Reid, *Memoirs of the Public and Private Life of Napoleon Bonaparte* (London, 1826).
61. John Ruskin, "The Exile of St Helena," in *The Works of John Ruskin*, ed. E. T. Cook and Alexander Wedderburn, 39 vols. (London, 1903-12), 2: 49-50.
62. See *Description of Haydon's Picture*, 6.
63. Haydon, *Diary*, 3: 503 (7 Jan. 1831).
64. For Haydon's insistence on viewing his own career through Napoleon's, see, e.g., his diary entry for 4 July 1821: *Diary*, 2: 346.
65. Haydon, *Diary*, 3: 499 (11 Dec. 1830); 3: 509 (5 March 1831; the dream occurred "about a month since"); 3: 510 (8 March 1831); 3: 182 (9 Feb. 1827); 3: 525 (18 June 1831).
66. For the Wellington dream, see Haydon, *Diary*, 4: 374 (30 Aug. 1836).
67. Haydon, *Diary*, 5: 334 (16 Dec. 1843); 5: 330 (28 Nov. 1843); 3: 407 (30 Dec. 1844); 5: 334 (13 Dec. 1843); 5: 339 (5 Jan. 1844, a later note); 5: 407 (31 Dec. 1844); 5: 351 (7 March 1844). For a list of Haydon's oils, see *Diary*, 5: 587-601.
68. Ibid., 5: 534-5 (30 April 1846); 5: 544 (18 May 1846).
69. Ibid., 5: 552-3 (18 June 1846); 2: 351 (29 July 1821). See also Haydon's letter to Mary Russell Mitford of 7 July 1828, sparked by the report of a banknote forger's suicide: "Don't you think that Cato was more of a hero than Napoleon by putting an end to himself?" *Benjamin Robert Haydon: Correspondence*, 2: 123. On Napoleon's failure to kill himself, see chapter 5.
70. "Last Thoughts" (shelfmark fMS Eng 1331.1 (91)), Haydon Papers.
71. *Description of Haydon's Picture*, 6.
72. On Thumb, see Haydon, *Diary*, 5: 355 (9 April 1844). Famously, Haydon's exhibition at the Egyptian Hall coincided with Thumb's own performance there; Haydon's takings were little more than one-hundredth of Thumb's. After Haydon's death, George Cruikshank captured the ironic contrast between the painter's failure and the sideshow artist's triumph in his caricature "Born a Genius and Born a Dwarf."
73. William Makepeace Thackeray, *Vanity Fair: A Novel without a Hero* (1847-48; Oxford, 1983), 812. See also the scene in Charles Dickens' *Our Mutual Friend* (1864-5; Harmondsworth, 1998) where Eugene Wrayburn notes that his own folded-arm pose resembles that of the exiled emperor (p. 663).
74. Add. MS 43025, f. 772.
75. William Wordsworth, "To B. R. Haydon, on Seeing his Picture of Napoleon Buonaparte on the Island of St Helena," in *Wordsworth: Poems*, 2: 707.
76. Arthur Conan Doyle, "The Six Napoleons," in *The Return of Sherlock Holmes* (1905).
77. Matthew Arnold to his mother, 7 May 1848, *Letters of Matthew Arnold, 1848-1888*, 2nd ed., ed. George W. E. Russell (London, 1901), 1: 12.
78. Matthew Arnold, *The Popular Education of France* (1861), in *Complete Prose Works*, ed. R. H. Super, 11 vols. (Ann Arbor, 1962), 2: 53, 56, 211.
79. Walter Bagehot, "Lord Althorp and the Reform Act of 1832" (orig. 1876), in *Bagehot's Historical Essays*, ed. Norman St John-Stevas (New York, 1966), 156-7.

80. Prochaska, *Republic of Britain*, 33. The Napoleonic threat was invoked in the (misquoted) Shakespearian epigraph to William Hone's *Buonapartephobia*: "With his name the mothers still beat their babes!" (*Henry VI, Part I*, II.iii). See also Thomas Hardy, *The Return of the Native* (1878: New York, 1999), 83–4.

81. See, among many others, Benjamin Bickley Rogers, *Napoleon III and England: An Enquiry* (Oxford, 1855); *France and her Emperor Considered Morally & Politically* (London, 1860); Ernst Veritas, *Dedicated to the Rifle Volunteers of England: The Inheritance of Napoleon the Third and the Legacy of Peter the Great* (London, 1860). Biblical exegetes were similarly concerned: see Whittemore, *The Seventh Head*; Hildebrand, *The Application of Prophecy to the Crimean War*. But see the sympathetic "Man of the World" [Charles Phillips], *Napoleon the Third* (London, 1854), and Joseph Mayer's description of the two Napoleons in *Catalogue of the Drawings, Miniatures, Cameos, and Other Objects of Art, Illustrative of the Bonaparte Family* (Liverpool, 1854).

82. W. C. Bennett, "The French Invasion" (April 1855), in *Poems* (London, 1862), 397–8. The poet calms the heroes' nerves by insisting that "Napoleon fights/For Europe's freedom by our side."

83. Including Carola Oman, *Napoleon at the Channel* (Garden City, NY, 1942); Arthur Bryant, *The Years of Endurance, 1793–1802* (London, 1942); Frank J. Klingberg and Sigurd B. Hustvedt, eds., *The Warning Drum: The British Home Front Faces Napoleon; Broadsides of 1803* (Berkeley, 1944); Bryant, *The Years of Victory*. Similarly, Alexander Korda's *That Hamilton Woman* (1941), a film beloved by Winston Churchill (who reportedly penned some of its dialogue), implicitly linked the contemporary threat of invasion to Napoleon's earlier one.

84. Jack Werner, *We Laughed at Boney (or; We've Been Through it All Before): How Our Forefathers Laughed Defiance at the Last Serious Threat of Invasion by Napoleon; A Striking Parallel with Our Present Position* (London, [1943]).

85. See, e.g., Desmond Seward, *Napoleon and Hitler: A Comparative Biography* (1988; New York, 1990).

86. Drawing such parallels was, needless to say, hardly a practice restricted to Britain. See Pieter Geyl's cautious comparison between Napoleon and Hitler in *Napoleon: For and Against*, 7–11.

87. Walter Scott, *The Life of Napoleon Buonaparte Emperor of the French*, 9 vols. (Edinburgh, 1827), 9: 103.

Epilogue: The Historical Napoleon

1. Helen Maria Williams, *Narrative of the Events Which Have Taken Place in France, from the Landing of Napoleon Bonaparte* (London, 1815), 278.

2. *Description of Haydon's Picture*, 4–5.

3. *Athenæum*, 3 Aug. 1850, 812–13.

4. Williams, *Narrative of the Events*, 277. On Williams, see Gary Kelly, *Women, Writing, and Revolution, 1790–1827* (Oxford, 1993), chaps. 2 and 6.

5. *Description of Haydon's Picture*, 4.

6. Benjamin Disraeli, *The Revolutionary Epick* (London, 1834), ii.

7. *Examiner*, 30 Sept. 1810, 609–10.

8. William Henry Ireland, *The Life of Napoleon Bonaparte*, 4 vols. (orig. pub. serially 1823–28; London, 1828), 1: xii–xiv.

9. [William Hamilton Reid], *Memoirs of the Public and Private Life of Napoleon Bonaparte*, 2 vols. (London, 1827), iv. A one-volume 1826 edition of the biography, with a different publisher (Sherwood, Gilbert, and Piper) and Reid's name attached, lacked the opening pages of this edition (published by George Virtue). On Reid's earlier writings, see chapter 3.

10. Bernard Barton, "Napoleon," in *Napoleon, and Other Poems* (London, 1822), 17.

11. Barclay de Mounteney, *The Case of a Détenu* (London, 1838), 7; Mounteney, *An Historical Inquiry into the Principal Circumstances and Events Relative to the Late Emperor Napoleon* (London, 1824), xiii.

12. Scott, *Life*, 9: 106–7.

13. Ibid., 1: iv–v, 9: 337, 9: xlvii, lxxiv (in Appendix V).

14. William Hazlitt, *The Spirit of the Age*, in *The Complete Works of William Hazlitt*, ed. P. P. Howe, 21 vols. (London, 1930–4), 11: 65. See Jones, *Hazlitt: A Life*, 372.

15. Hazlitt, *The Life of Napoleon Buonaparte* (vols. 13–15 of *Complete Works*), 13: ix. On Hazlitt, see chapter 6. On Hazlitt's *Life*, see Bainbridge, *Napoleon and English Romanticism*, 183–207; on this and Scott's biography, see Friedman, *Fabricating History*, 67–108.

16. Hazlitt, *Life*, 15: 198, 13: ix.

17. Ibid., 15: 131; 13: 105, 156, 184, 120.

18. Ibid., 15: 201, 232–3.

19. Scott, *Life*, 3: 341.

20. Hazlitt, *Life*, 14: 16, 188, 210; 15: 312–13.

21. R. H. Horne, *The History of Napoleon*, 2 vols. (London, 1840–1), 1: vii.

22. George Moir Bussey, *History of Napoleon*, 2 vols. (London, 1840).

23. Horne, *History of Napoleon*, 1: v, 81–2, 175, 327.

24. Bann, *Romanticism and the Rise of History*, xi. On how this problem was considered by contemporaries encountering landscapes and relics of the recent Napoleonic wars, see Semmel, "Reading the Tangible Past."

25. Morgan, *France*, 1: 181, 187–8.

26. Thomas Babington Macaulay, *Napoleon and the Restoration of the Bourbons*, ed. Joseph Hamburger (written 1831–2; New York, 1977), 56, 49, 55, 60. See John Clive, "Macaulay and the French Revolution," in Ceri Crossley and Ian Small, eds., *The French Revolution and British Culture* (Oxford, 1989), 103–22.

27. Macaulay, *Napoleon*, 50.

28. Ibid., 72.

29. Ibid., 71, 73.

30. Ibid., 72–3.

31. *Trial of John Peltier*, 110.

32. Yorke, *Letters from France*, 1: 125.

33. *ER* 23 (April 1814): 27–8. See also *ER* 25 (Oct. 1815): 507.

34. Edward Baines, *History of the French Revolution, from the Breaking Out of the War in 1792, to the Restoration of a General Peace in 1815*, 2 vols. (London, 1817), 1. See also "Philo-Brutus," *Political Metamorphoses* (London, [1814]), 3–4; Walter Scott, *Life of Napoleon*, 9: 33.

35. Macaulay, *Napoleon*, 68, 73.
36. Ibid., 98, 69, 74.
37. Ibid., 56.
38. Hobhouse, *Substance*, 1: 366; *The Political and Literary Observer* 1 (June 1815): 1–2.
39. *RYWPR*, 29 March 1806, 260.
40. See chapter 4.
41. See chapter 5.

Bibliography

I. Primary Sources

Pamphlets and Books

Pre-Napoleonic

Lloyd, Thomas. *An Essay on the Toleration of Papists.* London, 1779.

Thoughts on the Present State of the Roman Catholics in England. London, 1779.

Priestley, Joseph. *A Free Address to Those Who Have Petitioned for the Repeal of the Late Act of Parliament.* London, 1780.

A Reply to an Appeal from the Protestant Association. London, 1780.

Price, Richard. *A Discourse on the Love of our Country.* London, 1789.

Burke, Edmund. *Reflections on the Revolution in France.* Edited and with introduction by Conor Cruise O'Brien. Originally published 1790. Harmondsworth, 1968.

Mackintosh, James. *Vindiciæ Gallicæ: Defence of the French Revolution and its English Admirers against the Accusations of the Right Hon. Edmund Burke.* Originally published London, 1791. Oxford, 1989.

1797

Some Account of the Early Years of Buonaparte, at the Military School of Brienne; and of his Conduct at the Commencement of the French Revolution. London, 1797.

1798

Egypt Delivered; or, The Conqueror Conquered. Being a Full Account of the Whole Proceedings and Death of Buonaparte with Most of his Officers and his Whole Army (chapbook).

Irwin, Eyles. *An Enquiry into the Feasibility of the Supposed Expedition of Buonaparté to the East.* London, 1798.

———. *Buonaparte in Egypt: Or, an Appendix to the Enquiry into his Supposed Expedition to the East.* London, 1798.

"An Officer in the Service of the East India Company." *Reply to Irwin: or, the Feasibility of Buonaparte's Supposed Expedition to the East.* London, 1798.

Wakefield, Gilbert. *Reply to Some Parts of the Address of the Bishop of Llandaff to the People of Great Britain.* London, 1798.

1799

Bicheno, James. *The Signs of the Times, in Three Parts. A New Edition; with Additional Notes, to Illustrate the Subjects Discussed*, 5th ed. London, 1799.
Craig, W. *Anecdotes of General Buonaparte, Compiled from Original and Authentic Papers.* [1799].

1800

An Account of the French Expedition in Egypt; written by Buonaparte and Berthier; with Sir William Sidney Smith's Letters. To Which is Added, an Appendix, containing the Life of Buonaparte, Down to November, 1799, 2nd ed. Leeds, [1800?].
Bloomfield, Robert. *The Farmer's Boy: A Rural Poem.* London, 1800.
Burdon, William. *Various Thoughts on Politics, Morality, and Literature.* Newcastle upon Tyne, 1800.
Fox, Charles James. *The Speech of the Honourable Charles James Fox, in the House of Commons, on Monday, the 3d of February, 1800, on a Motion for an Address to the Throne, Approving of the Refusal of Ministers to Treat with the French Republic*, new ed. London, [1800].
Pitt, William. *Speech of the Right Honourable William Pitt* [3 Feb. 1800].
Witherby, Thomas. *Observations on Mr. Bicheno's Book, Entitled The Restoration of the Jews the Crisis of all Nations: Wherein the Revolutionary Tendency of that Publication is Shewn to be Most Inimical to the Real Interest of the Jews.* London, 1800.

1801

Bicheno, James. *The Destiny of the German Empire; or, an Attempt to Ascertain the Apocalyptic Dragon and to Shew that the Binding of the Dragon called that Old Serpent, the Devil, and Satan, and the Millenary State, are Likely to be Altogether Different from what Christian Writers have Taught us to Expect.* London, 1801.
Faber, George Stanley. *Horæ Mosaicæ; or, A View of the Mosaical Records, with Respect to their Coincidence with Profane Antiquity; Their Internal Credibility; and Their Connection with Christianity.* Oxford, 1801.
The Genius of France; or, the Consular Vision. A Poem, with Notes. London, [1801?].
Goldsmith, Lewis. *The Crimes of Cabinets; or, a Review of their Plans and Agressions [sic] for the Annihilation of the Liberties of France and the Dismemberment of her Territories. With Illustrative Anecdotes Military and Political.* London, 1801.
[Hankin, Edward], "A Kentish Clergyman." *Thoughts on the Preliminary Articles of Peace.* London, 1801.
Kett, Henry. *History the Interpreter of Prophecy, or, a View of Scriptural Prophecies and their Accomplishment in the Past and Present Occurrences of the World. With Conjectures Respecting their Future Completion*, 4th ed. 2 vols. London, 1801.
Mackereth, George. *An Historical Account of the Transactions of Napoleone Buonaparte, First Consul of the French Republic, from the Period he Became Commander in Chief of the French Army in Italy, in April 1796, until the Present, of his Having Compelled the Emperor of Germany, a Second Time, to Make the*

Peace with the French Republic, and Acknowledge its Independence, in February, 1801. London, [1801].

1802

Bicheno, James. *Estimate of the Peace: A Discourse Delivered at Newbury June 1, 1802, Being the Day Appointed by Proclamation for a General Thanksgiving to Almighty God for Putting an End to the Late War.* London, 1802.

Cobbett, William. *Letters to the Right Honourable Lord Hawkesbury, and to the Right Honourable Henry Addington, on the Peace with Buonaparté, to Which is Added, an Appendix, Containing a Collection (Now Greatly Enlarged) of all the Conventions, Treaties, Speeches, and Other Documents, Connected with the Subject,* 2nd ed. London, 1802.

Denon, Vivant. *Travels in Upper and Lower Egypt, During the Campaigns of General Bonaparte,* trans. E. A. Kendal. 2 vols. London, 1802.

[Hankin, Edward], *The Civil and Religious Advantages Resulting from the Late War. A Sermon Preached in the Parish-Church of Mersham, in Kent, on the Day Appointed for the General Thanksgiving.* London, 1802.

1803

An Address to the Mechanics, Artificers, Manufacturers, and Labourers of England. On the Subject of the Threatened Invasion, 2nd ed. London, [1803].

An Address to the People of the United Kingdom of Great Britain and Ireland on the Threatened Invasion. Edinburgh, 1803.

The Anti-Gallican; or Standard of British Loyalty, Religion and Liberty. London, 1803.

The Atrocities of the Corsican Demon; or a Glance at Buonaparte. London, 1803.

An Appeal from the Passions to the Sense of the Country, upon Buonaparté and Invasion. London, 1803.

Bicheno, James. *Preparation for the Coming of Christ; Inculcated: In a Discourse, Delivered at Newbury, October 19, 1803. Being the Day Appointed by Proclamation for a General Fast.* London, 1803.

Buonaparte in Britain! . . . Addressed to all Ranks. London, [1803?].

Burdon, William. *Unanimity Recommended.* Newcastle upon Tyne, 1803.

Butler, Charles. *A Letter to a Roman Catholic Gentleman of Ireland, on the Chief Consul Buonaparte's Projected Invasion.* London, 1803.

[Byerley, John Scott], "John Scott Ripon." *Buonaparte; or, The Free-Booter.* London, 1803.

Carr, John. *The Stranger in France: or, a Tour from Devonshire to Paris. Illustrated by Engravings in Aqua Tinta of Sketches, Taken on the Spot.* London, 1803.

Cobbett, William. *Important Considerations for the People of this Kingdom.* N.p., 1803.

Colman, George. *Epilogue to the New Play of The Maid of Bristol.* N.p., [1803].

An English Taylor Equal to Two French Grenadiers; or, Eternal Shame and Infamy on the Dastardly Coward, Who Would not Shed the Last Drop of his Blood in Defence of his King and Country. London, [1803?].

Hunter, William. *A Vindication of the Cause of Great Britain; with Strictures on the Insolent and Perfidious Conduct of France, since the Signature of the Preliminaries of Peace,* 3rd ed. London, 1803.

Invasion Defeated, 2nd ed. London, 1803.

"Job Nott." *The Lion Sleeps*. Birmingham, 1803.

King, J. *Letters from France . . . In the Months of August, September, and October, 1802. In Which Some Occurrences are Related Which are not Generally Known; and Many Conjectures may be Found that Seemed to Have Anticipated Recent Events*. London, 1803.

The Loyalist: Containing Original and Select Papers; Intended to Rouse and Animate the British Nation, during the Present Important Crisis; and to Direct its United Energies against the Perfidious Attempts of a Malignant, Cruel, and Impious Foe. London, 1803.

Mayer, Lewis. *A Hint to England; or, A Prophetic Mirror; Containing an Explanation of Prophecy that Relates to the French Nation, and the Threatened Invasion; Proving Bonaparte to be the Beast that Arose out of the Earth, with Two Horns like a Lamb, and Spake as a Dragon, whose Number is 666. Rev. xiii.* London, 1803.

Minto, Lord. *The Speech of the Right Honourable Lord Minto, at a General Meeting of the County of Roxburgh, held at Jedburgh the 15th August 1803, on Moving an Address to His Majesty. Ordered by the Meeting to be Printed and Circulated in the County*. Kelso, 1803.

Newenham, T[homas]. *The Warning Drum, a Call to the People of England to Resist Invaders*. London, 1803.

Publicola's Addresses. To the People of England; to the Soldiers; and to the Sailors. To Which is Added, his Postscript to the People of England. London, 1803.

Rassurez Vous; or the Improbability of an Invasion, and the Impossibility of its Success Demonstrated. Edinburgh, 1803.

Sarratt, [Jacob]. *Life of Buonaparte*. London, [1803].

Stewart, Charles Edward. *Obedience to Government, Reverence to the Constitution, and Resistance to Bonaparte: A Sermon, Preached at Bury St. Edmunds's, before the Right Hon. Lord Chief Baron MacDonald, and the Honourable Mr. Baron Hotham, at the Assizes, Held There July 29, 1803*. Bury, 1803.

The Trial of John Peltier, Esq. for a Libel against Napoléon Buonaparté, First Consul of the French Republic, at the Court of King's Bench, Middlesex, on Monday, the 21st of February, 1803. Taken in Short-Hand by Mr. Adams, and the Defence Revised by Mr. Mackintosh. London, 1803.

1804

Barré, William. *History of the French Consulate, under Napoleon Buonaparte; being an Authentic Narrative of his Administration, Which is so Little Known in Foreign Countries. Including a Sketch of his Life. The Whole Interspersed with Curious Anecdotes and a Faithful Statement of Interesting Transactions, until the Renewal of Hostilities in 1803*. London, 1804.

Buonaparteana; or, Sketches to Serve for an Inquiry into the Virtues of the Buonaparte Family. Bath, 1804.

Burdon, William. *The Life and Character of Bonaparte, from his Birth to the 15th of August, 1804*. Newcastle upon Tyne, 1804.

[Hankin, Edward]. *The Independence of Great Britain, as the First of Maritime Powers, Essential to, and the Existence of France, in its Present State, Incompatible with, the Prosperity and Preservation of all European Nations.* London, 1804.

The Life of Bonaparte, First Consul of France, Containing an Account of his Birth and Education, Assassinations, Battles and Sieges, Egyptian Expedition, his Intended Invasion of this Country, and Every Other Interesting Particular to the Day of his Coronation. London, 1804.

MacIndoe, D. *Our Sin, Danger, & Duty. A Sermon, Occasioned by the Present War with France, Preached Oct. 19, 1803, being the Day Appointed for a National Fast.* Newcastle upon Tyne, 1804.

Maclean, Charles. *An Excursion in France, and Other Parts of the Continent of Europe; from the Cessation of Hostilities in 1801, to the 13th of December 1803. Including a Narrative of the Unprecedented Detention of the English Travellers in that Country, as Prisoners of War.* London, 1804.

Mayer, Lewis. *The Emperor of the Gauls Considered as the Lucifer and Gog of Isaiah and Ezekiel: And the Issue of the Present Contest between Great Britain and France Represented According to Divine Revelation. With an Appeal to Reason, on the Errors of Commentators,* 3rd ed. London, 1804.

The Revolutionary Plutarch: Exhibiting the Most Distinguished Characters, Literary, Military, and Political, in the Recent Annals of the French Republic; the Greater Part from the Original Information of a Gentleman Resident at Paris. To Which, as an Appendix, is Reprinted Entire, the Celebrated Pamphlet of "Killing No Murder." 3 vols. London, 1804.

Rivers, David. *A Discourse on Patriotism, or the Love of our Country,* 4th ed. London, 1804.

Strange, T. *A Hint to Britain's Arch Enemy Buonaparte, an Effusion, Appropriate to Existing Circumstances,* 2nd ed. London, 1804.

[Yorke, Henry Redhead], "Galgacus." *The Anti-Corsican; or, War of Liberty: a Series of Letters Addressed to the People of the United Empire: First Published in the Star, under the Signature of Galgacus.* London, 1804.

Yorke, Henry Redhead. *Letters from France, in 1802.* 2 vols. London, 1804.

1805

Barré, William. *The Rise, Progress, Decline and Fall, of Buonaparte's Empire in France.* London, 1805.

Hunter, William. *A Sketch of the Political State of Europe, at the Beginning of February, 1805.* London, 1805.

[Orger, Thomas]. *The Nativity of Napoleon Bonaparte, Emperor of All the French, Calculated by a Professor.* High Wycombe, 1805.

[Rolleston, Matthew]. *The Anti-Corsican, a Poem, in Three Cantos; Inscribed to the Volunteers of Great-Britain.* Exeter, 1805.

A Sketch of the Present State of France. By an English Gentleman, who Escaped from Paris in the Month of May Last. London, 1805.

Worsdale, John. *The Nativity of Napoleon Bonaparte, Emperor of France; Calculated According to the Genuine Rules and Precepts of the Learned Claudius Ptolemy, from the Most Correct Astronomical Tables.* Stockport, 1805.

1806

Ensor, George. *The Independent Man: Or, an Essay on the Formation and Development of those Principles and Faculties of the Human Mind Which Constitute Moral and Intellectual Excellence.* 2 vols. London, 1806.

Faber, George Stanley. *A Dissertation on the Prophecies that have been Fulfilled, are now Fulfilling, or will Hereafter be Fulfilled, Relative to the Great Period of 1260 Years; the Papal and Mohammedan Apostasies; the Tyrannical Reign of Antichrist, or the Infidel Power; and the Restoration of the Jews.* 2 vols. London, 1806.

Mayer, Lewis. *Bonaparte the Emperor of the French, Considered as the Lucifer and Gog of Isaiah and Ezekiel: and the Issue of the Present Contest Between Great Britain and France, Represented according to Divine Revelation . . .* , 3rd ed. London, 1806.

——. *The Important Period, and Long Wished for Revolution, Shewn to be at Hand, when God will Cleanse the Earth by his Judgments, and when all Dominions shall Serve and Obey the Most High,* 3rd ed. London, 1806.

——. *The Woman in the Wilderness, or, The Wonderful Woman, with her Wonderful Seal, Wonderful Spirit, and Wonderful Child,* 2nd ed. London, 1806.

Southcott, Joanna. *The Long-Wished-For Revolution Announced to be at Hand in a Book Lately Published, by L. Mayer.* London, 1806.

Thoughts on the Relative State of Great Britain and of France, at the Close of Mr. Pitt's Life and Administration in 1806. London, 1806.

1807

Bicheno, James. *The Restoration of the Jews the Crisis of all Nations; to Which is now Prefixed, a Brief History of the Jews, from their First Dispersion, to the Calling of their Grand Sanhedrim* [sic] *at Paris, October 6th, 1806. And an Address on the Present State of Affairs, in Europe in General, and in this Country in Particular,* 2nd ed. London, 1807.

——. *A Supplement to the Signs of the Times; Containing a Reply to the Objections of the Rev. G. S. Faber. . . .* London, [1807].

The Crisis, 3rd. ed. London, 1807.

Hunter, William. *Reasons for Not Making Peace with Buonaparté. To Which is Added a Postscript,* 2nd ed. London, 1807.

[Reid, William Hamilton], "An Advocate for the House of Israel." *Sanhedrin Chadasha* [New Sanhedrin] *and Causes and Consequences of the French Emperor's Conduct towards the Jews: Including Official Documents, and the Final Decisions of the Grand Sanhedrin . . . With Considerations on the Question, 'Whether there is any Thing in the Prophetic Records that Seems to Point Particularly to England?'* London, 1807.

Southey, Robert. *Letters from England.* Edited by Jack Simmons. Originally published 1807. London, 1951.

[Stephen, James]. *The Dangers of the Country.* London, 1807.

Substance of the Speech of the Earl of Selkirk, in the House of Lords, Monday, August 10, 1807, on the Defence of the Country. London, 1807.

Transactions of the Parisian Sanhedrim [sic]*, or Acts of the Assembly of Israelitish Deputies of France and Italy, Convoked at Paris by an Imperial and Royal Decree, Dated May 30, 1806. Translated from the Original Published by M. Diogene Tama, with a Preface and Illustrative Notes by F. D. Kirwan, Esq.* London, 1807.

1808

Dale, John. *The Restoration of All Things; or, the State of a New World: Containing, Likewise, (in Chronological Order of Succession) a View of the Times Wherein Various Great Events Take Place*, 4th ed. London, 1808.

"An English Israelite." *A Letter to the Parisian Sanhedrin; Containing Reflections on their Recent Proceedings, and on their Venal Apostacy from the Mosaic Institutes: with Observations on the Conduct of Buonaparte, Relative to his Projected Subversion, and Final Extermination, of the Religion of Judaism, in France.* London, 1808.

Faber, George Stanley. *A General and Connected View of the Prophecies, Relative to the Conversion, Restoration, Union, and Future Glory, of the Houses of Judah and Israel; the Progress, and Final Overthrow, of the Antichristian Confederacy in the Land of Palestine; and the Ultimate General Diffusion of Christianity.* 2 vols. London, 1808.

Malcolm, James Peller. *Anecdotes of the Manners and Customs of London during the Eighteenth Century.* London, 1808.

Roscoe, William. *Considerations on the Causes, Objects and Consequences of the Present War, and on the Expediency, or the Danger of Peace with France.* London, 1808.

Whitbread, Samuel. *A Letter from Mr. Whitbread to Lord Holland, on the Present Situation of Spain.* London, 1808.

1809

Bonaparte No Universal Monarch, and Not Proved to be Favourably Noticed in Prophecy. Boston, 1809.

The Exposé; or, Napoleone Buonaparte Unmasked, in a Condensed Statement of his Career and Atrocities. Accompanied with Notes, &c. London, 1809.

Horner, William. *The Nativity of Napoleon Bonaparte, wherein is Predicted the Downfall of the Murdering Despot*, 2nd ed. Leeds, 1809.

Mayer, Lewis. *Death of Bonaparte, and Universal Peace; a New Explanation of Nebuchadnezzar's Great Image, and Daniel's Four Beasts. Rev. vi. viii. ix. xiii. and xvi. To Which is Added a Chronological Table of the Sovereigns Included in the Number 666*, 2nd ed. London, 1809.

Reid, William Hamilton. *Memoirs of the Life of Colonel Wardle; Including Thoughts on the State of the Nation, and the Final Issue of the Present Critical Juncture; with the Public Spirit of 1809, as Displayed in the Patriotic Proceedings throughout the British Empire; and Enumerating those Gentlemen who were most Conspicuous in Voting him Thanks, &c. Excited by his Inquiry into the Conduct of the Late Commander-in-Chief.* London, 1809.

Remarks on Some Parts of Mr. Faber's Dissertation on the Prophecies, Relative to the Great Period of 1260 Years. London, 1809.

1810

Bicheno, James. *The Consequences of Unjust War: A Discourse, Delivered at Newbury, February 28, 1810, being the Day Appointed by Proclamation for a General Fast: To Which Authorities are Appended, in Confirmation of the Facts Asserted.* London, 1810.

Byerley, John Scott. *The Prince: Translated from the Original Italian of Niccolo Machiavelli. To Which is Prefixed an Introduction, Shewing the Close Analogy between the Principles of Machiavelli and the Actions of Buonaparte.* London, 1810.

Channing, William Ellery. *A Sermon, Preached in Boston, April 5, 1810, the Day of the Publick Fast.* Boston, 1810.

A Concise History of the Origin, Progress and Effects of the Papal Supremacy, with Observations on the Alterations Made in it by Buonaparte. Dublin and London, 1810.

Goldsmith, Lewis. *An Exposition of the Conduct of France towards America,* 2nd ed. London, 1810.

——. *The Secret History of the Cabinet of Bonaparte; Including his Private Life, Character, Domestic Administration, and his Conduct to Foreign Powers: Together with Secret Anecdotes of the Different Courts of Europe and of the French Revolution. With Two Appendices, Consisting of State Papers, and of Biographical Sketches of the Persons Composing the Court of St. Cloud,* 4th ed. London, 1810.

Maistre, Joseph de. *Des Constitutions politiques.* Originally published 1810. Paris 1959.

Plumptre, Anne. *A Narrative of a Three Years' Residence in France, Principally in the Southern Departments, from the Year 1802 to 1805: Including some Authentic Particulars Respecting the Early Life of the French Emperor, and a General Inquiry into his Character.* 3 vols. London, 1810.

1811

[Aldred, Ebenezer], "Eben-Ezer." *The Little Book; (See the Tenth Chapter of Revelations) or, a Close and Brief Elucidation of the 13, 14, 15, 16, 17, and 18th Chapters of Revelations.* London, 1811.

Escape from France. A Narrative of the Hardships and Sufferings of Several British Subjects who Effected their Escape from Verdun. With an Appendix, Containing Observations on the Policy and Conduct of Buonaparte towards British Subjects. London, 1811.

1812

Colton, Charles. *Napoleon: A Poem; in Which that Arch Apostate from the Cause of Liberty is Held up to the Just Indignation of an Injured People; Concluding with an Address to France: Dedicated to the British Army in Spain.* London, 1812.

[Corfield, John], *Destiny of Europe!!! The Nativity of Napoleone Buonaparte, Emperor of France.* London, [1812].

[Egan, Pierce], *Boxiana; or, Sketches of Antient & Modern Pugilism.* London, 1812.

"Fingal." *Truth: Containing the Cast of the Seven Princes of Britain, Contrasted with that of the Seven British Merchants; with Suggestions for Opposing the Dynasty of Brunswick, and the British Constitution, to the Phantasmagoria of the Destroyer, and the Code Napoleon; and Instead of Catholic Emancipation, Suggesting the Great and Wise Policy of Endeavouring to Amalgamate the Different Christian Religions of Britain, into One Grand Hierarchy; and in Place of Renewing India Monopoly, Creating One of the British Princes Emperor of India, and another King of Canada.* London, 1812.

An Inquiry into the Justice of the Pretensions of Napoleon Bonaparte to the Appellation of "Great." London, 1812.

Reid, William Hamilton. *Memoirs of the Public Life of John Horne Tooke, Esq. Containing a Particular Account of his Connections with the Most Eminent Characters of the Reign of George III. His Trials for Sedition, High Treason, &c. With his Most Celebrated Speeches in the House of Commons, on the Hustings, Letters, &c.* London, 1812.

"Theourgos." *Plain Arguments Advanced to Convince the Nation of the Impropriety of the Restrictions at Present Imposed on the Royal Family.* London, 1812.

1813

Goldsmith, Lewis. *Buonaparte, an Outlaw!!! An Appeal to the Germans, on the Necessity of Outlawing Buonaparte.* London, 1813.

Heald, W. M. *Moscow: An Ode: According to the Arrangement of the Ancient Greek.* London, 1813.

Playfair, William. *Political Portraits, in this New Æra; with Explanatory Notes—Historical and Biographical.* 2 vols. London, 1813.

The Vision of Napoleon, a Poem. Edinburgh, 1813.

1814

Bonaparte's Journey to Moscow. (In the Manner of John Gilpin.) London, [1814?].

Buonaparte's Pedigree, Including his Collateral Branches, and Great Military and State Officers; from the Most Authenticated Account, 4th ed. London, 1814.

Byron, Lord. *Ode to Napoleon Buonaparte.* London, 1814.

[Landor, Walter Savage], "Calvus." *Letters Addressed to Lord Liverpool, and the Parliament, on the Preliminaries of Peace.* London, 1814.

The Christian Conqueror; or, Moscow Burnt, and Paris Saved. London, 1814.

England's Triumph: Being an Account of the Rejoicings, &c. Which have Lately Taken Place in London and Elsewhere. Including the Restoration of Louis XVIII, the Proclamation of Peace, and the Visit of the Emperor of Russia, and the King of Prussia, &c. &c. &c. Containing Several Original Documents. London, 1814.

Eustace, John Chetwode. *A Letter from Paris, to George Petre, Esq.,* 4th ed. London, 1814.

Irwin, Eyles. *Napoleon: Or, the Vanity of Human Wishes. Part II.* London, 1814.

"Philo-Brutus." *Political Metamorphoses.* London, [1814].

"A Protestant Spectator." *The Territories of Popery Invaded, Exemplified in the Conduct of Napoleon Buonaparte towards the Church of Rome. Ironically and Seriously Considered. A Poem. With an Introduction and Explanatory Notes.* London, 1814.

"A Royal Arch Mason." *The Corsican's Downfall. The Rise, Name, Reign, and Final Downfall of Napolean, Alias Nicolais Buonaparte; Shown Most Clearly to have been Predicted by the Prophet Daniel 2,400 Years Ago, and by St. John the Evangelist, 1,700 Years Ago. . . .* Mansfield, [1814].

Skeeles, G. J. *The Recent Events in France Considered. A Sermon, Preached on July 7, 1814, being the Day Appointed for a General Thanksgiving to Almighty God, for the Blessed Restoration of Peace.* Bury St. Edmunds, [1814].

Wedgwood, R[alph]. *The Book of Remembrance: The Outline of an Almanack Constructed on the Ancient Cycles of Time*. London, 1814.

1815

Cobbold, Elizabeth. *Ode on the Victory of Waterloo*. Ipswich, 1815.

The Duke's Coat; Or, the Night after Waterloo: A Dramatick Anecdote . . . Interdicted by the Licenser of Plays. London, 1815.

Explanation of the View of the Interior of the City of Paris, now Exhibiting in the Large Circle, Barker's Panorama, Strand, near Surry-Street. N.p., 1815.

Faber, George Stanley. *Remarks on the Effusion of the Fifth Apocalyptic Vial, and the Late Extraordinary Restoration of the Imperial Revolutionary Government of France: To Which is Added a Critical Examination of Mr. Frere's Combined View of the Prophecies of Daniel, Esdras, and St. John*, 2nd ed. London, 1815.

Frere, James Hatley. *A Combined View of the Prophecies of Daniel, Esdras, and St. John, Shewing that all the Prophetic Writings are Formed upon One Plan*. London, 1815.

Godwin, William. *Letters of Verax, to the Editor of the Morning Chronicle, on the Question of a War to be Commenced for the Purpose of Putting an End to the Possession of the Supreme Power in France by Napoleon Bonaparte*. London, 1815.

Hankin, Edward. *Political Reflections, Addressed to the Allied Sovereigns, on the Re-entry of Napoleon Buonaparte into France, and his Usurpation of the Throne of the Bourbons*. London, 1815.

Hone, William. *Buonapartephobia. The Origin of Dr. Slop's Name*. Originally published 1815. London, 1820.

A Letter, &c. An Account of the Conspiracy and Conspirators of Napoleon Buonaparte, of its Motives, Plan, and Progress; with the Biographic Notices of the Known and Suspected Conspirators, for the Purpose of Enabling the British Public to Form Just Conclusions as to the Probable Result of his Objects and Enterprise. London, 1815.

Lewis, James Henry. *Lewis's Orations, on the Battle of Waterloo, and on the Rise and Fall of Buonaparte*. Contains *The Battle of Waterloo. An Oration on the Military Exploits of the Duke of Wellington. Delivered at the Pauls' Head, Cateaton Street, on Monday, 18th September, 1815*. And *The Rise and Fall of Buonaparte. An Oration, Extracted from the Actions of the Life of that Extraordinary Man*. London, 1815.

Maclaren, Archibald. *Retaliation; or, A Hour and a Half in Paris. A Musical Entertainment, Founded upon Facts. In Two Acts*. London, 1815.

"A Native of Edinburgh." *The Battle of Waterloo: A Poem*. Edinburgh, 1815.

Richardson, Charlotte Caroline. *Waterloo, A Poem, on the Late Victory*. London, [1815].

Scott, John. *A Visit to Paris in 1814; being a Review of the Moral, Political, Intellectual, and Social Condition of the French Capital*, 2nd ed. London, 1815.

Scott, Walter. *The Field of Waterloo; A Poem*. Edinburgh, 1815.

A Short Description of the Island of Elba, and Town of Porto-Ferrajo; Illustrative of the View now Exhibiting in Henry Aston Barker's Panorama, Leicester Square. N.p., 1815.

Walker, George. *The Battle of Waterloo. A Poem*. London, 1815.

Walker, W. S. *The Heroes of Waterloo. An Ode.* London, 1815.

Waterloo. An Heroic Poem. London, 1815.

Williams, Helen Maria. *Narrative of the Events Which have Taken Place in France, from the Landing of Napoleon Bonaparte, on the 1st of March, 1815, till the Restoration of Louis XVIII. With an Account of the Present State of Society and Public Opinion.* London, 1815.

1816

[Alison, Archibald, et al.], *Travels in France, during the Years 1814–15. Comprising a Residence at Paris during the Stay of the Allied Armies, and at Aix, at the Period of the Landing of Bonaparte,* 2nd ed. 2 vols. Edinburgh, 1816.

Barrett, Eaton Stannard. *The Talents Run Mad; or, Eighteen Hundred and Sixteen. A Satirical Poem. In Three Dialogues. With Notes.* London, 1816.

Boyce, Edmund. *The Second Usurpation of Buonaparte; or a History of the Causes, Progress and Termination of the Revolution in France in 1815: Particularly Comprising a Minute and Circumstantial Account of the Ever-memorable Victory of Waterloo.* 2 vols. London, 1816.

Buchan, David Home. *The Battle of Waterloo: A Poem,* 2nd ed. London, 1816.

Byron, Lord. *Childe Harold's Pilgrimage. Canto the Third.* London, 1816.

The Campaign of One Day: A Poem, in Two Cantos. London, 1816.

Cargill, John. *Battle of Waterloo; a Poem.* Cupar, 1816.

The Coach that Nap Ran From. An Epic Poem in Twelve Books. Illustrated with Twelve Coloured Engravings. Price One Shilling and Sixpence; or, Embellished with a Ticket of Admission to the Exhibition of Buonaparte's Military Carriage, at the London Museum. Price Two Shillings. London, 1816.

Davidson, Henry. *Waterloo, A Poem. With Notes.* Edinburgh, 1816.

A Description of the Costly and Curious Military Carriage of the Late Emperor of France, Taken on the Evening of the Battle of Waterloo; with its Superb and Curious Contents, as Purchased by Government, and now Exhibiting (by Permission) at the London Museum, Piccadilly; with the Circumstances of the Capture, Accurately Described, by Major Baron von Keller, by whom it was Taken and Brought to England. London, 1816.

Description of the Field of Battle, and Disposition of the Troops Engaged in the Action, Fought on the 18th of June, 1815, near Waterloo; Illustrative of the Representation of that Great Event, in the Panorama, Leicester-Square. N.p., 1816.

Description of the Series of Pictures, Painted by Order of the Late Emperor of France, under his own Inspection, to Commemorate the Principal Actions of his Life. Also, Original Portraits, Busts in Marble, Bronze and Or-moulu, Superb Fire Arms, Services of Gold Plate, and other Magnificent and Costly Effects of Napoleon Buonaparte; Collected at Considerable Expense from the Louvre, and the Palaces of St. Cloud and Malmaison, and now Exhibiting at the London Museum, Piccadilly. London, 1816.

Elmes, James. *Description of the New Village of Waterloo; Formed into a Limited Number of Allotments for Building, on a Most Enchanting and Salubrious Spot Contiguous to the Regent's Park, near Primrose Hill, in the County of Middlesex.* London, 1816.

Ettrick, William. *The Season and Time: Or, an Exposition of the Prophecies Which*

Relate to the Two Periods of Daniel Subsequent to the 1260 Years now Recently Expired. London, 1816.

[Hobhouse, John Cam], *The Substance of Some Letters, Written by an Englishman Resident at Paris during the Last Reign of the Emperor Napoleon. With an Appendix of Official Documents.* 2 vols. London, 1816. A second edition, with revisions, is published the same year.

Hone, William. *Interesting Particulars of Napoleon's Deportation for Life, to St. Helena. His Treatment and Mode of Living since his Arrival, a Variety of Facts and Anecdotes, and a Description of Mr. Balcombe's Estate—the Briars.* London, 1816.

The Parallel: Nebuchadnezzar and N. Buonaparte. A Sermon, Preached . . . in a Parish Church, Bordering upon Torbay. London [printed Exeter], [1816].

Scott, John. *Paris Revisited, in 1815, by Way of Brussels: Including a Walk over the Field of Battle at Waterloo.* Boston, Mass., 1816.

Scott, Walter. *Paul's Letters to his Kinsfolk,* 2nd ed. Edinburgh and London, 1816.

Southey, Robert. *The Poet's Pilgrimage to Waterloo.* London, 1816.

The Voice of the People, as to the Waterloo Monument, with Observations on its Principles and Objects, its Funds and Management, and the Beneficial Effects Which may be Derived from it. London, 1816.

Warden, William. *Letters Written on Board His Majesty's Ship the Northumberland, and at Saint Helena; in Which the Conduct and Conversations of Napoleon Buonaparte, and his Suite, during the Voyage, and the First Months of his Residence in that Island, are Faithfully Described and Related.* London, [1816/17].

1817

Authentic Memoirs of the Life of the Late Lamented Princess Charlotte; with Clear Statements Showing the Succession to the Crown, and the Probability of the Wife of Jerome Buonaparte becoming Queen, and her Son, Jerome Napoleon, being Prince of Wales, and Afterwards King of these Realms. London, 1817.

Baines, Edward. *History of the French Revolution, from the Breaking Out of the War in 1792, to the Restoration of a General Peace in 1815.* 2 vols. London, 1817.

Barnes, John. *A Tour through the Island of St. Helena; with Notices of its Geology, Mineralogy, Botany, &c. &c. Collected during a Residence of Twelve Years; with some Particulars Respecting the Arrival and Detention of Napoleon Buonaparte.* London, 1817.

Bentham, Jeremy. *Plan of Parliamentary Reform, in the Form of a Catechism, with Reasons for Each Article, with an Introduction, Shewing the Necessity of Radical, and the Inadequacy of Moderate, Reform.* London, 1817.

Bicheno, James. *The Fulfilment of Prophecy Farther Illustrated by the Signs of the Times; or, an Attempt to Ascertain the Probable Issues of the Recent Restoration of the Old Dynasties; of the Revival of Popery; and of the Present Mental Ferment in Europe: as Likewise, how far Great Britain is Likely to Share in the Calamities by Which Divine Providence will Accomplish the Final Overthrow of the Kingdoms of the Roman Monarchy.* London, 1817.

[Croly, George], *Paris in 1815. A Poem.* London, 1817.

Letters from the Cape of Good Hope, in Reply to Mr. Warden; with Extracts from the Great Work now Compiling for Publication under the Inspection of Napoleon, 3rd ed. London, 1817.

Morgan, Lady. *France*, 2nd ed. 2 vols. London, 1817.

[Santini, Jean Noel], "Santine." *An Appeal to the British Nation on the Treatment Experienced by Napoleon Buonaparte in the Island of St. Helena.* London, 1817.

1818

Hornn, Jean. *The Narrative of Jean Hornn, Military Coachman to the Emperor Napoleon. Containing his Recollections of that Memorable Character, during the Ten Years in Which he was in his Personal Service,* 3rd ed. Newcastle, 1818.

Letters from the Island of St. Helena, Exposing the Unnecessary Severity Exercised towards Napoleon: With an Appendix of Important Official Documents. London, 1818.

Observations on Lord Bathurst's Speech in the House of Peers, on March 18, 1817. Sent Sealed to Sir Hudson Lowe, to the Address of Lord Liverpool, on the 7th day of October, 1817, 2nd ed. London, 1818.

Staël, Germaine de. *Considérations sur la révolution française.* 2 vols. Originally published 1818. Paris, 1862.

1819

Buonaparte, an Epistle in Metre from St. Helena; to Which are Added, 'Sauve qui peut!', Waterloo, &c. Holt, Norfolk, 1819.

Davenport, Allen. *The Kings, or, Legitimacy Unmasked, A Satirical Poem.* London, 1819.

Hazlitt, William. *Political Essays.* London, 1819.

Holmes, James Ivory. *The Fulfilment of the Revelation of St. John Displayed, from the Commencement of the Prophecy, A.D. 96, to the Battle of Waterloo, A.D. 1815: Containing a Refutation of the Systems Maintained by Mr. Faber, Mr. Cuninghame, and the Roman Catholic Author, Pastorini, in their Interpretations of this Prophecy.* London, 1819.

[Hook, Theodore Edward], *Facts, Illustrative of the Treatment of Napoléon Buonaparte in Saint Helena. Being the Result of Minute Inquiries and Personal Research in that Island.* London, 1819.

Letters from the Count de Las Casas [sic] . . . *To Which is Prefixed, a Copious Introduction; and the Whole Interspersed with Explanatory Notes.* London, 1819.

O'Meara, Barry E. *An Exposition of Some of the Transactions, that have Taken Place at St. Helena, since the Appointment of Sir Hudson Lowe as Governor of that Island; in Answer to an Anonymous Pamphlet, entitled, 'Facts Illustrative of the Treatment of Napoleon Bonaparte,' &c. Corroborated by Various Official Documents, Correspondence, &c.,* 2nd ed. London, 1819.

Whately, Richard. *Historic Doubts Relative to Napoleon Bonaparte.* Edited by Ralph S. Pomeroy. Originally published 1819. Berkeley, 1985.

1820s

Hegel, G. W. F. *Lectures on the Philosophy of World History, Introduction.* Translated by H. B. Nisbet. Originally delivered 1820s. Cambridge, 1975.

1821

Ireland, W[illiam]. H[enry]. *The Last Will and Testament of Napoleon Bonaparte, Late Emperor of the French, &c. &c. As Written with his own Hand, and Proved in the Prerogative-Court, Doctors' Commons; with a Prefatory Address and Copious Notes, Explanatory of Many Interesting Points Adverted to in this Singularly Curious Document.* London, [1821].

1822

Barton, Bernard. *Napoleon, and Other Poems.* London, 1822.
Bloomfield, Robert. *May Day with the Muses.* London, 1822.
Colton, C. *The Conflagration of Moscow: A Poem,* 4th ed. London, 1822.
Ireland, W. H. *France for the Last Seven Years; or, The Bourbons.* London, 1822.
Goldsmith, Lewis. *Observations on the Appointment of the Right Hon. Geo. Canning to the Foreign Department.* London, 1822.
O'Meara, Barry E. *Napoleon in Exile; or, A Voice from St. Helena. The Opinions and Reflections of Napoleon on the Most Important Events of his Life and Government. In his own Words,* 4th ed. 2 vols. London, 1822.

1823

Hazlitt, William. *Liber Amoris, or the New Pygmalion.* London, 1823.
Ireland, William Henry. *The Life of Napoleon Bonaparte.* 4 vols. London, 1828. Originally published serially, 1823–8.
The Sextuple Alliance. Glasgow, 1823.

1824

Amherst, J. H. *The Battle of Waterloo: A Grand Military Melo-Drama in Three Acts.* London, [1824].
[De] Mounteney, [Thomas J.] Barclay. *An Historical Inquiry into the Principal Circumstances and Events Relative to the Late Emperor Napoleon; in Which are Investigated the Charges Brought against the Government and Conduct of that Eminent Individual.* London, 1824.

1825

Amherst, J. H. *Napoleon Buonaparte's Invasion of Russia, or, The Conflagration of Moscow: A Grand Military and Equestrian Spectacle in Three Acts.* London, [1825].
Mackenrot, Frances. *A Letter to the Rt. Hon. Robert Peel, M.P., His Majesty's Secretary of State for the Home Department, upon the Detention of Anthony Mackenrot in New Bethlem Hospital, St. George's Fields.* Southwark, [1825].

1826

Chateaubriand, François-René, vicomte de. Preface to *Essai historique, politique et moral, sur les révolutions anciennes et modernes.* In *Oeuvres complètes,* ed. Ladvocat, 28 vols. [Paris, 1826].
Reid, William Hamilton. *Memoirs of the Public and Private Life of Napoleon Bonaparte: With Copious Historical Illustrations and Original Anecdotes.* London, 1826. A two-volume edition, without Reid's name on the title page, is published the next year.

1827

Scott, Walter. *The Life of Napoleon Buonaparte, Emperor of the French. With a Preliminary View of the French Revolution.* 9 vols. Edinburgh, 1827.

1828

Hazlitt, William. *The Life of Napoleon Buonaparte.* Originally published 1828–30. In *The Complete Works of William Hazlitt*, ed. P. P. Howe. Vols. XIII–XV. London, 1930–4.

1829

Lockhart, John Gibson. *The History of Napoleon Buonaparte.* Originally published 1829. London, 1906.

1830s (in chronological order)

Macaulay, Thomas Babington. *Napoleon and the Restoration of the Bourbons.* Edited by Joseph Hamburger. New York, 1977. The completed portion of Macaulay's projected *History of France, from the Restoration of the Bourbons to the Accession of Louis Philippe;* begun 1830–31 and abandoned.
Description of Haydon's Picture of Napoleon Musing at St. Helena; With Sketches of his Bed at Fontainbleau; Column of the English Garden, &c. &c. London, 1831.
A Family Tour through South Holland; up the Rhine; and across the Netherlands, to Ostend. London, 1831.
Lacy, M. Rophino. *Programme of the New Grand Historical Military Spectacle, (in Seven Parts), called Napoleon Buonaparte, Captain of Artillery, General and First Consul, Emperor and Exile.* London, 1831.
Carlyle, Thomas. *Sartor Resartus.* Originally published 1833–34. In *A Carlyle Reader: Selections from the Writings of Thomas Carlyle*, ed. G. B. Tennyson. Cambridge, 1984.
Disraeli, Benjamin. *The Revolutionary Epick.* London, 1834.
[Sainsbury, John]. *Catalogue of a Collection of Cameos; Marble Busts; Statues in Gold . . . Collected on the Continent and in England, during the Last Fifteen Years.* 1834.
A Hand-book for Travellers on the Continent: Being a Guide through Holland, Belgium, Prussia, and Northern Germany, and along the Rhine, from Holland to Switzerland, 2nd ed. London, 1838.
De Mounteney, [Thomas J.] Barclay. *The Case of a Détenu.* London, 1838.
Addison, Henry R. *A Rough Sketch of the Field of Waterloo.* Brussels, 1839.

1840s and after (in chronological order)

Carlyle, Thomas. *On Heroes, Hero-Worship and the Heroic in History.* Lectures given 1837–40. Published 1841. Ed. Carl Niemeyer. Lincoln, 1966.
Bussey, George Moir. *History of Napoleon.* 2 vols. London, 1840.
Sainsbury, John. *Sketch of the Napoleon Museum. The History of France Illustrated from Louis XIV to the End of the Reign and Death of the Emperor.* London, 1840.
Horne, R. H. *The History of Napoleon.* 2 vols. London, 1840–1.

The Military Carriage of Napoleon Buonaparte, Taken after the Battle of Waterloo; Together with its Superb and Curious Contents and Appendages; Now Exhibiting at the Bazaar, Baker Street, Portman Square. . . . Copy of Mr. Bullock's Original Catalogue. London, 1843.

Sainsbury, John. *Particulars of the Exhibition now Open at the Egyptian Hall, Piccadilly, from Ten till Dusk. Catalogue of the Napoleon Museum or, Illustrated History of Europe, from Louis XIV to the End of the Reign and Death of the Emperor Napoleon*, 2nd ed. London, 1843.

——. *The Napoleon Museum. The History of France Illustrated. From Louis XIV to the End of the Reign and Death of the Emperor. Comprising Marbles, Bronzes, Carvings, Gems, Decorations, Medallions, Drawings, Miniatures, Portraits, Pictures, Prints, Vignettes, State-Papers and Manuscripts, Coins, Medals, Books, Etc.* London, 1845.

Davenport, Allen. *The Life and Literary Pursuits of Allen Davenport.* London, 1845.

Napoleon Buonaparte: Sketches from his History. Adapted for the Young. London, [1846?].

Thackeray, William Makepeace. *Vanity Fair: A Novel without a Hero.* Originally published 1847–8. Oxford, 1983.

Walker, John. *Napoleon! Or, The Emperor and the Soldier! A Petite Drama, in one act.* London, [1840s].

Faber, G. S. *The Revival of the French Emperorship Anticipated from the Necessity of Prophecy.* Originally published 1852. 5th ed. London, 1859.

A History of the Sudden and Terrible Invasion of England by the French, in the Month of May, 1852. London, [1852].

Barham, R. H. Dalton. *The Life and Remains of Theodore Edward Hook*, new ed. London, 1853.

Whittemore, W. Meynell. *The Seventh Head: Or, Louis Napoleon Foreshadowed by Prophecy.* London, 1853.

Mayer, Joseph. *A Catalogue of the Drawings, Miniatures, Cameos, and Other Objects of Art, Illustrative of the Bonaparte Family, and the Principal Persons Connected with the Republic and Empire of France, Now in the Collection of John Mather, Esq., of Mount Pleasant, Liverpool: Arranged, and Illustrated by a Short History of that Eventful Period.* Liverpool, 1854.

[Phillips, Charles]. *Napoleon the Third.* London, 1854.

Rogers, Benjamin Bickley. *Napoleon III and England: An Enquiry.* Oxford, 1855.

France and her Emperor Considered Morally & Politically. London, 1860.

Veritas, Ernst. *Dedicated to the Rifle Volunteers of England: The Inheritance of Napoleon the Third and the Legacy of Peter the Great.* London, 1860.

Baxter, Rev. M. [Michael Paget]. *Louis Napoleon the Infidel Antichrist Predicted in Prophecy.* Toronto, 1861.

Bennett, W. C. *Poems.* London, 1862.

Hildebrand, G. B. *The Application of Prophecy to the Crimean War.* London, 1864.

Dickens, Charles. *Our Mutual Friend.* Originally published 1864–5. Harmondsworth, 1998.

Thiers, Adolphe. *Histoire du consulat et de l'empire.* Paris, 1874.

Hardy, Thomas. *The Return of the Native.* Originally published 1878. New York, 1999.

Bamford, Samuel. *Bamford's Passages in the Life of a Radical and Early Days.* 2 vols. London, 1893.

Conan Doyle, Arthur. "The Six Napoleons," in *The Return of Sherlock Holmes*. London, 1905.

Collected Editions

Arnold, Matthew. *Complete Prose Works*. Edited by R. H. Super. 11 vols. Ann Arbor, 1962.
Bagehot, Walter. *Bagehot's Historical Essays*. Edited by Norman St. John-Stevas. New York, 1966.
Lord Byron. *The Complete Poetical Works: Lord Byron*. Edited by Jerome J. McGann. 7 vols. Oxford, 1980–93.
Cobbett, William. *Selections from Cobbett's Political Works: Being a Complete Abridgment of the 100 Volumes Which Comprise the Writings of "Porcupine" and the "Weekly Political Register."* Edited by John M. and James P. Cobbett. 6 vols. London, [1835?].
Coleridge, Samuel Taylor. *The Collected Works of Samuel Taylor Coleridge*. Edited by Kathleen Coburn. Vol. III (in three parts), *Essays on His Times in the Morning Post and the Courier*. Edited by David V. Erdman. Princeton, 1969—).
Hazlitt, William. *The Complete Works of William Hazlitt*. Edited by P. P. Howe. 21 vols. London, 1930–4.
Keats, John. *The Poems of John Keats*. Edited by Jack Stillinger. London, 1978.
Macaulay, Thomas Babington. *Critical and Historical Essays*. 2 vols. London, 1907.
Moore, Thomas. *The Poetical Works of Thomas Moore*. 10 vols. London, 1840–1.
Rossetti, Dante Gabriel. *The Essential Rossetti*. Edited by John Hollander. New York, 1990.
Ruskin, John. *The Works of John Ruskin*. Edited by E. T. Cook and Alexander Wedderburn. 39 vols. London, 1903–12.
Shelley, Percy Bysshe. *The Complete Poetical Works of Percy Bysshe Shelley*. Edited by George Edward Woodberry. 4 vols. Boston, 1898.
Wordsworth, William. *William Wordsworth: The Poems*. Edited by John O. Hayden. 2 vols. New Haven and London, 1981.
——. *The Prelude*. Edited by J. C. Maxwell. Harmondsworth, 1971.

Electronic Databases

Literature Online. ProQuest Information and Learning Company. Internet database: http://lion.chadwyck.com.
Project for American and French Research on the Treasury of the French Language (ARTFL). University of Chicago. Internet database: http://humanities.uchicago.edu/ARTFL/ARTFL.html.

Letters, Diaries, Memoirs

Arnold, Matthew. *Letters of Matthew Arnold, 1848–1888*, 2nd ed. Edited by George W. E. Russell. 2 vols. London, 1901.

Bamford, Samuel. *Bamford's Passages in the Life of a Radical and Early Days.* Edited and introduced by Henry Dunckley. 2 vols. London, 1893.

Bentham, Jeremy. *The Correspondence of Jeremy Bentham.* Edited by Timothy L. S. Sprigge et al. London, 1968—.

Bowood Papers. Edited by the Earl of Kerry. *The First Napoleon. Some Unpublished Documents from the Bowood Papers.* London, 1925.

Burke, Edmund. *The Writings and Speeches of Edmund Burke.* Edited by Paul Langford. Oxford, 1980—.

Byron, Lord. *Byron's Letters and Journals.* Edited by Leslie A. Marchand. 12 vols. Cambridge, Mass., 1973–82.

——. *Lady Blessington's Conversations of Lord Byron.* Edited and introduced by Ernest J. Lovell, Jr. Originally published in *New Monthly Magazine,* 1832–3, then in book form 1834. Princeton, 1969.

Carlyle, Thomas and Jane. *The Collected Letters of Thomas and Jane Welsh Carlyle.* Edited by Charles Richard Sanders. Durham, NC, 1970—.

Coleridge, Samuel Taylor. *Collected Letters of Samuel Taylor Coleridge.* Edited by Earl Leslie Griggs. 6 vols. Oxford, 1956–71.

Croker, John Wilson. *The Croker Papers. The Correspondence and Diaries of the late Right Honourable John Wilson Croker, LL.D., F.R.S., Secretary to the Admiralty from 1809 to 1830,* 2nd ed. Edited by Louis J. Jennings. 3 vols. London, 1885.

Edgeworth, Maria. *Letters from England, 1813–1844.* Edited by Christina Colvin. Oxford, 1971.

Farington, Joseph. *The Farington Diary.* Edited by James Greig. 8 vols. London, 1922–8.

George IV. *The Letters of King George IV 1812–1830.* Edited by A. Aspinall. 3 vols. Cambridge, 1938.

Haydon, Benjamin Robert. *Benjamin Robert Haydon: Correspondence and Table-Talk. With a Memoir by his son, Frederic Wordsworth Haydon.* 2 vols. London, 1876.

——. *The Diary of Benjamin Robert Haydon.* Edited by Willard Bissell Pope. 5 vols. Cambridge, 1960–3.

Horner, Francis. *The Horner Papers: Selections from the Letters and Miscellaneous Writings of Francis Horner, M.P. 1795–1817.* Edited by Kenneth Bourne and William Banks Taylor. Edinburgh, 1994.

Hunt, Leigh. *The Correspondence of Leigh Hunt.* Edited by Thornton Leigh Hunt. 2 vols. London, 1862.

——. *Leigh Hunt's Political and Occasional Essays.* Edited by Lawrence Huston Houtchens and Carolyn Washburn Houtchens. New York, 1962.

Lovett, William. *The Life and Struggles of William Lovett, in his Pursuit of Bread, Knowledge, and Freedom; with some Short Account of the Different Associations he Belonged to, and of the Opinions he Entertained.* London, 1876.

Macaulay, Thomas Babington. *The Letters of Thomas Babington Macaulay.* Edited by Thomas Pinney. 6 vols. Cambridge, 1974–81.

Moore, Thomas. *The Poetical Works of Thomas Moore.* 10 vols. London, 1840–1.

Piozzi, Hester Lynch (Thrale). *The Piozzi Letters. Correspondence of Hester Lynch Piozzi, 1784–1821 (formerly Mrs. Thrale).* Edited by Edward A. Bloom and Lillian D. Bloom. Newark, 1989—.

——. *Thraliana: The Diary of Mrs. Hester Lynch Thrale (Later Mrs. Piozzi), 1776–1809,* 2nd ed. Edited by Katharine C. Balderston. 2 vols. Oxford, 1951.

Priestley, Joseph. *Life and Correspondence of Joseph Priestley.* Edited by John Towill Rutt. 2 vols. London, 1831–2.

Robinson, Henry Crabb. *Diary, Reminiscences, and Correspondence of Henry Crabb Robinson, Barrister-at-Law, F.S.A.*, 3rd ed. Edited by Thomas Sadler. 2 vols. London, 1872. Reprint, New York, 1967.

Shelley, Percy Bysshe. *Letters*. Edited by Frederick L. Jones. 2 vols. Oxford, 1964.

Southey, Robert. *The Life and Correspondence of Robert Southey*. Edited by Charles Cuthbert Southey. 6 vols. London, 1849–50.

——. *Journal of a Tour in the Netherlands in the Autumn of 1815*. Boston, 1902.

——. *New Letters of Robert Southey*. Edited by Kenneth Curry. 2 vols. New York, 1965.

Wordsworth, William and Dorothy. *The Letters of William and Dorothy Wordsworth*, 2nd ed. Edited by Ernest de Selingcourt. 8 vols. Oxford, 1967–93.

Manuscript Collections

British Library

Lord Broughton (John Cam Hobhouse) correspondence.
Supplementary Hardwicke Papers.
Warren Hastings Papers.
Holland House Papers.
Lord Liverpool Papers.
Nicholas Vansittart Papers.
William Windham Papers.
Arthur Young Papers.
Lord Chamberlain's Office Papers (plays submitted to the Lord Chamberlain's office since 1824).

Public Record Office

CO [Colonial Office] 247/17, CO 247/21, CO 247/35. Papers relating to Sir Hudson Lowe and Barry O'Meara.
FO [Foreign Office] 83/23. On Lewis Goldsmith's assassination proposal.
FO 97/169. Goldsmith's dispatches from France.
FO 97/205. Papers (1846–59) relating to the proposed French purchase of the land surrounding Napoleon's former tomb on St. Helena.

Houghton Library, Harvard University

Benjamin Robert Haydon Papers.

Huntington Library

John Larpent plays (submitted to the Lord Chamberlain's Office to 1824).

Periodical Publications

Daily and Weekly Newspapers

Antigallican Monitor and Anti-Corsican Chronicle (later *The British Monitor*)
Argus (Paris)

Black Dwarf
Champion: A London Weekly Journal
Cobbett's Annual Register (becomes Cobbett's Weekly Political Register in 1804)
Courier
Examiner
Independent Whig
Morning Chronicle
Morning Post
Mr. Redhead Yorke's Weekly Political Review
Oracle
Porcupine
Sherwin's Weekly Political Register
Statesman
Times
True Briton

Magazines

Annual Review
British Critic
Eclectic Review
Edinburgh Review
European Magazine, and London Review
Fraser's
Gentleman's Magazine
Monthly Magazine
Monthly Review
New Monthly Magazine and Literary Journal
Quarterly Review
Satirist
Scots Magazine, and Edinburgh Literary Miscellany
Scourge, or, Monthly Expositor of Imposture and Folly

Collections of Periodical Writing

Cobbett's Spirit of the Public Journals . . . For the Year 1804. Vol. I (only volume
    published). London, 1805.
The Spirit of the Public Journals . . . Being an Impartial Selection of the Most Ingen-
    ious Essays and Jeux d'esprits that Appear in the Newspapers and Other Publi-
    cations. With Explanatory Notes and Anecdotes of Many of the Persons Alluded to.
    London.

Almanacs

Merlinus Liberatus
Vox Stellarum

Parliamentary Debates

Cobbett's Parliamentary Debates, During the . . . Session of the . . . Parliament of the
    United Kingdom of Great Britain and Ireland. London, 1804–12.

The Parliamentary Debates from the Year 1803 to the Present Time. London, 1812—.

The Parliamentary History of England from the Earliest Period to the Year 1803. London, 1806–20.

Miscellaneous Publications

Broadsides, Songs, and Poems

Individual broadsides, songs, and caricatures are not separately listed. I list the three volumes that contain the British Library's large collection of 1,803 broadsides. The Houghton Library holds many broadsides not in the British Library collection, and the New York Public Library a few. Though many titles are duplicated in the several collections, endnotes cite only one location for each; my default citation is BL, since the British Library's collection is the largest.

The BL and Houghton volumes also contain songs of the period. Some later songs discussed in chapter 8 are separately listed in the BL catalogue. Others are in the Rare Book Library at the University of Pennsylvania.

A number of invasion broadsides are reproduced in Frank J. Klingberg and Sigurd B. Hustvedt, eds., *The Warning Drum: The British Home Front Faces Napoleon; Broadsides of 1803* (Berkeley, 1944). A valuable anthology of contemporary verse is Betty T. Bennett's *British War Poetry in the Age of Romanticism: 1793–1815* (New York, 1976).

Broadside Collections, British Library.
  "Broadsides Etc. Relating to the Expected Invasion of England by Bonaparte."
  "Loyal and Patriotic Hand-Bills, Songs, Addresses, Etc. on the Threatened Invasion of Great-Britain by Buonaparte."
  "Squibs on Buonaparte's Threatened Invasion."

Broadside Collections, Houghton Library, Harvard University.
  "Collection of broadsides" (*p FB8 N1627 Z803c).
  "Napoleon threatened invasion" (*p FB8 N1627 Z803n).

John Johnson Collection, Bodleian Library, Oxford University.

Caricatures

The British Library's unparalleled collection of British political caricatures, described in the *Catalogue of Political and Personal Satires Preserved in the Department of Prints and Drawings in the British Museum*, is widely accessible in its microfilm version. The Houghton Library, in addition, owns a good many Napoleonic caricatures not held by the British Library.

II. Secondary Works

Alexander, R. S. *Napoleon*. London, 2001.
Altick, Richard. *The English Common Reader: A Social History of the Mass Reading Public, 1800–1900*. Chicago, 1957.
Anderson, Benedict. *Imagined Communities*, rev. ed. London, 1991.

Andrews, Stuart. *The British Periodical Press and the French Revolution, 1789–99.* Basingstoke, 2000.

Aspinall, Arthur. *Politics and the Press, 1780–1850.* London, 1949.

Bainbridge, Simon. *Napoleon and English Romanticism.* Cambridge, 1995.

Bann, Stephen. *Romanticism and the Rise of History.* New York, 1995.

Barker, Hannah. *Newspapers, Politics, and Public Opinion in Late Eighteenth-Century England.* Oxford, 1998.

Barrell, John. *Imagining the King's Death: Figurative Treason, Fantasies of Regicide, 1793–1796.* Oxford, 2000.

Bate, Jonathan. *Shakespearean Constitutions: Politics, Theatre, Criticism, 1730–1830.* Oxford, 1989.

Baylen, Joseph O., and Norbert J. Gossman, eds. *Biographical Dictionary of Modern British Radicals.* Vol. I, *1770–1830.* 3 vols. Sussex, 1979.

Beedell, A. V. "John Reeves's Prosecution for a Seditious Libel, 1795–6: A Study in Political Cynicism," *Historical Journal* 36 (1993): 799–824.

Behrendt, Stephen C. *Royal Mourning and Regency Culture: Elegies and Memorials of Princess Charlotte.* New York, 1997.

Belchem, John. *"Orator" Hunt: Henry Hunt and English Working-Class Radicalism.* Oxford, 1985.

Ben-Israel, Hedva. *English Historians on the French Revolution.* Cambridge, 1968.

Bindman, David, et al. *The Shadow of the Guillotine: Britain and the French Revolution.* London, 1989.

Black, Jeremy. *Natural and Necessary Enemies: Anglo-French Relations in the Eighteenth Century.* London, 1986.

——. *The English Press in the Eighteenth Century.* London, 1987.

Blackburn, Julia. *The Emperor's Last Island: A Journey to St. Helena.* London, 1991.

Blagden, Cyprian. *The Stationers' Company: A History, 1403–1959.* Stanford, 1960.

Brewer, John. "Theater and Counter-Theater in Georgian Politics: The Mock Elections at Garrat," *Radical History Review* 22 (Winter 1979–80): 7–40.

Broadley, A. M. *Napoleon in Caricature, 1795–1821.* 2 vols. London, 1911.

Bryant, Arthur. *The Years of Endurance, 1793–1802.* London, 1942.

——. *The Years of Victory, 1802–1812.* London, 1944.

Burrow, J. W. *A Liberal Descent: Victorian Historians and the English Past.* Cambridge, 1981.

Butler, Marilyn. *Romantics, Rebels and Reactionaries: English Literature and its Background, 1760–1830.* Oxford, 1981.

Capp, Bernard. *Astrology and the Popular Press: English Almanacs 1500–1800.* London, 1979.

Christie, Ian R. *Stress and Stability in Late Eighteenth-Century Britain: Reflections on the British Avoidance of Revolution.* Oxford, 1984.

Clark, J. C. D. *English Society, 1660–1832: Religion, Ideology, and Politics during the Ancien Regime,* 2nd ed. Cambridge, 2000.

——. "Protestantism, Nationalism, and National Identity, 1660–1832," *Historical Journal* 43 (2000): 249–76

Clive, John. "Macaulay and the French Revolution." In *The French Revolution and British Culture,* ed. Ceri Crossley and Ian Small, 103–22. Oxford, 1989.

Colley, Linda. "The Apotheosis of George III: Loyalty, Royalty and the British Nation, 1760–1820," *Past and Present* 102 (Feb. 1984): 94–129.

——. "Radical Patriotism in Eighteenth-Century England." In *Patriotism: The*

Making and Unmaking of British National Identity, ed. Raphael Samuel, I: 169–87. London, 1989.

——. *Britons: Forging the Nation, 1707–1837*. New Haven and London, 1992.

——. "The Reach of the State, the Appeal of the Nation: Mass Arming and Political Culture in the Napoleonic Wars." In *An Imperial State at War: Britain from 1689 to 1815*, ed. Lawrence Stone, 165–84. London, 1994.

Collins, Marcus. "The Fall of the English Gentleman: The National Character in Decline, c. 1918–1970," *Historical Research* 187 (Feb. 2002): 90–111.

Connor, Walker. "When is a Nation?" *Ethnic and Racial Studies* 13 (1990): 92–100.

Cookson, J. E. *The Friends of Peace: Anti-War Liberalism in England, 1793–1815*. Cambridge, 1982.

——. "The English Volunteer Movement of the French Wars, 1793–1815: Some Contexts," *Historical Journal* 32 (1989): 867–91.

——. *The British Armed Nation, 1793–1815*. Oxford, 1997.

Cottrell, Stella M. Ní Ghallchóir. "The Devil on Two Sticks: Franco-phobia in 1803." In *Patriotism: The Making and Unmaking of British National Identity*, ed. Raphael Samuel, I: 259–74. London, 1989.

——. "English Views of France and the French, 1789–1815." D.Phil. thesis, Oxford University, 1990.

Cronin, Vincent. *Napoleon*. Originally published London, 1971; Fontana, 1990.

Crossley, Ceri, and Ian Small, eds. *The French Revolution and British Culture*. Oxford, 1989.

Curran, Stuart. "The Political Prometheus," *Studies in Romanticism* 25 (Fall 1986): 429–55.

Day-Hickman, Barbara Ann. *Napoleonic Art: Nationalism and the Spirit of Rebellion in France (1815–1848)*. Newark, Delaware, 1999.

Deane, Seamus. *The French Revolution and Enlightenment in England, 1789–1832*. Cambridge, 1988.

Dickinson, H. T. "The Eighteenth-Century Debate on the 'Glorious Revolution,'" *History* 61 (1976): 28–45.

——. *British Radicalism and the French Revolution, 1789–1815*. Oxford, 1985.

——. *Caricatures and the Constitution 1760–1832*. Cambridge, 1986.

——. ed. *Britain and the French Revolution, 1789–1815*. Basingstoke, 1989.

——. "Popular Conservatism and Militant Loyalism, 1789–1815." In *Britain and the French Revolution, 1789–1815*, ed. Dickinson, 103–26. Basingstoke, 1989.

——. "Popular Loyalism in Britain in the 1790s." In *The Transformation of Political Culture: England and Germany in the Late Eighteenth Century*, ed. Eckhart Hellmuth, 503–34. Oxford, 1990.

Dinwiddy, J. R. "Interpretations of Anti-Jacobinism." In *The French Revolution and British Popular Politics*, ed. Mark Philp, 38–49. Cambridge, 1991.

——. *Radicalism and Reform in Britain, 1780–1850*. London, 1992.

Donald, Diana. *The Age of Caricature: Satirical Prints in the Reign of George III*. New Haven and London, 1996.

Dozier, Robert R. *For King, Constitution, and Country: The English Loyalists and the French Revolution*. Lexington, 1983.

Duffy, Michael. *The Englishman and the Foreigner*. Cambridge, 1986.

Dyck, Ian. *William Cobbett and Rural Popular Culture*. Cambridge, 1992.

Eagles, Robin. *Francophilia in English Society, 1748–1815*. Manchester, 2000.

Eglin, John. *Venice Transfigured: The Myth of Venice in British Culture, 1660–1797*. Basingstoke, 2001.

Elliott, Marianne. "The 'Despard Conspiracy' Reconsidered," *Past and Present* 75 (May 1977): 46–61.

———. *Partners in Revolution: The United Irishmen and France*. New Haven and London, 1982.

Emsley, Clive. *British Society and the French Wars, 1793–1815*. London, 1979.

Epstein, James A. *Radical Expression: Political Language, Ritual, and Symbol in England, 1790–1850*. New York, 1994.

Evans, Eric. "Englishness and Britishness: National Identities, c. 1790–c. 1870." In *Uniting the Kingdom? The Making of British History*, ed. Alexander Grant and Keith J. Stringer, 223–43. London, 1995.

Finer, S. E. *The Life and Times of Sir Edwin Chadwick*. London, 1952.

Franklin, Alexandra, and Mark Philp. *Napoleon and the Invasion of Britain*. Oxford, 2003.

Friedman, Barton R. *Fabricating History: English Writers on the French Revolution*. Princeton, 1988.

Fruchtman, Jack. "The Apocalyptic Politics of Richard Price and Joseph Priestley," *Transactions of the American Philosophical Society* 73:4 (1983): 1–121.

Garrett, Clarke. *Respectable Folly: Millenarians and the French Revolution in France and England*. Baltimore, 1975.

George, M. Dorothy, ed. *Catalogue of Political and Personal Satires Preserved in the Department of Prints and Drawings in the British Museum*. Vols. VII–IX. 11 vols. London, 1942–49.

———. *English Political Caricature: A Study of Opinion and Propaganda*. 2 vols. Oxford, 1959.

Geyl, Pieter. *Napoleon, For and Against*. Translated by Olive Renier. New Haven and London, 1949.

Gilmartin, Kevin. *Print Politics: The Press and Radical Opposition in Early Nineteenth-Century England*. Cambridge, 1996.

Goodwin, Albert. *The Friends of Liberty: The English Democratic Movement in the Age of the French Revolution*. Cambridge, 1979.

Green, Daniel. *Great Cobbett: The Noblest Agitator*. London, 1983.

Greenfeld, Liah. *Nationalism: Five Roads to Modernity*. Cambridge, Mass., 1992.

Hampson, Norman. *The Perfidy of Albion: French Perceptions of England during the French Revolution*. Basingstoke, 1998.

Harling, Philip. "The Duke of York Affair (1809) and the Complexities of War-Time Patriotism," *Historical Journal* 39 (Dec. 1996): 963–84.

———. "Leigh Hunt's *Examiner* and the Language of Patriotism," *English Historical Review* 111 (1996): 1159–81.

———. "William Hazlitt and Radical Journalism," *Romanticism* 3 (1997): 53–65

Harris, Eileen. "Sir John Soane's Library: 'O Books! Ye Monuments of Mind,'" *Apollo*, n.s., 131 (April 1990): 242–7.

Harrison, J. F. C. *The Second Coming: Popular Millenarianism, 1780–1850*. New Brunswick, 1979.

———. "Thomas Paine and Millenarian Radicalism." In *Citizen of the World: Essays on Thomas Paine*, ed. Ian Dyck, 73–85. New York, 1988.

Hastings, Adrian. *The Construction of Nationhood: Ethnicity, Religion and Nationalism.* Cambridge, 1997.

Hill, Christopher. "The Norman Yoke." In *Puritanism and Revolution: Studies in Interpretation of the English Revolution of the 17th Century,* 50–122. Originally published 1958; New York, 1964.

Hilton, Boyd. *The Age of Atonement: The Influence of Evangelicalism on Social and Economic Thought, 1785–1865.* Oxford, 1988.

Hobsbawm, E. J. *Nations and Nationalism since 1780: Programme, Myth, Reality.* Cambridge, 1990.

Hobsbawm, E. J., and Joan Wallach Scott. "Political Shoemakers," *Past and Present* 89 (Nov. 1980): 86–114.

—— and Terence Ranger, eds. *The Invention of Tradition.* Cambridge, 1983.

Hole, Robert. "English Sermons and Tracts as Media of Debate on the French Revolution, 1789–99." In *The French Revolution and British Popular Politics,* ed. Mark Philp, 18–37. Cambridge, 1991.

Holmes, Richard. *Shelley: The Pursuit.* Originally published 1974; London, 1987.

Hone, J. Ann. *For the Cause of Truth: Radicalism in London, 1796–1821.* Oxford, 1982.

Hopkins, James K. *A Woman to Deliver Her People: Joanna Southcott and English Millenarianism in an Era of Revolution.* Austin, 1982.

Houghton, Walter, ed. *The Wellesley Index to Victorian Periodicals, 1824–1900.* 5 vols. Toronto, 1966–89.

Hyman, Paula E. *The Jews of Modern France.* Berkeley and Los Angeles, 1998.

James, Louis. "Inverted Emblems for Albion: Wellington and Napoleon on Stage." In *Patriotism: The Making and Unmaking of British National Identity,* ed. Raphael Samuel, vol. III, 243–51. London, 1989.

Jenks, Timothy. "Contesting the Hero: The Funeral of Admiral Lord Nelson," *Journal of British Studies* 39 (2000): 422–53.

Jones, Stanley. *Hazlitt: A Life, from Winterslow to Frith Street.* Oxford, 1989.

Jupp, Peter. *Lord Grenville, 1759–1834.* Oxford, 1985.

Kelly, Gary. *Women, Writing, and Revolution, 1790–1827.* Oxford, 1993.

Kinnaird, John. *William Hazlitt: Critic of Power.* New York, 1978.

Kumar, Krishan. *The Making of English National Identity.* Cambridge, 2003.

Lang, Timothy. *The Victorians and the Stuart Heritage: Interpretations of a Discordant Past.* Cambridge, 1995.

Langford, Paul. *Englishness Identified: Manners and Character, 1650–1850.* Oxford, 2000.

Langlands, Rebecca. "Britishness or Englishness? The Historical Problem of National Identity in Britain," *Nations and Nationalism* 5:1 (1999): 53–69.

Laqueur, Thomas W. "The Queen Caroline Affair: Politics as Art in the Reign of George IV," *Journal of Modern History* 54 (1982): 417–66.

Lean, E. Tangye. *The Napoleonists: A Study in Political Disaffection, 1760–1960.* London, 1970.

Lowenthal, David. *The Past is a Foreign Country.* Cambridge, 1985.

McCalman, Iain. *Radical Underworld: Prophets, Revolutionaries, and Pornographers in London, 1795–1840.* Originally published Cambridge, 1988; Oxford, 1993.

——. "The Infidel as Prophet: William Reid and Blakean Radicalism." In *Historicizing Blake,* ed. Steve Clark and David Worrall, 24–42. New York, 1994.

——. "New Jerusalems: Prophecy, Dissent and Radical Culture in England, 1786–1830." In *Enlightenment and Religion: Rational Dissent in Eighteenth-Century Britain*, ed. Knud Haakonssen, 312–35. Cambridge, 1996.

Maccunn, F. J. *The Contemporary English View of Napoleon*. London, 1914.

Macleod, Emma. *A War of Ideas: British Attitudes to the Wars against Revolutionary France, 1792–1802*. Aldershot, 1998.

Martineau, Gilbert. *Napoleon Surrenders*. Translated by Frances Partridge. London, 1971.

Mee, Jon. *Dangerous Enthusiasm: William Blake and the Culture of Radicalism in the 1790s*. Oxford, 1992.

——. " 'The Doom of Tyrants': William Blake, Richard 'Citizen' Lee, and the Millenarian Public Sphere." In *Blake, Politics, and History*, ed. Jackie DiSalvo, G. A. Rosso, and Christopher Z. Hobson, 97–114. New York, 1998.

Meisel, Martin. *Realizations: Narrative, Pictorial, and Theatrical Arts in Nineteenth-Century England*. Princeton, 1983.

Mitchell, Leslie. *Holland House*. London, 1980.

Morison, Stanley. *"The Thunderer" in the Making, 1785–1841. The History of The Times*, Vol. I. London, 1935.

Morris, Marilyn. *The British Monarchy and the French Revolution*. New Haven and London, 1998.

Muir, Rory. *Britain and the Defeat of Napoleon, 1807–1815*. New Haven and London, 1996.

Nairn, Tom. *The Enchanted Glass: Britain and its Monarchy*. London, 1988.

Newman, Gerald. *The Rise of English Nationalism: A Cultural History, 1740–1830*. New York, 1987.

——. "Nationalism Revisited," *Journal of British Studies* 35 (Jan. 1996): 118–27.

Nicholson, Eirwen E. C. "Consumers and Spectators: The Public of the Political Print in Eighteenth-Century England," *History* 81 (Jan. 1996): 5–21.

O'Brien, Conor Cruise. *God Land: Reflections on Religion and Nationalism*. Cambridge, 1987.

O'Leary, Patrick. *Regency Editor: Life of John Scott*. Aberdeen, 1983.

Oliver, W. H. *Prophets and Millennialists: The Uses of Biblical Prophecy in England from the 1790s to the 1840s*. Auckland, 1978.

Oman, Carola. *Napoleon at the Channel*. Garden City, NY, 1942.

Parrish, Stephen M. "A Booksellers' Campaign of 1803: Napoleonic Invasion Broadsides at Harvard," *Harvard Library Bulletin* 8 (Winter 1954): 14–40.

Pears, Iain. "The Gentleman and the Hero: Wellington and Napoleon in the Nineteenth Century." In *Myths of the English*, ed. Roy Porter, 216–36. Cambridge, 1992.

Philp, Mark, ed. *The French Revolution and British Popular Politics*. Cambridge, 1991.

——. "Vulgar Conservatism, 1792–3," *English Historical Review* 435 (Feb. 1995): 42–69.

Porter, Roy. *English Society in the Eighteenth Century*, rev. ed. Harmondsworth, 1990.

Prochaska, Frank. *The Republic of Britain, 1760–2000*. Harmondsworth, 2000.

Roberts, Andrew. *Napoleon and Wellington*. London, 2001.

Root, Christina. "Representations of Napoleon in English Romantic Literature." Ph.D. diss., Columbia University, 1991.

Rose, Jonathan. "Rereading the English Common Reader: A Preface to a History of Audiences," *Journal of the History of Ideas* 53 (1992): 47–70.

——. *The Intellectual Life of the British Working Classes.* New Haven and London, 2001.

Rosebery, Lord. *Napoleon: The Last Phase.* London, 1900.

Sack, James J. *From Jacobite to Conservative: Reaction and Orthodoxy in Britain, c. 1760–1832.* Cambridge, 1993.

Samuel, Raphael, ed. *Patriotism: The Making and Unmaking of British National Identity.* 3 vols. London, 1989.

Schoenbaum, S. *Shakespeare's Lives,* 2nd ed. Oxford, 1991.

Schofield, Thomas Philip. "Conservative Political Thought in Britain in Response to the French Revolution," *Historical Journal* 29 (1986): 601–22.

Schor, Esther. *Bearing the Dead: The British Culture of Mourning from the Enlightenment to Victoria.* Princeton, 1994.

Schroeder, Paul W. *The Transformation of European Politics, 1763–1848.* Oxford, 1994.

Schwarzfuchs, Simon. *Napoleon, the Jews and the Sanhedrin.* London, 1979.

Semmel, Bernard. *The Methodist Revolution.* New York, 1973.

Semmel, Stuart. "British Radicals and 'Legitimacy': Napoleon in the Mirror of History," *Past and Present* 167 (May 2000): 140–75.

——. "Reading the Tangible Past: British Tourism, Collecting, and Memory After Waterloo," *Representations* 69 (Winter 2000): 9–37.

Seward, Desmond. *Napoleon and Hitler: A Comparative Biography.* Originally published 1988; New York, 1990.

Shepard, Leslie. *John Pitts: Ballad Printer of Seven Dials, London, 1765–1844.* London, 1969.

——. *The History of Street Literature.* Newton Abbot, 1973.

Shine, Hill, and Helen Chadwick Shine. *The Quarterly Review under Gifford: Identification of Contributors, 1809–1824.* Chapel Hill, 1949.

Smith, Olivia. *The Politics of Language, 1791–1819.* Oxford, 1984.

Smith, R. J. *The Gothic Bequest: Medieval Institutions in British Thought, 1688–1863.* Cambridge, 1987.

Spater, George. *William Cobbett: The Poor Man's Friend.* 2 vols. Cambridge, 1982.

Starobinski, Jean. *Jean-Jacques Rousseau, Transparency and Obstruction.* Chicago, 1988.

Thompson, E. P. *The Making of the English Working Class,* rev. ed. Harmondsworth, 1968.

——. "Hunting the Jacobin Fox," *Past and Present* 142 (Feb. 1994): 94–140.

Thorne, R. G., ed. *The History of Parliament: The House of Commons, 1790–1820.* 5 vols. London, 1986.

Trumbach, Randolph. *Sex and the Gender Revolution, Volume One: Heterosexuality and the Third Gender in Enlightenment London.* Chicago, 1998.

Tulard, Jean. *Napoleon: The Myth of the Saviour.* Translated by Teresa Waugh. London, 1984.

Valenze, Deborah M. *Prophetic Sons and Daughters: Female Preaching and Popular Religion in Industrial England.* Princeton, 1985.

Vernon, James. *Politics and the People: A Study in English Political Culture, c. 1815–1867*. Cambridge, 1993.

———. ed. *Re-reading the Constitution: New Narratives in the Political History of England's Long Nineteenth Century*. Cambridge, 1996.

Vincent, David. *Literacy and Popular Culture: England, 1750–1914*. Cambridge, 1989.

Wahrman, Dror. *Imagining the Middle Class: The Political Representation of Class in Britain, c. 1780–1840*. Cambridge, 1995.

———. "*Percy*'s Prologue: From Gender Play to Gender Panic in Eighteenth-Century England," *Past and Present* 159 (May 1998): 113–61.

———. "The English Problem of Identity in the American Revolution," *American Historical Review* 106 (Oct. 2001): 1236–62.

———. "On Queen Bees and Being Queens: A Late-Eighteenth-Century 'Cultural Revolution?'" In *The Age of Cultural Revolutions: Britain and France, 1750–1820*, ed. Colin Jones and Dror Wahrman, 251–80. Berkeley and Los Angeles, 2002.

Webb, R. K. *The British Working Class Reader, 1790–1848: Literacy and Social Tension*. Originally published London, 1955; New York, 1971.

Wells, Roger. *Insurrection: The British Experience, 1795–1803*. Gloucester, 1983.

———. "English Society and Revolutionary Politics in the 1790s: The Case for Insurrection." In *The French Revolution and British Popular Politics*, ed. Mark Philp, 188–225. Cambridge, 1991.

Werner, Jack. *We Laughed at Boney (or; We've Been Through it All Before): How Our Forefathers Laughed Defiance at the Last Serious Threat of Invasion by Napoleon; A Striking Parallel with Our Present Position*. London, [1943].

Wichert, Robert A. "Napoleon and the English Romantic Poets." Ph.D. diss., Cornell University, 1948.

Wiener, Joel. *Radicalism and Freethought in Nineteenth-Century Britain: The Life of Richard Carlile*. Westport, Conn., 1983.

Wilson, Kathleen. "Inventing Revolution: 1688 and Eighteenth-Century Popular Politics," *Journal of British Studies* 28 (1989): 349–86.

Womersley, David. "Gibbon's Unfinished History: The French Revolution and English Political Vocabularies," *Historical Journal* 35 (1992): 63–89.

Wood, Marcus. *Radical Satire and Print Culture, 1790–1822*. Oxford, 1994.

Worrall, David. *Radical Culture: Discourse, Resistance and Surveillance, 1790–1820*. London, 1992.

Index

Note: Italicized page numbers refer to illustrations